Morning of Fire

Scott Ridley

Morning of Fire

America's Epic First Journey into the Pacific

WILLIAM MORROW
An Imprint of *HarperCollins*Publishers

A hardcover edition of this book was published in 2010 by William Morrow, an imprint of HarperCollins Publishers.

The map of Boston Harbor that appears on the verso page of Part I is courtesy of the Norman B. Leventhal Map Center, Boston Public Library.

The 1787 map of the United States that appears in the background of the title page and Parts I–IV was supplied by mapsofpa.com.

Gratitude is expressed for the permission of the Massachusetts Historical Society to quote from documents and microfilm records.

Grateful acknowledgment is made to the following for use of the images that appear throughout the text: courtesy of the Worcester Art Museum, Worcester, Massachusetts (p. 13); courtesy of the Washington State Historical Society (pp. 19, 71); courtesy of the Department of Rare Books and Special Collections, Princeton University Library (p. 40); courtesy of Beinecke Rare Book and Manuscript Library, Yale University (pp. 56, 80, 92, 117, 167, 170, 181, 335); and courtesy of the Estate of Hewitt Jackson (p. 224).

First William Morrow paperback edition published 2011.

Designed by Jamie Lynn Kerner
Map design by Eliza McClennen and Herb Heidt, © Herb Heidt, MapWorks 2010.

The Library of Congress has catalogued the hardcover edition as follows:

Ridley, Scott.
Morning of fire : John Kendrick's daring American odyssey in the Pacific / Scott Ridley.—1st ed.
p. cm.
Includes bibliographical references and index.
ISBN978-0-06-170012-5(hardcover) 1.Kendrick,John,ca. 1740–1794—Travel—Northwest Coast of North America. 2. Voyages to the Pacific coast. 3. Explorers—United States—Biography. 4. Northwest Coast of North America—Description and travel. 5. Northwest, Pacific—Description and travel. 6. Fur trade—Northwest, Pacific—History—18th century. 7. United States—Relations—Spain. 8. Spain—Relations—United States. 9. United States—Relations—Great Britain. 10. Great Britain—Relations—United States. I. Title.

F851.5.R53 2010
917.9504'24—dc22 2010019477

ISBN 978-0-06-170019-4 (pbk.)

11 12 13 14 15 OV/RRD 10 9 8 7 6 5 4 3 2 1

A voyage of such enterprise might truly be deemed a novel undertaking from a Country but so lately emerg'd from the ravages of a long, inhuman and bloody war . . .

—JOHN HOSKINS, BOSTON

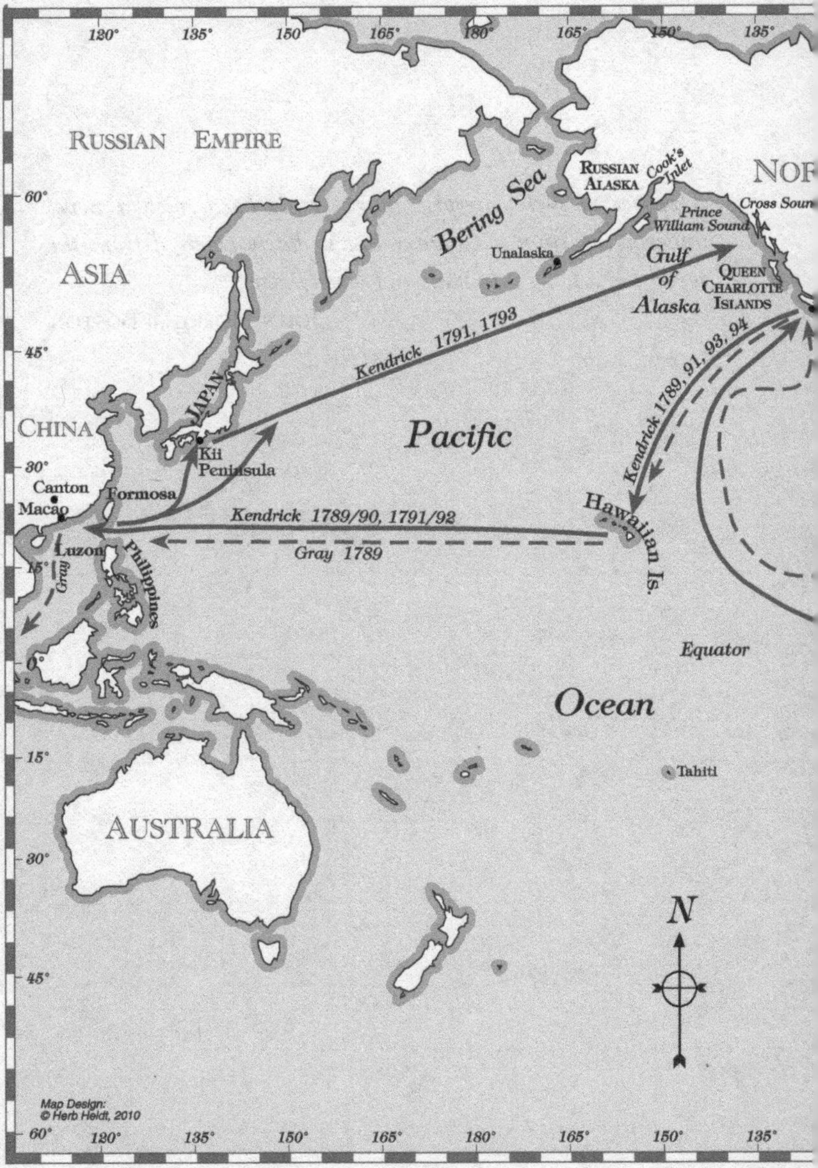

120°
135°
150°
165°
180°
165°
150°
135°
RUSSIAN EMPIRE
60°
ASIA
45°
CHINA
30°
Canton
Macao
15°
0°
15°
30°
45°
60°
Bering Sea
RUSSIAN ALASKA
Cook's Inlet
Unalaska
Prince William Sound
Cross Soun
NOR
Gulf of Alaska
QUEEN CHARLOTTE ISLANDS
Kendrick 1791, 1793
Kendrick 1789, 91, 93, 94
JAPAN
Kii Peninsula
Formosa
Luzon
Philippines
Gray
Pacific
Kendrick 1789/90, 1791/92
Gray 1789
Hawaiian Is.
Equator
Ocean
Tahiti
AUSTRALIA
N
Map Design: © Herb Heldt, 2010

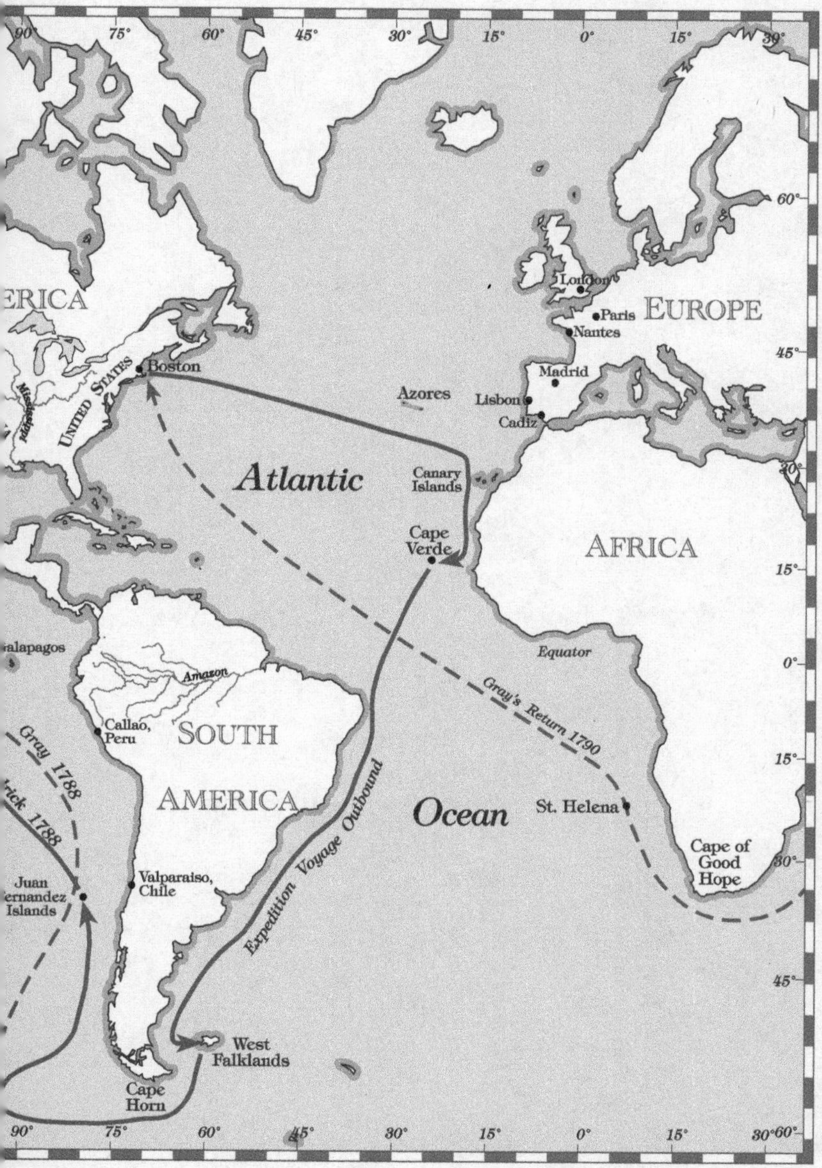

ERICA
UNITED STATES
Mississippi
Boston
Atlantic
Ocean
Azores
Canary Islands
Cape Verde
Lisbon
Cadiz
Madrid
London
Paris
Nantes
EUROPE
AFRICA
Equator
Gray's Return 1790
St. Helena
Cape of Good Hope
SOUTH AMERICA
Amazon
Galapagos
Callao, Peru
Valparaiso, Chile
Juan Fernandez Islands
Gray 1788
Kendrick 1788
Expedition Voyage Outbound
West Falklands
Cape Horn
90°
75°
60°
45°
30°
15°
0°
15°
30°
60°
45°
30°
15°
0°
15°
30°
45°
60°

Contents

Illustrations

PROLOGUE

Morning of Fire

MARCH 4, 1788—through a gray, cloudy morning and against a rising wind, two small American ships made their way off the coast of Staten Land near the tip of South America. The *Lady Washington,* a sixty-foot sloop carrying eleven men, and the *Columbia Rediviva,* a snub-hulled brig of eighty-three feet with a captain and crew of forty, scudded west like specks in the vast ocean. Under the rising wind the seas were running high and irregular, setting a strong current from the southwest. The ships were headed around Cape Horn and arriving late for this passage. Storm season had begun, and gales could appear out of nowhere, whipping swells to monstrous heights. For the next fifteen hundred miles, they would be in one of the most treacherous stretches on earth.

Beyond that danger lay the immense realm of the Pacific, the worlds of native people completely alien to them, and the enmity of the Spanish, who would soon issue orders to seize these ships. Although they seemed to be alone at a remote end of the earth, they were caught in a volatile tide of events from which there would be no turning.

THE LATE EIGHTEENTH CENTURY was a time of global turmoil. For three hundred years, a papal edict had largely prevailed as a backdrop to territorial treaties and agreements. In 1493, seeking to settle a conflict over the discoveries of new non-Christian lands, Pope Alexander VI had divided the globe, granting the seas and new lands in the Eastern Hemisphere—Cape Verde through Africa, India, and Asia—to Portugal, and the Western Hemisphere—ranging from the Americas to as far as the Philippines—to Spain. By the late 1780s, Portugal's fortunes had faded, and the overstretched Spanish Empire was starting to disintegrate. Driven by the ambition of merchants, a renaissance in science, and new philosophies of freedom and self-government, the myths and superstitions that held the Old World together began to fall away and modern nations started to stir.

At the heart of that change, the fledgling United States faced a future that was fragile and uncertain. The Revolution left the new nation weak, divided, and deeply in debt. Although America had won an impossible war against one of the world's superpowers, independence was not yet secure. Britain had largely shut down American trade. The economy was cash starved, and internal dissent was rising. In 1788, America's first ambassador to Britain, John Adams, headed home from London, frustrated that he was unable to break the British stranglehold. The prevailing opinion of the British court was that America's experiment with democracy would soon fail and the devastated colonies would come clamoring to rejoin the empire.

THE VOYAGE OF THE *LADY WASHINGTON* and *Columbia Rediviva* was a desperate bid to break the British stranglehold on trade and gain an American presence in the Pacific. It marked America's first expedition of enterprise and discovery. The commander, John Kendrick, had been a charismatic captain of privateers during the Revolution. A master navigator and visionary, he was a man fate had a habit of casting into the middle of events. In a historic letter to the Continental Congress in 1778, Benjamin Franklin informed the anxious delegates that France had at last decided to join the United States in its rebellion against Britain. As evidence of France's sincere faith, Franklin wrote that King Louis decided to grant Kendrick and another captain four hundred thousand French livres for capturing two prize merchant vessels. The award and stories of Kendrick's daring eventually made him a well-known figure on the Atlantic seaboard.

While no known portrait of John Kendrick exists, contemporaries describe him as being physically impressive and possessing great strength—a bold thinker, a trusted captain, a man who plunged into the unknown wilderness and, according to some, turned into a renegade and leader of a "banditti of renegadoes." Born of a stock of blue-eyed Yankee farmers and sailors, Kendrick had a clear gift to charm potential adversaries and win the loyalty of his men. His dry sense of humor easily took in more serious gentlemen and puzzled historians. The favor he showed his crews, at times over his officers, grew from his own rise from below deck and an egalitarian sense of humanity backed by a hatred of tyrants. In a time of stiff-necked and white-wigged ship's officers, Kendrick was the rare commander who was unafraid to break rules or protocol or to adopt the dress and learn the languages of the people he came among. His generosity and ability to entertain made him the favorite of native people. But he also possessed a patriarchal seriousness that could give way to fury. And sometimes that fury turned deadly. Although not strict in his religious beliefs, Kendrick was deeply ingrained with the sense of sacrifice and determination of his Congregational forebears. Through years of voyaging, he maintained an uncanny ability to persevere despite setbacks and fierce odds. Somewhere in him was a blind faith and an iron constitution that allowed him to survive the disease and deprivation that wasted many other men. He also possessed a subtlety that made him a surprisingly good strategist and frontier diplomat. From that generation which had achieved an unimaginable victory in winning independence, Kendrick remained dedicated throughout his life to what was known as the "glorious cause" of liberty. Franklin, Jefferson, and John Adams knew of him, as did George Washington. In time, other presidents would come to know his name as well, as they attempted for nearly fifty years to probe the events and claims left in his wake.

KENDRICK'S LIFE AND HIS LANDMARK VOYAGE embodied that harsh morning that was the turn of the eighteenth century. Born in 1740 on a small hilly farm in East Harwich, Cape Cod, John Kendrick was the third of seven children of Solomon Kendrick and Elizabeth Atkins. Their home bordered lands known as "Potonumecut" that stretched east along Pleasant Bay and held the remnant native tribes of the outer Cape: the Pamet people, the Nauset, the Monomoyick, the Saquatucket. Kendrick grew up among these native people and a close-knit group of relatives along the marshy shore. To the south was the farm of wild Sam Crook, a Monomoyick who ran his own whaling vessel. To the west were his cousins, the Snows. To the north on Tar Kiln Creek lived his uncle Jonathan Kendrick, the local physician. At the edge of Round Cove was the cedar bark *wetu* of old Wahenanun, who still spoke the Wampanoag language and practiced the ways of her people. And a half mile to the south was the grave of the Pilgrim guide Squanto, hidden on the high bank of Muddy Creek.

Kendrick's grandfather, Edward Kendrick, had arrived in Harwich around 1700 and married Elizabeth Snow, the granddaughter of Nicholas Snow, a holder of extensive lands and one of the "old-comers" from Plymouth who first settled the Cape. Kendrick's father, Solomon, born sometime during the winter of 1705/6, was master of a whaling vessel who was famous in local lore for having his boats attacked by a whale they had wounded far offshore on Georges Bank. "Tis a wonder they were not all destroyed," a contemporary account read, "for the Whale continued striking and raging in a most furious manner in the midst of them," destroying one boat and killing a man. Kendrick's boyhood was spent in his father's formidable shadow. Following local tradition, Kendrick went to sea with him by the time he was fourteen. By his late teens, he was sailing with crews of native men from Potonumecut. In 1762, he came ashore briefly at the end of the Seven Years' War to serve under a cousin, Jabez Snow, on a militia mission to the frontier of western New York.

As trouble with Parliament and the king mounted in the 1760s, his father moved off to Nova Scotia where he became one of the proprietors of the town of Barrington.

Staying behind, John Kendrick came of age in the defiant atmosphere of the coffeehouses and taverns of Boston. Here, he was in the midst of the firestorm of opposition to Parliament's Stamp Act of 1765 and the hated Townshend Acts, which usurped local authority and levied an array of onerous taxes. As strife increased on the waterfront, he may have been involved in the widespread boycott of British goods and the burning of Boston's customs house, or riots over seizure and impressment of American sailors for British ships.

During this time, Kendrick also frequented the south coast of Massachusetts, where talk of liberty and independence was rife and smuggling was rampant. Perhaps through his grandmother Atkins's family on Martha's Vineyard, he met Huldah Pease, the daughter of an Edgartown seafaring clan. Shortly after Christmas in 1767 they married and settled for a time on the island. Subsequent colonial records show that Kendrick mastered the whaling brig *Lydia* to the grounds off Cape Verde, and took the schooner *Rebecca* into the Gulf of Mexico, where he negotiated his way out of being seized by the Spanish *garda costa*.

Family tradition holds that on the rainy night of December 16, 1773, John Kendrick was part of the legendary band that boarded two East India Company ships at Griffin's Wharf in Boston and dumped 342 chests of tea into the harbor. Thumbing his nose at the British shortly after, he is said to have been master of the brig *Undutied Tea*.

At the outbreak of the Revolution, Kendrick may have smuggled powder and arms from the Caribbean with the sloop *Fanny,* whose owners were under contract with a secret committee of the Continental Congress. In May 1776, the *Fanny* delivered a cargo of muskets, double-brided gun locks, and cannon and pistol powder for the secret committee. In December, the owners applied to the Massachusetts Council for Kendrick to embark on the *Fanny* as a privateer. Onshore at Dartmouth (New Bedford), Kendrick made the sloop into a brigantine by adding a second mast and rerigging her sails. On July 10, 1777, he departed with 104 men for the English Channel and the French port of Nantes, where American privateers gathered. Here the *Fanny* became known as the *Boston,* and his crew the "Boston men."

His first large British prizes were the West Indiamen *Hanover Planter* and the *Clarendon,* which Kendrick and the *General Mercer* out of Cape Ann took after a battle with two twenty-eight-gun frigates. The prizes were carrying rich cargoes of muscovado sugar and rum from Jamaica to London, and tried to disguise themselves as vessels from a neutral port. Brought into Nantes in mid-August 1777, the captured ships caused an international stir. France had not yet entered the war, and Kendrick's prizes tested French neutrality and engaged Benjamin Franklin in correspondence with King Louis XVI and Congress. Discussion of the prize ships among the king's ministers helped to precipitate the entry of France into the war. In the fall of 1778, Kendrick returned home a hero and was initiated into St. Andrew's Lodge of Freemasons, which owned the Green Dragon Inn where the Boston Tea Party had been planned. Members of the lodge included Paul Revere and many of Boston's revolutionaries. With his prize money from the French king, Kendrick bought a house, wharf, and store at a riverfront site called the Narrows in the village of Wareham on the south coast of Massachusetts and built the first public school there.

Settled in the Narrows that winter, Kendrick's family was safe from the British fleet that had raided the coast, stripping Martha's Vineyard of livestock and food stores and reducing the population to near starvation. Up the tidal Warnico River, the warehouse and store were also safe from warships shelling the shore and burning ships and fishing vessels where they lay at anchor. Anguished at what was happening, Kendrick sailed off in late winter to command another privateer, the *Count d'Estaing,* which he owned in partnership with the New York patriot Isaac Sears. Southwest of the Azores island of Flores, he encountered a British frigate, the twenty-eight-gun *Brutus,* and her tender with ten guns. Kendrick was forced to strike his colors, and he and his crew were locked below as prisoners on the *d'Estaing* from April 8 to 22. The British captain forced as many prisoners as possible to sign on with him. Finally, impatient with those who held out, he set Kendrick and thirty of his men in a boat. They made a thirty-mile trip to Graciosa—one of the central islands of the Azores—where they were well treated by the inhabitants. After two weeks, they embarked in their boat again for the main island of Terceria, where the governor of the islands hosted them for two weeks and arranged passage on a Swedish vessel to Lisbon, a thousand miles to the east.

At Lisbon, with no money and only the shirt on his back, the affable Kendrick won the support of a local American sympathizer, Arnold Henry Dohrman, who fed and housed him and his men. On Sunday afternoon, June 13, 1779, Kendrick wrote to Benjamin Franklin from Lisbon reporting the capture of his vessel and praising the kindness of the people of the Azores and Dohrman, "a Sensiar Friend to the Cause of Liberty." Kendrick said he and his men were setting out that day for Spain, the first leg of a long trek back to France.

After surviving a two-month, thousand-mile journey with his remaining crew, Kendrick returned to America with the French fleet. He then left for the Caribbean with the *Marianna* to take at least one more rich prize, a Dutch merchant vessel from the plantations of Surinam carrying five tons of cotton, eight tons of cocoa, and one hundred fifty tons of coffee.

Shortly before the British surrendered at Yorktown in 1781,

Kendrick came ashore. In his sporadic visits home he had managed to father six children, and now he buckled down to making his way in the new nation. Like many of those who survived the war, the rich and dangerous life he led seemed to become part of a storied past. He had no idea that his greatest adventures still lay ahead. In the harsh morning that was rising, as much as any major military campaign or act of government, the odyssey he would embark on would spark changes that would shape world history and the future of the new nation.

Part I

The Journey Outward

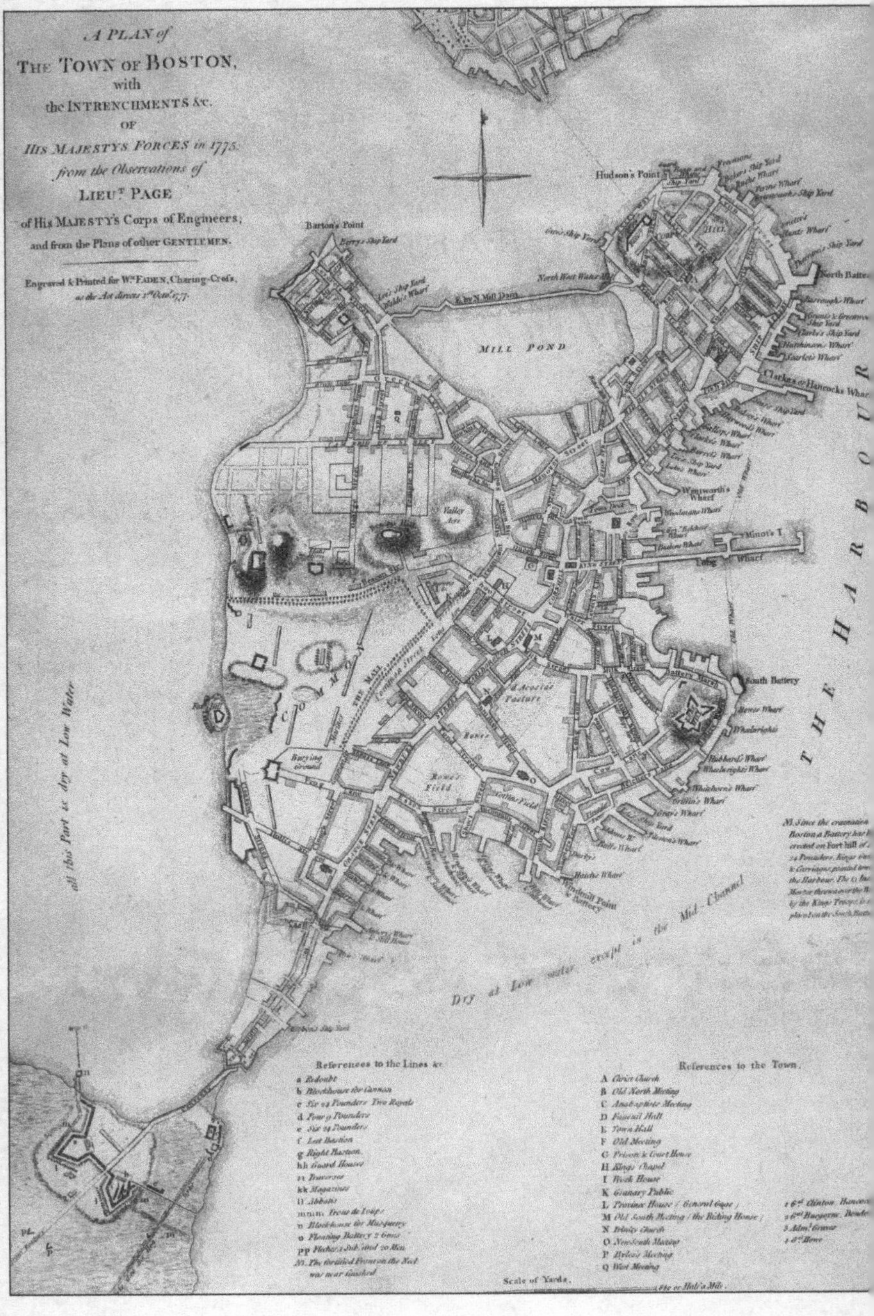
A PLAN of
THE TOWN OF BOSTON,
with
the INTRENCHMENTS &c.
OF
HIS MAJESTYS FORCES in 1775:
from the Observations of
LIEUT. PAGE
of His MAJESTY's Corps of Engineers;
and from the Plans of other GENTLEMEN.
Engraved & Printed for Wm. FADEN, Charing-Cross,
as the Act directs 1st Octr. 1777.
Hudson's Point
Barton's Point
MILL POND
North Battery
Clarkes or Hancocks Wharf
Wentworth's Wharf
Minot's T
Long Wharf
South Battery
THE HARBOUR
Valley Acre
Buying Ground
Bowes Field
Windmill Point Battery
all this Part is dry at Low Water
Dry at low water except in the Mid-Channel
References to the Lines &c.
a Redoubt
b Blockhouse for Cannon
c Six 24 Pounders Two Royals
d Four 9 Pounders
e Six 24 Pounders
f Left Bastion
g Right Bastion
hh Guard House
ii Traverse
kk Magazines
ll Abbatis
mmm Trous de Loups
n Blockhouse for Musquetry
o Floating Battery 2 Guns
pp Fleches 1 Sub. and 20 Men
N.B. The fortified Front on the Neck was near finished
References to the Town.
A Christ Church
B Old North Meeting
C Anabaptists Meeting
D Faneuil Hall
E Town Hall
F Old Meeting
G Prison & Court House
H Kings Chapel
I Work House
K Granary Public
L Province House (General Gage)
M Old South Meeting (the Riding House)
N Trinity Church
O New South Meeting
P Hollis's Meeting
Q West Meeting
1 Genl. Clinton
2 Genl. Burgoyne
3 Adml. Graves
4 Genl. Howe
Scale of Yards.
880 or Half a Mile.

Chapter One

Out of a Time of Great Peril

Boston

February–October 1787

Joseph Barrell hurried along the snow-crusted lane of Marlborough Street in the weak light at the end of the day. It was early February, 1787, and the chill wind off the harbor carried the smell of the tide. Under his greatcoat, Barrell clutched a packet of papers, a detailed plan he had worked out to launch a daring expedition of two ships into a little-known part of the world. The voyage would be America's first across the broad expanse of the Pacific, and shipmasters in the next generation would regard it as one of the most remarkable journeys ever undertaken by the United States. It marked a desperate venture in a perilous time.

After the victorious Revolution and euphoria of the Peace Treaty of 1783, an economic depression had settled over villages and farms. Port cities and their harbors were left reeling from the war. Inflation was rampant. There was no common currency, state governments were weak, and representatives to the Congress of the Confederation bickered over fundamental issues, threatening to secede. Heavy debts owed to Britain for damages in the war were due, and the prospects for international trade and revenue were bleak. In a punishing move, the king had closed all British ports from Canada and the British Isles to the Caribbean to the remaining American ships. France and Spain, likewise, offered no viable trade agreements for their harbors or colonies. Each of those kingdoms wanted the United States as a dependent client nation hemmed in between the Appalachians and the Atlantic.

Securing independence was far from certain, and Barrell, a prominent merchant who had been a member of the clandestine Sons of Liberty, feared along with many others that the blood and suffering of the long revolution might come to nothing. Frustration in the countryside had grown to the point that a popular uprising had broken out. As he trudged along the street, hired militia were hunting through heavy snows in the hills of western Massachusetts, searching for farmers and shopkeepers who had taken arms against what they saw as a corrupt state government. The unrest had been spreading for a year and a half in Massachusetts, Connecticut, Rhode Island, and New Hampshire over high taxes, controversial court procedures, and the taking of farms and homesteads for nonpayment of bills. Armed farmers had blocked courts from holding session in order to stop the seizures. And in a violent confrontation on January 25, three rebel regiments totaling fifteen hundred men attempted to capture the Springfield Armory. They were led by Captain Daniel Shays, a veteran who was once honored by the Marquis de Lafayette for his bravery. Some believed a new revolution was brewing.

At Mount Vernon, where he had retired after the war, the usually reserved George Washington became apoplectic when he was told there were as many as fifteen thousand disaffected yeomen in New England ready to take up arms. To his friend Henry Lee, Washington wrote, "I am mortified beyond expression when I view the clouds that have spread over the brightest morn that ever dawned in any country. . . . What a triumph for the advocates of despotism, to find that we are incapable of governing ourselves . . ."

A push was on for a new federal government. But without trade, without customs revenue, without taxes, it would be impossible to support a new central government and succeed in securing independence. Shipping was the soul of early commerce, and breaking the Old World stranglehold on American vessels was essential to the survival of the fledgling nation. Barrell's plan held a way to travel beyond the Atlantic ports closed to American ships, open an American gateway to the Pacific, and establish a base for the new nation on the far side of the continent. It was an audacious leap to send two ships and a relatively small crew of fifty men into the largely unknown reaches of the globe.

When he arrived at the home of Thomas Bulfinch on Bowdoin Square, Barrell was brought into the parlor before a warm fire. Among a circle of trusted friends he laid out his plans. Next to Barrell's packet of papers, Bulfinch opened a leather-bound copy of James Cook's journal from his third voyage, which described the exotic and unknown expanse of the Pacific and served as the inspiration for Barrell's expedition. In 1776, Britain's King George III had dispatched Cook to the Pacific with two ships in search of the Northwest Passage, rumored for centuries to be a link between the Atlantic and Pacific Oceans. While Cook didn't find the prized passage, he "discovered" the Hawaiian Islands and a treasure of rich furs on the northern Pacific

Joseph Barrell *by John Singleton Copley. Joseph Barrell was a member of a large Boston merchant family with relatives posted at offices in the Caribbean, London, and India. An ardent federalist, he supported the vision of an expanding nation and later became a prominent land speculator in Ohio, Kentucky, and Georgia.*

coast of America. In China, furs that Cook's men had purchased from the American natives in return for trinkets sold for as much as one hundred and twenty Spanish dollars for a single sea otter pelt. This was more than double a full seaman's wages for a year. The prospect of gathering fortunes sent the crews of Cook's two ships into near mutiny to return to the American coast. Two seamen "seduced by the prevailing notion of making a fortune" stole a fixed-oar cutter and disappeared, never to be seen again. Duty and the lash drove the rest of the crew homeward. The fortune in furs was still waiting for those daring to venture out.

Barrell had already been involved with the first two American ships sent to China on the established track eastward around Africa's Cape of Good Hope. The *Harriet* had gone out from Massachusetts on an aborted voyage in 1783. And the *Empress of China,* which carried thirty tons of Barrell's New England ginseng, left New York in 1784. Although the *Empress* made a moderate profit, Barrell found that the market for ginseng was limited and Chinese merchants wanted silver and gold coins, which were scarce in the new republic. Reading Cook's journal, he seized upon the idea of using the highly prized furs as a subsitute for money. Following the pattern described in Cook's journal, Barrell outlined a triangular trade of New England goods and trinkets for sea otter furs from Pacific Northwest tribes; an exchange of furs for tea, silk, and other goods at Macao; and a homeward voyage laden with rich Chinese cargo. There were two chances at profits, and Barrell worked out costs and contingencies in detail. He concluded that in a short time a rich trade with the East could prove "superior to any the country enjoys at present." To firmly secure this trade, the Pacific expedition would also seek to purchase lands on the Northwest Coast. Barrell wanted to establish an American outpost "at least equal to what Hudson's-bay is to Great Britain," and extend the new nation by claims of possession. And even more dramatic, Barrell proposed that the expedition search for the legendary Northwest Passage. If it could be found, the waterway would unlock the vast interior of the continent and open a new trade route to the East for Americans.

The brazen plan reflected Barrell's personal ambition and his broader desperation for the new nation to succeed. He calculated that the expedition's ships, supplies, men, and trade goods would need an investment of forty-nine thousand dollars, a small fortune at the time. But despite the cost and wild reach of Barrell's plan, his reasoning was convincing and the prospect for trade was attractive. Fourteen shares were soon divided among his circle of friends as a joint venture. Barrell took four shares, and two shares each went to his new partners: young Charles Bulfinch, who would become America's premier architect; Crowell Hatch, a Boston captain; Samuel Brown, a Boston merchant and shipowner; John Derby, a Salem merchant whose family owned and provisioned ships; and John M. Pintard, a financier based in New York.

They knew that carrying out the voyage was fraught with difficulty. Spain would resist any encroachment in the Pacific, and the route westward around South America's Cape Horn was greatly feared. The two ships would have to withstand immense punishment, and there were few vessels available. Boston, like other port cities, had been devastated by the British during the first two years of the war. Shipyards were wrecked, and hundreds of ships up and down the coast had been seized and taken to auction at Liverpool or burned to the waterline where they lay anchored. New ships were hard to come by. The shipyards that survived were shorthanded, and the few ships being framed were going to foreign owners who could pay in cash. Adding to the expense, the hulls of the expedition's ships would need to be sheathed in copper to ward off wood-boring teredo worms, barnacles, and rot.

The voyage would also be extraordinarily long—more than two years—and require a large amount of provisions, as well as a mountain of trade goods and ship stores to maintain the vessels. There was also a question of whether seasoned men would sign on. Although there was an exotic allure to the Pacific, colored by tales of island paradises and unrestrained sex with beautiful women, the ships were headed for dangerous, uncharted waters, and it was well-known that long voyages like this commonly lost a quarter or more of the crew to scurvy and other diseases.

The key to attracting good men and ensuring success for the expedition rested on finding the right commander. New England was full of blue water captains, but this one would have to be both a seasoned warrior and a diplomat who could negotiate dangers at sea and along unknown coasts. It would take someone experienced in the care of a crew on such a long journey, someone who could hold the hearts of his men and fire their determination through soul-wrenching events. Moreover, he would have to be a master navigator who appreciated the dream of an American outpost on the Pacific and was willing to risk his life in this venture. Whatever candidates they considered, the choice came down to one broad-shouldered captain who literally stood above the others.

By the early summer, Barrell sent word for John Kendrick to meet him at his counting house at Boston's Town Dock. Kendrick had been a whaling captain for twenty years, and was well-known for his command of privateers during the Revolution. Upstairs from the cavernous storeroom, they sat in Barrell's office overlooking the waterfront. Dressed in his velvet jacket and ruffled shirt, Barrell appeared very much the wealthy patrician. Kendrick, a rough-hewn counterpart, was tanned and wrinkled and worn by years at sea. He was tough, but possessed a charm and confidence that easily won others over. The two men were nearly the same age: Barrell forty-eight years old and Kendrick forty-seven. They had come to manhood during the turbulence and protests in Boston before the Revolution, and both had risked their lives and fortunes in the war. Barrell knew that Kendrick would see the expedition as more than just a trading mission. Like many of the founding fathers, they shared the naive belief that the Revolution could be carried out into the world through open ports and free trade. Markets opened by American ships, as much as the concept of liberty, would undermine secret pacts between Old World in nations and topple corrupt monarchies. This new trade with China was a stroke in that direction. If they were successful, they would gain the money they were desperate for and contend with the ancient empires that sought to contain the new republic. Barrell rolled out a map, and Kendrick watched his keen eyes and fine hands as the merchant traced out the voyage.

The two ships would carve an American trade route around Cape Horn to the Far East, Barrell told him. They would sail the whole coast of the Americas and barter for furs in the north, then cross the Pacific and stop at the Sandwich Islands on the way to Macao, China. The trip homeward would cross the Indian Ocean and round Africa's Cape of Good Hope. It would be the first circumnavigation by American ships, and more than just a historic trading voyage, Barrell explained he wanted to establish an American presence in the Pacific. He said the captain would have to evade Spanish warhips and ports, and build ties with native people in order to purchase lands from them for an outpost on the Pacific. If land could be purchased, Barrell assured Kendrick, he could get Congress to approve it. Added to this was the tantalizing prospect of finding the legendary Northwest Passage before Britain, Spain, or Russia, to secure a permanent advantage.

The plan offered a grand vision, undoubtedly considered madness by some captains. Beyond the formidable dangers of the voyage, the expedition put the ragtag former colonies in the position of challenging the Old World empires. Compared to the wealth and power of Spain, Britain, and Russia, the new American republic was an impoverished backwater. Boston had a population of only eighteen thousand, Philadelphia, twenty-eight thousand, and New York was the largest city with about thirty-three thousand people. Aside from state militias, there was only a token remnant of the Continental army and no navy; the two ships would be on their own on the other side of the world. They would be sailing into unknown waters peopled by tribes rumored to be cannibals, remote Asian coasts infested with pirates, and a region that would be jealously guarded by Spain.

Kendrick surely recognized what they were up against, and the odds might have been part of what appealed to him. Listening to Barrell, he saw this as the voyage of a lifetime. The prospect of adventure and glory made a stark contrast to the monthly packet run he was currently mastering up and down the coast between Boston and Charleston, South Carolina. This venture could help set a new course for the nation. It was an opportunity to make his mark in trade and carry the seed for an "empire of liberty" envisioned by Thomas Jefferson and others to the Pacific coast. He knew a chance like this would not come again, and soon after their discussion, Kendrick agreed to command the expedition.

BARRELL SENT HIS PARTNER John Pintard to Congress on August 18 with a request for a sea letter for the voyage, a document intended to ensure passage and protection in foreign waters. The request was put aside. Congress had recently passed a law to allow the creation of new states, and tensions with Spain had increased over the disputed "middle lands" between the Appalachians and the Mississippi River. Talk of war with Spain was in the air. And pressed by popular unrest in New England over Shays' Rebellion, Congress was also anxiously awaiting the results of the constitutional convention in Philadelphia. Within a few weeks, the Constitution proposing a new national government was received at Federal Hall in New York. Congress approved it on September 17, and the following weekend, a committee consisting of Melancton Smith of New York, John Kean of South Carolina, and Nathan Dane of Massachusetts reviewed Pintard's letter. Although they were aware that the expedition would need to pass through hostile Spanish waters, the committee noted only that the ships were "bound on a voyage to the Northwest coast of America" and were owned and manned by Americans. On Monday, September 24, the twenty-eight members of Congress gathered at Federal Hall, approved and issued the sea letter. Pintard immediately dispatched the document by post rider to Boston, more than two hundred fifty hard miles away.

AT BOSTON HARBOR, the expedition's two ships were tied up at Hancock's Wharf. Barrell had purchased the best vessels available and had them hauled out on the ways to be refitted. The command ship, the *Columbia Rediviva,* was a stumpy three-masted ship, eighty-three feet six inches long on deck, with a 212-ton carrying capacity, snub-bowed and deep in the hull like the whalers Kendrick had once taken into the icy North Atlantic. Tradition claims she was built at the Scituate shipyard of James Briggs on the North River in 1773, where she escaped destruction by the British during the Revolution. Her name meant

The Columbia Rediviva *and* Lady Washington, *sketched by Hewitt Jackson.*

"dove reborn," which was symbolic of the new nation and perhaps also implied the biblical dove sent in search of new land and prosperity.

The *Lady Washington* was a coastal sloop of sixty feet and ninety tons, built low and tough in the shipyards north of Boston as early as 1750, probably with two-inch oak planking on her hull. Her single, gaff-rigged mast was stepped at an angle and she had a certain romance to her. Commissioned as a privateer in 1776, she took at least one prize ship near Boston and once escaped four British war barges sent to sink her. Kendrick undoubtedly noted her similarity to his brigantine the *Fanny*, with which he had captured his first prizes in the Revolution. To the eye of any sailor, the *Washington* was much more the dove, and *Columbia* akin to the Ark.

As a steady stream of chandlers, riggers, and carters provisioned the ships, the sea letter arrived—it was a ribboned document, embossed with the seal of the Congress of the Confederation and signed by Arthur St. Clair, who presided over the chamber. The letter placed the ships under the patronage and protection of Congress and was addressed in a flourish to kings, princes, and officials of foreign ports. Although the document appeared official, it could mean very little in the farther reaches of the earth. Despite the peace and prosperity implied by the image of the dove, fitting out for sea included installing on the *Columbia* ten cannons, as well as several swivel guns that fired grapeshot. More cannons and a half-dozen swivel guns were placed aboard the *Lady Washington*.

News of the voyage appeared in Boston newspapers and spread down the coast. To most Boston merchants, the expedition sounded like a trip to the moon. Not only were they sailing around the Horn into unknown and hostile waters but the chance of success in that frightening void seemed to be pure speculation. Nevertheless, enthusiastic articles appeared and were reprinted from one newspaper to the next. They stated that the ships would be sailing for New Albion, or Kamchatka, or Northwest America. The truth was that the expedition was bound for an exotic wilderness harbor named Nootka by James Cook. It was located on the Northwest Coast at 48° north latitude, well within the domain claimed by the Spanish Empire.

The prospect of adventure and word of Kendrick's mastering the expedition brought on veterans of the Revolution and seasoned hands as well as young sailors. The voyagers were divided generally into four groups: ship's boys, seamen, craftsmen, and officers and "gentlemen." They came from Cape Cod, the North Shore of Massachusetts, Boston, and Rhode Island. Signing on were sailmaker William Bowles of Roxbury, gunner James Crawford of Georgetown, blacksmith Jonathan Barber of Boston, and carpenter Isaac Ridler, a British émigré who had served on privateers during the Revolution. Also brought on were up-and-coming Boston sailors: the highly regarded second mate Joseph Ingraham, whose father was a controversial merchant captain; the *Washington*'s first mate, Robert Davis Coolidge of Roxbury; and carpenter's mate Joshua Hemmingway, who was Isaac Ridler's brother-in-law. From the North Shore came the cooper Robert Green, Otis Liscomb of Gloucester, and Miles Greenwood of Salem, whose father had owned privateers. Among younger sailors were the sons of two of Barrell's associates, John Cordis and Andrew Newell, and several ships' boys as young as twelve years old. Kendrick also enlisted two of his sons for the historic venture: Jonathan, eighteen years old, as fifth officer, and Solomon, sixteen, as a common seaman.

The "gentlemen" signed by Joseph Barrell included Richard S. Howe, the ship's clerk, and the Boston furrier Jonathan Treat. The third officer, nineteen-year-old Robert Haswell, whose father had been a Loyalist and lieutenant in the British navy, would become the unofficial chronicler of the first two years of the voyage. And the *Columbia*'s first officer, Simeon Woodruff, whom young Haswell referred to as "the aged gentleman," came aboard as a kind of celebrity. Woodruff was a Connecticut native who served in the British navy during the American Revolution and sailed with Captain James Cook on his third voyage of discovery. He had already seen the rich furs of the Northwest and the amorous women of the Pacific islands, and had fought off native attacks.

Serving under Kendrick as captain of the *Lady Washington* was thirty-three-year-old Robert Gray, who had grown up on Narragansett Bay and was the nephew of Samuel Gray, one of four men killed in the Boston Massacre in 1770. Gray was a brash, one-eyed Rhode Islander who was said to have sailed in the Continental navy. He thought himself to be the better choice to command the voyage. Headstrong, arrogant, and focused on the merchant purpose of the expedition, he would continually chafe under Kendrick's command.

On Friday, September 28, with the sea letter in hand, as well as letters from the Massachusetts Legislature and the French and Dutch consuls, Kendrick moved the ships to the channel off Castle Island. Under a nearly full moon, final preparations for the voyage went on late into Saturday night. On Sunday morning, September 30, freshly rigged and with their hulls painted black with a broad yellow band above the waterline, the ships sat at their moorings. Through the morning the crew's families and guests came aboard. At noon, Kendrick arrived in a boat with the harbor pilot, accompanied by Joseph Barrell, the ship's clerk Richard Howe, and others. They had come from a service at South Church where a solemn prayer had been offered for the voyage.

With a light breeze out of the southwest, Kendrick gave command for the ships to make sail; the pilot took them out past Spectacle Island, faring seven miles to Nantasket Roads off the village of Hull. Anchored that night near the entrance channel to the great harbor, they staged a celebration. Pennants lay slack as speeches and song went rising into the still air. Seabound ships anchored nearby enjoyed the din as lanterns hung in *Columbia*'s rigging glowed above the deck, dappling the black water. In the first entry of his journal, young third mate Robert Haswell wrote, "The evening was spent in murth and glee the highest flow of spirits animating the whole Company."

Barrell presented Kendrick with instructions granting him broad authority:

> *The ship Columbia and sloop Washington being completely equipped for a voyage to the Pacific Ocean and China, we place such confidence in you as to give you the entire command of this enterprise. It would be impossible upon a voyage of this nature to give you with propriety very binding instructions, and such is our reliance on your honor, integrity and good conduct, that it*

would be needless at any time. You will be on the spot, and as circumstances turn up you must improve them . . .

Barrell also handed out medallions engraved in pewter, copper, and silver to commemorate the voyage. One side of the medallions depicted the two ships under sail and read: "Columbia and Washington Commanded By J. Kendrick." The reverse held the names of the ships' owners and around the rim read: "Fitted At Boston, N. American For The Pacific Ocean."

One of those who received a medallion was the commander's wife, Huldah Pease Kendrick. She would have come up the day before from the village of Wareham. Still at home were three boys: Benjamin, Alfred, and Joseph, all under age twelve, and little six-year-old Huldah.

Although she was accustomed to frequent separations during twenty years of marriage, Huldah Kendrick faced a much deeper emotional strain now that two of her sons were shipping off. Torn between pride in their mission and apprehension at such a long journey, it was likely she lingered with her boys and husband and was among the last passengers rowed ashore.

Below deck, the men and boys arranged themselves, taking a measure of one another in the dim, lamplit space under the foredeck. Haswell made notes in his journal as the other officers settled into their narrow cabins. Amid the high hopes and emotion of the evening, no one could imagine what would unfold in an odyssey driven by Kendrick's perseverance and vision. In the years to come, word would drift back in scant letters and news from other ships of this man who became part legend, buying up a huge tract of land that would benefit the new nation, allegedly going renegade, and helping to push the world toward a global war. The obscure wilderness harbor they were headed for at Nootka would become a flashpoint around which the destinies of European empires would turn. For America, more than a decade and a half before Lewis and Clark, Kendrick would inspire voyagers and open a gateway to the

Pacific. But that was far ahead, unforeseen in the night's mix of anticipation and high emotion.

If they slept at all, it was not long. At the edge of this great harbor, in the early dark before dawn with a purple-gray light rising, the two ships made their way out of the channel for open sea.

CHAPTER TWO

Passage to the Underworld

Cape Horn

MARCH–APRIL 1788

TUESDAY, MARCH 5, east of Cape Horn—Five months into the voyage, memories of the last festive night in Boston had long faded. Kendrick had taken the ships on a shakedown cruise across the Atlantic to Cape Verde, off the western coast of Africa, where he reorganized the *Columbia*'s hold and rested and fattened his men for the arduous months ahead. At the turn of the year, they ran down the coast of South America, staying well offshore to avoid Spanish patrols. At the desolate Falkland Islands they stopped for water and final preparations.

With more than a little trepidation, on February 28, 1788, they set out on a flood tide at dusk from the West Falklands and made their way into blustery winds and mountainous seas to round Cape Horn. Five days later, the bold, barren outline of Staten Land loomed north of them and a gale rapidly approached from the west.

The irregular seas began to lengthen into large, thick swells. From the pitching quarterdeck of the *Columbia,* John Kendrick watched the *Lady Washington* heeling and plunging in the waves behind them. Ahead, the gray mass of clouds was blackening into twisted peaks along the horizon. Kendrick ordered his crew to tack and the *Washington* followed.

Climbing over these steep southern swells, the *Columbia*'s hold was filled with the bulk of their provisions for two years and an assortment of trade goods: tin mirrors, beads, calico, mouth harps, hunting knives, hatchets, files, and bar metal that could be worked into chisels. Despite breaking up the hold and repacking the ship at Cape Verde, she still handled like a box on ice. Kendrick could only hope they would not encounter the mammoth storms that could gather as the southern winter approached. It would be cold. It would be bitterly cold, the only certainty of the days ahead.

THE SHIPS RAN SOUTHWARD, trying to skirt the edge of the storm, making good headway through cold rain and spray. They had prepared for this for months, but there was no imagining the extreme conditions they would face. Everyone had heard tales in port about rounding the Horn. It was like a passage into the underworld. Ceaseless wind. Blinding ice storms. Utterly black nights. Immense waves. Exhausted men washed overboard. Some could name the ships lost. Nineteen-year-old mate Robert Haswell recalled in his journal that Britain's Lord Anson, seeking to raid Spanish ships and settlements along the Pacific, had led a squadron here in March 1741 and met disaster. Only four of seven ships made it through and hundreds of men perished. Haswell thought it improbable that the *Lady Washington* and *Columbia* attempting passage at the same time of year could succeed where Anson in the finest ships had nearly failed.

Kendrick stayed on deck watching the approach of the storm and then went below, where the air was filled with the scent of pipe smoke and bilgewater and the incessant sound of the waves pounding on the hull. Goats brought on board at Cape Verde bleated in a makeshift pen. Around them planks groaned and creaked, and seawater began to drip overhead from the seams of the deck.

Kendrick knew another part of Lord Anson's story that painted an even more dismal picture than Haswell had noted in his journal: Five large Spanish warships, each more than twice the size of the *Columbia*, under the command of Don José Pizzaro, had pursued Anson's squadron. In the region they were crossing through now, the ships had been stuck by a brutal storm that raged for three days. The Spanish ships became scattered, and then the *Hermosa* with five hundred men went down. Pizzaro's surviving ships were driven west. The *Guipscoa* split her mainsail, and in the rolling seas the mainmast was sprung. Battering from huge waves opened her upper works, and seams and bolts were drawn from the upper timbers. With a foot of snow on deck and unable to keep up with the leakage, the upper deck was cut away and the cannons and an anchor jettisoned. Fearing the ship was coming apart, the captain wrapped six turns of an anchor cable around the hull to keep it together. More gales followed. After three weeks of continual horror, the crew drove the ship onto the shore of Brazil. Two hundred fifty of her seven hundred men were dead. Pizzaro's command ship, the *Asia*, ultimately made it back to Brazil in May after sixty days and losing half the seven hundred men aboard. The *Esperanza* followed with only fifty-eight alive of four hundred fifty men, and the *Estevan* suffered similarly.

Kendrick knew that Anson had weathered that storm just ahead of Pizzaro's ships, escaping the full force of the seas by running south. Anson believed that the Andes Mountains funneled the strongest storms and highest seas closest to shore. Four hundred miles below the Horn at 62° south latitude, halfway to the edge of the Antarctic Circle, he found that the storms were severe but moderated, with intervals of sun in the bright, hard cold.

Kendrick was racing toward that line now, outrunning the gale coming on, and trading the brutal winds and high seas for the bitter cold, hopeful that it would give him and his men a few days of intermittent respite and headway to the west.

TWO NIGHTS LATER, ON MARCH 7, they encountered the first frost forming on the sails and deck. Still laboring in heavy weather, they came across swimming penguins and a small whale. The wind intensified, forcing them down to reefed topsails and storm jibs. As the seas built, the decks became awash.

As much as contending with the seas and storms buffeting the ships, they were in a race against time. Prolonged fatigue, injuries, and scurvy were what had broken the men of Anson's and Pizarro's ships. And they were still far from the point where Anson had met the worst storms.

Kendrick had far fewer men than Anson, almost a skeleton crew by comparison, who bore the work in two alternating watches. On the *Lady Washington,* with Captain Robert Gray and ten men, one watch was led by Davis Coolidge and one by Robert Haswell. On the *Columbia,* with Kendrick and forty men and officers, one was led by first mate Joseph Ingraham and the others by Robert Green and John Cordis. Usually the watches would come on deck every four hours, with all hands on from 4 to 8 P.M., but shorter watches would be set in the fierce cold and storm conditions, and the free watch could be called out of an exhausted sleep at any time, swallowing a jigger of rum before going topside to shake out reefs or furl sail.

By Sunday, March 9, the ships had made three hundred miles south-southwest from where they first encountered the gale, and were now midway to the tip of the Antarctic Peninsula. Twenty-foot swells and sleet made the deck slick with ice and it became hard to stand watch.

Kendrick worried about the punishment the ships were taking, especially the *Washington*. As she struggled to follow into the wind, he watched the sloop's hull disappear underwater. Swells surged over her until only the mast and reefed sail were visible, and then whitewater rushed off as she resurfaced to meet the next wave. Although the *Co-*

lumbia's freeboard was higher, intermittent waves washed waist deep down her deck. Bedding and everything below on both vessels was soaked. Men were constantly working the bilge pumps.

Watch was kept in the cold by men clinging to lines strung on deck, but proved futile when the wind finally moderated and a heavy fog blew in. The mist closed around them and turned the night blind. They tried to hold their course by compass but had no opportunity for a sextant reading on the sun or moon. With the *Washington* intermittently passing out of sight at night, Kendrick was greatly concerned that the two ships would become separated. But by some miracle, mornings found the sloop still on the southern horizon.

During the week of March 17 the weather turned excessively cold. Large "islands of ice" appeared, and blowing sleet and snow caked everything. On deck, men struggled to clear the rigging and halyards that controlled the sails. For the topmen, who tended the upper courses of sail, conditions aloft grew incredibly treacherous. Climbing fifty or seventy feet in the air, they clung to an icy yard and looped footropes as they took in sail, the ship rocking them far out over the lurching swells, and the wind shrieking and cracking around them.

Anson had lamented the loss of one of his best seamen overboard, something that haunted all captains and sailors. Fighting through a storm and unable to turn back for him, they watched as he swam vigorously. Anson later anguished that the men grew more grieved "as we lost sight of him struggling with the waves, and concerned that he might continue long sensible of the horror of his irretrievable situation."

Kendrick undoubtedly watched his sons on deck amid the increasing hazards. As frost and snow hardened in the intense cold, they worked with the crew to clear the blocks and lines and hack ice off the yards, mast, and rails with belaying pins. If ice built up a thick rime, the ship could become impossible to handle. Mountainous seas could easily broadside them and send the hull over on her beam ends. Or if the lines clogged in the frozen blocks, the voyagers could find themselves facing an iceberg they would be helpless to avoid. After the first two weeks, squalls and constant headwinds began to wear them down. Haswell wrote on March 17: "Winds have allowed us to gain but little Westing and at this time our prospect of weathering the Cape is very unfavorable."

A MONTH BEHIND THEM, a British ship known as the *Bounty,* captained by William Bligh, would sail through five weeks of howling weather and nearly round the Horn before a massive storm drove her hundreds of miles backward to start over. With a number of his crew suffering from exhaustion, cracked ribs, and dislocated shoulders, Bligh turned toward South Africa's Cape of Good Hope to take the long way through the Indian Ocean into the Pacific. This decision, which added months to the *Bounty*'s frustrating voyage, helped bring about the infamous mutiny that was to come.

On Kendrick's ships, numbing cold increased the grumbling among the men. As on most vessels, there were divisions among them. Perhaps because of their Loyalist leanings, Robert Haswell, first mate Simeon Woodruff, and the ship's surgeon, Dr. Roberts, formed a clique among the officers. Haswell identified another group as "the captain's people," which included second mate Joseph Ingraham and many of the seamen.

Problems were evident at the outset of the voyage, according to Haswell, and after the forty-two-day passage to Cape Verde, Kendrick had gotten into a heated disagreement with first mate Simeon Woodruff, who seemed to be at the forefront of dissent. Kendrick disliked the way the *Columbia* handled in Atlantic squalls and likely faulted Woodruff, who was responsible for the packing of the hold. In the harbor at Praia, Cape Verde, Kendrick ordered the hold broken up and repacked. The order received little cooperation from Woodruff, so Kendrick took on the work with the men himself. Woodruff's British navy background and the haughty attitude of royal officers differed greatly from Kendrick's style, and Woodruff's celebrity status may have prompted him to act like something of a peacock. At the end of the first week of December, Kendrick removed him from his position as first officer of the *Columbia*. He offered Woodruff the choice of staying aboard as a passenger and undertaking tasks he was set to, or leaving the expedition. Woodruff requested that he be allowed to go on board Gray's ship, the *Lady Washington*. After more bickering, Woodruff refused to sign departure papers. Kendrick ordered him before the mast, where Woodruff spent the night in the open air without bedding. In the morning he signed the papers and was set ashore at Praia.

Haswell felt Woodruff's departure as a personal blow, and he protested bitterly in his journal: "This Gentleman was of known abilities as a navigator and greatly experienced as a Seaman he had Commanded several ships out of London, he was an officer under the Great Captain James Cook on his last Voyage to the Pacifick Ocean." Woodruff had clearly puffed himself up. Whatever he had told Haswell or the crew, he was not listed as an officer on Cook's ship, but a gunner's mate.

The day after Woodruff was set ashore, the ship's surgeon, Dr. Roberts, claimed that his health was declining and asked Kendrick for a discharge. Kendrick responded that he'd grant the request if Roberts would pay for his passage from Boston to Cape Verde. Roberts refused. Nevertheless, the next day Kendrick gave him permission to go ashore. Roberts did not return, and Kendrick received a note from the governor of the island saying that Roberts had sought his protection, complaining of "inhuman treatment." Kendrick attempted to have Roberts returned, at one point finding him in the street and encouraging him at sword point toward the beach, but Roberts cried out for the militia and refused to go back to the ship.

As they were preparing to leave Cape Verde on December 21, an officer of a Danish East India vessel came on board the *Columbia* and said that Dr. Roberts had changed his mind and was willing to return to the ship if he would not be flogged. Kendrick knew better than to take malcontents or those unable to handle adversity on an extended voyage. Kendrick was also confident that they had the skills on board to minister to the crew's health as well as the unpredictable doctor could. He refused to let Roberts reboard and left him at Praia.

Tensions continued to mount as the ships bounded southward toward Cape Horn. One day Haswell struck and bloodied one of the men, Otis Liscomb, for not responding to his orders to come up on deck. When Kendrick saw Liscomb's bloody face, he exploded and grabbed Haswell and slapped him. He told him that he would take his pistol and blow his brains out if he found him on his quarterdeck again. Haswell was removed from his cabin to common quarters with the men. He requested that Kendrick allow him to leave the ship for another vessel, and Kendrick agreed he could take the first vessel they encountered. Unfortunately, no other ship appeared. At the Falklands, Haswell was transferred to the *Lady Washington* to serve under Gray.

Haswell's bitterness and Gray's brash ambition would reinforce one another in the close quarters of the *Lady Washington*. Both Haswell and Gray thought that the time spent at Cape Verde was an unnecessary delay, bringing them late into their passage around the Horn. They would go on to pose a lasting problem for Kendrick. Like the discontent on the *Bounty*, their animosity would take time to deepen. Kendrick paid them little attention. On these pitch-black nights in wild seas, what Haswell and Gray might think was the least of his concerns.

On March 19, the ships were nearly five hundred miles south of Cape Horn at Anson's line of 62° south latitude. Quick, freakish storms clouding blue skies with blinding sleet and snow flashed past them and then broke into sunshine again in less than an hour. In those intervals they managed to press forward. Three days later, on March 22 they were about 670 miles south-southwest of Cape Horn. Having passed the halfway point in rounding the Horn, they shifted their course northwest. They were just approaching the region where Anson had met the most dire storms and seas.

Between four and five in the morning on April 1, nearly four weeks after they had encountered the first gale, the night watch on the *Co-*

lumbia found the wind reversing from the northwest to the south and stiffening. Kendrick knew this was a sign of dangerous weather. The *Columbia* took the shifting winds full on the stern and changed course, attempting to race ahead of it, running with huge seas where the wind disappeared in the troughs and gusted again as the ship climbed to the top of the next swell and sledded down its face. In a maneuver known as "wearing ship," the sails swung with sudden violence across the mast exerting a force that could strain stays, snap lines, shred canvas, and dismast a ship. In the turbulent darkness, the *Columbia* fired a signal gun for the *Washington* and she followed. Swells were rising out of the blackness, bigger than any they had seen thus far, probably topping forty feet.

While the *Columbia* plowed heavily, the *Washington* raced over the massive waves as the winds increased. Lamplight on the *Lady Washington* dropped in and out of sight, and by daylight, with the full force of the storm approaching, she was nowhere to be seen.

Aboard the *Washington,* Haswell used the same language as Anson to describe the devastation that had struck his ships near this spot: "a perfect hericain." In the first few hours, huge breaking swells stove in the *Washington*'s port side quarterboards. With the deck surging underwater, and towering swells breaking nearly on top of her, Haswell huddled with Gray and his crew below deck, believing they faced certain destruction at any moment. Both officers cursed Kendrick for delaying so long at Praia, for keeping them at the Falklands, and for leading them into a storm they might never escape. In three days of raging seas and fierce blizzard, the ships became entirely lost to one another. Neither knew if the other survived, or if the dreams they had embarked with six months earlier were now doomed.

The men on board the *Washington* were exhausted, soaked to the bone, and cold, with no hope of getting dry. The sloop's jib stay was carried away, and only the first mate, Davis Coolidge, and Haswell were in good enough health to go aloft to attempt repair in a wind that pummeled and stung them. For the next ten days they continued through a constant series of violent squalls, and on April 12 Haswell wrote that a gale arose "greatly sirpassing any thing before I had aney Idea of." Immense swells lifted the entire length of the *Washington.* They lashed the wheel and kept the sloop facing west and hunkered down under bare poles, waiting, and expecting a final thundering wave to sink them at any moment.

On board the damaged *Columbia,* Kendrick kept a standing order to watch for the *Washington*. Day after day she failed to appear. When night closed down over the icy, windblown hell, the crew lay caught between hope and despair for their shipmates, and uncertainty about their own fortunes. As the fury continued, Kendrick doubtless wondered what he had brought his sons into. If they survived to return home, they would carry word of the loss of the *Washington* and her captain and crew, something he dreaded as much as the failure of the voyage.

In the few distracted moments he had, Kendrick might have marveled at how close their experience had been to Anson's. The same first gale, the same frozen westing, the same brutal storm as they turned northward. At this point, with his ships scattered and his crew debilitated, Anson had feared Pizarro's Spanish warships coming upon him, unaware that they had been devastated in the storm behind him a month earlier. At least he did not have to fear the Spanish out here, Kendrick might have thought; there was only the howling wind and sea to contend with. Little did he know that, not far ahead, Spanish ships would soon be searching for them.

Chapter Three

Spain's Frontier

Mexico City

March–April 1788

After Pizarro's squadron was destroyed chasing Lord Anson, Spain had sent ships around the Horn during the southern summer, in December and January, and built up a meager fleet to protect and supply Pacific ports. Foreign vessels attempting passage to the coveted Spanish domain in the winter were left first to the ravages of the Horn, but messages about strange ships stopping at ports in Brazil or farther south were often passed to Spanish officials. Approaching from the Falklands, far offshore, Kendrick's ships remained unreported. But despite any precautions Kendrick had taken, his voyage was an open secret.

Don Diego de Gardoqui, Spain's minister in New York, was the first to find out about Kendrick's expedition, and he promptly sent word to Madrid on the weekly packet that ran from New York to Cadiz. A brilliant and beguiling diplomat, Gardoqui had arrived in the United

States in late 1784, after sailing to Havana with José de Galvez, the minister of the Indies who had won him this post. Dressed in a richly brocaded coat and a perfumed and powdered wig, Gardoqui was presented to Congress in its chamber on Wall Street on Saturday, July 2, 1785. To the members attending, he embodied Old World Europe and the complicated and tenuous relationship between the confederated states and Spain.

Although now in decline, Spain remained a global superpower and held a vast domain, drawing tribute and taxes from an empire that reached from islands in the Caribbean to Mexico, Central America, nearly all of South America, and across the Pacific to the Philippines. In North America, Spain's territory dwarfed the thirteen states. Spanish Florida included the future states of Mississippi, Alabama, Florida, and disputed lands in Georgia and along the Mississippi River north to Natchez. The Louisiana Territory encompassed the present states of Louisiana, Arkansas, Oklahoma, Missouri, Kansas, Iowa, Nebraska, Minnesota, the Dakotas, Wyoming, Montana, and Idaho. To the west, New Spain combined the areas of Texas, New Mexico, California, Arizona, Utah, and Colorado. Additionally, Nuevo Galicia contained northern California, Oregon, and Washington and ran north through British Columbia into Alaska.

Administration and protection of the immense Iberian domain was organized in an elaborate structure in the hands of viceroys in Havana, Mexico City, Lima, Buenos Aires, and Manila. The tiered bureaucracy under them was made up of provincial governors, captaincies general, *alcaldes* (mayors), *consejos* (local councils), and local leaders of missions, parishes, and villages. Positions were inherited, purchased, or granted as honors or signs of favor. Maintaining fleets and militias was costly, and within this complex administration, communication was slow and cumbersome. Advance intelligence was vital, and foreign ministers and consuls were the critical eyes and ears of the empire. Their first task was to maintain control of the far-flung colonies and the vital stream of tribute and taxes. To do this, they kept all unlicensed foreigners out of Spanish waters and territories.

Congress was divided and cautious in its judgment of Spain. Its dealings with Gardoqui were complicated by the fact that his family bank had channeled funds to the Revolution and that King Carlos III had eventually committed troops and warships to help defeat the British. Spain had entered the war late in 1779, bound by the "Family Compact" treaty to protect France, not to support American independence. Spain's chief interest was in regaining lands it had lost to Britain in the Seven Years' War, more than a decade earlier. Shortly after entering the war, Spanish troops opened a second front along the Mississippi, securing Baton Rouge and Saint Louis and fighting as far north as Fort Saint Joseph in present-day Michigan. In the Gulf, they captured British settlements at Mobile and Pensacola, and Spanish ships took the Bahamas and other British islands in the Caribbean. At the war's end, with the common British enemy defeated, Spain had regained some of her former lands, but feared an independent American republic acting as a hostile neighbor and a model for increasingly rebellious South American colonies. Spain's goal was for the United States to become a dependent client nation, and to prevent its expansion.

A steady stream of American settlers was already coming over the Appalachians into the "middle lands" east of the Mississippi River. They viewed the river as their great highway, and a route to ship trade goods from settlements southward through New Orleans. This made the river a particular source of contention. In 1784, Spain shut down the lower Mississippi, preventing Americans from proceeding overland or down to the Gulf without a passport from Spanish officials. When Gardoqui came before Congress, discussions had been deadlocked for two years over America's right to navigate the river and settle the "middle lands." In the Peace Treaty of 1783, Britain had granted this frontier territory to the United States with the tantalizing prospect that Congress would then sell millions of acres to settlers and speculators to finance America's war debt. Britain expected the lion's share of the income to be paid to its subjects who had suffered losses in the war, one of the treaty's terms. Britain also knew that the grant of this territory would create deep conflicts with Spanish land claims in the region and would disrupt any alliance between Spain and the rebellious Americans.

Gardoqui was presented to Congress as the minister King Carlos III had empowered to resolve these disputes. However, his private instructions were to keep any progress in negotiations at bay and to disrupt union between the states. Word of Garodqui's intent had been secretly noted in Europe. The French minister at Madrid, Armand Marc, Count de Montmorin, wrote to foreign minister Charles Gravier, Count de Vergennes, in Paris: "The cabinet of Madrid thinks it has the greatest interest not to open the Mississippi to the Americans, and to discourage them from making establishments on that river, as they would not delay to possess themselves of commerce with New Orleans and Mexico, whatever impediments should be opposed to their progress, and that they would become neighbors the more dangerous to Spain, as even in their present weakness they conceive vast projects for the conquest of the western shore of the Mississippi."

Gardoqui took a house in New York City's Vauxhall Gardens, at the lower end of Broadway near Federal Hall. To advance his mission he built up a network of agents and friendly informants. Generations of experience in European diplomacy had refined spying and coercion to a subtle art. The viceroy in Mexico City sent a small fortune of fifty thousand pesos to him annually for his work. From that fund, desperate American merchants, frontiersmen, and elected officials received an array of payments and favors.

In 1786, Gardoqui was nearly successful in having Congress relinquish a claim of rights to navigate the Mississippi. Secretary of State John Jay had recommended acceptance of a treaty that would relinquish rights to the river for twenty-five years in return for rights of commerce with Spain, which would largely benefit the New England states. This angered pioneers in the "middle lands." The Revolutionary

War hero George Rogers Clark gathered militia, and scattered incursions and attacks began mounting on Spanish settlements in contested areas. Gardoqui believed that state officials and members of Congress had encouraged some of the attacks.

BY THE SUMMER OF 1787, Gardoqui was plotting with James Wilkinson, a former general in the Continental Army who was referred to as the "Washington of the West," to set up a Spanish colony in the middle lands. Wilkinson would lead settlers in Kentucky and Tennessee, which were not yet states, to form an independent government loyal to Spain. The citizens of the new colony would have rights on the Mississippi River and act as a buffer to halt American expansion. Wilkinson warned Spanish officials that the move could result in war, and as talk of the plan spread, the prospects of war indeed heated up. While Congress tried to restrain states and independent pioneers, Britain offered one hundred thousand pounds and support of a ten-thousand-man militia in the Appalachian region to invade Louisiana and take control of the region from Spain. The pioneer militia would proceed south, and British ships would capture New Orleans from the Gulf. Britain wanted George Rogers Clark to lead the invasion. Clark was no friend of the British, but he was determined to rid the area of Spaniards and push down the Mississippi, with or without the support of Congress.

THIS AGITATION FOR WAR was part of the political atmosphere in September 1787 when Congress granted the sea letter for the *Columbia* and *Lady Washington*. For Gardoqui, Joseph Barrell's venture to the Pacific Northwest Coast intensified the difficulty of stopping expansion of the United States. The voyage posed a new affront to Spain's efforts to maintain dominion in the Pacific, which had been held under a papal grant for more than two centuries.

The largest potential crack in Spain's ancient claim was the leg-

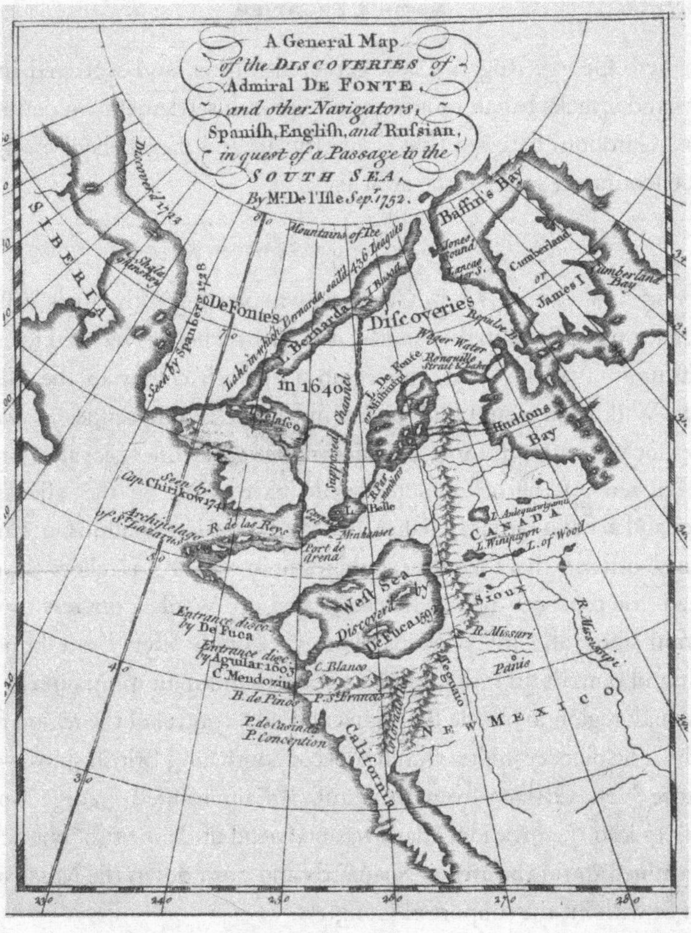

Created by Guillaume de l'Isle, this 1752 map, and copies later made from it, set off a wave of interest to discover the Northwest Passage connecting the Pacific and Atlantic oceans. The map shows the coast of California north to the Bering Strait with the legendary Strait of Juan de Fuca opening to a "West Sea" or "Inland Sea" close to the headwaters of the Mississippi. To the north, the Straits of Admiral de Fonte connect through long waterways to Hudson's Bay. Benjamin Franklin as well as other leading scientists and hydrographers of the time believed in the existence of the fabled passage.

endary Northwest Passage, said to cross North America and connect the Atlantic and Pacific Oceans. Ancient texts called it the "Strait of Anian." Discovery of the passageway had long been sought by many nations. Giovanni Caboto, sailing under the name John Cabot for the

English, had looked for it in the North Atlantic as early as 1497. After raiding the Spanish coast in 1579, Francis Drake searched for the strait from the Pacific, as a shortcut home to England. He ended up on the Oregon coast and named the area "New Albion." When the Spanish found out, they sent their own expeditions northward from Mexico.

In one of the prevalent Spanish stories, Juan de Fuca (Ioannis Fokas), a Greek captain sailing for Spain in 1592, discovered what he believed to be the Strait of Anian leading to an inland sea, which he sailed for twenty days. He said a tall stone column rising from the sea marked the entrance. Fuca told his tale to the British consul in Venice, Michael Lok, who sent it to the English court. From there it was incorporated in the popular book *Purchas His Pilgrimes,* published in London in 1625.

According to another story, in 1640 Spanish admiral Bartholome de Fonte discovered a strait leading from the Pacific into the northwest American coast. There he encountered a ship captained by a man named Nicholas Shapley, who said he had sailed westward from Boston and through Hudson's Bay.

Following these stories, maps of the seventeenth and eighteenth centuries showed the Straits of Admiral de Fonte arcing northward to Hudson's Bay. Farther south, the Strait of Juan de Fuca was believed to lead from the Pacific to a great "river of the west" spoken of by Native Americans. It was suspected to reach eastward to the headwaters of the Missouri River. In 1745, the British Parliament offered a prize of twenty thousand pounds to the explorer who could locate it.

The Loyal Company of Virginia, a group of land speculators that included Thomas Jefferson's father and the grandfather of Meriwether Lewis, began planning an expedition to the Missouri River in 1756 to see if rumors that it "communicated with the Pacific Ocean" were true. Nearly a decade later, at the close of the Seven Years' War, the American frontier hero Robert Rogers, who had engaged in campaigns on the western frontier around the Great Lakes, said that after studying the subject and talking with Indians, he was convinced of the existence of the Northwest Passage. In 1765, Rogers proposed taking two hundred men on an expedition to find it. One of his captains, Jonathan Carver, eventually made the journey west and allegedly reached the headwaters of the Missouri River. Carver applied in vain for Parliament's twenty-thousand-pound reward in 1773 and delivered a report and map to the King's Board of Trade, which published it in 1778. Carver's account names the "river Ouragon" for the first time and describes it as flowing into the mythical Strait of Anian. Thomas Jefferson read Carver's account, and while awaiting a gathering of Congress at Annapolis in 1783, he wrote to George Rogers Clark suggesting that he lead an American expedition to find the legendary passage, one of many efforts Jefferson would make over the next twenty years.

ANY NATION VENTURING to the Pacific Northwest Coast was assumed by Spain to be searching for the entrance to the legendary passage and attempting to claim the territory surrounding it. This posed a dire threat to Spain's dominion over the region. The Americans were already pushing the frontier westward in the Mississippi Valley, and now were about to appear in the Pacific. After receiving information on Kendrick's expedition, Mexican viceroy Manuel Antonio Flores Maldonado wrote a warning to Antonio Valdes, minister of the Marine and the Indies, at Madrid: "We should not be surprised if the English colonies of America, republican and independent, put into practice the design of discovering a safe port on the South Sea [Pacific Ocean], and try to sustain it by crossing the immense land of this continent above our possessions of Texas, New Mexico, and the Californias. Much more might be expected of an active nation that bases all its hopes and resources on navigation and commerce; and, in truth, it would obtain the richest trade of Great China and India if it were to succeed in establishing a colony on the west coast of America."

Flores believed that although it would take several years to establish an American port on the Pacific, Kendrick's expedition, along with probes from the English and Russians, had to be stopped.

The Count of Floridablanca *by Francisco Goya. Don José Monino y Redondo, first Count of Floridablanca, was Spain's foreign minister and chief statesman from 1777 to 1792. Much of his effort served to forestall decline of the once-dominant Spanish empire.*

Diego de Gardoqui's report to Madrid on Kendrick's expedition from Boston would have been forwarded to Antonio Valdes as well as chief minister José Monino Floridablanca. The lean, sunken-faced Count Floridablanca had spent his career protecting the empire from internal and external threats. For more than a decade, reports had been filtering in concerning the plans of Russian merchant companies to extend their fur-trading operations down the Pacific coast from outposts that were established in 1761 off the coast of Alaska and expanded in 1784 to the mainland. He knew that at the urging of those Russian merchant companies, Russian empress Catherine II was now looking at the expanse of Canada to Hudson's Bay and south to California.

Spain had settled its string of California missions along the Pacific coast at San Diego, Santa Barbara, Monterey, and San Francisco between 1769 and 1782 to secure its northern territory. Spanish warships were also sent north from Mexico in 1774 and 1775 to keep an eye on the Russian stations in Alaska and make explorations of the Northwest Coast. And in 1779 an expedition was sent to stop British captain James Cook from exploring for the Northwest Passage and making land claims. Cook concluded that a northern passage between the Pacific and Atlantic did not exist. But belief in the old stories was strong and when his journal was published in 1784, many, including Spanish officers in the Pacific, regarded Cook's conclusion as mistaken.

Russian empress Catherine II ordered an immediate translation of Cook's journal, and gathered an expedition under one of Cook's former officers, Joseph Billings. A number of Cook's other officers enlisted in British merchant ventures to launch from London and Macao for the Northwest Coast. They were interested in the fabled passage, but primarily sought the treasure in furs that Cook had discovered. Floridablanca recognized that the immense wealth that might be gained from trading sea otter furs to China created what seemed to be a real-life quest for the fabled golden fleece. Viceroy Flores had noted this would be "the richest trade of Great China and India." Whoever captured the sea otter trade would control riches, territory, and possibly the legendary passage through North America.

For Britain, the quest for this treasure became part of a larger Pacific campaign to "swing to the East" after the American Revolution. Through the exploration and claims of James Cook and Francis Drake, the British believed they had a valid claim to the Pacific coast of America. Consistent with what Spanish officials feared, the sea otter trade would soon become an important part of London's strategy to assert that claim and break Spain's ancient dominion over the Pacific.

To counter the surging interest in the Northwest Coast of America, Floridablanca reaffirmed a standing policy to exclude foreign ships from Spanish waters and set out a plan to send war frigates into the region. At the City Palais in the dusty valley of Mexico City, Viceroy Flores received a royal order issued from Madrid on November 9, 1787, six weeks after Kendrick had sailed from Boston. Flores, a stout naval commander who had spent his career hunting pirates in the Mediterranean and the West Indies, knew how to deal with illegal ships. The first step was to stop the Russians who were already established to the north. He reviewed Floridablanca's order, which coincided with instructions already sent to the port of San Blas, a naval station three hundred miles from Mexico City on the Pacific coast south of the Baja Peninsula. Ships were to be prepared for a mission to search as far as 61° north latitude, the vicinity of the Kenai Peninsula at the northern end of the Gulf of Alaska.

Conditions at the royal port at San Blas reflected how thinly Spanish men and material were spread. The harbor was a shallow channel carved out of a tidal river surrounded by mangrove swamps and rain forest. The main town was on a hill a mile up the river and contained a ramshackle village, military warehouses, a customs house, and a church. Those stationed there considered it an unhealthy place. Most of the year the woods were thick with mosquitoes and black-throated magpies. Crocodiles lurked in the inlets and muddy lagoons. Grass huts on stilts clustered along the shore. The inner harbor in the river was barely accessible and could only moor four ships. Other vessels had to anchor in the bay, outside the swells that broke onshore.

Despite its threadbare appearance, for nearly twenty years San Blas had been a critical base for shipbuilding and support of the missions in California. José Camacho, an aging navigator, was in charge of the port. Like other officers, he kept a ranch in the healthier upland climate at Tepic, thirty miles inland. With his lieutenants, he commanded the local militia and three armed frigates: the *Santiago* (225 tons), the *Favorita* (193 tons), and the *Princesa* (189 tons). In addition there were two armed packets, or supply ships, the *Aranzazu* and *San Carlos El Filipino*. These ships patrolled the coast, supplied the missions in California, and carried out periodic trans-Pacific voyages to Manila.

When Flores's order to send ships to Alaska arrived in early 1788, Estevan José Martinez, captain of the *Princesa,* was the only officer available to lead an expedition. A portly, balding man with a neatly trimmed beard, Martinez was raised to command. He had been trained at the naval center of San Telmo in Seville, a city with ancient seafaring traditions. Somehow he had ended up here, patiently serving his king during the past fifteen years in San Blas, and awaiting an opportunity to make his mark. He was said to be a nephew of Viceroy Flores and was known as a garrulous man, clever, and accustomed to handling rough crews. As a pilot under Juan Perez he had gone north in 1774 but had not been included in the 1775 expedition or the mission to stop James Cook's exploration. He was familiar enough with the thousands of cold foggy bays and coves along the northern coast to recognize how difficult it would be to locate the Russians. His orders were to discover their outposts, gather intelligence on their operations and plans, check the accuracy of maps of the coast included in Cook's journal, and to take possession of harbors and other sites that offered advantages for Spain along the coast.

In view of the pressure building in this region, he knew that the viceroy and court ministers would be watching the outcome of his mission. The difficulty of the task presented a challenge that both vexed and excited him. After studying Cook's journal and the charts provided by Flores, on March 8, 1788, Martinez departed for the north. On board the *Princesa* were ninety-two men and officers and two chaplains. The *San Carlos,* commanded by pilot Gonzalez Lopez de Haro, carried another chaplain and eighty-six crew and officers. Slipping offshore, they passed Cabo San Lucas at the tip of the Baja Peninsula and by mid-April were halfway to the Gulf of Alaska.

Chapter Four

Refuge

April–June 1788

In the southern Pacific, forty-five hundred miles south of San Blas, the *Columbia* was struggling in the aftermath of the harrowing storm. As hurricane winds bore down and parted the two ships, the *Columbia* had been driven back toward the east. Her mainmast had cracked, the hull was leaking, and the sternpost holding the rudder was damaged. As they lay stalled below Cape Horn, the crew worked to make repairs in continuing squalls. Kendrick kept a signal lantern lit for the *Washington* and fired periodic shots from a cannon, but received no response. The nights were gloomy and frozen, and fear settled among the crew as they headed back into the winds

Far to the southwest, Robert Gray welcomed the empty horizon as the storm cleared. He was enraged that Kendrick's delay at Cape Verde had led him into this winter passage and so close to death, but he now saw an opportunity to escape Kendrick's command. Just before leaving the Falklands, Kendrick had written orders for what Gray should do if they were separated, or if the *Columbia* perished. The first step was a rendezvous at the remote island of Mas Afuera, 540 miles off the coast of Chile. After repairing a split mainsail, Gray aimed the sloop for the island. During the next week, as they made their way northward, the air warmed. Ice crusted on the hull slowly melted. Intermittent gales continued, but nothing like the thundering deluge the sturdy little ship had survived. Once beyond the west entrance to the Straits of Magellan, the strong Humboldt Current and prevailing southwesterlies carried them into more temperate seas and the vast serenity of the rolling Pacific.

They fell into a steady routine, accompanied by thick schools of porpoises running beside the ship, and the first flying fish they had seen in this ocean. Three weeks after parting with the *Columbia,* clouds on the horizon indicated land. Then, at 1 P.M. on April 22, the peak of Mas Afuera poked up into the sky thirty miles off. They brought the ship within four or five miles of shore and scanned the steep, forbidding cliffs that stood partially shrouded in clouds. The great hunk of volcanic rock towered up hundreds of feet along the shore. Far above them the profile of the bare, humped mountain ridge broke above the cloud mass at more than four thousand feet. Before sunset they hove to, waiting through the night to search out a landing spot and take on water and wood.

The next morning Gray scanned the horizon. As he expected, the slow-sailing command ship, if she still existed, was nowhere in sight. He determined that he had fulfilled his orders from Kendrick, and was now on his own.

THROUGH THE GLASS in the early daylight they could see flocks of wild goats grazing on upland precipices and thousands of seals swarming over the rocks along the steep shore. Many streams of fresh water were pouring down the cliff face where brush and trees grew along the edge. In the ship's boat, first mate Davis Coolidge circled the island, which was only six or seven miles long, and found it uninhabited, with steep cliffs, heavy surf, and no place to land without great danger.

Twenty years before, British captain Philip Carteret had noted that the only way to get water from the island was to anchor a boat outside the surf and swim ashore with empty casks and a line to haul filled casks back out. Haswell mentioned Carteret's daring maneuver, and most likely had an account of his Pacific voyage on board. Nevertheless, the *Washington* lacked equipment to haul the casks. Having crewmen plunge into the icy shorebreak wasn't an option. Frustrated, Gray briefly considered stopping at Mas a Tierra, the main island of the Juan Fernándes archipelago, about 120 miles east, but there was a greater risk in taking on water there. They were lightly armed and alone, and could easily lose their ship to the Spanish.

Several hundred miles north lay a pair of uninhabited islands. The latitude was fairly certain, but the longitude was vague. Gray thought they could find them. Measuring longitude was still a trial-and-error process for all ships. A sextant, the triangular handheld sighting instrument that gave optical fixes on the sun, moon, and stars, functioned well for calculating latitude. Longitude, however, required accurate chronometers, which were still being experimented with. The common method of calculating longitude was to plot a course from the last known point, using compass direction and estimated speed, with an allowance for drift and variance of currents, to locate the new position. Measuring speed was a matter of tossing a log tied to a knotted line overboard and timing the "knots" drawn out behind the ship. Miscalculation of longitude on long voyages frequently resulted in wrecks or a course that missed an island or harbor altogether. Ships could end up hundreds of miles from their destination and wander at sea far past the time that provisions and water gave out.

Without waiting a day longer at the planned rendezvous, Gray took the *Lady Washington* northward. He assumed the uninhabited islands would be nearly due north of Mas Afuera, which meant they could run by compass alone. As a precaution, during the next week he reduced water rations to two quarts per man per day. After a few days of anxious sailing, on the morning of May 3 they sighted Ambrose Island sixty miles to the northwest. It took more than a day to approach in light winds. The shore was swarming with seals. And the banks above the shore were eroded, showing brilliantly colored layers of sediment that delighted the men, who, aside from Mas Afuera, had seen little but the sea and sky for two months. High up on top of the banks was a plain with sparse vegetation where they hoped to find water. They took the longboat ashore on the lee side of the island. As they attempted to climb the crusty volcanic slope while carrying empty water casks, rocks crumbled and shifted beneath them, setting off landslides and cave-ins that frightened them. They retreated to the narrow shore and then spent fruitless hours trying to find another way up. Finally they resigned themselves to staying along the shore, where they killed a number of seals and sea lions for their oil and skins. Fish also abounded in the shallows, and at the end of the day they returned to the ship with a welcome supply of fresh meat, but no water.

Gray pressed on. During the next three weeks they made almost sixteen hundred miles and by May 24, under variable winds, passed far west of the Galapagos Islands without seeing them. They had run out of islands that might have offered some chance to replenish wood and water, and eagerly watched for the approach of rain clouds.

A MONTH BEHIND THEM, the *Columbia* paused offshore at Mas Afuera. Not finding the *Washington* at the rendezvous gave Kendrick deepened concern for her crew's fate. He had been ordered by Joseph Barrell "not to touch at any part of the Spanish dominions on the western continent of America, unless driven there by some unavoidable accident." With the *Columbia* still needing repairs, his water and wood running low, and hoping for some word of the sloop, Kendrick decided to risk putting in at Mas a Tierra. Hauling off to the east, they soon saw its folded ridges and craggy line of peaks rising out of the ocean, desolate and barren. This was the island where Alexander Selkirk had been marooned for four years beginning in 1704, which was the inspiration for Daniel Defoe's *Robinson Crusoe.* To the Spanish it was known as Juan Fernándes Island, after the sailor who discovered it in 1574. The isolated location had made it a frequent haunt for pirates, and Lord Anson had taken refuge there after his battered passage around the Horn in 1741. Anson's lost sloop, *Tryal,* caught up with him at anchor in the harbor. On the verdant north shore, he had nursed his men and ships back into a raiding force, and later succeeded in taking Spain's Acapulco treasure galleon, which was laden with taxes and tribute. Following this, the viceroy in Lima occupied the island and established a settlement in 1750 with the dual purpose of serving as a penal colony and discouraging foreign use as a haven for privateers raiding the South American coast.

Kendrick was headed toward the island's Spanish colony in Cumberland Bay. He thought the treatment the *Columbia* would receive depended on the temper of periodic uprisings and unrest along the coast, and even more on the personality of the local governor. He was unaware of the danger they were in, and did not call the crew to prepare the guns. They were in no shape to fight, and it made more sense to be prepared to run, if events fell to that.

Coming around the high, barren mountain on the north side in a bright morning light, Kendrick stopped a mile offshore, scanning the harbor, which opened to a bay and a broad green valley spilling onto a beach. Sparse trees climbed up to the base of the eroded ridges. A small fort with yellow-brown stone walls occupied a high bank on the west side. Across a creek, a scattering of tiny houses and fenced gardens of convicts and outcasts dotted a grassy field. A few small fishing boats sat at anchor, but there were no ships. The *Washington* was not there.

From the fort, the governor of the island, Don Blas Gonzales, recognized a ship in distress. Gonzales was sergeant major at the Isla Juan Fernándes military post and leader of its civil government. He was a plain man and tried to be a just and pious administrator. Foreign ships were sometimes seen passing offshore, but rarely entered the bay. This was the first ship he had seen flying the red-and-white striped colors of the United States. He quickly summoned an officer, Nicholas Juanes, to put out in a fishing boat with an armed guard.

Kendrick was comforted at the sight of only one small boat approaching with a few armed men. As it came alongside, he made signs of peace and invited the two Spanish soldiers on board. Juanes questioned Kendrick in Spanish, which no one among the officers or crew fully understood. Kendrick tried to explain in French that he needed safe anchorage to make repairs and take on fresh water and wood. He said they were sailing in company with a packet boat that had become separated from them in a storm. In Juanes's account, Kendrick said that General Washington of the United States had sent him on this expedition to inspect the Russian settlements north of California.

Juanes noted that the ship carried three officers and a crew of forty. Eighteen of the crew seemed to be boys between twelve and sixteen years old. For armament there were ten cannons: two large stern chasers, and two canons on each side of the ship, interspersed with four smaller cannons. Juanes noted that none of the younger crew appeared trained in the use of weapons. The captain and crew seemed friendly and nonthreatening. Kendrick offered copies of the ship's papers. Juanes took the first mate, Joseph Ingraham, back into the harbor with him to request permission to enter. Juanes reported what he had found and said he believed there was little cause for suspicion. Don Blas Gonzales was intrigued by the American ship, and he decided to inspect this curious *Bostonesa Fragata* himself.

The *Columbia* moored less than a pistol shot off the wharf, under the guns of the fort. Gonzales watched the captain boldly come ashore to meet him, taking his hand and asking in French for his hospitality. He had not yet received instructions from the viceroy to seize the *Columbia* and *Washington*. Although royal law dating from 1692 required Gonzales to consider all foreign ships in Spanish waters as enemies, there was also a universal code of mercy for those in distress at sea. And it was clear the Americans were in distress.

Although communication was difficult, Kendrick was affable and charming, and his deference led to mutual respect between the men. Gonzales inspected the damage to the ship and noted gun placements and the structural differences with European ships. The high quarterdeck gave officers a clear view of the whole ship and created ample quarters below it. Gonzales marveled at the fine woodworking in the ship's cabins, and concurred with Juanes that these voyagers meant no harm. He was impressed that they had weathered the Horn. Putting the ugly prospect of seizing this ship aside, he granted six days for repairs and provisioning, though he warned that there was a scarcity of wood and almost everything else. No one was to go ashore without his permission, and all contact with the island's inhabitants was to be avoided. When Kendrick asked about his missing sloop, Gonzales had no information to offer.

Relieved for the moment by a chance to repair and resupply, Kendrick set the ship's carpenters, Isaac Ridler and James Hemmingway, to work on the mast and the damaged sternpost and rudder. Cargo was shifted in the hold to find the source of leaks, and a boat was sent to the little creek to fill water casks under the noses of the fort's soldiers.

Four days after the Americans arrived, a Spanish packet, the *Delores,* appeared with provisions for the settlement and dispatches from Callo, Peru. The packet was headed to Valparaiso, Chile. A Frenchman on board was sent for by the governor to assist in examining the *Columbia*'s papers. In addition to the sea letter from Congress, Kendrick showed him an official letter of the Sieur l'Etombe, the French consul at Boston. Kendrick also undoubtedly regaled him with memories of his privateering days in Nantes a decade earlier. The Frenchman did not want to end up in the middle of an imbroglio, and so he found nothing amiss. Through the captain of the packet, Kendrick sent a brief letter to Joseph Barrell, telling him they had arrived at Juan Fernándes after a "fatiguing passage of eighty-six days from Falkland Islands, and the misfortune of parting with the Sloop Washington on the first of April." Wanting to deliver only good news, as was typical of his messages, Kendrick added a postscript that he believed the *Washington* was safe.

The crew did what they could in the six days Gonzales had allotted. The *Columbia* needed to be hauled out to fully repair seams that had opened, but that would have to wait. Some of the work was hampered by strong winds from the south, funneling violent gusts down the ravines and out onto the bay. These microbursts, lasting only one or two minutes, disrupted replacement of chafed lines and tore apart anything on deck not lashed down. As they prepared to leave on the sixth day, a heavy rainstorm and winds from the north drove into the harbor, keeping them at anchor until June 3.

Meanwhile, word of the *Columbia,* carried by the packet, had reached Valparaiso and set off a panic. The primary warship in the region, the thirty-four-gun *Santa Maria,* was not prepared for sea. A merchant brig, the *San Pablo,* was quickly armed and sent off in pursuit on June 12, followed by the *Maria*.

WITH A HEAD START OF SEVERAL DAYS, the damaged *Columbia* limped northward along the course Kendrick had instructed Gray to take, keeping far off the coast of the continent until they reached variable winds on the coast of California. Meanwhile, the *San Pablo* patrolled inshore and missed the *Columbia* entirely. After days of searching northward, she put into Lima with news of the *Bostonesa Fragata*. As panic spread up the coast, Peru's viceroy, Teodoro de Croix, sent out another ship from Callao. De Croix was outraged that Gonzales had not seized the armed American ship. "We cannot ignore the strangers who penetrate into these seas with no license from our court," he wrote. "They must be tried like enemies . . . Regardless of how innocent the designs of the American Republic . . ." de Croix believed it was right to be suspicious "to protect the King's serene and pacific possession." He pointed to invading pirates who could easily disrupt commercial shipping and raid coastal towns. Behind his concern was the reality the *Columbia* made obvious—that without a huge Pacific fleet of warships, Spain had no way to protect shipping and the numerous coastal villages and towns of this sprawling domain.

After the pursuit ships returned empty-handed, Gonzales was stripped of his office for not seizing the *Bostonesa Fragata* and arresting her crew. Gonzales argued that he had carried out his office with diligence and obeyed the law with an interest in promoting peace between the two nations. It was a case that would go on for years. Eventually, Kendrick would enlist Thomas Jefferson to help restore Gonzales to the Spanish court's good graces, but Jefferson's efforts too would prove futile.

Viceroy Teodoro de Croix sent a warning north to Viceroy Flores in Mexico City that the American *fragata Columbia* had appeared at the island of Juan Fernándes. He also dispatched the warning to officials in Guatemala, with copies to minister Antonio Valdes in Madrid. Mexico's viceroy Flores sent the message on to San Blas, Acapulco, and the missions north to San Francisco: "A ship named Columbia which belongs to General Washington of the American states, and under the command of John Kendrick sailed from Boston September 1787 to make discoveries and inspect the establishments of the Russians . . ." If the *Columbia* or its consort, *Lady Washington,* appeared, they were to be seized and the crews arrested as pirates.

UNAWARE OF THE EVENTS THEY HAD SET IN MOTION, Kendrick and his crew continued slowly northward on their seventy-five-hundred-mile course, averaging less than a hundred miles a day. They planned to land near "New Albion," along the coast of northern California and southern Oregon, the area Britain claimed was discovered and named by Francis Drake in 1579.

A Night Dance by Women in Hapaee *by John Webber. Published as part of James Cook's journal of his third voyage, engravings of this type fed the fantasies of sailors and the public alike about the exotic nature of the Pacific.*

Eight months into their voyage and far into the Pacific, the *Columbia*'s crew likely grew enamored with the idea of visiting islands described by James Cook. They also became eagerly focused on their destination—Nootka. The exotic-sounding wilderness harbor where Cook's crew had traded for prized furs lay midway between San Francisco and the Gulf of Alaska. Spanish captain Juan Perez, who had briefly traded with natives there in 1774, called it San Lorenzo. In typical imperial fashion, Cook renamed it King George's Sound four years later as part of Britain's efforts to lay claim to the coast. London mapmakers reportedly borrowed from Cook's notes and gave it the name of Nootka, by which it had become known.

Although Joseph Barrell had issued specific instructions that no man was to trade on his own account, talk of how James Cook's crew had traded buttons and nails for prime skins was common below deck.

The Russians called sea otter furs "liquid gold" because of the high payments they received from Chinese traders. Few of the Americans had seen the furs, but they were known to possess a mesmerizing beauty and were marveled at for their thickness, softness, and near-luminous sheen. Glossy black or brown on the outer surface, the inner fur held a silvery underluster that looked incredible when rippled in the wind or by the hand. It was the choice of royalty, and the Chinese treasured it for exclusive clothing for wealthy mandarins. Native people of the Northwest Coast prized it as well, and sewed three five-foot skins into robes for chiefs, or trimmed collars and capes with it. Each *Columbia* crew member undoubtedly hatched plans for trading and smuggling a few prime skins that could be worth ten times his wages. Kendrick let them dream, knowing there was great uncertainty ahead and they could soon be tested by a daunting enemy.

JUNE PASSED INTO JULY as they plodded northward. Cold water from the north and hot, steamy days created thick fogs. Despite manning a close watch, the *Columbia* went far west of the Galapagos. Rain kept the water barrel full, and albacore and turtles provided fresh meat, a break from the last of the goats on deck and the meat they had salted and packed six months earlier at Cape Verde. As they sailed with a prevailing northwesterly wind guiding them, their good fortune gave out.

Two of the crew showed purple blotches on their skin. Others complained of bleeding gums and aching in their joints; some seemed unusually pale and their eyes were sunken. This was the curse of long-distance voyages that any captain feared more than hostile ships or storms: scurvy. The disease was unpredictable, and superstition held that it came from "sea vapors." Although at first it would affect only a few members of the crew, given enough time it could disable most of them. Kendrick knew that as the disease advanced there would be shivering and trembling, listlessness, bleeding under the skin, and boils and open sores that would not heal. Old wounds could reopen.

Eventually, a man's feet, legs, hands, and even bones would begin to rot. At an advanced stage the disease led to an agonizing death. Although it was generally believed to be accelerated by the unsanitary conditions that prevailed below deck on most ships, some physicians and captains believed it could be cured or prevented by a good diet. The disease, in fact, resulted from the body's inability to make collagen when it did not receive vitamin C from fresh fruit and vegetables. James Cook was among the early mariners to try various foods to cure scurvy, but packing oranges, lemons, and limes aboard ships for long voyages was not a common practice until the early nineteeth century. Not until the early twentieth century was the connection between vitamin C deficiency and scurvy conclusively proved.

John Hammond and Hanse Lawton, two of the three seamen who had signed on just before sailing from Cape Verde, were in the worst condition. They had not fattened and rested with the crew as Kendrick prepared for the long voyage. Isolated from the other men and confined in the sick bay, Hammond's condition steadily worsened. Kendrick and Ingraham had the crew wash down the ship with gunpowder and vinegar, hoping the fumes would kill the contagion and whatever other opportunistic disease might be lurking. Two other common ship illnesses, typhus and dysentery, could appear at the same time and further disable the crew.

The haunting presence of disease increased the crew's eagerness to reach land. Many believed that solid earth restored a man's vitality. Often, sailors tried to cure the disease by burying a scurvy victim in sand up to his waist, a treatment that exacerbated infections and death.

As the symptoms of scurvy became more prevalent among the men, watches were unable to get aloft to change sail, and the topsails remained reefed. This conserved the men's energy but prolonged their suffering since the ship was now making slower headway. It was a different kind of hell from the thrashing they had received coming around the Horn. Kendrick watched his sons and others for signs of the disease, and tried to give heart to Lawton and Hammond. The condition of *Columbia*'s men deepened his concern over the fate of the *Washington,* if she had survived the storms around the Horn.

THE *WASHINGTON'S* MEN WERE also afflicted with scurvy, and her progress had slowed as well. When the *Columbia* was departing Cumberland Bay on June 3, the *Washington* was seven hundred fifty miles southwest of Manzanillo on the Mexican coast. She had been too far inshore and was caught in the strong southward-flowing current. More than two weeks later, on June 19, the sloop had made only twenty miles of headway. Finally, giving up this course, Gray took the ship westward about nine hundred miles and then swung northeast again. It was a roundabout route, but the trade winds and currents would favor them.

The weeks wore on, and the rainfall that Gray and his men prayed for replenished their water casks, but seven of the eleven men were suffering from scurvy. Three or four developed very serious cases. Salted meat seemed to add to the problem. They caught turtles, whose strong flavor and stringy flesh was judged "not very delicate eating." Gray knew they needed to find land soon.

The crew was kept busy braiding anchor cables in anticipation of reaching shore. The unrelenting work of making rope by picking apart old strands and reweaving the threads into new braids went on for hours each day when there was nothing else to do. Gray took sextant readings, noting their drift and the changing winds that finally allowed them to make steady progress.

On July 31 came the surprise they had long hoped for: they sailed into a dense flock of birds. Hours later, they sighted a haze to the east. The following day the water changed from blue to a greenish hue. Huge strands of kelp torn from the bottom by some storm floated on the surface. Piling on a press of sail they made what speed they could toward the haze, and on the morning of August 2, with "inexpressible joy," they saw the dark blue line of the American coast appear nearly thirty miles off. Haswell took a sextant reading. They were in 41°38' north latitude (approximately twenty miles south of the Oregon border near the Klamath River).

The morning of August 4 was foggy. Riding a light breeze, they closed with the coast of North America. Green hills huddled all along the shore and stretched across the entire eastern horizon. That night they waited anxiously offshore to avoid shoals, sunken rocks, or reefs. The following morning, a light breeze carried them in, then died, and they lay in a calm about two and a half miles out. The current carried them slowly southward, where they could see a river through the glass. Gray put out the anchor, and they were planning to lower the longboat to explore the river when they sighted a canoe approaching.

They primed the swivel guns, and the men loaded their muskets as the broad redwood canoe came over the swells. The canoe was long—maybe twenty feet—with square ends arching inward at the bow and stern. There were ten men inside. As they approached the ship, a few rose and made signs of friendship. They stood several yards off, gesturing and talking. They were brown-skinned and naked except for deerskin loincloths and blue beads of European manufacture. Some were marked with various tattoos. Haswell noted that they were "well-limbed" and was impressed by their strength and ability to handle a canoe at sea. Gray coaxed them to the ship. They came alongside, and a few offered short pipes stuffed with tobacco or sweet-scented herbs. Gray gave them presents, keeping the crew on guard. As they attempted to converse, the wind gusted up from the west bearing signs of a squall. Fearing they would be driven onto shoals inshore, Gray cut short the encounter and turned north, looking for a harbor.

They searched for hours and found only an endless stretch of beach. There seemed no safe place to land, which was all the more agonizing for those suffering the worst cases of scurvy.

For the next few days they coasted, finding the land "thickly inhabited by the maney fiers we saw in the night and Culloms of smoak we would see in the day." All the tribes were down at their summer camps along the shore. As the sloop cruised past, men came off in canoes, and others fled from their houses into the woods or ran along the shore, shaking their spears and shouting in defiance. All the signs seemed to show that traders had been on this shore at some time.

Near midday on August 9, four days and about two hundred miles north of their first encounter, two men in a small canoe with pointed ends came toward them. They hung out of pistol range until one of them stood. A "very fine looking fellow," Haswell noted, "delivered a long oration, accompanying it with actions and Jestures that would have graced a Europan oritor." Gray believed they were offering fish and fresh water on shore and he let them know that he and his men were seeking furs, which they indicated they would bring the next day. The *Washington* ran offshore again that night for the safety of deeper waters. The next morning, in fog and wet weather, they set down the longboat to search out a landing place. While the longboat was exploring the shore, two canoes paddled out to the sloop, one carrying the two men from the previous day and the other holding six men armed with bows and spears. They offered several sea otter skins, and one man came on board. Haswell noted that a few were pitted with smallpox scars and carried metal knives, more signs of previous traders.

It wasn't until the evening of August 13 that they found a harbor large enough for the sloop. Heading offshore at dusk, they returned the next day and armed the longboat with a swivel gun. Then they sent First Mate Coolidge and a few of the crew to sound the entrance and mark bearings to the channel. The *Washington* anchored a half mile from shore, near what is now Tillamook Bay. Smoke rose from a village in a clearing in the trees. A few natives appeared and stared at the ship. Gray was reluctant to send anyone in. After great amounts of gesturing and enticement a canoe finally ventured out. Gray handed them presents over the side. Others followed, bringing with them boiled crabs and baskets of berries as return gifts. Haswell noted, "these were the most acceptable things they could have brought to most of our seamen who were in a very advanced state of the scurvey and was a means of a restoration of health to three or four of our Companey who would have found one months longer duration at sea fatal to them so advanced were they in this malignant distemper."

By evening there was a brisk trade of sea otter skins for knives, axes, adzes, and other goods. And the next day the crew took on several boatloads of wood and refilled water casks. While the crew worked onshore, the natives cautiously approached, bringing more berries, but always with their knives gripped, ready to strike. There was fear and fascination on both sides. Haswell noted that the crew knew nothing of the manners and customs of these people, and observed "the women wearing nothing but a petticoat of straw about as long as a highlanders kilt."

News of the sloop went from the village into the countryside, and on the third morning, amid pleasant weather and a breeze from the ocean, an "amazing number of the natives" came alongside offering boiled and roasted crabs and dried salmon and berries, which the men bought with buttons or other stray metallic objects. Growing uneasy about the number of natives surrounding them, or perhaps due to some unnoted incident, Gray decided to depart. They weighed anchor and started out on the tide, only to go aground on a rocky reef in the channel.

They would have to wait for the next flood tide to refloat the ship. In the meantime, Gray sent out the longboat with seven men to gather grass and fodder for the few goats still on board. The landing party of seven men included victims of advanced scurvy. Haswell later noted that they had only two muskets and three or four cutlasses with them. Haswell and Coolidge were armed with swords and pistols, and brashly walked into the village. There they found a group of men demonstrating their skill with spears and arrows. To their horror a war dance began, "accompanied with frightful howlings" and threatening gestures that convinced the two young officers to leave.

Marcus Lopius, a young black servant Gray had taken on at Cape Verde, was scything grass near the shore, his cutlass stuck in the sand. As he turned to carry a bundle to the boat, a native who had been loitering nearby grabbed the cutlass and began to run. The men yelled, threatening to shoot him if he didn't drop the cutlass. Lopius took off after him. No one could call him back.

Hearing the commotion, other natives rushed out of the village. The shouts carried down the beach to Haswell and Coolidge. Realizing the danger they were in, Coolidge ordered the longboat to follow them, and the two officers and a crewman ran back to the village to find Lopius. Despite offering gifts, no one would tell them anything. Then, "turning a clump of trees that obstructed our prospect the first thing which presented itself to our view was a large groop of the natives among the midst of which was the poor black with the thief by the colour loudly calling for our assistance . . . when we were observed by the main boddy of the Natives to haistily approach them they instantly drenched there knives and spears with savage feury in the boddy of the unfortunate youth. He quited his hold and stumbled but rose again and staggered towards us but having a flight of arrows thrown into his back he fell within fifteen yards of me."

A second shower of arrows then fell on Coolidge, Haswell, and the crewman as they ran for the boat. The tide was low and they splashed into the shallows with the natives chasing them. Haswell turned and shot the closest pursuer with his pistol. Coolidge did the same and called to those in the boat to cover them as they waded out. The natives plunged in after them, hurling spears and shooting more arrows. Coolidge was wounded slightly, as was Haswell, and the crewman with them took an arrow that made a seemingly fatal wound. He fainted from sudden loss of blood as they ran. They grabbed him and dragged him aboard the boat as it pushed out.

The natives launched canoes to cut them off from the ship. It was a race, with the natives quickly gaining until musket fire from the longboat began to hold them back. Haswell was convinced that they had walked into an ambush. If the men ashore had been killed, Gray and the three men onboard the *Lady Washington* would have been easily overwhelmed.

Musketfire from the longboat continued to hold off the canoes, and as the frightened men reached the sloop, Gray fired three swivel shots, which drove the last of the canoes to shore. The crewman who had been wounded on the beach was unconscious. Gray feared he was near death, but he recovered after the arrowhead was removed and his bleeding stopped.

All that night the sloop helplessly waited for the tide as the sleepless men listened to "hoops and houlings" from the village. There was a large fire on the beach near where Lopius was killed and they could see a great number of men passing back and forth in front of it. Haswell wanted vengeance, and he wished Gray would rake the fire and village with swivel guns. But Gray thought that would only make matters worse. Right now, the men were vulnerable, and firing on the villagers would only inflame the situation.

At 4 A.M., just before first light, the *Washington* raised sail in a desperate attempt to get offshore. She lifted from the shoal, but as they passed the sandy point of the harbor, the wind died and the current dragged the sloop out into the surf breaking over another bar. They dropped anchor too late and the swells drove them hard onto the shoal, breaking over the stern, shattering the transom windows, and flooding the captain's quarters. The men were tossed about on deck. Those watching from the shore must have believed the sea was vanquishing their new enemies. All seemed lost.

Despite the pummeling on a flooded deck, the men held on. As the pintals and gudgins that kept the rudder in place were bent by repeated crashing on the hard shoal, the crew could only hope they remained workable and the hull stayed sound. As the tide slackened, Gray put the longboat over the side carrying an anchor they could use to kedge themselves into the channel. As they labored to move the sloop, a large war canoe slipped out of the harbor, staying out of gun range and taking a position between them and the open ocean. Hauling on the anchor proved fruitless. Now they were grounded and blocked.

For a second night they awaited the wind and another high tide.

The next morning, August 18, was foggy and still. In the mist, a great crowd of natives gathered by canoes on the beach and shouted out to the war canoe beyond the bar, which answered soon after. The fog did not burn off, and about noon the *Washington*'s crew saw three large war canoes carrying thirty men each emerging from the mist with bows bent and spears ready. Gray fired three swivel shots. The war canoes turned. Gray did not want to risk the possibility of attacks from both sea and shore, so they hurriedly raised anchor and strained frantically to scrape off the bar. With the help of a light breeze and a surging wave, the sloop lifted. Onshore, a mix of relief and dismay probably passed among the warriors as the strange vessel slipped beyond the waves and disappeared into the fog.

The shock of those long hours of the encounter most likely left Gray and his crew exhausted and wondering if this was what they should expect all along the coast. How would they survive, let alone trade? Nootka, where James Cook had described the natives as friendly, was two hundred fifty miles north, if they could find it. Even there, they would be vastly outnumbered. They were on their own, and the situation was so desperate that Haswell mentioned nothing of it in his journal. The reality was that Gray's and Haswell's headstrong drive to part from the *Columbia* and their naive blundering had left them badly exposed.

CHAPTER FIVE

Halting the Incursion

Northwest Coast

MAY–DECEMBER 1788

AS THE *WASHINGTON* WAS FLEEING TILLAMOOK, the *Columbia* was logging slow and steady headway a thousand miles off the Mexican Baja coast. The pursuing ships had dropped off long ago, but the alarm about the American expedition was still spreading. From the north, Estevan José Martinez aboard his war frigate *Princesa* was coming down the Pacific coast. He had not learned of Kendrick yet, but he was already convinced he had found a dire threat to the Spanish Empire, and had in his hands a plan to defeat it.

Three months earlier, in May, Martinez had sailed north to reach the sprawling archipelago of southern Alaska, with the armed packet boat *San Carlos* trailing him with supplies. He cruised past the eerie maze of fog-shrouded inlets and islands, believing that somewhere here might be the legendary Straits of Admiral de Fonte. But there was no time to search, and the land gave no clear sign of a passageway into the continent. When the fog burned off at midday it revealed only immense mountains and dense green forests coming out of winter.

Estevan José Martinez Fernández y Martinez de la Sierra was the temperamental founder of Spain's fateful settlement at Nootka. (Portrait from the Spanish Royal Navy)

Fixed on his mission, Martinez pressed northward, and at the mouth of Prince William Sound, on May 17, he began the search for Russian outposts.

Problems with his officers and those of the *San Carlos* were dogging the voyage. The difficulties ranged from silent animosity to direct disobedience of orders. An apprentice pilot argued with Martinez for a few days over the identification of Isla del Carmen. The pilot insisted it was Montague Island, as marked on the British map by James Cook. Frustrated by the apprentice's persistent refusal to record the correct name in his journal, Martinez struck the young man, knocking him flat on the deck and ordering him to go aboard the *San Carlos*.

For Gonzalo Lopez de Haro, the pilot commanding the *San Carlos,* the incident added to the reasons he disliked being under Martinez's command. Lopez de Haro was ordered to keep in visual contact with the *Princesa,* but like Robert Gray in the *Washington,* he evaded his commander and sailed north on his own. On the Kenai Peninsula, the *San Carlos* pilot encountered Aleut natives who indicated where the Russians might be found. The Aleuts showed him letters written in Russian and one in English from William Douglas, the captain of a British ship that had recently traded in local villages.

Although Martinez and Lopez de Haro had not seen them, there were three British fur-trading ships prowling the Alaskan coastal waters as part of an effort to monopolize the fur trade: the *Iphigenia Nubiana,* which Douglas commanded, and the *Prince of Wales* and *Princess Royal* commanded by James Colnett, a former officer of James Cook.

On June 30, Lopez de Haro found the Russian settlement the natives had described in Three Saints Bay on Kodiak Island. The commander told him there were six other outposts in Alaska, a Russian sloop on the mainland, and more than four hundred men. Another Russian ship, *Trekh Sviatitelei,* commanded by two imperial naval officers, was also cruising the region. The ship carried painted posts, copper plates, and medals to stake out and claim the Russian domain at 52° north latitude, halfway south to Nootka. An expedition from Siberia was expected in the coming year. It would be led by Joseph Billings, another one of Cook's officers who was now serving Russian empress Catherine II. The Russians were intent on putting a halt to British trading ships, and they planned to make a settlement at Nootka.

With his new information, Lopez de Haro hurried to rejoin the *Princesa*. But Martinez had found an even richer source of intelligence. As he cruised north and west along the Aleutians, he happened upon the Russian outpost at Dutch Harbor on the island of Unalaska. In the shadow of a looming mountain, twenty native huts on the shore surrounded a crude warehouse and a long building used to shelter Aleut hunters. A single grizzled Russian, Potap Zaikov, commanded the outpost. Martinez had been anchored in the harbor for ten days when the *San Carlos* appeared, and during that time had developed a warm relationship with Zaikov.

When Lopez de Haro gave his report, Martinez angrily told him that the information was of little use. His figures on the Russian men were not accurate, and from Zaikov, Martinez had learned more of the Russian and British plans. There were four additional Russian men-of-war coming around the Cape of Good Hope to reinforce the Billings expedition. And the Russians wanted to establish a settlement at San Lorenzo de Nuca during the next summer, in July or August of 1789, to block British trading and assert their claims.

Even though some of Lopez de Haro's information confirmed what Zaikov had said, it didn't matter. Martinez viewed Haro's excursion as insubordination and began a formal process to remove him from command of the *San Carlos,* an action that sparked further dissent among Martinez's officers and crew. At one point a pilot and pilot's apprentice went down on their knees, pleading with Martinez to go no further on his charges against Lopez de Haro. He resisted their appeals and told them they could lodge a formal complaint against him when they returned to San Blas.

Following the viceroy's instructions, on August 5 Martinez held a small ceremony onshore, surreptitiously taking possession of Dutch Harbor despite the Russian settlement. His spirits seemed to brighten, and the officers' appeals concerning Lopez de Haro finally succeeded. He restored de Haro to command of the *San Carlos,* warning him again to remain in visual contact, and if separated to rendezvous with the *Princesa* at Monterey. On August 15, the two Spanish ships left Dutch Harbor and started homeward.

Martinez was deeply disturbed by the threat the Spanish Empire faced at Nootka in light of growing British interests and the Russian intent to establish a settlement there. On the return trip he began work on a plan to deliver to José Commacho, his commander at San Blas, and to Viceroy Flores. At the center of the plan, he believed San Lorenzo de Nuca (Nootka Sound) should be fortified as soon as possible to act as the main base for Spain's defense in the North Pacific. Ships stationed there could explore south to San Francisco and north to Cook Inlet, Alaska, securing the coast and making special note of any inlets that would appear to be the straits of Admiral de Fonte or Juan de Fuca. He also added the possibility of Spanish companies taking over the fur trade and extending Spanish control to the Sandwich Islands (Hawaii). To assert his devotion, Martinez capped the plan with an oath to sacrifice his "last breath in the service of God and King" to carry out the plan.

If Martinez had received the warning from Teodoro de Croix about Kendrick and the American expedition, he would have considered the situation even more critical. He also might have lingered on this part of the Alaskan coast to take these vessels. But he had been gone from San Blas a few months when de Croix's warning arrived.

As he voyaged south, Martinez missed the *Washington,* which was making her way up the Oregon coast north of Tillamook. Two weeks later, he passed the track of the *Columbia,* sailing farther offshore and headed for her American landfall.

Things were still going wrong with his officers. Not surprisingly, Lopez de Haro had parted with the *Princesa* again at the first opportunity in heavy southern Alaska fog. While Martinez waited for him at the planned rendezvous at Monterey, Lopez de Haro pressed southward, eager to be the first to bring news about the Russians to San Blas and to file a complaint against Martinez for brutality and drunkenness. What he didn't contemplate was that the urgency of his news would override consideration of his complaint.

When Martinez arrived at San Blas a month after Lopez de Haro, he repeated the news from Alaska and delivered his plan to defend the empire. Viceroy Flores agreed that having an armed presence in those northern waters was now vital. Although it would be difficult to support on a permanent basis, a Spanish base could secure the empire's claim and counter the threat of the Russians and British, as well as the Americans.

Flores understood the critical nature of the American expedition and their desires for a port on the Pacific. He embraced Martinez's recommendations and instructed the sharp-tempered captain to make the *Princesa* and *San Carlos* ready for sea, granting him the rank of commander-in-chief for the new expedition. Short of men and supplies, Martinez would have to draw some of his crew from the local population who had never been to sea. The pilots who had just failed in their official complaints against Martinez would now be required to serve under him once again.

In his instructions to Martinez, Flores denigrated the validity of any claims Russia or Britain might make to the Northwest Coast by citing previous Spanish expeditions, which established "our just and preeminent right to occupy the coasts discovered to the north of the Californias, and to defend them against foreign colonizing powers." Flores considered it a "delicate undertaking" for Martinez, who was to

Spanish Frigate *Princesa* off Neah Bay 1792 *by Hewitt Jackson.*

halt any foreign trading with native villages and to attempt to reason with Russian or English commanders. He was to remember the serious consequences of arousing the hostility of the Russians, and to remain firm with the English. Flores also warned Martinez that he might encounter Kendrick's *Bostonesa Fragata* and "a small packet which was sailing in her company." For these American ships he could use "more powerful arguments." If the Americans were to try to use force, Martinez was to repel them. Although not stated in the instructions, Martinez knew that royal standing orders allowed him to seize any foreign ship in Spanish waters as an enemy.

The new command was an ambitious undertaking. In addition to securing Nootka, Martinez was also ordered to send the *San Carlos* to explore ports and inlets north of Nootka from 50° to 55° north latitude, in the vicinity where the Straits of Admiral de Fonte were thought to lie. When the *Aranzazu* and *Conception* arrived later in the year with supplies, they were to examine the coast from Nootka south to San Francisco and take possession of harbors while looking for the Strait of Juan de Fuca.

No one could have guessed that Martinez's plan would soon make the wilderness harbor at Nootka an international flashpoint. Completely unaware of what lay ahead of them, John Kendrick and the American expedition were sailing into the middle of it.

Part II

Infinite Wilderness

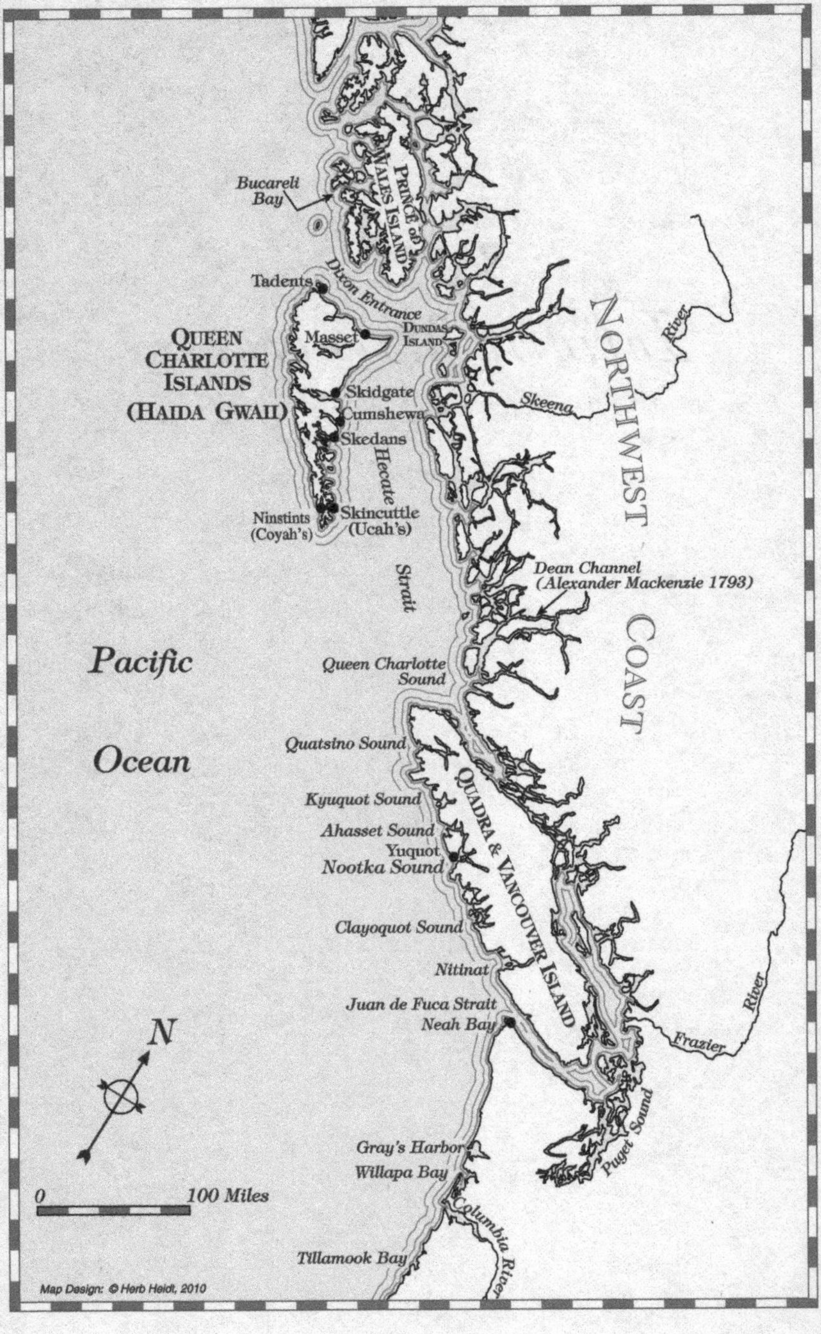

Bucareli Bay
PRINCE of WALES ISLAND
Tadents
Dixon Entrance
QUEEN CHARLOTTE ISLANDS (HAIDA GWAII)
Masset
DUNDAS ISLAND
Skidgate
Cumshewa
Skedans
Hecate Strait
Ninstints (Coyah's)
Skincuttle (Ucah's)
NORTHWEST COAST
River
Skeena
Dean Channel (Alexander Mackenzie 1793)
Pacific Ocean
Queen Charlotte Sound
Quatsino Sound
Kyuquot Sound
Ahasset Sound
Yuquot
Nootka Sound
QUADRA & VANCOUVER ISLAND
Clayoquot Sound
Nitinat
Juan de Fuca Strait
Neah Bay
Frazier River
Puget Sound
N
Gray's Harbor
Willapa Bay
0
100 Miles
Columbia River
Tillamook Bay
Map Design: © Herb Heidt, 2010

CHAPTER SIX

Nootka

Northwest Coast

SEPTEMBER 1788–MAY 1789

UNDER A CLEAR HALF-MOON the American landmass rose on the night of September 22 as the *Columbia* approached the mountainous coast. Kendrick took a lunar observation and fixed within a few miles how far north they had come. Not wanting to fight the southward current, he had kept his course far offshore until they were in the vicinity of Nootka. The past few days, progress had been agonizingly slow. When the night watch changed, word of landfall spread through the ship greatly lifting the spirits of the crew.

Dawn broke with high clouds and moderate winds as Kendrick brought the *Columbia* in along the southwest-facing coastline. The vast green land stirred excitement, with men watching over the rail, and a few aloft, examining the shore for a break or inlet. This was not the American paradise of ancient explorers, but an infinite wilderness of northern coastal rain forest swept by fourteen-foot tides and hemmed in by harsh rocky terrain. It looked incredibly majestic from the sea. Low, rounded ridges close to the shore stood in the shadows of a continuous chain of taller peaks behind them, one reaching into the sky a mile or more. Along the shore, the forested ridges fell to weather-beaten headlands and sandy pocket beaches hedged in undergrowth and thick cedar hummocks.

The entrance they were looking for, known as San Lorenzo de Rada (Road of Saint Lawrence) to the Spanish, was easily lost in the ragged folds of the shore. It lay about two miles wide in a lowland gap near a rocky point. They cruised slowly to the southeast and by midday they found it. After almost a year of voyaging, this channel in the wilderness meant release from the sea and the ship, a return to health, and perhaps fortune. Arrival had come none too soon. Many of the crew were in advanced stages of scurvy, exhausted and barely able to move, with open sores and badly swollen legs and joints. The two Cape Verde men had suffered the most. One of them, John Hammond, had succumbed four days earlier. The other, Hanse Lawton, was near death as well.

Kendrick ordered a launch put out to explore the channel. But before they could lower it, the sail of a ship's boat appeared coming out of the sound. The crew's jubilation peaked when someone called out that it was the longboat from the *Washington*. As the boat approached, Kendrick was overwhelmed with relief. The months of doubt that haunted him as they plodded northward now vanished. Everyone was elated. They had an expedition once more.

Gray had arrived at Nootka only a week earlier, on September 16. For a month he had cruised the coast north of Tillamook, cautiously trading offshore after Marcus Lopius was killed and they narrowly escaped losing the sloop. In foul weather he overshot the sound and then spent days doubling back to find it. When he first took the *Washington* into the sound, Gray had seen a sail, and for a brief time believed the *Columbia* had beaten them to their destination. Much to his surprise, it was a boat from an English ship, the *Felice Adventurer,* commanded by a former British navy lieutenant, John Meares. Meares was sailing with two other ships he owned, all under Portuguese colors to evade monopoly rights granted to the British South Sea Company and the East India Company for Pacific trade. His fine features and sparsely bearded face held an attitude of pompous self-assurance. As he helped guide the *Washington* to safe harbor, Meares told Gray that his coming was a mistake; there were few furs to be had in this area. During the next few days the Americans found Meares to be calculating and duplicitious. Haswell complained in his journal that he tried to scare them off by "fabricating and rehursing vague and improbable tales" about "vast dangers" in navigating the coast and "the Monsterous Savage dispositions of its inhabitants." He said it would be madness for the Americans to attempt to winter among the local Mowachaht people, who were cannibals. After days of this, Meares finally departed for Macao. Gray had been preparing the *Washington* for a cargoless voyage to China when the *Columbia* appeared.

FROM LAND, GRAY HAD NOTICED that the *Columbia*'s topsails were reefed and the topgallant masts that stood above them were down. It was a sure sign that no one could climb to set the upper sails. Now, as he came on board, Gray could see widespread scurvy among the men. There is no record of the conversation between Kendrick and Gray, but the health of the crews and the condition of the sloop would have been foremost. Gray undoubtedly related the skirmish at Tillamook and that his journey had taken 103 days from Masafeuro to New Albion and another month along the coast to Nootka. The *Columbia* had been 109 days at sea from Juan Fernándes, making about the same forward progress as the *Washington* over the 7,457-mile journey.

IN THE AFTERNOON, GRAY GUIDED the *Columbia* into Nootka Sound. Before them sat a cluster of islands where the broad bay branched into large inlets running through gorges to the north and east. Although the sound was only six or seven miles across, with a large island in the middle, the raw expanse of the mountains and sky made it seem immense.

TEN YEARS EARLIER, JAMES COOK had arrived here with the *Discovery* and *Resolution* to take on water and make repairs. A canoe ventured out from the shore, and according to legend, the natives saw some of Cook's men who were burned red by the sun and thought they were salmon in human form. Hearing of this, the local village chief sent out a spiritual leader to learn who these people were and what they wanted. Three canoes approached Cook's ships, with two men in one, six in another, and ten in the last. When they got close enough, a man stood and made a long oration, throwing handfuls of feathers, while others in the boats cast red dust into the air. As the leader spoke, he shook a rattle and made forceful cries. When he finished, others stood and spoke briefly. Cook's men called back to them, but the two groups didn't understand each other. A breeze sprang up pushing the ships nearer to shore, and more canoes came out filled with curious men and women. Among the many canoes, one appeared remarkable for the bird's head carved on its prow and the manner in which it was painted. A distinctive man stood in it—assumed to be the chief—with many feathers hanging from his head, and his face and body wholly painted. Shaking a rattle, he harangued the men on the ships in the same way as the first speaker.

One large canoe appeared, filled with men who began singing as they paddled, evoking an ethereal mood as evening fell. The men echoed the words of a lead singer and kept rhythm by clapping their paddles on the side of the canoe. Cook's men responded with a fife and drum and then French horns, which the Mowachaht regarded with rapt attention. Despite the oncoming chill of a cold March night, many of the canoes stayed clustered around the ship until 10 P.M. As some of them departed, they made a circuit around the ships and the men sang out *halloo,* on a single note, drawing it out in the middle and letting the sound die away.

The people overcame their fear the next day and trading flourished. Cook was apparently using a Spanish map of 1774–75 that had been secretly acquired and identified this bay as San Lorenzo de Rada. Cook renamed it King Georges' Sound. Later he asked a native the name of the place. The man repeated "itchmenutka, itchmenutka," making a sweeping gesture with his arm. Cook assumed that "nootka" was the name of the whole sound. However, the man was saying that the ships should "go around" to the main village and better harbor. Nootka was the name ultimately recorded by Cook's mapmakers. Despite the initial language barriers and misunderstandings, trade was vigorous over the next month, especially for furs that would provide warmth as the ships sailed north. Fabulous sea otter skins were purchased for bits of metal: buttons, odd coins, and nails; anything the men could scavenge or pry loose.

When the furs were sold later at Macao, stories of magnificent profits at Nootka spread by word of mouth at first and then through a few unofficial journals written by Cook's men. With publication of Cook's journal in 1784, the stories were confirmed. The British government began supporting merchant expeditions to Nootka at the urging of the scientist Joseph Banks, who inherited Cook's mantle for Pacific exploration, and Alexander Dalrymple, the hydrographer for the East India Company and the British Admiralty. The first British trading ship, the *Harmon,* captained by James Hanna out of Macao, arrived at Nootka in 1785. Several others followed in 1786 and 1787 captained by George Dixon, Nathaniel Portlock, and James Colnett, all former officers under James Cook. Gray undoubtedly told Kendrick that two English ships lay there now.

JUST INSIDE THE SOUND, Gray led the *Columbia* toward a small, snug cove on the western shore. It was only a quarter mile long and a quarter mile wide and was protected by three small rocky islets hooking northward. As they came around the islets, Kendrick could see the masts of the two English ships that Gray had described: Meares's small, newly built schooner, *Northwest American,* and his brigantine, *Iphigenia Nubiana,* which was about the size of the *Columbia*. The late afternoon sun and long shadows from pines on shore stretched darkly over the edges of the cove as Kendrick dropped anchor in clear shoal water. After nearly six months apart, Haswell noted that at five o'clock in the afternoon the *Columbia* came to rest "within forty yards of us."

Thick post frames of about twenty houses stood staggered along a bank on the western shore. This was Yuquot, what Cook called "Friendly Cove," a seasonal village and ceremonial center where people had lived for more than four thousand years. It was now deserted. They had arrived too late in the season to trade, Gray told Kendrick. The fifteen hundred Mowachaht people who lived here had recently packed their canoes with the planks from their walls and roofs and had gone to their winter camp twenty miles up one of the inlets.

A View of the Habitations in Nootka Sound *by John Webber. The village of Yuquot, on the shore of what James Cook named "Friendly Cove," was a ceremonial center that had been occupied seasonally for more than four thousand years.*

The two English ships were also planning to depart. Gray likely repeated to Kendrick that Meares said it would be madness to stay for the winter; the weather was horrendous, there was an endless haunting quality to the wilderness, and the natives were cannibals. Believing the *Columbia* lost, Gray said, he had planned to sail to Macao for trade goods and to return to Yuquot in the spring for furs. Wood was already stacked in the *Washington*'s hold for the voyage.

But Gray's dream of an independent trading mission, if that was what he truly intended, vanished as Kendrick began issuing orders. Despite whatever joy he and Haswell may have felt at reunion with the *Columbia,* Gray was no longer in charge. After half the voyage on their own, they were back under Kendrick's command. There is no record that Kendrick took Gray to task for going off on his own and risking the sloop, an argument that Haswell would have recorded. More likely, Kendrick recognized that there was too much at stake for continued strife, and better ways to manage the two headstrong officers. When asked by Gray what his plans were, Kendrick kept his own counsel and said he would announce nothing until the English ships had departed.

Out of self-interest as much as generosity, Kendrick sent ship carpenters Ridler and Hemmingway, his blacksmith Jonathan Barber, and his caulkers to help the captains of the two English ships, William Douglas and Robert Funter, prepare their vessels for sea.

In the native tongue the village name Yuquot means "the wind blows from all directions," and the Americans got a taste of it now, as rain squalls battered them for several days, hampering their work. On September 28, the weather cleared and they buried Hanse Lawton onshore. Others with advanced scurvy, possibly including Kendrick's sons, were quickly recovering.

October 1, 1788, was the anniversary of their departure from Boston, and Kendrick staged a formal celebration. Although the festivities did not include the orations and songs shared with loved ones on their last night in the channel of Boston Harbor, the event marked how far the men had come in the months since then. They had lost time at Cape Verde preparing the ships, resolving dissent within the crew by firing Woodruff and Dr. Roberts, and they had unfortunately lost the astronomer John Nutting overboard off the coast of Brazil in an apparent suicide, but all the other men who had departed from Boston were safe. Green and seasoned sailors had survived a passage that few dared. Kendrick's sons had grown and hardened. And blessed with relatively good fortune, they had unwittingly escaped capture by the Spanish and more losses to scurvy. On this far side of the world, they could now begin the mission of trade and discovery Kendrick saw before them.

At noon, with all men on deck, James Crawford, the gunner on the *Columbia,* lit a taper and fired thirteen guns. The *Washington* did the same. British captain Robert Funter answered with seven guns from a makeshift house Meares had built onshore, and the Scotsman William Douglas fired six guns from the *Iphigenia*. The rumbling of the cannonade rolled through the sound, pealing off the mountainsides.

After the booming tribute, Douglas and Funter and their officers came aboard the *Columbia* for a feast. Among the *Iphigenia*'s crew were a Chinese man and a striking Sandwich Islander, a young chief named Kaiana, whom Meares had brought to Macao and Douglas was supposed to return to the islands. The handsome six-foot-four-inch warrior was gathering an arsenal of guns to take back, and undoubtedly enticed the Americans to barter while he told stories of the amorous Sandwich Island women. More serious discussion among the officers focused on the fur trade and also perhaps on the Nootka natives, who had been seen only in fleeting glimpses.

The *Columbia*'s first mate, Joseph Ingraham, ship's clerk Richard Howe, and the furrier Jonathan Treat were invited to go along with Douglas on the *North West American* to a village on the east side of the sound to purchase fish and oil and whatever other provisions they might gather. They left the cove on October 14 and heavy wind and rain followed. After a few days, Ingraham and the others returned embittered. On the other side of the island was a village where Douglas's armed crew had gone ashore and plundered all the fish and oil they could find in the houses, leaving the families with little food for the winter. In return, the crew had left the villagers with small pieces of copper. When they came upon canoes with men fishing, they would lower a boat and chase the canoe, firing on the natives as they fled. If Douglas's men captured them, they would demand the fish in the canoe. Now the Americans knew why the Mowachaht quickly disappeared whenever they approached.

Douglas traded cannon to Kendrick for additional provisions, dismantled the makeshift house Meares had constructed onshore, and threw in boards from the roof for the Americans to use as firewood. On Sunday, October 26, Kendrick's longboats towed the *Iphigenia* and *North West American* out of Friendly Cove. Douglas expected Kendrick to follow them to the Sandwich Islands. Natives watching the cove from the woods noted the English departure and word quickly spread. Haswell wrote that the *Iphigenia* had no sooner cleared the mouth of the sound than natives appeared and "flocked to us in great numbers with fish oil and some venison and a very friendly intercourse soon commenced by which we were plenteously supplied with provisions and some skins."

With the English ships gone, Kendrick announced his decision. He took the broad authority Joseph Barrell had granted him to make judgments based on their circumstances and began to reshape the expedition. They were three years behind the earliest trading ship to visit this cove, as well as the ships of three of Cook's officers and the wily John Meares. The competing ships made it necessary for the Americans to create an advantage for themselves. They needed to set up trade for the spring and talk with natives about what they might know of the great "river of the west," the fabled Northwest Passage. Moreover, they needed to develop relationships that would allow them to establish an American outpost for the longer-term "Hudson's Bay Company" effort Joseph Barrell had envisioned. If Kendrick had ever intended to make this a single trip and circumnavigation (which is doubtful, given his interest in the deeper goals of the expedition), that intent had changed.

Unlike the glancing contact and pillaging that would doom the success of other traders, Kendrick was going to immerse himself in the native world. They would winter here. He would spend time with the Mowachaht and learn their language. He would attempt to understand their ways and beliefs. Although Meares had claimed that Maquinna, the Mowachaht chief, was a fearsome cannibal, Kendrick would open an effort to befriend him. The men, in the meantime, were to deal fairly with the people and avoid all conflict and disputes, particularly over Mowachaht women.

As events at Tillamook had demonstrated, it was unknown and potentially deadly terrain they were entering. They knew nothing of these people and their customs. Encounters were rife with taboos, misunderstanding, and temptation for the crew to be lured into clandestine meetings and secret trading. Kendrick knew he could try to protect the men and contain what they did, but he couldn't stop them. Despite any measures and cautions he may have laid down, it is likely that hidden trading and sex with the women at Yuquot took place soon after the English left. James Cook's surgeon, David Samwell, had noted that six days after the *Discovery*'s arrival, Cook's men had made known the acts they were interested in with native women. While Mowachaht customs required women to be modest and chaste, slaves captured from other villages were offered in what Nootka men soon learned was a very lucrative trade. Although some sailors reportedly feared oral sex because the women were cannibals, officers nonetheless purchased nights with the young women. Showing a hint of evil, Samwell, a Welsh parson's son, recorded the pleasure he took in "cleansing a naked young Woman from all Impurities in a Tub of Warm Water, as a young Confessor would to absolve a beautiful Virgin who was about to sacrifice that Name to himself." One girl was said to have been a week or ten days on board his ship.

Those first transactions had a lasting effect. When the ships *Experiment* and *Captain Cook* arrived in 1786, they were not greeted with the same ceremony and singing Cook had encountered. Instead, the men coming aboard promptly offered women as well as furs. It was a dire exchange. Slave women sold to the trading ships would return to their villages with venereal disease. The ships then moved on to other villages. The steady enticement of trading and the subtle perniciousness of disease brought outbreaks of sickness and sterility, jeopardizing the world that the Mowachaht had inhabited for millennia.

Kendrick tried to keep his men busy. He knew he couldn't stop them from trading whatever loose metal objects they could gather for sex or furs in clandestine meetings, so he set them on preparations for the uncertain winter ahead. He sent one group to fell trees for a storehouse and shelter on shore, and others to cut and shape new spars. Part of his plan was to rerig the *Washington* with a second mast, making her a brigantine like the privateer *Fanny* he had rebuilt and captained a decade earlier. He also set men to work on a kiln to make charcoal for the blacksmith's forge and bricks for a new chimney for the *Columbia*. They would need all the heat and shelter they could get. In his journal, Haswell scoffed at Kendrick's undertaking, but had apparently learned from Robert Gray not to openly challenge their commander.

Aware of their hostility toward him, Kendrick shared little of his plan with Gray and Haswell. He formed a general strategy and anticipated which native alliances he would need to pursue, but much was uncertain and he needed to remain flexible. This adventure into the unknown wilderness was much the same as sailing with a vague awareness of one's latitude but not longitude. Where they were headed would take them much farther and longer, and demand much greater sacrifice, than he could have imagined.

DESPITE FREQUENT RAIN AND CONSTANT WIND, natives came almost every day to trade fish, venison, oil, and a few furs. In return, they wanted copper, but Kendrick had only precious copper sheathing for the ships. Instead, he offered them "chisels"—strips of bar iron Jonathan Barber hammered on the forge and ground sharp on one edge. Although not bright and malleable like copper, tools such as these had high value for woodworking or weapons.

The furs received in exchange had been gathered and prepared with great difficulty. Elk, bear, and other furs came from deep inland over a trail eastward into the mountains. Here in the sound, sea otters had become increasingly skittish and more difficult to capture or kill as hunting intensified. To approach and shoot an otter with arrows as it fed on fish or shellfish at the water's surface and then to harpoon it to keep it from sinking or diving required great skill. Hunting was best on windless days when the sound was like glass and several canoes could track the otters underwater, keeping them down until they were exhausted and could be more easily shot or driven into nets. Once on shore, the extraordinary care taken in skinning, stretching, and drying a three- to five-foot-long prime pelt was largely left to the Mowachaht women.

In stark contrast to the luxurious sea otter furs they brought, the men often appeared garish to the Americans. They rubbed their bodies all over with an oily red pigment that had a fine claylike consistency. Their faces, which were full and rounded, with high cheekbones and small dark eyes, were stained black, bright red, or white. Fish oil mixed in the paint turned rancid after a time, yielding a strong odor that may have been just as rank as the sailors', who rarely bathed.

The natives' ornaments differed by individual. Many had their ears pierced with bone, shells, tassels, or a piece of copper. Others had their noses pierced and strung through with a thin cord. Their long black hair usually hung loose, but could at times be bunched up and tied with a thread or branch of cedar at the top of the head, or tied in multiple thin braids. For ceremonies, some would add sandy mica to the paint, which made their faces glitter. For special occasions they also wore carved visors, or masks, some with human faces and hair, which made them seem ferocious or bizarre.

The women were usually stout like the men, although many were described as tall and beautiful. They did not wear the same paint, but often groomed their hair with deer grease, giving it a bright sheen. While the men often went about fully naked, the women covered themselves in knee-length skirts woven from cedar bark cloth, and with a cape tied at the front. Some children who had never worn paint were noted to have skin as pale as southern Europeans.

They were a fishing people who focused their spiritual activity on whales and whaling. The chief they spoke of and feared was Maquinna, a master whaler and shaman, whose hunting skills helped to provide for the tribe. He was a regional leader, and he and his family ruled a band divided in European perception into "nobles" (*taises*) and "commoners" (*meschimes*) served by slaves captured from other tribes. Maquinna kept his rule by spreading the wealth he acquired—feeding the hungry in lean times, and during times of plenty giving away his most valuable possessions in a potlatch celebration. The more he gave, the greater his status and regard.

The name Maquinna was handed down to each chief. The man holding power now was about thirty years old and had taken the place of his aged and blind father about the time Cook had arrived. Legend says his father had been killed in a raid on their village, and Maquinna exacted revenge by decimating the attackers' village and taking many captives. The rumors that Meares spread about Maquinna and his people being cannibals had been handed down by Cook's men, who said they were offered skulls and a roasted and dried hand. There were further stories of Maquinna, blindfolded, grasping at a group of captured children for one he would eat. Haswell believed these stories to be true, noting that Maquinna's people "eat the flesh of their vanquished enemies and frequently of their slaves who they kill in Cool blud." He professed to have witnessed an instance of this. The prospect of being killed and eaten, and thus losing the chance of resurrection along with one's soul, horrified and haunted sailors. Investigating these rumors, the Spanish would later find no truth in them, except for ritual acts, but the lurid belief remained, and relationships were charged with a dark undercurrent of fear and suspicion.

By the middle of November, the days were turning cold, and at night frost settled over the ground and the decks of the ships. In addition to the shelter built onshore, Kendrick set up a house on the deck of the *Columbia*. They maintained their system of watches and took hunting excursions. The land proved nearly impenetrable. The cove lay in a clearing behind which the deep-shadowed forest stood like a wall. Heavy rainfall supported dense vegetation, and thick moss grew over a maze of fallen branches and rocks. Deep gorges and steep cliffs that crisscrossed the woods made them a shadowy, impassable haunt of owls and bear, lynx, raccoon, and deer.

In the light snow along the shore, Haswell found where deer came down at night and he waited in the cold with a musket, proudly returning with a big buck. Kendrick traveled up the sound, shooting geese and exploring the coast from the longboat. The tailor, Bartholomew Ballard, made him a deerskin coat, and Kendrick spent time with the Mowachaht learning their customs and language. His behavior was far outside the bounds of the usual dandified, stiff-necked ships' officers of his day. It is uncertain whether or not he became intimate with their women, but he began to learn about these people and their ways. The Mowachaht cosmology was complex, with many gods that infused the earth and water. From what Kendrick could understand, a supreme being, Qua-utz, had come in a copper canoe and created the first woman. They believed in an afterlife from which dead relatives and friends acted as guardians sending them fish and animals. Those at peace with the gods provided well for their families and were held in high esteem. Those not at peace feared an enormous fiery-eyed devil, Matlox, who dwelled in the woods and hopped on one leg and would devour those he caught.

Despite the stories they had heard from Meares, Kendrick found the Mowachaht docile and friendly, and his regard for them grew paternal. Because he had spent his youth among the remnant tribes at Potonumecut, he was comfortable among native people, and like many early American explorers, he did not possess the racial hatred that would permeate the actions of later pioneers. Kendrick probably foresaw a difficult future for these people. They had no firearms with which to defend themselves, and exploitation by traders and trading posts could easily destroy their world. Within a few generations, diseases such as smallpox and the "French pox" of syphilis, along with liquor and abuse, could also decimate them. And more subtle and sweeping changes could reverberate among the interrelated bands of the Mowachaht in the region, altering the balance of relations and stirring trouble between them. There were twenty-two villages on the shores of the sound. To the west was the chief Hannape, Maquinna's father-in-law. To the east were Tlupanantl's bands, and people known as the Muchalaht. To the southeast were Wickaninish's people. Intermarriage and raiding mixed the bands and kept their world locked in tensions between familial ties and mutual jealousies and feuds. Maquinna was the ceremonial chief of all the Mowachaht and attempted to maintain control of the region by having all trade carried on through him. But shutting out other chiefs increased competition and jealousies. With Maquinna in winter quarters far up the sound in these first few months, there was no one to control interactions with Kendrick and his men; the door at Yuquot was open for opportunity and mischief.

DESPITE THE PRESENCE OF A CONSTANT GUARD, on the night of December 11 fifteen water casks stored on shore in a shed roofed with an upturned longboat were stolen along with five small cannon from Captain Douglas. Losing the cannon was troubling, but water casks were essential for voyaging and marked a greater loss. The natives that traded with Kendrick told him that "the people of the opposite side of the sound with hoom they were at war were the agressers." Not wanting to inflame the situation by punishing innocent people, Kendrick let the matter go for a time and ordered new casks made.

Haswell recorded nothing of a Christmas celebration. Kendrick was not a commander to require prayers, although a special dinner would have been served, perhaps flour pudding with whortleberries, which were apparently harvested well into the winter. They would have gathered in the house built on the deck of the *Columbia* and sung songs and told stories. It was familiar rituals and schedules, Kendrick knew, that would keep them sane in the overwhelmingly gray, unknown wilderness.

FOURTEEN MONTHS FROM PORT, little or nothing had been heard in Boston from men of the expedition. In their home villages, the year 1788 had been one of heated arguments over a new federal government. As a state delegate, Joseph Barrell had strongly advocated ratification of the Constitution and tried to sway his brother Nathaniel Barrell, Sam Adams, and a large contingent that feared the power of central government. "You were always on the side of a Federal Government," Barrell said in a letter to Nathaniel. "Judge then my surprise when I am told that my brother is the most decided Antifederalist in the Eastern Country, that he declared in Town Meeting he would loose his right hand before he would acceed to the proposed Constitution." Joseph Barrell harangued Nathaniel, and eventually he came around. Sam Adams, too, finally acquiesced after freedom of the press and the right to bear arms were added to the Bill of Rights. Massachusetts voted 187 to 168 for the Constitution in February. A few months later, in June, New Hampshire became the ninth state to approve it, achieving the threshold of nine out of thirteen states that were required for federal adoption. Public debates then broke out over the candidates for Congress and the presidency. Just days before Christmas, New Hampshire and Massachusetts voters had chosen electors who would cast ballots for the nation's first president, whom everyone anticipated would be George Washington. The official vote would not come until January 7. Kendrick would have been ecstatic about a new government led by Washington, but being so far off the world's map, he would not learn of these events for almost a year.

The letter Kendrick had sent in June from Cumberland Bay to Joseph Barrell was kept for review by Spanish officials and had not yet reached Boston at the close of 1788. The only news families received in the last year was from a New York ship that found a letter tucked into a wall at the Falklands, summarizing the expedition's Atlantic voyage to that point. Fathers, mothers, and wives undoubtedly wondered whether and how the men had survived. Meanwhile, snug in their winter quarters, joined in thoughts of home, the voyagers awaited the year ahead and what it might bring.

The first event to occur boded disaster. On January 13, an alarm went up over a fire below deck on the *Columbia*. Coals dropped down in the afterhold set ablaze sails that were stored against the bulkhead of the powder magazine. The men who came running found the fire so intense that heat was searing through the deck. It was worse below deck. No one could approach the smoky, burning area. If fire reached the powder magazine, the whole ship would go up, taking lives and all the trade goods and supplies of the expedition with it. The men worked frantically, chopping a hole in the foredeck. It was a desperate act that would feed more air to the flames, but the only way to get access to the area ablaze. On the smoking deck above the hole, men placed themselves in harm's way, splashing down buckets of seawater and pulling out burning sails. The risk paid off and the men extinguished the fire, although the scorched deck and bulkhead went on steaming and smoldering for hours. It was a sobering reminder of how suddenly fate could turn.

Fifteen days later, on January 28, a large canoe appeared at the mouth of the cove. As the watch called out its approach, the canoe moved directly toward the *Columbia* and slipped alongside. In command was a tall, thickly muscled chief in his midforties who came onto the ship with a serious, intimidating presence. His name was Wickaninish, and with him were his brother and several persons of distinction. Nearly all of them were more than six feet tall, and much more handsome than the men of Nootka. They had traveled from Clayoquot Sound, about forty miles southeast on the coast. Bundled in the canoe were more than two dozen excellent sea otter skins. Few were traded, because Wickaninish wanted copper and muskets, which the Americans weren't prepared to pay. As a subchief to Maquinna, Wickaninish did not linger, but invited Kendrick and Gray to visit him at his village. Word of the meeting most likely traveled up the inlet, and within the next few days some of Maquinna's people began to appear early from their winter quarters. Across two or more canoes they carried broad hand-hewn cedar and pine planks, some four or six feet wide, on which they placed their possessions. When they unloaded, they laid the planks on the huge permanent frames standing on the high bank above the cove. The upright posts that held the roofs were carved into human and animal spirit figures called "*klummas.*" Some of the doorways were carved as imaginary animals with open mouths. Kendrick's men watched in awe as the village of Yuquot took shape and more than a thousand people gathered.

Chief Maquinna *by Fernando Selma. Maquinna was the regional chief of the Mowachaht people, and a shaman and whale hunter with whom John Kendrick built an alliance.*

Maquinna's arrival was not recorded, but Kendrick was soon summoned to meet with him. He occupied the far end of the largest house, which stretched a hundred feet long and thirty feet wide. Several families lived there. Sleeping platforms covered with finely woven blankets and furs and mats lay along the walls in dim, smoky light. Fires burned in a wide corridor down the middle. Overhead, dried and smoked fish were strung through the gills on sticks hung in the low roof joists.

Maquinna sat on a raised platform in an ankle-length black otter skin robe. Quelequem (Callicum), whom he designated to deal with foreigners and was said by some sources to be his brother, sat beside him. Their hair was covered with oil and fine white down. Maquinna's broad face was painted red except for the area around the eyes, and his cheeks were sprinkled with fine mica. Callicum was taller and leaner. Also present were Maquinna's wife and two children, a girl and a boy. Kendrick learned that he'd had an infant daughter who had died several months earlier in the fall of 1787 and was still mourned by the family.

Gifts were presented, and a meal of fish steamed in a wooden box was set before them. They conversed with the few words each knew of the other's language. Kendrick found Maquinna highly intelligent and thoughtful.

From his years of whaling, Kendrick had great admiration for anyone who pursued the earth's largest creature miles at sea from a canoe. As he appraised and sought to befriend this dark-eyed young man, he might have tried to share stories of his own whale hunts. Kendrick learned at some point that there was a mystical dimension to the Mowachaht relationship with the whales, and a spiritual ceremony, replete with cleansing and sometimes human sacrifice. Men abstained from sex to prepare for a hunt. And if the hunt was successful, the lanced whale would be towed ashore, where the whole village would partake in shares of meat and blubber.

Maquinna had been told much in advance of the arrival of Kendrick and his "Boston men," as all Americans after Kendrick would come to be called on the Northwest Coast. He listened to Kendrick's offers of trade and friendship, and questions about the stolen cannon and water casks. As a gesture of friendship, Maquinna agreed to help find the thieves. Although both men were striving for prestige for themselves and security for their people, Maquinna may also have feared the new power of those who now held the cannons.

Whatever queries Maquinna sent out, he soon had information for Kendrick. On Sunday, February 22, Kendrick took Gray, Haswell, and several crew members in two armed boats across the sound. The village where they were told to look, however, proved much more distant than expected. Not wanting to engage an unknown enemy in an inlet so many miles from the ships, or perhaps realizing it was all merely a gesture of goodwill by Maquinna and no one would be caught, they returned empty-handed.

Defense of the ships became a heightened concern. As the *Washington* prepared for the first trading voyage, the crew built a new bulwark around the railing with more ports cut for gun emplacements. In early March, the hull was caulked and painted and men brought provisions and trading goods on board from the *Columbia*. On the morning of Monday, March 16, Kendrick and others towed the *Washington* out of the cove to the mouth of the sound for a trip to Clayoquot to meet with Wickaninish. They would also cruise farther south to begin a search for the Strait of Juan de Fuca. Six months earlier, as the *Washington* was coming northward from Tillamook, Haswell had noted being forced out by a strong current as they passed along a foggy shore. "I am of [the] opinion the Straits of Juan de Fuca exist," he recorded, observing a "very Deep Bay" in the vicinity. Haswell's observation had undoubtedly been related to Captain Kendrick, who wanted Gray to take a closer look. Kendrick had most likely received some information from Maquinna's people, and watching the sloop depart, he hoped they might return with some lead on the Northwest Passage.

BY NOON THE *WASHINGTON* WAS WELL OUT, cruising offshore to avoid numerous rocks and reefs. At sunset they stood off the entrance to Wickaninish's domain at Clayoquot Sound and spent the night offshore under light breezes. The next morning, the wind died as they approached the bay, and as they lay idled, Toteescosettle, Wickaninish's brother, came out to the ship. After a long, still morning, the wind freshened and they entered Clayoquot and at four o'clock anchored in about fifty feet of water. Unlike Nootka Sound, Clayoquot did not have a broad bay, and lay instead in a maze of channels behind three large rocky islands and a series of islets facing the sea. From villages on the islands, several of the local chiefs and their men came to the ship to trade and stayed on board until sunset. Wary of deception, Gray asked everyone to depart as it grew dark and then stiffened his request by firing a gun.

The next day trading continued and the *Washington* gathered many fine sea otter skins. Relations with Wickaninish's people relaxed, and Haswell found their manners and customs identical to those of the people of Nootka. As they had noticed when Wickaninish first visited, these people appeared taller and better proportioned than those at Nootka. They now found that their villages were also larger and more populous. The carved pillars of the longhouses were more numerous and ornately executed. Here too, some were so large that a carved and painted mouth of a creature served as a doorway. Their images showed great regard for the sun, and on one wide board Gray's men found the painting of a plump sun with eyes, a nose, and a mouth, and rays extending from it in a manner similar to what they might find from a country painter at home.

After ten days of trading among the maze of islands and villages, on March 28 the *Washington* left Clayoquot and headed farther southeast. Forty miles down the coast they entered another bay. In a single canoe, natives speaking a dialect like the Mowachaht cautiously approached and offered their friendship. The sailors learned that the summer before Meares's longboat had fired on people in this harbor. This group seemed poorer than those at Clayoquot or Nootka, and they told Gray they had no otter skins because they sold them all to chief Tatooch, who lived to the south. Gray named the bay, known as Patchenat by the natives, Poverty Cove.

Gray kept seeking out inlets and villages as they sailed down the coast. Cautious about venturing onshore, they remained on board to trade, swivel guns ready in the new gun ports as canoes paddled out to them.

On March 31, the *Washington* cruised along a shore running eastward in a broad inlet. Scanning the full breadth of it, Haswell rapturously determined that this was the fabled Strait of Juan de Fuca. They labored through treacherous seas several miles to the southern shore. The next morning as the sun rose clear from the horizon, Haswell believed he saw the strait stretching into the east, and as he had noted the day before "no land to obstruct the view as far as the eye could reach." This was consistent with the belief that the fabled passage was part of an inland sea. They were reluctant to proceed farther into unknown waters, and as they beat in place, a heavy squall struck from the southwest. Afraid of being driven ashore, Gray ran the *Washington* northward to Poverty Cove, where they rode out the rain and sleet that night.

For the next two weeks intermittent storms chased them as they shifted back and forth along the coast. They cruised around the mouth of Juan de Fuca, along the coastline of what would become Washington State, and north again to Barkley Sound and Poverty Cove. They gathered furs, but did not extend their exploration into the strait any deeper than twenty miles. Gray's interest was in the challenges of trading, not discovery. On April 22, after a voyage of five weeks, they left the mouth of the strait for Nootka to reprovision and load more trading goods. At Friendly Cove a surprise was waiting for them.

William Douglas was at anchor in the *Iphigenia*. The *Columbia* was nowhere to be seen. Douglas had arrived three days earlier after wintering over at Hawaii. He told them that Kendrick had taken the *Columbia* six miles up the western shore to a cove known as Mawina. Gray borrowed a ship's boat from Douglas and under thickening clouds and haze went to report to Kendrick. But when he reached Mawina he was stunned to see that Kendrick had not readied the *Columbia* for trading. Instead he had constructed an outpost.

During his hunting expeditions, Kendrick was taking full stock of the inlets and coves in the sound. Mawina had a beautiful sandy beach and an island protecting it, and was less exposed than Yuquot. It offered fresh water from two streams and deep anchorage fifty feet from shore. Moreover, the cove was away from Maquinna's direct oversight and from rival British ships. From here, small boats were free to trade through the whole sound. Although there was a village nearby, it may also have been easier to limit the men's dealings with the Mowachaht. Kendrick had settled in and built a "Good house," with a gun battery, a blacksmith forge, and outbuildings to store provisions on the island at the mouth of the cove—the first American-built structures on the Pacific coast. He named the island St. Clair and the outpost Fort Washington.

ALTHOUGH KENDRICK HAD NOT SHARED his plan with Gray, the outpost was to be the expedition's cornerstone for trade and a longer-term American presence. The sight of the rough-hewn log buildings and the flag flying over the island only intensified Gray's and Haswell's frustrations with Kendrick. The *Columbia,* Haswell observed, "was now mearly a Hulk." She had not been hauled out to have her bottom graved and caulked. Her topmasts were still down. Kendrick had judged her to be too unwieldy for close sailing and trading along the shoal-ridden coast and bays, where currents and sudden winds off steep slopes could ground her. They would prepare for sea in good time, but her main function was to be a storehouse. Trade could proceed quite well at the outpost with her anchored here. The *Washington,* which had a shallower draft and much greater maneuverability, would be the primary trading vessel for coastal inlets and bays.

Gray burned with suppressed rage as the *Washington* was brought up to Mawina from Friendly Cove and prepared for a second voyage.

But he did not have long to stew, because the need for a quick departure soon became urgent.

The schooner *Northwest American*, the *Iphigenia*'s sister ship, had followed Douglas into port on April 23. The two British ships found that Kendrick had already taken the winter's furs and secured advance trading commitments from Nootka Sound villages. Douglas also realized that the *Washington* had gathered furs to the south and would soon head north, so he hurriedly sent the schooner northward to trade in the Queen Charlotte Islands. The *Washington* set off after her on May 2.

After the sloop passed through the entrance to Nootka Sound on the tide, the wind shifted head-on from the northwest, and the crew spent the night beating back and forth without making much headway. The following day they were still making slow progress under winds from the northwest when, at four in the afternoon, a strange ship appeared inshore. She fired a gun to bring them around. Through his glass Gray could see that she was a warship, and she was running up the red and yellow colors of Spain.

CHAPTER SEVEN

Seizure

Nootka

MAY–JUNE 1789

THE SPANISH SHIP TACKED into the wind and made for the *Washington*. She was a black tar–washed frigate of twenty-four guns, about the same size as the *Columbia*. Within a short time she came within speaking distance, her cannons trained on the sloop. Gray was apparently stunned. Contending with a Spanish warship was something he and Kendrick may have spoken of, but the reality threw him into confusion.

A voice called across the short, heaving distance between the two ships, instructing the American captain to put down a boat and come on board. Either Gray did not understand the order or was purposefully evasive. He sent first mate Davis Coolidge and another officer.

On board the *Princesa,* Estevan Martinez was taken off guard as well. He had started out from San Blas on January 17 on his mission to secure the Spanish Empire in the North Pacific. He expected to encounter four Russian frigates, not this small American sloop, although he was aware from the warnings received in Mexico that the *Washing-*

ton might be on the coast. Viceroy Flores had given Martinez broad latitude to use "powerful arguments" against the Americans. Trading in Spanish waters without a license from the king was just cause to seize the sloop and imprison her crew.

When Coolidge arrived on the *Princesa*'s deck, he found fifteen soldiers fully armed. Also on board were four friars, and a crew of eighty-nine. Lashed to the quarterdeck was an Eskimo kayak. In the hold, Martinez was hauling supplies and armament for a garrison that would be the heart of Spain's defense in the North Pacific. After rapidly endorsing Martinez's plan in December, Viceroy Flores had sent it on to Madrid. Final approval from Foreign Minister Floridablanca was forthcoming; the official communication would take months. In the meantime, Martinez was to make his outpost appear like a permanent settlement. The Spanish captain was confident the plan would succeed. He had endured his years of humble service in the backwaters of the empire awaiting such a mission. Martinez envisioned ships exploring and making claims from San Lorenzo de Nuca into the Gulf of Alaska, and south to the California missions. Through careful exploration he was confident the Northwest Passage would be found and secured. He also believed that a private commercial company could be formed by Spanish merchants to monopolize the fur trade. And to the west, he proposed that an outpost be established in the Sandwich Islands, making them a valuable Spanish possession.

It was a grand scheme, born of an earlier time in Spain's glory, and hampered by San Blas's meager resources. During the voyage, Martinez found that the port commissary had shortchanged him on supplies, and many of the men enlisted to fill out the crew were native Mexicans who suffered in the cold climate. A significant number of them had venereal disease, and two men, including his "leech," or bloodletter, died on the passage from San Blas. When Martinez was told that a "dropsical" ship's boy was covered in sores, he ordered his officers to "get rid of him" in open sea.

As in his last voyage north, Lopez de Haro and the support ship *San*

Carlos once again had difficulty keeping company with him and had become separated in a storm off the California coast nearly a month earlier. The *Princesa* was alone. Although the ship was well armed, Martinez had no support onshore. His plan was highly vulnerable at this point and he needed time. He had to find a way to stall these American interlopers until he could become established.

BURLY AND OFFICIOUS IN HIS BLUE CAPTAIN'S COAT, Martinez informed the two young American officers through his translator, Gabriel del Castillo, that they were trespassing in Spanish waters and demanded to know their business. Standing on the deck of a foreign warship and ignorant of what was being said around them, the two young Americans were reluctant to reveal their mission. They showed him the *Washington*'s passport, which Martinez noted was signed by John Kendrick and General Washington. He asked for their instructions, and their reply was a weak half-truth: their water casks had been stolen and they were seeking materials to replace them. Martinez concealed his disbelief. He held the two men and sent his pilot and del Castillo on board the *Washington* to question Gray and examine the ship's papers.

Del Castillo demanded that Gray explain his presence in Spanish waters, and also asked if they had come across any Russian or British vessels. Although no Russians had been sighted, Martinez learned from Coolidge that their command ship, the American brig *Columbia,* lay at anchor in Nootka Sound. Also moored there, Coolidge told him, was a British ship, the *Iphigenia.* The *Iphigenia*'s captain "was a Portuguese, the first mate a Scotchman, and the crew English" and she was engaged in collecting sea otter skins. Martinez made no comment on the *Columbia,* but mused that the British ship would make him a good prize.

Though he knew Gray and his officers were lying about their mission, Martinez let their shoddy dissembling go. The American command ship was trapped, and there would be more time for him to decide what to do with the sloop. Martinez charmed the crew by sending aboard presents of brandy, wine, hams, and sugar. Gray responded by giving him an assortment of artifacts, including two precious red feather robes from Hawaii, and bows, arrows, and harpoons from Nootka. Haswell naively observed, "this gentleman endeavored to do everything to serve us." Martinez's generosity guaranteed that the *Washington* would remain unsuspecting and return soon. Parting with him, Gray fired a seven-gun salute, which the *Princesa* answered.

The encounter made Martinez aware of how little he knew of what was transpiring at Nootka. While his orders focused on halting Russian colonization, he would soon find that the most immediate threat to Spanish dominion would come from the British ships of John Meares.

DURING THE WINTER AT MACAO, Meares had formed a new business partnership, merging his ships, which were veiled under a Portuguese flag, with those of a competing group, the King George's Sound Company. The new venture was called the "Company of Free Commerce of London," and it gave Meares financial leverage, legitimacy, and a unified British presence. Meares's new business partner, Richard Cadman Etches, was a well-connected London merchant whose ships had been among the first to arrive at Nootka and were captained by former officers of James Cook: Nathaniel Portlock, George Dixon, and James Colnett. Through Etches, the powerful group had ties to members of Parliament and possessed licenses to trade in the Pacific from the British East India Company and the South Sea Company. Etches was also said to be associated with the British secret service. The new company was ready to provoke a confrontation by aggressively proposing trade "in all the territories that are looked upon as belonging to the Crown of Spain" and by taking "possession of all new discovered parts for the King and Crown of Great Britain." At Nootka, they sought to turn Meares's previous camp into a permanent settlement for fur trading, and they authorized their ships to engage and capture any opposing vessels.

Meares directed the venture from Macao. Two of his ships, the *Princess Royal* and the *Argonaut,* were already en route from Macao to spearhead the British settlement. The commander was a blunt and volatile British navy lieutenant, James Colnett, who had been a junior officer with Cook at Nootka in 1778 and had traded in the waters around Nootka for Etches for the last two seasons. On board the *Argonaut* with him were thirty British and Portuguese seamen and officers and twenty-nine Chinese tradesmen: carpenters, bricklayers, blacksmiths, shoemakers, and others who would form the core of the commercial outpost, which was to be called Fort Pitt after the British prime minister.

THE *ARGONAUT* WAS STILL A MONTH AWAY as Martinez approached Nootka Sound early on the morning of May 5. In the harbor at Friendly Cove, shortly after sunrise, Douglas, who was ill in his cabin on the *Iphigenia,* received word of an unknown vessel. After wintering over in the Sandwich Islands, he was unaware of Meares's ambitious new venture. Nonetheless, Douglas was expecting Meares's ships. He was desperately in need of supplies, and assuming that this was the vessel carrying them, he sent a boat to pilot her into the harbor. At some point during the next two hours, Douglas realized that the ship was a Spanish war frigate. The *Iphigenia*'s crew went on alert. Before noon, the *Princesa* rounded the point and entered Friendly Cove, led by Douglas's boat and a Spanish launch. The black-hulled ship dropped anchor in the lee of one of the islets, known as Hog Island. The deck was crowded with men, including soldiers at arms. Douglas's crew and the Mowachaht people watched in astonishment as the Spaniards raised banners and a cross and held a religious ceremony on deck.

Martinez wrote, "We sang the Salve to Our Lady of the Rosary, the patroness of this frigate for having conducted us prosperously to the port of our destination." They followed with a fifteen-gun salute and three cheers for his Catholic Majesty King Carlos III. Douglas concealed the nationality of his ship by unfurling the Portuguese flag and responding with fifteen guns. Kendrick most likely heard the distant cannon fire and soon saw Callicum, who had been dispatched by Douglas, approaching Mawina in a canoe.

Haswell later recorded: "On the morning of the [5th] of May they saw an Indion Canoe paddled by six naked natives coming towards them with grate haste. When she came alongside they found our Friend Calecum in her with a letter from Captain Douglas to Captain Kendrick . . ." Learning of the Spanish warship, Kendrick may have feared that the American expedition's base at Nootka would need to be abandoned. It was one thing to anchor a vessel in these waters, and quite another to have a gun emplacement, a house and outbuildings, and a flag flying. On the way down to Friendly Cove, he must have pondered what plausible explanation he might offer.

The Spanish ship was in a flurry of activity. Kendrick found Douglas and the *Iphigenia*'s nominal Portuguese captain, Francisco José Viana, at lunch on board the *Princesa*. Martinez generously made a place for Kendrick. As he had done with Robert Gray and the *Washington*, Martinez plied the captains with delicacies and hospitality. Through his translator, del Castillo, Martinez told them he was waiting for two other ships to catch up, and that he had encountered Kendrick's *Lady Washington* less than a day to the north.

The Spanish commander tested Kendrick on the purpose of his expedition. Uncertain about what Gray might have said, Kendrick told him another half-truth: the *Columbia* was on a voyage of discovery and had suffered extensive damage and put into Nootka for repairs. A fire on board had delayed them further. With many of his men suffering from scurvy, he had built a house onshore, and a blacksmith forge to repair his ship, and a gun emplacement to protect the crew through the winter. He confirmed that he had sent the *Washington* north in search of material for barrel hoops, and to look for the Straits of Admiral de Fonte. This comment caught Martinez's attention, but he said nothing. Kendrick's story seemed to be acceptable because he readily acknowledged Spanish dominion over the region and said he was prepared to leave as soon as the *Columbia* was fit for sea.

Douglas told Martinez a similar story—that the *Iphigenia,* leaking badly and in need of pitch and tar, had taken refuge at Friendly Cove. Martinez generously offered help to repair the ship. He never mentioned that Gray had told him the *Iphigenia* was trading for furs but did ask Douglas and Viana to let him see their ship's papers. The documents were in Portuguese, and Martinez held them for translation.

Among those at the table, Martinez may have recognized Kendrick as a kindred spirit. They were nearly the same age, and in a time of dandified ship's officers they had a casual style and a shared dislike of the English. Moreover, Martinez saw this seasoned American captain as a potentially useful ally. Kendrick had gained a great deal of knowledge of the native people and spoke some of their language, which offered an entry to the Mowachaht world.

After lunch, Martinez accompanied Kendrick and Douglas to Maquinna's longhouse. As they climbed the embankment onshore, the squad of armed Spanish soldiers that accompanied them provoked strong objections from Maquinna's men who stood naked in full red and black body paint. After a brief conference, Martinez sent the soldiers back to the ship. Maquinna's men, presenting a fierce spectacle at the doorway, stepped aside. Inside, slats of daylight fell on the dirt corridor that led between family cubicles along each wall. Kendrick was familiar with this place and the people living here. At the far end, Maquinna, his brother the warrior Quatlazape, and Callicum sat on their raised platform in the smoky light. Their heads were covered in oil and fine white bird down, from which their black eyes peered at the Spanish commander. After food and dancing and song, there was an exchange of gifts. Maquinna presented Martinez with a beautiful sea otter skin, and Martinez gave him woolen and flannel cloth, glass beads, and a pair of scissors. Their discussion was laboriously translated from Spanish to English to Mowachaht and back again. Martinez and

Maquinna recalled the time he had come to this port in 1774 with the expedition led by Juan Perez. Maquinna was just a teenager at the time, but he remembered that Martinez had tossed abalone shells down to the canoe and hit his brother. He still kept the shells in the house as prized possessions and brought them out. Martinez also mentioned silver spoons that had been taken from him, and later found by James Cook. Maquinna recalled these as well, saying that the man who had stolen them was now dead.

The meeting established warm relations, and the Mowachaht eagerly paddled out to the *Princesa* the next morning at 6 A.M., calling for Martinez, who gave them small gifts. Kendrick was pleased with how things had begun with the Spanish commander, and saw an opportunity to ingratiate himself and encourage mutual benefit. Before returning to Mawina, he invited Martinez, Douglas, and the Portuguese captain, José Viana, to come dine with him at his outpost.

Kendrick spared no effort to impress Martinez. During the course of the meal, he offered three toasts to the Spanish monarch, each followed by a thirteen-gun salute. Kendrick presented his ship's letter from Congress, which Martinez believed was signed by George Washington. He also gave Martinez a letter documenting what he had already told him—"In answer to your request how I came to be riding at anchor in Nootka Sound belonging to the King of Spain . . ."—where he repeated the conditions that made him settle in the area for the winter and finally assured him, "now as you may Observe we are getting our Ship in readiness for Sea . . ." Kendrick offered use of his forge and the cove for Martinez to build a schooner. He sold him canvas for sails, and deck fixtures, nails, and caulking. He also loaned Martinez his blacksmith, Jonathan Barber, who was set to the ominous task of making leg shackles.

At the small village onshore at Mawina, Kendrick organized a feast where he introduced Martinez to a group of lesser chiefs as "their brother who had come to live with them for some time." He said the Spanish commander would protect them from foreign nations that might try to attack them, a subtle reference to the plundering by Meares's ships. "Wacass, wacass" (friend), they said, clasping Martinez's hand. Martinez was impressed by this and by first mate Joseph Ingraham's knowledge of Nootka Sound and its people. He asked Ingraham for a report he could forward to the viceroy.

The celebrations continued in a warm drizzle on May 10 as the three captains and their officers were invited to a naming ceremony for Maquinna's son, Prince Hauitl. Maquinna's two brothers, his father-in-law, Hannape, and chiefs of other tribes were in attendance. Kendrick sat with Martinez and explained the ceremony as it unfolded. The rhythmic beating of sticks, dancing, and singing echoed across the cove far into the night.

Early the next morning, partly sleepless from the din of the party, Martinez took his bedding and went up to visit Kendrick. The burly Spanish commander saw himself in a difficult position. If he expelled Douglas from Nootka, it was likely the British would try to establish themselves in another cove or bay along the coast. There was no way he could patrol the intricate shoreline and islands to prevent it. He had to halt them here, although he could not accomplish it without the neutrality of Kendrick and the Mowachaht.

Douglas later claimed that Martinez and Kendrick made an alliance against him during this visit. It is not clear whether Kendrick agreed with Martinez's plan to seize the *Iphigenia*. Nevertheless, Martinez told Kendrick that he would take Meares prisoner when his ship appeared and gained Kendrick's complicity. Later, when events were slipping toward war, Meares would allege that it was John Kendrick who convinced Martinez to take the British ships. Though Kendrick denied the allegation, he did have a reasonable motive for encouraging a conflict between Martinez and the British. If control of the Northwest Coast was uncertain at this point, he could gain time and a better opportunity to settle an American outpost.

No doubt Kendrick recognized the sensitivity of the situation and its possible repercussions. The nine-year War of Jenkins' Ear in the

1740s that had sent Lord Anson's squadron into the Pacific to raid Spanish villages and ships took place after Spain's *garda costa* in the Caribbean seized a British ship they claimed was a privateer. Parliament had been tipped into a frenzy to declare war when the alleged severed ear of the ship's captain, Robert Jenkins, was displayed in a jar in the House of Commons.

While taking any ship was a sensitive matter, the success of the American mission depended on Martinez's goodwill. At this point Kendrick wanted nothing more than to keep his favor and to push the British traders off the coast. The strategy was consistent with the view of Thomas Jefferson and other leaders who believed that Britain posed the greatest threat to the United States and that it was better to keep the western lands in the hands of the weakening Spanish Empire and then take it later piece by piece.

ON MAY 12, MARTINEZ'S MISSING CONSORT, the *San Carlos,* came in from the fog at the mouth of the sound, guided by boats from the *Princesa*. The Spanish vessels saluted one another with five cannon salvos, and the *Iphigenia* responded as well. Hearing the rumbling cannons, Kendrick and Martinez came down from Mawina to Friendly Cove in the afternoon.

Officers of all the ships were invited to lunch on the *San Carlos.* With reinforcements from the sixteen-gun support ship now on hand, Martinez wrote an affidavit recording why he would seize the *Iphigenia.* She was anchored in Spanish waters without a license from the king, and her instructions were in direct conflict with his own. The *Princesa*'s orders were to intercept and evict foreign ships from these waters. Douglas's Portuguese instructions ordered him to take any Spanish, Russian, or English ship that might oppose him. He was to bring the belligerent ship to Macao and sell it as a prize. The officers and crew were to be punished as pirates. Martinez saw these instructions as an extreme insult and direct challenge to Spanish claims and honor.

Martinez sent for Douglas, who later wrote, "As soon as I was on board he took out a paper, and told me, that was the king of Spain's orders to take all the vessels he met with on the coast of America; that I was now his prisoner." Douglas argued that Martinez misinterpreted his Portuguese instructions, and "to take me prisoner, in a foreign port that the king of Spain never laid claim to, was a piece of injustice that no nation ever attempted before." Although the angry Scottish captain said he would leave Nootka, Martinez ordered his men to seize him.

Forty armed Spanish men then climbed into longboats and rowed the short distance to the moored *Iphigenia.* The crew was utterly surprised, and surrendered as soon as the Spanish came on board. Once the ship was disarmed, the Portuguese flag came down and the Spanish colors ran up amid cheers and a salvo from the *Princesa.* Martinez divided *Iphigenia*'s crew, imprisoning them below deck on the two Spanish ships. Douglas was enraged, railing at Martinez, saying that if he had entered any other port in Spanish America with a ship in similarly poor condition, he would have been granted assistance and allowed to go on his way. He also ranted at the double standard that allowed Kendrick and the American ships to remain free, and he accused Kendrick of plotting with Martinez.

The Spanish commander had fallen into a dangerous game, in which any action he took was open to criticism. The Treaty of Paris concluding the Seven Years' War in 1763 made it illegal for British ships to trade in Spanish waters. But Viceroy Flores had also instructed Martinez to stay clear of harsh contention with other nations where it could be avoided. Seizing the *Iphigenia* could make him appear either bold and prudent, or a blundering fool. Letting her go posed the same problem. He may have been aware that the governor of Juan Fernándes Island had been stripped of his post for not taking the *Columbia* when she came to Cumberland Bay, and she was much less of a threat to Spanish dominion than British ships with false Portuguese papers. Martinez had no easy answers, and he began to document his actions with great care, taking an extensive inventory of the contents of the

Iphigenia. His plan was to send her and her crew south to San Blas to see if she would be condemned by the viceroy as a legal prize.

The seizure of the ship and the imprisonment of Douglas and his men shocked Maquinna's people. They became increasingly worried as the Spanish presence changed the atmosphere of the cove. The problems went far beyond the hostility between foreigners. In the hasty preparations for sailing at San Blas, the *Princesa* had not been fumigated to reduce the number of rats she carried. On her arrival, the infestation had swarmed ashore and attacked food stored in the longhouses. More than two hundred Spaniards and British had also fouled the waters of the cove and the tidal flats with the sewage and garbage they dumped overboard. The sound of woodcutting parties echoed out from the forests, and armed soldiers ranged along the beach. Women were said to have been assaulted, and fish in the cove were disappearing.

The seizure of the *Iphigenia* was the final straw. Maquinna expressed concern over whether Douglas and his men were now slaves and worried about other ships coming to the cove and trading. Almost overnight, most of the Mowachaht packed up and abandoned Yuquot. They resettled at an inlet three miles up the west side of the sound at a village known as Coaglee. Prisoners from the *Iphigenia* who had friends among the Mowachaht sent verbal messages to them, asking that they warn the *Northwest American* and any approaching ships from Meares that they had been captured.

Over the next two weeks, prisoners from the *Iphigenia* watched the Spanish fortifications take shape on the rocky islets enclosing Friendly Cove. Martinez named the rough log and stone-terraced *castillo* on Observatory Island San Miguel and planned to put ten cannons there to face over the sound and the cove. Across a marshy tidal creek by the western shore, the Spanish built a barracks, a forge, and a warehouse to store supplies. They also began work on the commandant's house. In a crash effort to get the port's defenses in order, Martinez set any man who could wield an ax to work. A half-dozen structures were under way, including a second gun emplacement called San Rafael, holding seven cannons and a lookout on the crest of Hog Island, facing the sea. Martinez knew that Meares's ships would be coming, and the Russians by the end of July or early August. He needed to be ready.

Douglas kept arguing with Martinez, refusing to select from his men those who would help sail the *Iphigenia* to San Blas under Spanish command. He also refused to sign an inventory for the ship. And he refused at first to see Kendrick. He noted in his journal that the Spanish commander had told him in confidence that "his orders were to take Captain Kendrick, if he should fall in with him any where in those seas; and mentioned it as a great secret that he would take both him and the sloop *Washington* as soon as she arrived in port."

It's not clear whether Kendrick caught wind of this, or if Martinez was lying to placate Douglas, but regardless, Martinez was in no position to take the Americans. Already, he brooded over the *Iphigenia* prisoners consuming his provisions at a rapid rate and began to have second thoughts about seizing the ship. The *Iphigenia* was in poor condition for a long voyage and would have little value as a prize. Recalling the viceroy's warnings to be cautious, Martinez perhaps listened to a suggestion of compromise from Kendrick that would force Douglas from the coast. He began to reconsider his interpretation of the *Iphigenia*'s instructions, and finally conceded that maybe the translation of the Portuguese orders was not as clear as it first appeared.

Douglas and his crew were released after he and Viana agreed to sign a bond stipulating that the value of the *Iphigenia* and its contents would be surrendered if she were found by the viceroy to be a legal prize. Joseph Ingraham and Kendrick witnessed the agreement, and appeared to mediate the deal. To ensure payment, Martinez tried to pressure Douglas to sell the *Northwest American* to him at a price set by Kendrick. The schooner was still somewhere to the north, and Douglas told Martinez ambiguously that "he might act as he thought proper" on her return. Trying to ameliorate Douglas's resentment, Martinez provided him with supplies that would take the *Iphigenia* to the Sandwich Islands.

Kendrick and Ingraham attended a dinner Martinez hosted for the glowering Scot and his officers. The Spanish commander ordered him not to cruise the coast for furs and never to trade in these waters again. Douglas vaguely acquiesced. That afternoon the *Iphigenia* was towed out through the entrance of the sound. Once he was beyond sight of land, Douglas immediately broke his word and turned northward to trade for furs to carry to Macao. As he sailed the coast, he also searched for the *Northwest American* to stop her from returning to Nootka. There was no way he would yield the schooner to Martinez. He said he would bring her crew and cargo on board and "set her on fire, if I find I cannot carry her with me" to the Sandwich Islands.

Somewhere along the storm- and fog-laden coast, Douglas missed the schooner. A little more than a week later, on June 8, she appeared at the mouth of Nootka Sound. Martinez sent out boats. He was wary of Douglas's vagueness in accepting his decree, and so he confiscated the ship as security for payments for the repairs and supplies given to the *Iphigenia*. As he had done with the *Iphigenia,* he made the *Northwest American*'s crew prisoners and divided them between the *Princesa* and the *San Carlos*.

LATE IN THE AFTERNOON ON JUNE 17, nine days after the *Northwest American* was captured, Robert Gray brought the *Lady Washington* into the sound on a following wind. Much had changed in the six weeks since he left. The crude bastion called San Miguel stood on Observatory Island at the entrance to Friendly Cove, and the gun emplacement called San Rafael was under way on the crest of Hog Island. Cannons to defend the cove and the bay were nearly in place. Along the shore southwest of the village, buildings under construction were visible. As they passed by the entrance channel, Haswell wrote that "the Spanish Ship [*Princesa*] was laying in the Cove with a Spanish Snow [*San*

Carlos] and an English Sloop . . ." The *Princesa* fired a gun to halt the American sloop, but Gray ignored the shot. Not knowing what might have happened to Kendrick, he hurried his damaged and leaking vessel toward hoped-for sanctuary at Mawina.

During the cruise northward, once again he had almost lost the sloop, this time venturing too close to shore and grounding on a rock ledge where the surf pounded her. A lesser ship would have gone to pieces. It was another touch-and-go situation, but she held, and they finally warped themselves off with an anchor.

Gray came along under the steep, rugged slopes of the six-mile stretch of shore, anxious about what he might find. With great relief he saw the American flag flying amid the treetops of St. Clair Island. Gray should by now have recognized John Kendrick's wisdom in setting up Fort Washington in this cove removed from Yuquot. More sheltered from the squalls off the ocean, and with a better source of fresh water, the rough-hewn compound also offered a semblance of protection from the Spanish. Moreover, Kendrick and the "Boston Men" had developed strong alliances among the Mowachaht that made them formidable. Kendrick had a reputation for fairness, and people from other villages across the sound came to Fort Washington to trade without going through Maquinna. The log house and forge and gun emplacement had quickly become the first American outpost on the Pacific.

While Gray had cruised up and down the coast seeking furs, Kendrick had gathered hundreds of skins here. And from the native people he had learned vital information: they were not on the mainland coast of America, but on an island. A trail led eastward from the village at the head of Tahsis Inlet to vast waters filled with many islands. Maquinna purchased furs there for a trifle and carried them back overland to Nootka in two days and a night. The image of an "inland sea" to the east fit with what the *Washington* had found in her first cruise to the south to the Strait of Juan de Fuca, and offered a tantalizing prospect for finding the Northwest Passage.

As Gray approached Mawina he could see that the *Columbia* was finally ready for sea. A puff of smoke billowed from the deck, and then came the delayed boom of a salute. Gray was happy to answer. Before he could work the *Washington* into the cove, a boat came out carrying Kendrick and—much to his surprise—the Spanish commander and a British captain, Thomas Hudson.

TWO DAYS EARLIER, ON JUNE 15, Hudson had appeared with the sloop *Princess Royal,* the first of Meares's ships. She was a low-slung vessel, a third smaller than the *Washington,* and carried a crew of only fifteen. She was highly vulnerable, and Hudson concealed from Martinez that Meares was one of her owners and that he was bringing instructions for Douglas and the *Northwest American.* He also did not disclose that his command ship, the *Argonaut,* would soon arrive. At the urging of Martinez and the Americans, Hudson accepted Spain's dominion over the region. After 116 days at sea from Macao, all he wanted was permission to undertake repairs and replenish his water and wood and then depart. Martinez saw this small vessel as no threat and was most likely relieved by Hudson's willingness to comply with his orders. After viewing the ship's charts, the Spanish commander began to focus on talk of the Strait of Juan de Fuca, where the *Princess Royal* had sailed in the summer of 1788 under a previous captain, Charles Duncan.

When Gray arrived, Martinez recalled that Kendrick had told him the *Washington* would be searching for the Straits of Admiral de Fonte. He asked if they had found them. Haswell said they had. Two weeks after Gray encountered the *Princesa,* they had taken the *Washington* into a broad bay and Haswell noted, "we discovered that the straits of Adml de font actually exist . . . I believe all the Range of coast North of Juan de Fuca Straits as far north as we went is a vast chain of Islands and entrances . . ." Reflecting the images on contemporary maps, Haswell believed that "it is probable when [the straits] shall be penetrated . . . large rivers and Lakes may be found that may overlap the western bound of the Lakes that have their vent in our Eastern coast . . ." Haswell and Gray most likely related what they had seen in the broad bay to the north and mentioned that in their earlier trip south they had found and coasted into the Strait of Juan de Fuca and seen the mythical "inland sea."

Martinez was enthralled and alarmed at what American and British traders had discovered in the bay to the north and at Juan de Fuca. Just a few days before, on June 14, he had noted in his diary (perhaps backfilling and revising after seeing Hudson's charts from the *Princess Royal* or talking with Gray):

> *I have recalled that in the year '74, when I was in this harbor on my return to the Department [San Blas], while sailing close to the coast, I had sighted in this sound in latitude 48 degrees 20 minutes, though at a distance, an opening of considerable size extending inland. At that time I was not able to reconnoiter it, since I was under orders of the first pilot and frigate's ensign Don Juan Perez, who did not wish to approach the coast . . . Considering now, according to the reckoning which I made then, that the opening must be some forty leagues, a little more or less, distant from this port, I determined to carry out the reconnaissance. For this purpose, I planned to avail myself of the schooner [the Northwest American] . . . This must, I am persuaded, be the Strait of Juan de Fuca, the existence of which the European nations, and particularly the English, have denied.*

The parallel myths of the Strait of Juan de Fuca to the south and the Straits of Admiral de Fonte to the north of Nootka offering a gateway between the Atlantic and Pacific must have stirred Martinez's thoughts of glory. Charles Barkley, commanding the *Imperial Eagle* under Austrian colors, was reportedly the first fur trader to sight the unusual column of rock marking the entrance to Juan de Fuca in 1787. Believing the column consistent with the ancient myth, he bestowed the legendary name on the strait. Charles Duncan with the *Princess Royal* visited the mouth in 1788. Within weeks of Duncan, John Meares supposedly used Barkley's charts to follow his track to the mouth of the strait. Gray entered with the *Lady Washington* in April 1789. However, none of these ships penetrated farther than the first twenty miles of the strait. For Martinez, discovery seemed to beckon. Reaching the strait and the inland sea and proving James Cook wrong would ensure him great honor from his king and a place in seafaring legend. But he had some catch-up to play with the British and the Americans in this search.

Exploring the mythical strait was important enough for Martinez to suddenly shift the carpenters, caulkers, and others from the crash effort on the port's defenses. They were set to work on the *Northwest American* to prepare a journey to Juan de Fuca. Although only a year old, the schooner's bottom was not sheathed in copper and had suffered extensive damage from worms and rot. She was hauled out on the Yuquot beach and careened, and in less than a week she was relaunched. Martinez had her towed alongside the *Princesa* and blessed and rechristened as the *Santa Gertrudis la Magna,* a name he felt suited a ship of discovery, and one that honored his distant and long-patient wife, Dona Gertrudis Gonzalez de Martinez.

On Sunday, June 21, Martinez held a special dinner to celebrate the ship and crew at the start of what he hoped would be a historic voyage. He invited Kendrick and Gray, the British captain Thomas Hudson, and all their officers. Kendrick offered Davis Coolidge to accompany the schooner as a pilot. Coolidge had previous experience in the strait with the *Washington,* and for the benefit of the American expedition he would be able to note anything the Spanish found. Martinez accepted the offer and Coolidge joined the Spanish crew. After the dinner, the *Santa Gertrudis* was towed out of Friendly Cove and set sail from the sound at 4 P.M.

Following the departure of the *Santa Gertrudis,* and feeling triumphant about what the world would soon hear, Martinez decided to stage a ceremony marking Spain's possession of San Lorenzo de

As the Spanish settlement took shape, gun emplacements covered both the entrance to Nootka Sound and the inside of Friendly Cove. (Drawing by José Cardero)

Nootka. He planned it as a grand pageant and invited the Americans, the captive *Northwest American* officers, and the native chiefs to attend.

The morning of Wednesday, June 24, dawned warm and clear. The ten cannons were in place at San Miguel. The hut on the hill for storing powder and ball and arms was complete. A large wooden cross had been hewn from timbers and engraved with the names of Jesus Christ and King Carlos III and the dates of 1774 (when Martinez said he had first entered this sound) and the present year, 1789. Although the commandant's house had not been completed, yellow banners and flags were raised from the structure.

Martinez went ashore at 9 A.M., and before his assembled officers and chaplains and the entire garrison, he declared formal possession of the port of San Lorenzo, its coasts and adjacent islands, all in the name of His Most Catholic Majesty Don Carlos III. A document of possession was placed in a bottle that was stoppered with pitch and buried at the foot of a low stony hill on the beach. As the towering cross was hauled up into place, Fray Severo Patero delivered the church's blessing of these acts.

Kendrick and his officers, as well as the British sailors, watched the ceremony, which ended with the troops firing a volley. The *Princesa,* the *San Carlos,* and the bastion of San Miguel answered with a salute of fifteen guns, and when Martinez returned aboard ship, another round of cannon was fired. Men posted in the rigging gave seven cheers for the king, followed by cheers Martinez had requested from the Americans and the British. The exuberant Spanish commander then served a banquet for his officers, the friars, and the foreigners, firing more salvos and raising further cheers to the king.

ON THE MORNING OF SUNDAY, JUNE 28, at 8 A.M., the *Lady Washington* and the *Columbia* came down to Yuquot and anchored in Friendly Cove. Thomas Hudson's *Princess Royal* was there as well, preparing to depart. Unaware of the approach of the *Argonaut,* Martinez granted Hudson leave with a stern warning not to trade south of the Alaskan waters of Prince William Sound. If he was found below that region, his ship would be taken.

After being towed out of the sound on July 2, the *Princess Royal* fell becalmed in a listless summer fog. Perhaps Hudson stalled, hoping to warn the *Argonaut* to seek out another harbor. He missed her arrival by hours.

Chapter Eight

The Golden Fleece

Nootka Sound

July 1789

MORE THAN A MILE AT SEA, a voice called out of the dark asking in Spanish for permission to come aboard. The watch on the *Argonaut* peered into the foggy blackness and sent for the captain, who came up as a launch filled with men slipped alongside the ship. Standing in the boat under the lamplight was a large, balding man, dressed like a common sailor. He claimed he was the commandant of the Spanish settlement at Nootka. James Colnett, a Royal Navy lieutenant and commander for Meares, had cruised these waters the past two seasons and knew of no Spanish settlement here. Blustering with a distinct air of superiority, he challenged the sailor, who seemed to be an imposter. A second boat then appeared, and two Americans, the *Columbia*'s supercargo, Richard Howe, and first mate, Joseph Ingraham, assured him that this was indeed Captain Martinez, the Spanish commandant at Nootka.

Colnett bristled at the prospect of Spain claiming the sound and wasn't sure what to think. The past few hours had grown increasingly confusing. Before sunset, two canoes had come offshore to the ship with a garbled warning about a captured ship that he could not make sense of. Then, as the *Argonaut* approached Nootka's rocky entrance, Colnett saw what he thought was the *Princess Royal* slowly heading south through the fog, or maybe it was an American sloop he had been told was on the coast. Colnett found now that it had been the *Princess Royal*.

Martinez gave him a letter from Thomas Hudson confirming the good treatment he had received from the Spanish commander. "Should you go into the Port," Hudson assured Colnett, "I am confident the Commodore would order you every Assistance in his power as he had done me." However, the letter mentioned that the *Northwest American* had been taken. Still puzzled, Colnett invited Martinez down to his cabin, where he examined his seemingly good-natured face in the lamplight as they talked.

The Americans came down to the cabin as well. After an exchange of pleasantries through the translator, Gabriel del Castillo, Colnett bluntly told Martinez that he was serving the Company of Free Commerce of London and his plan was to erect a fortified trading settlement at Nootka. Martinez noted, "He was entrusted to prevent other nations from taking part in this fur trade, both in this port and in other harbors of the coast, and moreover he brought orders from his sovereign, the king of England, to take possession of the port of Nootka and its coast . . ." Martinez may have mused that the *Argonaut* was aptly named. As in the old myth, whoever controlled the treasured golden fleece would control the land.

Martinez informed him that this was the domain of Spain and observed Colnett's expedition was a private venture; the *Argonaut* did not belong to King George, and Colnett did not have any authority to transact public business such as taking possession of land.

Colnett responded that he was a king's officer, and insisted he could act in the king's interest.

Martinez was already familiar with Britain's tactic of blurring the line between private purpose and public authority as a way to extend territory through exploration and trade. In fact, there was a broad dispute between European nations as to what constituted a valid claim of possession. The common starting point was the ancient Roman law of *terra nullius* ("nobody's land"), which had for centuries allowed an explorer to take possession of desired territory. Land not already claimed by a Christian prince was deemed "nobody's land" by European courts. This meant that when a European nation took control of land considered *terra nullius,* the rights of any indigenous people, such as the Mowachaht, who had occupied the Nootka area for millennia, could be ignored. Any dispute over claimed territory was thus one purely between "Christian princes."

Spain held that its fundamental rights to lands in the Western Hemisphere came from the papal grant of 1493 and formal acts of possession undertaken by its explorers. The British court rejected the pope's authority and argued (when it was convenient) that land also had to be settled and used to have a proven claim of possession. Colnett held that Cook had first entered Nootka in 1778, which gave title for this coast to Britain, and that John Meares had purchased and built an outpost on the land at Yuquot a year before Martinez arrived.

Martinez informed him that he had been at Nootka before Cook, in 1774. His expedition had named the area San Lorenzo de Rada, and the local chief, Maquinna, could confirm that he had been there. He recited the evidence of the abalone shells and said that the Spanish silver spoons Cook wrote of finding here had been stolen from him. Further, he said that there was no British house at Yuquot when he arrived. Howe or Ingraham could confirm that the hut was pulled down after Meares left and that they had used the roof boards for firewood. Confronted with this information, Colnett shifted to a more concilatory tone and asked Martinez "in a friendly manner to permit him to construct a strong building for the security of his own person and those who accompanied him, so that they could take some precautions and be protected from irruptions, raids, and thievery of the Indians."

"I divined his intentions," Martinez said, "and answered him that I could under no consideration permit it, since it was contrary to the orders which I carried."

Martinez was worried that Colnett would sail off to another spot. Unlike the *Iphigenia,* the *Argonaut* was a well-stocked ship that could establish a very substantial hidden outpost elsewhere on the coast. As Martinez later related to Viceroy Flores, if Colnett had carried out his designs, "we would have had a bad neighbor, and in time of war, an enemy at hand, to whose attacks Old and New California would be exposed on account of their weak defenses."

Seeking a way around their impasse, Martinez turned on his charm and played at seduction. He had none of the usual brandy, ham, and sugar to offer. Instead, he appealed to the British captain's sense of superiority. He told Colnett that he was in dire need of supplies and awaiting the long-overdue arrival of his supply ship, *Aranzazu*. Indeed, he had mistaken the sail of the *Argonaut* for that of his ship.

Colnett offered to supply whatever Martinez needed from the *Argonaut*'s supplies. Martinez politely thanked him and at the same time offered "all the assistance in his power" to Colnett. He entreated Colnett to anchor in Friendly Cove where the Spanish vessels lay. But Colnett hesitated. Recognizing his anxiety at being lured into a trap, Martinez assured Colnett that he was "a man of honour, Nephew to the Vice king and Grandee of Spain." Martinez continued that if he "would go in on those declarations of his honour" the *Argonaut* could depart whenever Colnett pleased.

"It was late and thick weather; I took his word and honour," Colnett wrote later.

Colnett stayed below with Martinez in the cabin, talking and drinking as the American boat and the Spanish launch towed the *Argonaut* into the sound. Colnett had ordered his pilot, Robert Duffin, to keep the *Argonaut* outside the cove at Yuquot. Duffin either ignored him or was not able to separate from the Spanish launch without a confrontation. At midnight Kendrick was called from his cabin on the *Columbia* and watched the British ship enter Friendly Cove. The *Argonaut*'s bow was tied to the *Princesa*'s stern mooring, and her stern to the *Columbia*. Soon after, Howe and Ingraham returned aboard the *Columbia* and reported the argument between Martinez and Colnett.

Late into the night, Martinez kept up his drinking and friendly banter with Colnett, who was surprised when he came on deck to find his vessel in Friendly Cove under the guns of Fort San Miguel and secured between the Spanish frigate and an American ship. To soften the shock, Martinez made a show of granting Colnett permission to erect a tent onshore and replenish the *Argonaut*'s water and wood.

Colnett retired but did not sleep. He chastised his pilot, Robert Duffin, for disobeying orders and allowing the ship to be towed into the cove. And he criticized himself as well for having only two swivel guns mounted and his dozen cannons still stored in the hold. Just before departing the ship, the American Richard Howe had given him a second, more candid warning letter from Thomas Hudson. When he read it, Colnett found that the *Iphigenia* had been captured because her instructions were to make prizes of foreign vessels. He had to be very careful in revealing his own instructions. Looking for a way out of their predicament, Colnett took a few men over the side in his captain's boat, rowing out of the calm dark cove and along the beach, scouting the Spanish gun emplacements at San Miguel and San Rafael, and returning before daylight. A guard Martinez had set to watch the British ship reported on Colnett's movements the next morning.

From the *Columbia,* Kendrick looked out over his bow in the dawn light to see the *Argonaut* within a pistol shot of his deck. He knew that Martinez planned to take Meares's command ship. The only question was whether the capture would be bloodless. There was no way Kendrick could get free of this, and he sent younger crew members to the shore camp and made certain his men were prepared. The atmosphere in Friendly Cove was tense as the pale sun rose, burning off the night's fog.

The flags of the two Spanish ships hung limp in the damp stillness. The American sloop and brig had raised their flags, and onshore the

American crew, camped where Meares's hut had stood, hoisted their red, white, and blue flag on a pole. Robert Duffin, who had been there the previous summer, looked at the crude Spanish forts atop Observatory and Hog Islands, and the buildings being constructed along the shore. He could see no sign of Meares's house remaining where the Americans had a large sailcloth tent. Patches of trees near the shore had been clear-cut and the Mowachaht village seemed empty.

Aboard the *Princesa,* Martinez took offense that Colnett had not followed tradition by raising his flag as a sign of respect for the Spanish king. He sent an order to Colnett. A few minutes later, blue English flags were run up at the bow and stern. At the main masthead, a broad blue pennant with a white square in the center was raised, "giving us to understand he was an officer of high rank," Martinez noted with greater irritation.

He sent a second message, inviting Colnett to breakfast and asking him to bring his ship's papers. The Americans watched the messenger passing between the ships, and Colnett going aboard the *Princesa.* They knew that Martinez was toying with him.

Short on sleep, and in no mood to joust with the Spaniard, Colnett said he could not present the papers requested because his chests were in disorder, and that he would search for them. Martinez went back to the *Argonaut* with Colnett and followed him to his cabin. He noticed great rolls of sailcloth stowed below deck, and asked again why Colnett had come to Nootka. The sails were for a one-hundred-foot sloop (the *Jason*) whose frame was aboard, Colnett told him. She was the first of several vessels they would launch on the coast.

"He informed me he bore the title or commission of governor of the port of Nootka," Martinez noted. "He further said that of the officials who accompanied him, some were to take command of the company's vessels, and others were to have charge of the books of the factory, for which purpose they had left London.

"I answered him, saying that he should consider his commission discharged since there was no place for the company's pretensions, and I could in no wise allow him to carry out his instructions."

Colnett began a search for his papers, and Martinez returned to the *Princesa*. At some point in the early afternoon Martinez spoke with Kendrick, asking him to prepare to deliver a favor. Until this point, Kendrick had kept his distance from Colnett. He probably had no liking for the fancy airs of the British "governor" of Nootka, and remained wary of what might transpire. Two of Kendrick's officers lingered aboard the *Princesa* to gather intelligence, probably Howe and Ingraham, whom Martinez admired.

At three o'clock in the afternoon, Colnett asked through a messenger to borrow Martinez's launch so he could tow the *Argonaut* out into the sound where he could catch the early wind off the land and set sail the next morning.

The pretenses were over. Martinez sent a reply message: "My friend, in the present circumstance it is necessary that you put into my hands at once your passport, instructions, and other papers that I have asked of you. Such are the orders of the king of Spain, my sovereign."

From the American ship, Kendrick and his men could see Colnett come up on deck, dressed in the London company's uniform and wearing his sword. Colnett was furious at having to acquiesce to someone he regarded as a treacherous Spaniard who was challenging British rights. Colnett later noted, "I received an order from Don Martinez, to come on board his ship and bring with me my papers. This order appeared strange, but I complied with it, and went aboard the *Princesa*."

Martinez was in his cabin with his pilot, the two Americans, and a padre. Colnett went in and showed the "passport" given to him by John Meares. Martinez asked for his other papers, and Colnett said that his instructions were directed to him alone and he was not authorized to show them. He haughtily demanded to know if Martinez was going to lend him the launch.

Martinez's temper flared. "I have no thought of doing so unless you first disclose the contents of the passport and other documents I requested," he said. As the argument heated up, the Americans left.

Martinez glanced over the passport papers, and "although he did not understand a word of the language in which they were written," Colnett said that he "declared they were forged, and threw them disdainfully on the table." Martinez told Colnett he would not sail until his request for documents was satisfied.

Colnett slapped the table with his palms and shouted, "Goddamn Spaniard," and then accused Martinez of breaching his trust and "that word and honour which he had pledged to me." He said Martinez would have to fire on him to stop him from sailing, and then he placed his hand on his sword. "I now saw, but too late, the duplicity of this Spaniard," Colnett said.

Martinez rose in anger and went out. "I was conversing with the interpreter on the subject," Colnett wrote, "when having my back towards the cabin door, I by chance cast my eyes on a looking-glass, and saw an armed party rushing in behind me. I instantly put my hand to my hanger, but before I had time to place myself in a posture of defense, a violent blow brought me to the ground. I was then ordered into the stocks . . ."

Up on deck, Martinez sent del Castillo to Kendrick with a message. The *Columbia*'s bow guns were manned, and so were the *Princesa*'s stern chasers. Colnett's crew looked with astonishment at cannons facing them on each side. This was the moment that would tell whether Colnett had prepared his crew for a conflict. It quickly passed; the Portuguese sailors and Chinese laborers wanted no part of the fight. Outnumbered and outgunned, the dozen British officers and sailors also yielded. Looking at Kendrick's guns loaded with shot, *Argonaut* pilot Robert Duffin wrote, "It was impossible to make any resistance against such superiority; indeed it would have been insanity to have attempted it." The overwhelming show of force by Martinez had prevented bloodshed.

Spanish soldiers climbed on board, seized the ship, and imprisoned Colnett's men in the irons made by Kendrick's blacksmith, Jonathan Barber. The Chinese laborers and most of the Portuguese sailors were taken ashore to the garrison, and the ten English sailors were confined in their forward quarters on the *Argonaut*. Colnett was beside himself. Martinez ordered that he be kept in stocks, but apparently Haswell intervened. "[A]n Officer that had been in the British navy, but at this time belong'd to the American ship, Advis'd them not to put me in the Stocks," Colnett later recalled. He was held for a time on the *Princesa*, raving that he would be hanged. He seemed to be going mad. The Spanish locked him in a cabin. Through the dusk and into the night he could be heard shouting that he would be executed and that two British war frigates would arrive to deliver a reckoning.

KENDRICK SAW THIS AS a very serious turn of events. Given the opposing views of Britain and Spain, the conflict might have seemed inevitable. And he most likely saw his own part in it as unavoidable. It wasn't possible for Martinez to ignore the direct challenge to his orders. Similarly, the Americans could not let the British take this sound or any other on the coast. Given the aggressive intent of Colnett's expedition, provocation of the Spanish must certainly have been among the possibilities John Meares and Richard Etches contemplated. Given that the South Sea Company license granted them approval to trade "in all the territories that are looked upon as belonging to the Crown of Spain," perhaps it was a confrontation the London merchants were seeking. The ramifications of the action were huge and, unlike the taking of the *Iphigenia*, could not be undone. The *Columbia*'s furrier, John Treat, noted an opinion among the Americans that "this will undoubtedly occasion Some altercation between the two Powers, particularly Should She [the *Argonaut*] be condemned at St. Blaz . . ."

As troubling and monumental as the taking of the *Argonaut* appeared, Kendrick would not let it stand in the way of his own long-pending plans.

At dawn the small harbor erupted in a volley of cannon fire. The booming shook everyone from sleep, or from the breakfast of gruel they had settled down to. Just thirty yards from the *Argonaut,* smoke from the blasts rose above the decks of the *Columbia* and *Lady Washington.* The roaring went on for more than a minute as the guns resounded and smoke drifted across the *Argonaut.* It was July 4, and Kendrick was opening the day with a salute to his new nation. Even if it was seen as rubbing in the humiliation of the British captives, he wanted to match the celebration Martinez had held a week earlier.

Kendrick hosted a feast aboard the *Columbia,* attempting to lighten the personal rancor by inviting not only Martinez and his officers and padres, but also the captured officers and men of the *Argonaut* and *Northwest American.* Throughout the day, the American ships fired volleys and the *San Carlos* and Fort San Miguel responded. Martinez and Kendrick proposed toasts to the Congress of the Confederated States and to His Catholic Majesty Carlos III. Both commanders were badly out of touch in this remote part of the world. King Carlos III had died seven months earlier. In the United States, the members of Congress were now part of a federal government. And in April, just two months before, George Washington had been inaugurated as the nation's first president.

The Mowachaht came to watch the booming celebration from the edges of the woods and the shore. Although a few natives continued trading with the ships, a strong chill had fallen over the relations between the Spanish and the native people since the Mowachaht had left the cove, made obvious by the fact that Maquinna was not here.

Colnett was absent as well. According to Robert Duffin, madness ran in Colnett's family. By Colnett's own account, he contracted a fever that threw him into delirium. He raved uncontrollably, and the Spaniards deemed him insane. In the morning he came on deck ostensibly to urinate over the side, but when the chance came, he climbed the ship's rail and had to be prevented from jumping into the harbor.

A few days later, in the early morning, Colnett broke his small cabin window, crawled out, and plunged into the harbor in an attempt to drown himself. When rescuers reached him, he fought them, and they had to pull him from the water by his hair.

THE STEADY TENSION SURROUNDING COLNETT and the *Argonaut* was broken on July 5, when the *Santa Gertrudis* returned from her two-week exploration of the Strait of Juan de Fuca. It was an exciting and welcome distraction for Martinez. José Maria Navaez, who commanded the schooner, confirmed finding the entrance to the strait. Following Martinez's instructions, he said they had sighted the "inland sea" and traded for seventy-five furs, but sailed no farther than the American sloop had ventured in the spring. A thorough survey would require at least two ships, ample provisions, and a force of armed men.

Martinez was elated at the discovery. That same day he wrote one of the longest entries in his diary. "There is ground for believing that this strait forms a connection with the Mississippi River in an ESE direction, although according to reports, it divides into two arms," one of which he believed "communicates with the strait of Admiral Fonte" in the north. After speculating on various inlets, he wrote, "From all this, it is evident that up to this expedition, neither Spaniards nor foreigners have been able to give a definite account of the above mentioned straits, although most so far have denied its existence. While in some accounts I have read that there never were any such persons as Admiral Fonte or Juan de Fuca, I have been disposed to think that these navigators did make their discovery, but the observations taken with their instruments were not true and the longitudes of the places mentioned by them were in fact much less." He noted that James Cook believed the straits to be imaginary, and accurately observed that Cook did not approach the land in the regions where the straits had been found. From this, he concluded, "The English have maintained two opinions on this question. One denies the existence of the passage from Hudson Bay to this gulf, and the other concedes that there is such a strait." Following the *Santa Gertrudis* exploration, Martinez wrote that he was "of the belief that the existence of these two straits is certain. The mouth of Juan de Fuca has been reconnoitered by me, and that of Fonte is assured from the reports that have been given of it, and finally because I saw one of its mouths in the year '74, to which entrance I gave the name of Don Juan Perez." Martinez glowed with triumph: "If Captain Cook had lived until the present time there is no doubt that he would be set right as to the existence of these straits, as in a short time it will be demonstrated to all Europe. Even he who circumnavigates the globe does not see all lands." Martinez believed that these straits, offering entry to the Northwest Passage and the interior of North America, provided all the more reason to follow his plan and stop the British, the Russians, and the Americans.

John Kendrick learned from Davis Coolidge what the *Santa Gertrudis* had seen, and he knew from Gray's cruise to the north the inlet where de Fontes's straits might lie. These observations seemed to confirm waterways Kendrick had likely seen on maps published more than a decade earlier. He had remained in the background and been careful to assist Martinez for the past two months, and he would continue to do so for a short time longer now. However, he also wanted to pursue these straits for American claims.

Over the next several days, Martinez took a detailed inventory of the *Argonaut*'s cargo, expropriating and noting stores needed for his own men. He also seized armaments and equipment intended for Colnett's Fort. Among his personal effects, Colnett would later claim that he lost his "sextant, charts, and drawing paper and all . . . his nautical instruments . . . [and a] time piece of Mr. Arnold's making," which Martinez apparently gave to Kendrick. Colnett was overcome with despair and kept asking who his executioner would be. Command of the *Argonaut* was turned over to Robert Duffin, who watched bitterly as the Spanish took his stores and ordered his men into forced labor. In secret, Duffin began to write a series of letters to John Meares on events as they unfolded.

With the exception of Colnett, who had to be kept under constant watch, the Americans said that Martinez treated the *Argonaut*'s officers and crew liberally, letting them go ashore during the day and only locking them up at night. In the British version of events, their time ashore was spent in work parties, and they were beaten if they didn't comply. Apparently, however, they had enough freedom to meet their Mowachaht friends and complain about Spanish treachery. They warned the Mowachaht that Spanish control of the harbor would soon close down all trade and the tribe would suffer under Martinez.

At their new summer village at Coaglee, three miles up the sound, Maquinna and his chiefs pondered what to do. The Mowachaht chief had gone back to the harbor once, to complain that Martinez's men were stealing longhouse boards at Yuquot for construction of the Spanish buildings. Martinez did nothing in response. Since the Mowachaht had left Yuquot, Martinez had become more distrustful and suspicious of them. The padres found no willing converts to Catholicism; men and boys insisted on going about naked; the chiefs still worshipped idols and practiced polygamy. Worse, rumors continued to circulate about Maquinna eating captured children. Kendrick assisted Martinez in purchasing slave children brought to him by the Mowachaht. Martinez then passed the children to the friars, who renamed them and sought to bring them into their faith.

What Martinez first saw as stubborn, savage behavior now grew to a fear that Callicum and Maquinna were plotting against him. He was most likely aware that Mowachaht canoes had carried a warning out to Colnett's ship as it lay offshore in the fog. He had also heard that

Callicum met with Colnett at dawn before the *Argonaut* was captured. Colnett had allegedly told Callicum that Martinez "had come to be the master of this land, and that he would expel us all from this port." Martinez wanted a stop to the intrigue and plotting. With the Russians coming soon, his authority had to be absolute and the port secure. He had no more time or patience for a policy of seduction for Maquinna and Callicum. His suspicions were about to trigger a deep and deadly schism.

LATE IN THE AFTERNOON ON SUNDAY, JULY 12, the watch at San Miguel reported sighting a ship anchored far offshore. It was not the Russians. Through their glass the soldiers saw that she had lowered a boat, which was making for the shore with several men. The Spanish dispatched two armed launches to intercept it. Once outside the sound, the men in the launches saw that the vessel was the *Princess Royal,* which had departed ten days earlier. In violation of Martinez's warnings, Thomas Hudson had taken the ship to Clayoquot to trade for furs, and now brought her back toward Nootka. Perhaps from natives traveling to Clayoquot he had heard that the *Argonaut* was captured and Colnett had fallen into a dire situation.

The launches approached the boat two miles from the *Princess Royal.* Hudson was aboard with five men. He was disguised as a seaman and armed with a pistol. Reaching the boat, the Spanish officers recognized Hudson and asked him to step into the launch. In the midst of a struggle, his pistol was seized and discharged. However, the boat raced away from the launches and headed toward the sound. As it came into the cove and approached the *Argonaut,* Martinez appeared on deck and ordered the men in the boat to be captured. Martinez believed that Hudson had returned to gather information from Colnett on the capture of the ship, which he would report back to Macao. From papers found on the *Argonaut,* Martinez now knew that Hudson had misled him. The *Princess Royal,* as well as the *Northwest American* and *Iphige-*

nia, were all owned by the London company and were part of Colnett's mission to take possession of the coast.

When Hudson was delivered to the commandant, Martinez asked him to write a letter to his crew to bring the *Princess Royal* in. He refused, and Martinez told him that "if his crew offered any resistance," he would be "hanged from the yard arm as a warning to the other prisoners in the port." Hudson then wrote to his first mate: "Mr Jaques, As I am a Prisoner and Captain Colnett also I would not have you make any resistance but comply with everything relative to the fortune of War." In a postscript he added: "don't make any resistance but comply with this in every respect otherwise things of worse consequence may Commence."

An armed Spanish launch was sent out to the *Princess Royal* in the dark. Martinez cautioned the launch's pilot "to use all care, since the vessel's guns were loaded, and the crew under orders to fire." Martinez wrote, "I commanded him that if they did, he should board and seize her by force, putting the crew to the sword without quarter." Colnett said later that Martinez already had a "Yard Rope rove to hang Captain Hudson . . ." Although the Spanish pilot commanding the launch did not have a good command of English, the message to surrender got through. The sloop and the ten men aboard were taken without resistance at three in the morning and brought into Friendly Cove.

AT MAQUINNA'S VILLAGE OF COAGLEE, word arrived that another ship had been seized and its crew made captive. Callicum, who was the tribe's designated ambassador to the foreigners, had had enough of Martinez's belligerence; the Spaniards had gone too far. The Mowachaht people had been pushed from their traditional home and spiritual center. Now, just as they had been warned by the British prisoners, their ability to trade was being cut off. They were losing their wealth and prestige. Something had to be done.

In the late morning, Callicum arrived at Friendly Cove and paddled out to the *San Carlos* in a canoe with his wife and child. He complained to the pilot, Lopez de Haro, who still held his own grudges against Martinez. Lopez de Haro tried to placate the chief with gifts. As he paddled back across the cove, Callicum saw Martinez on the *Princess Royal*. "Martinez Pisec! Martinez Capsil!" he shouted at him, calling the Spanish commander a robber and thug. He charged that Martinez was not content to take the vessels that came into the cove, but had to rob those outside the sound as well. Prisoners on the sloop interpreted for Martinez what the chief said. Martinez called to Callicum, but he continued to chastise the Spanish commander. Everyone in the cove stopped to watch what was taking place.

When the prisoners began laughing, Martinez snapped. He grabbed a musket from one of his men guarding the sloop and fired it at Callicum, but missed. "I took another and fired it, killing him," Martinez later wrote. The ball passed through Callicum's chest, knocking him into the water. Watching his body quickly sink, his wife and child became hysterical, screaming until someone came out to help them. Callicum had been unarmed. Everyone was stunned, but Martinez regarded the act as justifiable. He rationalized that the chief was conspiring with the English. He was making an example, as he would have made of Hudson. He would accept no insult to his honor, or plotting against Spanish authority in this harbor.

KENDRICK WAS HELPLESS TO DO ANYTHING, and it was probably not in his interest to intervene. On one side, his reputation and the American relationship with the Mowachaht were well established. And on the other, his dealings with Martinez had grown very entwined. Given Martinez's increasingly hostile temperament, and the potential of being drawn into the Spanish showdown with the Russians, it was time to leave port and continue with the expedition, but Kendrick didn't want to close the door on Fort Washington.

Kendrick told Martinez that he had not completed his mission and asked to return the following year after stopping at the Sandwich Islands and China. Martinez said yes, if he carried "an official Spanish passport." Martinez asked Kendrick to take the prisoners of the *Northwest American* to Macao on the *Columbia* and offered ninety-six sea otter skins to cover their expenses. Kendrick agreed. Martinez also asked Kendrick to sell 137 prime otter skins for him at Macao and to "entrust the proceeds to the Spanish ambassador at Boston to the credit of the crown." As an additional condition of Kendrick's return to the coast, Martinez requested that he "buy on my account in Macao two altar ornaments for the mass, and seven pair of boots for the officers of the San Carlos and of my own ship."

A personal connection between them emerged as well. In what must have been a difficult surprise, John Kendrick, Jr., now twenty years old, well versed in navigation, and fluent in the Mowachaht language, announced that he had decided to remain at Nootka and join the Spanish navy. There is little record of a discussion between father and son, but in a touching scene noted by one of the Spanish officers, the weathered American commander stood with tears streaming down his cheeks as he told his son that life held no greater fortune than to be a man of goodwill and to faithfully follow that path.

MARTINEZ GAVE THE AMERICANS an opportunity to dispatch a bundle of letters on the *Argonaut,* which was about to be taken to San Blas. For most of the men, it was the first chance to write home in two years. For Kendrick it had been thirteen months since he had written to Joseph Barrell from Cumberland Bay after rounding the Horn. In the midst of all the drama at Friendly Cove, he had made a fateful decision about the expedition. But knowing the letter could easily be opened and read, Kendrick was hesitant to divulge any meaningful information. He told Barrell that he would cruise northward and proceed to China where he would receive Barrell's instructions and let him know of the voyage's success, which to this point was "not by any means equal to your expectation." Kendrick also enclosed a letter to his wife, Huldah, and asked Barrell to forward it by "the first safe conveyance" to the village of Wareham.

AS KENDRICK MADE FINAL PREPARATIONS, the *Argonaut* was towed out of the cove and anchored in the sound. Manned by Spanish sailors, the captured ship departed for San Blas on the tide at 2 A.M. on July 14 carrying Colnett, Duffin, and the other captives locked below. A headwind from the south-southeast forced the ship to tack most of the day, until it finally dropped out of sight at sunset. The departure must have seemed like watching a slow-burning fuse. There was a globe-rattling blowup coming: it was just a matter of when, and whether the Americans would remain caught in the middle.

The Taking of the Bastille *by Jean-Pierre Houël. Events in Europe, such as the storming of the Bastille in Paris on July 14, 1789, would ultimately affect what would unfold in the far Pacific, just as events at Nootka would shape the lead-up to war in Europe and ambitions of the United States.*

Chapter Nine

Divided Dreams

Nootka, Clayoquot, Queen Charlotte Islands

July–October 1789

At 10 a.m. on July 15, the Spanish woodchoppers were at work along the shore as the longboats from the *Columbia* and *Lady Washington* towed the ships out of the harbor. Kendrick looked up and could see the men clearing the ground for gardens and the Mowachaht village standing dismantled and nearly empty. Perhaps for the first time in thousands of years, this site was uninhabited by native people during the summer.

The expedition had waited on the tide, and men at the oars got an added lift from the current out of the cove and through the entrance of the sound. Martinez went along with his boat, accompanying the ships "a distance of five or six miles in order to take leave of the Americans," who he said were continuing "their voyage of discovery." It was a strange parting. The Spanish commander seemed to grow more belligerent as his outpost took shape. His attitude would continue to darken. A few months after the Americans left, he reflected on his tangled relationship with Kendrick and noted: "I treated this enemy as a friend" and "could have taken his sloop and the frigate Columbia." Keenly aware of Martinez's unpredictable behavior, the Americans were glad to be gone.

After nearly a year in what seemed an infinite green wilderness, Kendrick was at last looking ahead at a flat, clear horizon. This was the first time the *Columbia* and many of the men had been to sea in ten months. Though she had been overhauled, reballasted, and packed for a long Pacific voyage, the ship still handled like a sluggish box on ice. Like Martinez, the men believed the expedition was headed north, but once out of sight of land Kendrick turned southeast for Clayoquot. He had personal reasons perhaps: Callicum's father-in-law, Wickaninish, was there, and the Americans needed to preserve good relations after the chief's killing. But more importantly, Kendrick had decided on a dramatic change in the course of the expedition.

Off Clayoquot, surf was breaking over submerged rocks. Kendrick lowered a boat to guide the *Columbia* through the half-mile-wide channel between two rugged islands. Three miles inside the sound the summer village of Opitsat lay on a low slope above a sandy beach. There were five main villages off the three large arms of the sound. Opitsat was the largest. More than twenty-five-hundred inhabitants lived here, in ancient carved houses that stood in a winding cluster about a half mile across. The Americans noted that the village seemed to be growing, as people who had formerly lived at Yuquot settled there. Kendrick and his men knew many of them, and their canoes came to trade once the two ships were anchored. At nightfall, when they were gone, Kendrick spoke with his men, taking the most seasoned hands aside for confidential discussions.

He then sent a messenger to the *Lady Washington,* inviting Gray to his cabin. The relationship between the two men had deteriorated further. Gray had written a letter of complaint to Joseph Barrell, attacking Kendrick's character, and sent it to Boston on the *Argonaut*. The complaint started with their landing at Cape Verde at the beginning of the voyage, "where we lay forty-one days, which was thirty-six more than I thought was necessary . . ." He also brazenly told Barrell: "I had the good luck to part Company the first day of April in a severe gale and thick snow storm to the Southward and Westward of Cape Horn." However, he failed to mention that under the "good luck" of going off on his own he had lost a man and almost sacrificed the entire crew and sloop at Tillamook. Gray told of scurvy on the *Columbia,* but nothing of the disease on his own vessel, and claimed that Kendrick prevented him from making "the best voyage that ever was made on this Coast." He went on to boast of the "considerable success" of his cruises while "the Columbia has rid it out here all the time." He concluded by writing, "I have nothing more to inform you except the voyage will not turn out to the Owners expectation, all for want of a nimble leader." And in a snide postscript, Gray asked Barrell to "present my best respects" to the other owners "and inform them that we have orders not to write to them, we must refer them to Capt. Kendrick's Letter for all information relative to the voyage."

During the past year, Kendrick may have wondered if it would have been better to sack Gray at Cape Verde. The sniping and sarcasm started then, but the disobedience didn't appear until Cape Horn. The seasoned commander may have hoped he could win the headstrong young captain over, but that had failed, and Gray's resentment built. Kendrick had recognized that the best way to manage Gray and Haswell was to send them off on missions and tell them only what they needed to know. That was what he would do now. He explained to Gray that there were not enough provisions for both ships to cruise north, and an early start to the market at Macao with the *Columbia* might bring a better price for furs. Much to Gray's surprise, Kendrick then told him they would switch ships. Gray would take the *Columbia* to Canton. Kendrick would take the *Washington* north. Kendrick didn't tell him when he would follow him to China, and Gray had no idea that Kendrick had asked Martinez about coming back the following year. Gray did understand that with the British ships captured and driven off the coast, the Americans had at least a brief opportunity to be in sole possession of the fur trade. As he absorbed the full scope of what Kendrick was saying, Gray undoubtedly recognized that the new orders presented an opportunity to escape Kendrick's command once more.

All the furs for market were shifted over to the *Columbia,* plus the bundle of ninety-six furs Martinez had given to Kendrick to cover the expenses of the *Northwest American* prisoners. Kendrick took the 137 furs that Martinez had asked be sold on the Spanish account.

Kendrick was now embarking on something more than an American trading adventure. It would become an odyssey, extending into the unknown, and bent on securing a presence for the new nation in the Pacific. He divided the men to give the *Lady Washington* a full complement of skills and the most seasoned hands. The *Washington*'s first mate, Robert Davis Coolidge, would go with him, as would the blacksmith Jonathan Barber, carpenter Isaac Ridler, sailmaker William Bowles, gunner James Crawford, cooper Robert Green, and Thomas Foster, John Cordis, John McCay, Samuel Thomas, and ten others, a total of twenty-one men, including himself.

Haswell, Ingraham, and Solomon Kendrick would go with Gray, who would have a total of thirty of the expedition's members plus the prisoners from the *Northwest American.* Kendrick pressured the most experienced prisoners to serve as seamen on the *Columbia* and threatened to leave them onshore in the wilderness if they did not sign on. Perhaps out of admiration for the charismatic commander, or out of a desire for adventure, a few of the *Northwest* crew volunteered to sail with Kendrick's select group.

THE STAY AT CLAYOQUOT lasted two weeks. During that time Maquinna came down with Callicum's grieving wife and family. Hearing rumors that Martinez would be looking for an excuse to shoot him next, he remained at Clayoquot. Callicum's murder deepened Wickaninish's distrust of the Spanish and European traders, but he and

Maquinna reaffirmed a special friendship with Kendrick. As much as trading partners, they would become important allies.

ON JULY 30, THE MEN on the *Washington* fired a thirteen-gun salute and watched the *Columbia* and their crewmates sail out of Clayoquot. Solomon Kendrick was among them. No one recorded what advice Kendrick might have given Solomon, or what personal message he might have asked him to carry home. He might have confided that the future was wildly uncertain, depending on what happened in the next several weeks.

As the *Columbia* disappeared, Kendrick was filled with excitement and dread at what he was undertaking. It was a dangerous combination he was setting loose, sending Haswell and Gray off together to deliver a group of resentful and enraged prisoners from the *Northwest American* to Macao. Unknown to him, the prisoners were carrying the secret letters Robert Duffin had written to Meares about the capture of the *Argonaut* and the *Princess Royal*. Meares's wrath could be expected, but the depth to which it would go was impossible to foresee. Kendrick regarded the risk as more than worth what was at stake.

Fort Washington at Mawina offered an opportunity to gain a beachhead for the new nation on this coast. Kendrick's reputation and the alliances the "Boston Men" had built with native people could provide security against the Spanish and the British and a steady flow of furs. Moreover, Kendrick now had a chance to mount his own search for the Northwest Passage. Staying behind to achieve these larger goals would mean giving Gray the honor of the first American circumnavigation, but Kendrick hoped that what would come later would carry a greater glory. He had the right men willing to stay with him. For all of them, this was still the voyage of a lifetime, and for those close to Kendrick and charmed by his dreams, it was a chance to sail into history.

What Kendrick did next has stirred controversy among historians. The prospect of entering the Strait of Juan de Fuca, just a day's sail south of Clayoquot, was extremely tempting. Coolidge had been in the strait twice now, and Wickaninish, who ruled the region below Nootka, traded with people on the inland sea and had ties to tribes in the south, including a niece married to Tatooch, whose domain lay at the mouth of the strait. Kendrick could take on some of Wickaninish's men at Clayoquot to help pilot the *Washington* into the inland sea and lead him to natives who could in turn direct them farther.

Wickaninish had already told Colnett that "The Straits of Juan de Fuca ran 5 days sail to the Eastward." There was "a large Passage to the North . . . and also a large sea to the South." The Clayoquot chief's canoes could not enter the passage, but by carrying them over an isthmus of land "he had been as far down in this Southern Sea as to get wood as sweet as my Sugar."

Colnett concluded, "It's the general Opinion of Capt. Duncan & of all that saw those Inlets that they Communicate with Hudson Bay's nearest Settlement of the Hudson Bay Co. Which is Hudson House is Lat 53d Long. (blank) Bears (blank) West dis 400 leagues. I have also every reason to think that the Straights of Juan de Fuca Joins with all those Inlets to the Northward & that all the Coast of America as far north as Prince William Sound is only a body of Isles & that the Main lays much farther to the E.ward than is generally believed . . ."

Wickaninish most likely shared the same information with Kendrick. If Martinez was requesting more ships to find and claim the passage for Spain, Kendrick knew that this was his opportunity to press on. He would not have been interested in a survey and detailed mapping, but in discovering a targeted passage through the region with native guides. Coolidge, or Wickaninish, may have cautioned him about taking the sloop so far into potentially hostile waters. Given his limited provisions, he might also have been forced to choose between exploring Juan de Fuca here in the south, or the Straits of Admiral de Fonte to the north.

According to John Meares, after the *Columbia* sailed for China, the *Lady Washington*

> *entered the Straits of John de Fuca, the knowledge of which she had received from us; and, penetrating up them, entered into an extensive sea, where she steered to the Northward and Eastward, and had communications with the various tribes who inhabit the shores of the numerous islands that are situated at the back of Nootka Sound, and speak, with some little variation, the language of the Nootkan people. The track of this vessel is marked on the map, and is of great moment, as it is now completely ascertained that Nootka Sound and the parts adjacent are islands, and comprehended within the Great Northern Archipelago. The sea also, which is seen to the East is of great extent; and it is from this stationary point, and the most Westerly parts of Hudson's Bay, that we are to form an estimate of the distance between them.*

If Kendrick had in fact traveled up the Strait of Juan de Fuca and followed the route marked by Meares, the four- or five-hundred-mile distance could have been traversed in four weeks. It would have been quite difficult for Kendrick to tow the *Lady Washington* for much of the eighty-mile transit through the narrow channels of Discovery Passage and the Johnstone Strait, or similar channels to the east. But with native assistance he could have accomplished the trip.

Backing up his statements, Meares published a narrative and map, showing for the first time what would become known as Vancouver Island. Traced onto the map was the *Washington*'s approximate route in the autumn of 1789. However, Kendrick never made a public claim that he circumnavigated the island, or that he had searched for the Northwest Passage at any time. Outnumbered by the British and Spanish, the American commander may have maintained his practice of keeping his own counsel. It would have been logical for him to protect information on the fur-rich villages on the east side of the island, to avoid admitting that he had misled Martinez, and to keep secret any information about an inland passage.

It is also possible that Meares fabricated the report of the *Washington*'s inland cruise to prod Parliament and the British Admiralty to act (which it did) out of fear that the Americans or the Spanish would soon discover the passage. At the southeast end of the "inland sea" (near Puget Sound), Meares indicated on his map the great "river of the west" extending eastward toward the Missouri River.

CONSIDERING THE LACK OF ADDITIONAL EVIDENCE and Meares's reputation for lying, some historians do not believe that Kendrick made the journey around Vancouver Island. Others, who have considered the collateral evidence and take Meares at his word, believe that the *Washington* was the first vessel to pass through the "inland sea," which presents a great inconvenience for the later claims of British captain George Vancouver.

The next confirmed report of Kendrick was in September, more than a month after he had left Clayoquot. He was a day's sail above where he would have come out from the "inland sea" through Queen Charlotte Sound. Thomas Metcalf, of the tiny twenty-six-ton schooner *Fair American,* was looking for his father's ship when he encountered Kendrick. Metcalfe later told Martinez that he spoke with Kendrick at 54°20' north latitude, four hundred miles up the coast from Nootka. Martinez jealously observed that Kendrick was in "one of the mouths of the strait of Fonte."

Kendrick was near the present-day Alaskan border (just below Dundas Island), among a bewildering string of fog-enshrouded bays and inlets winding seventy or a hundred miles among huge forested islands. Three months earlier, the *Washington* had entered this area during Gray's cruise northward in the early summer. Haswell thought a survey of the branching channels that teased far inland would prove "an almost endless task," needing to be undertaken by a nation willing to bear the expense. Coolidge, who had been here with the *Washington,* would have been of some help in the search, but the task was daunting. Kendrick could ask native people about a passageway as he traded along the coast, but by September, time was a factor in acquiring the information he was looking for. The rainy season was starting. Salmon were in the upper reaches of the rivers and streams. Snow lay on the mountaintops, and most of the native people were headed into their winter quarters. Moreover, if Kendrick wanted to catch up with the *Columbia* at Macao to send communications homeward, he would have to leave the coast and his initial explorations aside. Equally vital, he had to finish gathering enough furs to fund a return to the coast the following year.

BY THE END OF SEPTEMBER, Kendrick took the *Washington* from the foggy archipelago to the Queen Charlotte Islands, about forty miles offshore. While the islands close to the mainland had a fierce and rugged wildness, the Queen Charlotte Islands seemed to have a more ethereal and mysterious quality. The native people knew them as Haida Gwaii ("the islands of the people"), or Xhaaidlaglia ("the islands at the borders of the world"). The Spanish were said to be the first Europeans to see them, during the expedition of Juan Perez in 1774. James Cook had missed them. Cook's officers Nathaniel Portlock and George Dixon were the first to trade there and named them after Britain's queen in 1786. Robert Gray had called them the "Washington Islands."

Several villages rich in furs lay along the eastern shores of the islands. The *Lady Washington* may have stopped at Masset and the villages of Skidegate and Skedans as Kendrick made his way down the shore. At the southern end of the islands, Kendrick went into "Congethoity," named "Barrell's Sound" by Gray when he traded there in June. The sound lay about fifteen miles above the southernmost point and had two entrances. The eastern entrance (the Houston-Stewart Channel) was flushed by dangerous currents and tides that dropped as much as twenty-four feet during a full moon. Sunken rocks lay hidden in the channel and thick beds of kelp choked the open water. Kendrick took the *Washington* into the sound below several small islands, some of them barren rocks stained black by the sea. Nature here was much starker than in the rocky wilderness at Nootka. The black silence and stillness of the bays coupled with the raw beauty of the forests and the strands of slowly twisting fog inspired a kind of reverence. The eastern shore of the island, which the Haida called SGang Gwaay (Anthony Island), held dark, sea-worn headlands framed with thick hemlock and pine and thickets of wild rosebushes. Farther in, stands of huge tideland spruce, hundreds of years old and as much as sixty feet in circumference soared two hundred feet out of the mossy ground. No branches grew on the lower half of the massive trunks. At least one was reported to have a dwelling carved into it.

Smoke rose from a small sandy cove at the village of Ninstints, two-thirds of the way along the shore on the island. The *Washington* fired a cannon as a signal to trade. Soon after, numerous canoes took to the water. Kendrick ordered the *Washington* to anchor well offshore. Unlike the Mowachaht, the Haida were regarded as aggressive and treacherous. Many still came out to the ships singing and left with a song after trading, but jealousy and sour negotiations were common.

Both men and women were in the canoes. The men had partially painted faces but did not paint their bodies as they did at Nootka. Instead they were smeared with a thin film of grease and the dirt it collected, insulating their skin from the cold and insects. They climbed on board the *Washington* without the least reserve. The men wore various raccoon and otter mantles over their shoulders. They also had cast-off sailors' garments with shells, buttons, thimbles, or Chinese coins sewn onto them. Around their necks, each man wore an iron dagger, polished bright and sharp, with a handle wrapped in leather. Some were pointed at each end to strike a double blow.

The women wore long-sleeved leather frocks with a skirt down to their knees. Their hair hung loose or lay tied in braids a finger-width thick and covered in paint. Most of the women's faces, from their cheekbones to their chin, were painted black. On another ship, a group of sailors enticed a young "perfect beauty" to wash off her face paint. They found her skin as pale as their own, and her amused friends mocked her as she hurriedly repainted herself. What fascinated the *Washington*'s crew was that some of the women displayed an extremely odd fashion—a labret, or oval, piece of wood inserted into the lower lip, extending it like "a small shelf" by as much as four inches. When pushed up it would cover her upper lip and nose. When it fell, the labret entirely covered the chin and exposed the lower teeth. The practice seemed a mark of distinction worn by both lower-class women and chiefs' wives.

With his sons gone and few of the younger crew on board now, Kendrick may have been more lax in managing the men. As the *Washington*'s crew had learned from trading here in the early summer, these women were less reserved than the Mowachaht. In the midst of barter, they were said to be "always ready and willing to gratify the amorous inclinations of any who wish it."

Trading at Ninstints was conducted through one chief, Coyah, an apparent tyrant who controlled SGang Gwaay, the adjacent island of Kunghit, and the region just north of the channel. He was described by one ship's officer as "a little diminutive savage-looking fellow as ever trod." A leader of the Raven clan, Coyah may have modeled himself on the mythical Raven, who was a magician and transformer, the greediest and most lecherous antihero among the mythical Haida characters. Two years earlier, with Colnett's support, Coyah had taken a raiding party north, looting furs from villages as far north as Skidegate and trading them to the British. He was cruel and imperious, and Kendrick apparently took an immediate dislike to him.

After a few days anchored off the village, someone stole the captain's linen that had been washed and left hanging to dry. Petty thievery had been going on since their arrival, and Kendrick decided to send for Coyah and Schulkinanse, an older chief who may have been his father-in-law. When they climbed on board, Kendrick confronted Coyah about the thefts and, learning nothing, took both men hostage. The crew sat them on the deck and clamped their legs into the notches of a cannon carriage. Kendrick told them and others in a canoe alongside that if they did not return the stolen goods, he would kill them. The canoe carried Kendrick's threat to shore, and people of the village soon appeared with some of what had been taken. Recognizing that trading would be at an end when they released the two chiefs, Kendrick forced them to bring out all the furs they had left, and gave the same rate in goods he had previously paid.

The native version of the story, told later by a woman of the village, offered harsher details, saying that Kendrick "took Coyah, tied a rope round his neck, whipt him, painted his face, cut off his hair, took away from him a great many skins, and then turned him ashore." Humiliated, Coyah lost his chieftainship when he came ashore and was made an "Ahliko," or one of the lower class.

While beating Coyah seemed out of character for Kendrick, who was usually singled out for his humanity toward native people, he may have wanted to see the tyrant deposed in favor of another chief, or maybe the wilderness or desperation for funds was bringing out the bloody work he was capable of.

As in the killing of Callicum, violence in trading was becoming all too common. James Hanna, the first British fur trader at Nootka, reportedly killed fifty Muchalaht on the northeast side of Nootka Sound in 1786. As a prank he had also lit gunpowder underneath a chair Maquinna was sitting on, which launched him into the air and scarred his backside. Meares had fired on natives to get their furs, as did Colnett. By the time the *Columbia*'s first mate, Joseph Ingraham, and the clerk, Richard Howe, witnessed the *Northwest American* crew shooting and robbing natives and houses in Nootka in October 1788, violence was already a common trade tactic.

Of all the native people he would encounter, the one with Coyah was Kendrick's only recorded case of brutality. Left in humiliation, the diminutive Raven clan chief developed a festering hatred of traders that would result in a string of deadly retaliations, and far-reaching personal consequences for Kendrick.

Chapter Ten

A Place of Skulls

San Blas, Mexico

August–October 1789

As the *Washington* traded near the Queen Charlotte Islands, nearly three thousand miles to the south James Colnett had fallen into deep despair and resigned himself to fate.

The *Argonaut* arrived at San Blas on August 15, two weeks before the *Princess Royal*. Colnett was suffering from scurvy, and many of his imprisoned crew were in deplorable condition. Each night during the month-long voyage down the California coast, Colnett was locked in Duffin's cabin. He said he was hungry and parched much of the time and watched helplessly while the Spanish and one of his own men broke open "every case of the cargo that was in the [captain's] Cabin out of which what they thought proper was taken." He said he was taunted and "almost suffocated" in the heat as they sailed south. As bad as his condition seemed, he had freedom most days and was treated far better than the ten English crewmen locked in irons in the bread room. Their condition deteriorated to a point where Colnett described them as "half Starved and [bathed in] constant perspiration, their Bones Crawling through their flesh, Stark naked, and no one could discern the Colour of their Skin, for the conveniency they had to ease the calls of nature was never emptied, till by the roll of the Ship it upset on them and their bedding, and even not allowed to Shift themselves. Lice, Maggots, and every other vermin that this filth Collected, made them prefer being stark naked rather than keep Clothes on them to harbour additional Plagues. Their Victuals that they gave them were frequently thrown into them like Dogs, and the Door lock'd on them again . . ."

Since Colnett's episodes of delusion, Robert Duffin had taken on the role of captain. Duffin and the other officers, confined in their own cabins, rarely visited Colnett, who accused Duffin of siding with the Spanish and doing everything to distress him. He also charged that Duffin had many occasions to retake the ship when the Spanish were drunk at night, but failed to do so.

At San Blas, they were held a night and a day at anchor in the bay before being taken off the *Argonaut* and up the river at dusk. The Spanish ushered Colnett onto a barge with the aging port commandant, José Comacho, while Colnett's men crowded into a second boat. Colnett lamented the miserable figures the dirty and naked crew cut before the people who lined the shore to see them. Mosquitoes swarmed over them as they proceeded a mile upriver. Stick and grass huts appeared along the darkened shore. They seemed wretched to Colnett—far below the quality of the grass houses of the Sandwich Islanders. As they approached the village, many more people appeared along the shore and the road where they landed. Colnett estimated there were about eight hundred inhabitants of the town. "It being a Market day . . . I do not believe there was a single person that could walk but our arrival had brought to the water side."

They were marched into the town and held at first in a house off the square. Nearby was the slaughterhouse, "which was it not for the Turkey Bustards [buzzards] which destroy all the Offals that the pigs do not, this place would become more pestilential than it is." Colnett described it as a "golgotha or Place of Skulls" and said their sleep was disturbed by bells that announced the deaths of villagers, a common occurrence during what was now the "unhealthy season."

Commandant José Comacho read with alarm a letter from Estevan Martinez on the seizure of the British ships, and forwarded the large package of the *Princesa*'s reports and inventory lists of the captured ships to Viceroy Flores. At Mexico City, the ailing viceroy received Martinez's request to have the British ships declared prizes at about the same time he received orders from Madrid. Floridablanca and minister of the Marine and Indies Antonio Valdes had at last responded to Martinez's original plan. They agreed on the urgent need to defend Spanish dominion in the North Pacific, which they knew the British wanted to test.

Count Juan Vincente de Revillagigedo, the son of a previous viceroy, was coming to replace Viceroy Flores. A new commander, Juan Bodega y Quadra, would be installed at San Blas with five other naval officers. And new ships were to be constructed for actions to keep out foreign vessels, which might extend to removing the Russians from Alaska.

The news of Revillagigedo's appointment arrived as he journeyed overland from Veracruz to Mexico City. The new viceroy would soon issue orders to build up the outpost at Nootka and begin extensive exploration of the Strait of Juan de Fuca. The decision fulfilled at least part of Martinez's recommendations, but the shift did not bode well for the temperamental captain. His wife, Gertrudis, had petitioned the royal court to have her long-absent husband returned to Spain. He would lose not only his mission, but also the protection of Flores as the result of allegations that would soon be leveled at him concerning the captured ships. Despite what Martinez might suffer personally, the Spanish ministers' decision was well timed and appeared to anticipate the heightened tensions about to erupt.

At San Blas, many of the prisoners contracted fever. First mate James Hansen committed suicide by slitting his throat with a razor in the privy, and eighteen of the thirty-one men eventually died or deserted. As time elapsed, Colnett noted, "We now had no remedy left but to resign ourselves to fate and depend on the Court of Great Britain for our release which we were well-assured would happen as soon as the news by the way of China thro' the Americans that were at Nootka when we were Captured."

As Colnett despaired, Robert Gray was en route to China. On November 17, the prisoners and the news of the capture of the *Argonaut* and *Princess Royal* arrived at Macao. Stories about the Spanish seizure spread through the city. An enraged John Meares read the letters from Douglas and Duffin, took depositions from the prisoners, and set off on the next ship for England. He would take this to the prime minister, he would take it to Parliament, and regardless of what he had to do, he was determined to break Spain's three-hundred-year-old claim of dominion over the Pacific.

Far from Colnett's hell, and oblivious to the ominous events in the making, Kendrick was about to depart the Queen Charlotte Islands, his men eager to exchange the cold rains of the coast for their long-held fantasies of the solace of the Sandwich Islands.

Part III

Odyssey

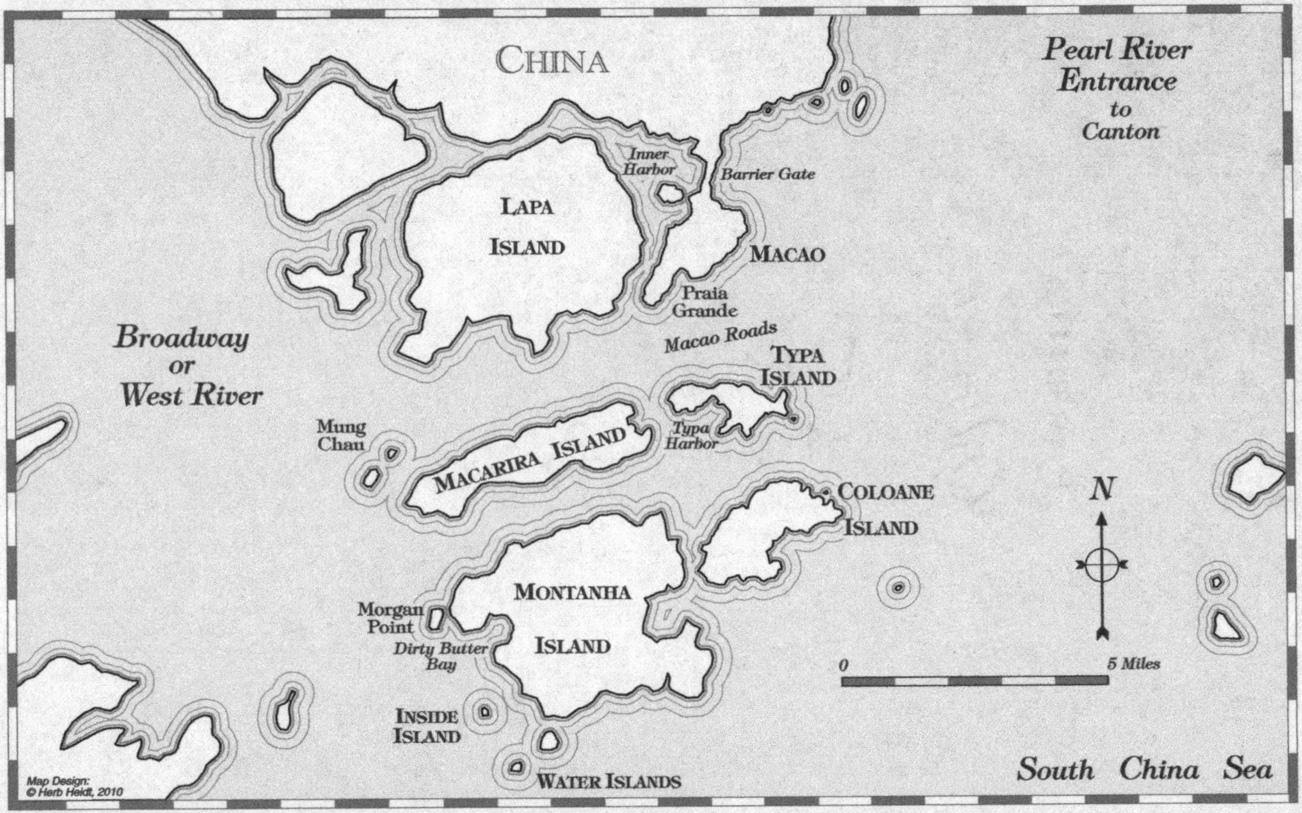
CHINA
Pearl River
Entrance
to
Canton
Inner
Harbor
Barrier Gate
LAPA
ISLAND
MACAO
Praia
Grande
Macao Roads
TYPA
ISLAND
Broadway
or
West River
Mung
Chau
MACARIRA ISLAND
Typa
Harbor
COLOANE
ISLAND
N
MONTANHA
ISLAND
Morgan
Point
Dirty Butter
Bay
0
5 Miles
INSIDE
ISLAND
WATER ISLANDS
South China Sea
Map Design:
© Herb Heidt, 2010

CHAPTER ELEVEN

Volatile Paradise

Sandwich Islands

OCTOBER–DECEMBER 1789

THREE OR FOURS DAYS out from the Queen Charlotte Islands, the *Washington* eased into trade winds from the northeast that would carry her on the twenty-seven-hundred-mile passage to the Sandwich Islands. As Kendrick and his crew made their way toward the mid-Pacific, large flocks of birds resembling plovers appeared, and lone albatrosses soared under the high thin clouds. For men who had voyaged nearly a year and then spent another year in the deep northern wilderness, the good weather sparked anticipation of a long-awaited paradise. The stories of Sandwich Island women they had heard in Boston were colored with glowing detail by the men of the *Iphigenia* and by Kaiana, the young Hawaiian chief who accompanied Douglas. New members of their crew who had wintered in the islands aboard the *Northwest American* now boosted their expectations further. A single nail bought copious quantities of roast pork and fruit, and beautiful women would come aboard each evening for sex. These women were said to possess arts Western women knew nothing of and would initiate former farm boys and lowly jack-tars into life on the far side of the world. Even the reluctant officers of arriving ships were said to find themselves unable to resist.

Aside from the anticipated paradise, Kendrick was concerned about the more serious uncertainties that awaited them. He knew that a war was under way in the islands and they had to take care in their alliances with local chiefs. He also knew that these islands were an extremely valuable prize for any nation because they were ideally situated to command voyaging and trade routes in the North Pacific. Like an outpost at Nootka, or the elusive Northwest Passage, the harbors and shores they were headed for could easily become a source of contention between European courts.

Estevan Martinez had already urged that Spain take possession of these islands. He reported that the island group, "which abounds in everything that is necessary, is placed in the center of the Pacific Ocean at an almost equal distance from San Blas, Nootka, Prince William, Siberia, Japan, the Philippines, and Canton. The voyage each way requires but a month, and it is an advantageous stopping place where ships sailing between this coast and Canton can take on a store of provisions."

As part of his intelligence-gathering, the Nootka commandant kept Matuturay, a young Hawaiian chief who had been aboard the *Northwest American*. With Matuturay, Martinez created a short Spanish-Hawaiian dictionary and told the viceroy that the young chief "is very inclined toward us, and realizes the difference between our treatment and that of the English. We could probably accomplish the reduction of all the islanders, and our sovereign would have new subjects" if a Spanish outpost were established.

At present, the British were far ahead of Spain. Although London had not adopted a formal policy toward possession of lands in the North Pacific, merchant adventurers were leading the way to create one. In 1786, James Cook's former officers Nathaniel Portlock and George Dixon visited the islands in the large fur traders *King George* and *Queen Charlotte*. They began the practice of reprovisioning there on voyages between America and China. The King Georges Sound Company, which they were part of, saw this as an important link for much more than resupply.

When Richard Cadman Etches applied to the East India Company for trading privileges for the King Georges merchants in April 1785, he envisioned the Sandwich Islands becoming "the grand emporium of Commerce between the two Continents and the innumerable Islands of that immense Ocean." In the monopoly British merchants sought in the Pacific, the islands would be an essential midocean marketplace. John Meares went so far as to claim that providence intended the islands to belong to Great Britain, an attitude that was widely shared in England.

Kendrick undoubtedly wondered what it might mean for American trade in the Pacific and Asia if other nations controlled these islands. Britain's policy of closing her ports to American ships did not bode well. And if the belligerence of Martinez was any indication, Spanish possession would also pose problems. The American expedition's instructions were to purchase lands that appeared beneficial and offered a base for trade. This left Kendrick to discover what foothold, if any, he might find there. His efforts to keep Hawaii open held great portent for the new nation.

BACK HOME, THE IMPOVERISHED FORMER COLONIES were just beginning to stir from the devastation of the Revolution and the ensuing economic depression.

As the *Washington* headed south for Hawaii, Joseph Barrell was entertaining President George Washington. In late September, Washington had left New York City for a tour through the New England states. The journey for many was a triumphant march, symbolic of the new federal government now in place. For others, it was vital for peacemaking.

Despite ratification of the Constitution and the first federal election, there was deep-seated rancor among the states and hostility in the countryside. There was a fear of new tyranny and that an elite class—an American royalty—was forming to run the country. In the wake of Shays' Rebellion, Washington wanted to bolster the support of merchants and the goodwill of yeoman farmers for the federal government. In a time with no mass media other than regional newspapers, he had to venture out, using his charismatic image to capture local loyalty and build unanimity by riding through the villages and farms where Shays' armed rebellion had risen up and opposition to the Constitution had been widespread.

Joseph Barrell was appointed to a committee of three to manage Washington's visit to Boston, which would include a ceremony for Washington to review troops gathered on the Cambridge Common, the spot where he had first taken charge of the Continental Army in 1775. Barrell rode out to Worcester to escort Washington's entourage along the Upper Post Road. There is no record of their conversation, but they most likely touched on foreign trade, and Kendrick's expedition.

A year earlier, Barrell had sent Washington one of the medallions commemorating the expedition. Like Jefferson, John Adams, and others, Washington wanted open ports and free global trade so the United States could make full use of her growing population and rich resources to contend with the Old World empires. In response to the gift of the medallion, Washington offered Barrell his hearty wishes for success in the Pacific, with the hope "that the day will arrive (at no very distant period) when the sources of commerce shall be enlarged and replenished; and when the new Constellation of this Hemisphere shall be hailed and respected in every quarter of the terraqueous globe!"

IT WAS THE RAINY SEASON in the islands. As the rugged sloop continued southward, intermittent thick weather clouded the horizon. During the second week of November, three weeks from the Queen Charlotte Islands, the snowy peak of Mauna Kea ("white mountain") on Hawaii appeared through the glass as a broad hump, rising nearly 13,800 feet. Mauna Loa lay hidden to the southeast. The men undoubtedly wanted to put in at the first harbor on the north shore. But wary of the local warring, and seeking Kaiana and other chiefs he had been told of, Kendrick kept far offshore. He rounded the southern end of the island, staying wide of Ka Lae, an area said to have raging currents and strong winds that could sweep unsuspecting vessels onto reefs and hidden rocks.

The shoreline grew steeper as they ran up the southwest Kona shore, broadside to swells that had rolled thousands of miles across empty sea. The *Washington* was the fifteenth ship of record to arrive after James Cook's landing a decade earlier. Kendrick would find memory of the British explorer still fresh, and as at Nootka, the people still absorbing the impact of that contact.

FOR CENTURIES THE HAWAIIAN ARCHIPELAGO was nearly unknown. In the east was the big island of Hawaii. To the west lay the seven main islands of Maui, Kahoolawe, Lanai, Molokai, Oahu, Kauai, and Niihau, and other scattered islets. People from the southern Marquesas twenty-three hundred miles to the southeast are believed to have arrived here as early as A.D. 400. An invasion from Tahiti, or several migrations, occurred around the year 1200, and oral histories tell of at least one homeward voyage. Cook had stopped at Tahiti on his way to the American coast. When he asked about islands to the north, the Tahitians reportedly told him they knew of none. Perhaps they had forgotten their oral history, or wanted to be the focus of Cook's attention and so misled him. Or perhaps he didn't record their answer.

Cook is commonly recognized as the first European to discover the islands—in January 1778. However, local historians believe that Spanish sailors and possibly Chinese, Dutch, or Japanese seamen arrived in earlier shipwrecks or expeditions. A common tale was that, while crossing the Pacific from Mexico to the Philippines, Spanish pilot Juan

Gaetano had reached the islands in 1542. Estevan Martinez mentioned Gaetano in his recommendations to Viceroy Flores for a Spanish outpost in the islands. Gaetano's story had never been proved, because Spain's practice was to keep all its discoveries and maps as state secrets. However, enough facts about the islands had leaked out to make their existence more than speculation. The first world atlas, *Theatrum Orbis Terrarum,* published in 1570, shows an isolated island group called "Los Bolcanes" (the volcanoes) at nearly the same latitude and about ten degrees of longitude east of Hawaii's actual location.

Cook certainly knew the rumors of Los Bolcanes and had studied Anson's maps of the Pacific, which included islands with the Spanish names Los Majos, La Mesa, and La Desgracida near the same isolated location. Regardless of what the Tahitians had told him, as Cook sailed for the American continent, he arced westward out of his way as he approached the region, and picked up sightings of birds and other signs of land.

AT DAYBREAK ON JANUARY 18, 1778, Cook's crew noted clouds and the blue haze of land bearing northeast-by-east. The ships' accounts show that during the next several hours more clouds showed as distinct islands. The men were fresh from Tahiti, where many had been reluctant to leave what one officer described as "tasting Joys and Bliss that seemed More than Mortal." The appearance of these islands seemed to offer solace and a temporary reprieve from the frozen reaches of the earth they were headed toward in search of the Northwest Passage.

That night amid slack winds the current carried them northward toward Kauai. Off the eastern end of the island the following afternoon the appearance of the two ships drew a few daring native men to venture out in canoes. Cook found the words they spoke as they sat alongside the ship similar to Tahitian. Very timidly they traded fish for what little was offered them, and seemed to recognize iron and brass. Sailing on along the coast, Cook's officers noted villages on the rising hills. Native people onshore, sighting what seemed to be moving islands, fled into the distance or stood in awe at the water's edge.

On January 20, the *Resolution* and *Discovery* came to anchor near the Kauai village of Waimea. An early native historian noted that there was panic and debate over what the ships might be. A kahuna (priest) argued that they were temples of Lono, a god of prosperity and peace whose banner was a triangular-shaped white cloth hung from a pole with a crosspiece. With a warrior at his side, the kahuna courageously went aboard the *Resolution* and offered a prayer to lift any *kapu,* or spiritual power, on the ship. It was the right gesture, but it didn't stop what was coming.

Voyage records show that more than half of the 112 members of the crew and officers on the *Resolution* showed signs of venereal disease. Another seventy crewmen on the *Discovery* most likely carried similar infections. The disease had spread quickly at Tahiti, where relationships with native women had grown into "marriages" and romantic entanglements that drew some men to attempt desertion. Concerned that there would be the same problems here, Cook decreed that no women would be allowed aboard the two ships. He did not want the dishonor of introducing the disease to these islands. Men with venereal symptoms could not go ashore, under any pretext, and those who did go ashore were to have no connection with the women. No one was to stay onshore overnight. Anyone found breaking the order would receive twelve lashes.

In the harbor at Waimea, men came aboard trading pigs and sweet potatoes, and marveled at all the metal that might be made into knives and weapons. Thievery was rampant. Any metal object not nailed or tied down was taken. One man carried off a butcher's cleaver and escaped his pursuers. Another was shot and killed when Cook's men believed he was trying to steal from a boat as it was landing. Despite this, trading continued through the afternoon and evening, and women swam or paddled out to the ship. Cook's men rebuffed them, and the women left shouting epithets as they turned back toward shore.

During a two-week stay, Cook learned of other islands to the east of Kauai, but could delay no further. On February 2, the two ships departed for the north. The impression made by the Hawaiian people and their lush landscape stayed with Cook's men for the next nine months.

Kealakekua Bay *by John Webber. Despite its reputation for violence and James Cook's death, the bay at Kealakekua would become a frequent stop for visiting ships.*

ON NOVEMBER 26, 1778, after voyaging to the American coast, north into the Gulf of Alaska, and through the Bering Strait, Cook returned. His search for the Northwest Passage had halted when they reached unending walls of pack ice. Now they were seeking rest and repairs to ships worn by the fierce North Pacific. They sailed around Molokai and Maui, where Cook was greatly discouraged to find signs of venereal disease among the natives who came on board. He believed it had been left by a watering party that was stranded ashore overnight. Some of his officers argued that Cook was fighting the inevitable—that the disease would spread—and that it was perhaps indigenous (although the natives knew their disease was linked to the ships).

Finally agreeing to land and make repairs, Cook headed for a bay on Hawaii's west shore in early January. The bay was known as Kealakekua—the "pathway of the gods." Using information from Maui natives on board, Cook apparently knew the impact his arrival might have. This was the annual four-month period of *makahiki,* when warfare was prohibited; the time for celebration of the god Lono, who had left the island in ancient times and sailed off over the horizon from this very bay. Crowds gathered for the annual festival were astonished as they beheld Cook's approaching sails, which seemed nearly identical to Lono's triangular white tapa banner hung on a cross-shaped pole. As at Kauai, priests regarded the ships as emissaries of Lono. Some believed Cook to be the god himself returning. Thousands of people swarmed onto the water in canoes or swam to the *Discovery* "singing and shouting and exhibiting a variety of wild and extravagant gestures." The great number who went climbing up the side and into the rigging made the ship heel.

Coming ashore a short time later, Cook found villagers falling on their faces as he approached. Taken by priests, he was put through a ritual at their temple, fed part of a rotting, roasted pig, and given a bitter drink, most likely the slightly narcotic *awa.*

As expected, the rule against women on board the ships did not hold. According to officers' accounts, the ships were filled with women engaging in sex. The crew also engaged in numerous liaisons near the stone temple where they were allowed to camp. Angered by breaches of local customs, steady demands for food, spreading disease, and jealous friction, goodwill toward the foreign men wore down.

As incidents of physical scuffles and threats began to occur, Cook determined that "these people will oblige me to use some violent measures" and that "they must not be left to imagine, that they have gained an advantage over us."

On February 14, 1779, the *Discovery*'s large cutter was stolen from her mooring. In retaliation, Cook proposed seizing and holding all the canoes in the bay until the cutter was returned. He sent out boats and armed men to block escape from the harbor, then went ashore with nine marines to the village of Kaawaloa to take the old chief Kalaniopuu hostage. On the way back to shore with the chief, hundreds and ultimately as many as three thousand people surrounded Cook's party. Word came ashore that a chief attempting to leave the bay had been shot and killed in a canoe by men in one of the ships' boats. The crowd was enraged. One warrior threw a rock and struck Cook. Another threatened him with a knife. A marine officer was attacked and beat back a man with the butt of his gun. Cook fired his pistol. More stones began to fly and Cook fired again. As Cook turned to shout to the launch, he was struck with a club or stabbed in the neck or shoulder and fell forward into the water. The crowd surged around him, killing him and four marines as others scrambled into the launch and rowed out of reach.

Astronomers and carpenters who were ashore across the bay conducting an astronomical observation heard the musket shots and received orders to abandon their camp. The ships fired cannons into the village, scattering people into the hills. The expedition's grieving officers wanted Cook's body returned and they threatened to destroy the village if it were not delivered. A few days later, two priests of Lono, who lamented the killing, came to the ship with a piece of flesh from Cook's buttocks wrapped in a bundle. His skull was said to be in the possession of the chief Kalaniopuu. The priests related that the rest of him was burned, dismembered, and distributed; his intestines were said to have been used to rope off a temple. In retaliation, armed parties of mariners went ashore, burning houses and killing several natives. Two warriors' heads were cut off and hung on the bows of ships' boats. Order was finally restored several days later before the ships sailed, but a reputation for violence hung over this harbor.

Nathaniel Portlock, who made a brief visit in May 1786, concluded that it was not safe to land at Kealakekua without a strong guard. George Dixon apparently communicated this warning to James

Colnett and others. However, this was the harbor William Douglas frequented with the *Iphigenia*, and where Kendrick would have the best opportunity to meet Kaiana and other important island chiefs.

THE AMERICAN COMMANDER WAS FAMILIAR with the stories of Cook's death, and prepared the *Washington*'s guns as they made for Kealakekua Bay. After passing villages along the shore, they came toward the most densely populated part of the island. Smoke drifted from groves of coconut trees as they rounded Palemano Point. At the blunt head of the mile-wide bay, an immense, steeply sloping cliff, pocked with caves, rose six hundred feet above the water. The abrupt shore below it cut off low peninsulas to the north and south.

Arriving at Kealakekua, the Lady Washington*'s crew would have found a greeting that matched their expectations. (Drawing by Sigismund Bacstrom)*

Little had changed since Cook was here. On the barren north peninsula was the royal village of Kaawaloa, a hundred or so houses with walls and roofs of thatched pili grass. On the south side was Waipunaula (now known as Napo'poo'o), where farmers and fishermen lived. Over the rugged rising land to the south, cultivated enclosures and more huts were scattered among groves of coconut trees. The shore all around the bay was enclosed with blackened volcanic rock and lava beds. At Waipunauloa there was a sandy beach and a well of fresh water.

The village dogs barked as double canoes and single hulls with outriggers launched out. Unlike the seasonal Mowachaht villages, which subsisted on hunting and gathering, the people here lived a settled life on parcels of land known as *ahupuaa,* which were subdivided and granted according to a sophisticated feudal system. Shares of crops from the *ahupuaa* went to the local chief, who then passed shares to the district chief for this section of the island. The chiefs were interrelated members of ruling families with inherited divine powers, or mana. The ruling families, known as *ali'i,* were tiered by the purity of their royal blood and stood at the top of a rigid caste system. Beneath them were the kahunas, who were priests or masters in certain crafts. The fields were worked by the *maka'ainana,* or people of the land, and the *kauwa,* who were outcasts and slaves. Daily life was controlled by a system of religious instructions and taboos (*kapu,* or spiritual power) that dictated how each person should act at a particular time and place, shaping each person's destiny from birth to death. These instructions influenced planting of the fields, fishing, eating, drinking, sex, dancing, games, trade, and war. Violations could result in bad fortune, or an array of punishments, including death. Life was a journey among spiritual powers guided by *kapu* and the whims of chiefs and their queens. The *ali'i* and some of the kahuna could declare or lift *kapu* to control events, although there were certain restrictions even they had to observe or risk the wrath of the gods and the disruption of the social order.

The *Washington* anchored not far from the spot where Cook had lost his life. Onshore were men who had taken part in the attack. One of them, Pelea, who may have been on Kauai at the time Kendrick arrived, was said to have been the first who stabbed Cook, and he kept a white ruffled shirt rent with holes that he claimed belonged to the explorer. For some visitors, he would bring it out and describe the order in which the wounds had been delivered.

As when Cook arrived, Kendrick and the *Washington*'s crew found themselves in the midst of the four-month *makahiki* season at Kealakekua, which had begun in October. Their arrival lived up to everything they had been told. In the clear waters of the bay, brown-skinned women in a "state of nature" came alongside in canoes or swam around the ship. Some wore only a short skirt of grass or a bark-cloth loin skirt—a *pa'u*—which they readily stripped off. The young, unmarried women were crowned by flowers, with long brown or black hair flowing over their shoulders. Most of the women coming to the ship had their hair cut short in back and long in front, some with bangs stained white with clay or crushed lime from coral. They wore necklaces of shells or polished black wood. A number of them had their front teeth knocked out—a sign of mourning for a husband or loved one lost in battle. With local warfare taking a heavy toll, so many of these young widows and mourners swam out to the ships that their toothless smiles were mistaken by the sailors for an odd local fashion. Unlike the barter for women on the Northwest Coast, romance was the custom here, and women who were widowed by war were eager to ally with a man who had some degree of power.

On board the *Washington,* the women flirted with the crew. In the modest words of one officer, they "seemed not to esteem chastity a virtue." Another officer observed "that few could but admire them and none resist the impulse of the moment." According to native history, even James Cook was seduced when a chieftess offered her daughter, Lelemahoalani, to him. Whatever seductive dancing or sensual arts the women might have practiced were never recorded or were washed out in the wave of missionary fervor that followed the merchant traders decades later. However, deep affection was common. Foreign men became bound to the islands and chiefs in part through the women. And in certain cases, women betrayed a chief to report to sailors a plot brewing against their lives.

Woman of Sandwich Islands *by John Webber. Hawaiian women often formed strong bonds with foreign sailors who in turn stayed and supported chiefs.*

Man of Sandwich Islands *by John Webber. This figur is noted to be Kaiana, the young chief with a wide varying reputation.*

Kendrick had put up boarding nets, which ran eight feet up from the deck to control access to the ship. The men coming on board were affable and ready to trade hogs, taro, plantains, and fish held in the canoes. They were stout and well muscled, with black hair tied in many finger-width braids or cut short on the sides and long on top. Most wore only a *malo,* a sash tied around the waist that secured a narrow breechcloth. Some were tattooed, and all of them appeared incredibly clean. They paid little attention to the women around them.

Kendrick sent for the Hawaiian chief Kaiana, who was at Kawaihae Bay on the northwest corner of the island. He was expecting the sloop. The *Columbia* had stopped there in August and left a letter for the American commander before departing for Macao. When Kaiana paddled out to the *Washington,* he was bearing the letter. Kendrick took it below and opened it. In a quick, urgent message the *Columbia*'s clerk, Richard Howe, warned of the duplicity of the natives. He said that a month before the *Columbia* arrived, the *Iphigenia* had been attacked and Douglas and his men barely escaped. Despite the laughter and amiable trading on deck, what the chiefs wanted was not beads or looking glasses or nails. They wanted guns and powder and shot. Kendrick could expect that any pistols or muskets bartered might suddenly be turned on the ship and her crew.

Security on the *Washington* had to remain tight. Kendrick could forbid canoes coming to the ship after dark, and they would have to closely guard against their anchor cable being cut. The reality was that they were on a small sloop with less than thirty men, surrounded by hundreds of warriors. Their best chances for survival rested on Kendrick's negotiating ability and the behavior of the crew.

From Kaiana and Douglas, Kendrick learned that Hawaii had been ruled until a few years before (1782) by the supreme chief, Kalaniopuu, the old man Cook had attempted to take hostage. As he lay dying, he designated his son, Kiwalao, as his heir, and his nephew, Kamehameha, as war lord.

Kamehameha was a great bull of a man, about thirty years old, and one of the most talked-about figures in the islands. People feared his approach and his scowling and fierce countenance. His life was enveloped in an aura of violence and legend, and he was seen as a man of destiny. He was said to have been born to a queen of Kona during a time of storms and strange lights in the sky, which some historians believe was the passage of Haley's Comet in 1758, but others date his birth to February 1753. Spirited away as a child, he was later trained by his uncle, supreme chief Kalaniopuu, in religion, navigation, the arts of ruling, and warfare. He soon earned a reputation as a fearless warrior, and as the one foretold to rule over all the islands.

The arrangement of shared power with his cousin, Kiwalao, raised old jealousies and created shifting alliances for power and land. Fighting soon broke out. Because he was an *ali'i* of lesser royal blood, Kamehameha had difficulty attracting and maintaining allies. To bolster his stature and diminish his cousin, Kamehameha took Kiwalao's daughter captive and made her his wife. Then, adding insult to injury, he captured and married a girl that Kiwalao had betrothed. Finally, Kiwalao was killed in battle in 1786 after four years of fighting. Nevertheless, control of the island remained divided. Kiwalao's brother, Keoua, who ruled the northern part of the island, now became Kamehamha's rival.

Kaiana sided with Kamehameha when he was brought back to the islands by Douglas in 1788. Kaiana was a noted warrior who had collected a small arsenal of pistols and muskets during his time among the traders. He was made a district chief at Kawaihae, a village likely to face the first onslaught of attack from Keoua's northern district, or from Maui. Kaiana was also the leader for an inter-island battle with Maui that was anticipated to happen soon. This would not be like the bloodless clash and taking of ships at Yuquot, or the village raiding of the Mowachaht. It would involve everyone. Kamehameha was about to wage war on two fronts with more than ten thousand warriors under his subchiefs.

Beyond the conflict with Keoua for control of Hawaii, Kamehamha wanted to rule all of the islands. Kahekili, the most powerful old chief in the four kingdoms of the islands, was his primary foe. He ruled Maui, Oahu, and Lanai and controlled Kauai with his half-brother Kaeokulani (Kaeo). The old island lord was rumored by some to be Kamehameha's father, and many believed he was also the one foretold to control all the islands. His name was associated with lightning, and half his body was tattooed black. The troop of fanatical warriors he led were tattooed in the same way and wore their eyelids propped up. They were called *pahupu'u,* and mention of their name and the vicious attack dogs that accompanied them struck fear into native hearts.

From the villagers, Kendrick and his men heard that Kamehameha would attack Kahekili after the close of the *makahiki* period. Kaiana was particularly interested in acquiring muskets, powder, and shot from Kendrick in preparation for the war. Kendrick most likely

Kamehameha, King of the Sandwich Islands *by Louis Choris. Kamehameha I, the legendary ruler of the Hawaiian Islands, at about age sixty.*

traded the few arms he could spare at this point. He recognized the circumstances and set out to build alliances as he had on the Northwest Coast.

Kaiana and weapons were Kendrick's entry to the world of the *ali'i*. Keaweaheulu, one of the five chiefs of the Kona district, befriended Kendrick. The American commander may have indicated to him that he wanted to establish regular trade with island chiefs instead of just gathering provisions for his ship.

How the first opportunity for permanent trade came about is not known, but one tale says it was a coincidence: firewood brought to the *Lady Washington* burned with a sweet-smelling smoke. Perhaps women brought the wood aboard to fumigate the foul odors below deck, or to soothe aching joints. Kendrick recognized it as sandalwood (*santalum*). The natives called it *la-au-ala* ("sweet wood") or *iliahi* ("fiery surface") for its reddish blooms and red-tinted new leaves. They used it for scenting bark cloth, for making dyes, and for medicinal purposes.

Somehow Kendrick knew that the Chinese prized this wood and used it in religious rituals and as an aphrodisiac. He also knew that no sandalwood grew in China; it was shipped from India. Like the sea otter furs of the Northwest Coast, Kendrick believed this scented wood might offer a key to trade in these islands and the chance to gain a foothold here. Permission to cut trees and cure the wood would have to come from the chiefs, and in particular from Kamehameha.

The royal house at Kaawaloa sat apart from the others, surrounded by a fence that commoners could not cross on pain of death. Not even a blade of grass could be bent by a commoner. The short walls and high peaked roof were thatched with dried golden-brown pili grass. Inside was a large, airy space standing open to the ridgepole. The floor was covered with printed leaf and rush mats. A large opening was cut in the high peak of the wall for light and ventilation. Kamehameha's companions were all about the room, people called the *mako'u* after the torch that burned all night as they stayed up telling stories, gossiping, or playing games. At the head of the room was Kamehameha, wrapped in a long, scented *tapa* (bark cloth) robe. James King, who had sailed with Cook, described him as having one of the most savage faces he had ever seen. His broad, squat head atop a massive body was marked by a wrinkled forehead, down-turned mouth, and fiercely bright eyes.

Accompanied by Kaiana, Kendrick probably presented his gifts and attempted to explain his wishes. With little to trade except a few guns, Kendrick would have offered a share in the profits, seeking to make Kamehameha, Keaweaheulu, and Kaiana partners. This was consistent with local sharing of island harvests and ensured that the chiefs would protect the venture. Kendrick may have proposed more as well. He was ultimately seeking an outpost here, as with Fort Washington at Nootka. He would leave a man in the Kona district to start that outpost, to harvest trees and help train Kamehameha's men in warfare with muskets. Kamehameha may have perceived the deal as a way to put his profits toward a shipment of guns. Whatever the final terms, Kamehameha agreed.

Many of the *Washington*'s crew most likely vied to stay, though the logical choice was one man who had experience in warfare aboard privateers and knew how to prepare and cure wood: the carpenter Isaac Ridler. Given the danger inherent in remaining, Kendrick would have given Ridler a partnership in the enterprise. There were no extra provisions to trade other than bits of metal. Ridler would need to make his own way, trading, fishing, and foraging, and directing the harvest of sandalwood under the protection of Kamehameha and the unpredictable and jealous lesser *ali'i*. Although Ridler had a wife and children in Boston, he was enthralled. With two younger crew members, James Mackay and Samuel Thomas, he agreed to take up Kendrick's effort to gain the first American foothold in this volatile paradise.

Despite any misgivings about Kaiana, and perhaps to direct other captains through a man he was allied with, Kendrick wrote a letter of recommendation for the young chief on December 11, 1789: "During the stay of these three weeks at this place we have received every attention of the chiefs . . . Cianna [Kaiana] (who accompanied Capt. Meares to China and back again) he having supplied us with every refreshment the islands afforded. It is therefore recommended to the notice of any commanders who may here after stop here to refresh he being a chief of consequence in whom the greatest trust may be placed as was ever experienced."

WITH THE DEAL SETTLED, Kendrick left Kealakekua and passed westward through the island chain, stopping at Kauai for water, and at Niihau, the last westward island, for yams and hogs. Once fully provisioned, the *Washington* sailed due west. The five-thousand-mile trip to Macao, across the western Pacific and threading through the islands between Formosa and the Philippines, would take about five weeks with fair weather.

Kendrick had somehow skated through danger once again. The rapid launching of the American presence in the islands, with little or no resources, was more evidence of his ability to garner the confidence of his men and win the cooperation of chiefs who considered themselves in part divine.

Kamehameha had come away impressed with the American captain's comfort with power. But the situation remained volatile, and quickly deteriorated. Kamehameha wanted much more than muskets—he wanted a European ship with cannon to attack the canoe fleet of Kahekili. He did not have long to wait. Three months after the *Washington* left, the New York brig *Eleanora* came to the islands. At Maui, her boat was stolen and a sailor was killed. Captain Simon Metcalfe sought revenge. He had a chief put a taboo on the port side of his ship, and lured canoes to trade at the starboard side where he had mounted all his guns. When the canoes came crowding in, he opened fire with grapeshot, killing more than a hundred men, women, and children. Some accounts put the number as high as three hundred.

At Hawaii, Metcalfe continued his harsh treatment of native people, punishing the district chief Kameeiamoku with a rope for some perceived slight. Humiliated, the chief vowed to destroy the next foreign ship that arrived. That ship was the thirty-three-foot schooner *Fair American,* which had a crew of four and was captained by Metcalfe's nineteen-year-old son, Thomas.

While the *Elenora* was anchored at Kealakekua, Thomas Metcalfe brought the *Fair American* into Kawaihae Bay, about forty or fifty miles to the northwest. Both Kaiana and Kameeiamoku went aboard. They placed a brilliant feathered cape around young Metcalfe as a gift, and then one of the chiefs picked him up and tossed him overboard. Warriors alongside in canoes speared and clubbed him. The four remaining crew were quickly seized and thrown overboard. Three were killed. The fourth, a young Welshman named Isaac Davis, tried to swim off and they beat him with paddles and pushed him underwater. Regardless of how long they held him down, he refused to succumb. He was finally hauled ashore and beaten mercilessly until he was blind and fell unconscious. He was left for dead, tied facedown in a canoe.

Ridler received word of the attack and of one possible survivor. After finding Davis in the canoe, terribly bruised and bleeding but still alive, he had him carried to his house. Ridler realized that he and the two younger crew members with him were in grave danger.

Fearing that the elder Metcalfe would find out what had happened, Kamehameha restricted the movements of Kendrick's men and made it taboo for anyone to go out to the *Eleanora*. He also seized one of her crew who was ashore, an English boatswain, John Young. When no canoes would come out to the ship and Young failed to return, Metcalfe sent a message ashore to Ridler, which threatened "to take ample revenge" unless Davis was brought to the ship. Getting no response, he sensed that something was terribly wrong and hauled out of the bay. Kamehameha took the *Fair American* from Kaiana and hid it in a cove. To save his own life, as well as that of Davis and Young, Ridler continued to serve Kamehameha, teaching his warriors how to fire cannons and sail the small schooner.

With the *Fair American*, and assistance from the foreigners, Kamehameha invaded Maui. Kahekili was away at Oahu. Kamehameha's forces pursued Kahekili's son, Kalanikupule, and other chiefs deep into the Iao Valley. Battles were traditionally fought with a volley of short spears, then at close range with long spears, shark-toothed clubs, slings, swordlike knives, and shields. Kamehameha had the cannons hauled overland and slaughtered so many of Kalanikupule's warriors that their bodies dammed a stream. The battle became known as Kepaniwai—the battle of the dammed waters of Iao.

The victory had little meaning, however, because while Kamehameha was warring on Maui, his rival Keoua took the opportunity to come down from the north and ravage Kamehameha's villages on Hawaii's west coast. Kamehameha returned to fight two battles against Keoua in the expanding island war. In the midst of it, Ridler, along with Davis, Young, and the other two *Washington* crew members, Mackay and Thomas, lived under constant threat of death and prayed for Kendrick to soon return.

Chapter Twelve

House of Cards

Macao

January 1790

Off the coast of China, the *Washington* sailed into a dawn light that unveiled a forest of fishing boats on the horizon to the north and west. Through his glass, Kendrick could see vessels of all sizes, some with high broad sterns, fishing in pairs. With her flag snapping in the breeze, the sloop made her way to them, calling out and receiving little or no intelligible response. The shoals they were on lay two days offshore, and the *Washington* was seeking a lone white rock jutting from the water, known as Pedro Blanca, that marked the approach to the Pearl River Delta and Macao. By the end of the day, a scattering of small islands appeared—the Ladrones (Spanish for "thieves")—showing they were on the correct course. Douglas had warned that pirates lurked here, hunting in packs and preying on unsuspecting vessels. The crew armed themselves and loaded the swivel guns.

The wind stiffened and the weather grew cloudy as they came toward the long, mountainous shore. At night they saw lights of many fires dotting the horizon, and boat traffic thickened again. In the morning, amid the hubbub of so many vessels, from tiny fishing boats, to junks, to huge seven-hundred-ton merchant ships, no one took much notice of a small sloop. Most foreign ships took a Chinese pilot on board from one of the junks that approached flying a marked flag. Kendrick could afford nothing at this stage and most likely wanted to make his own way in. Smoke and the smells of the land came over the water as Kendrick followed the inbound ships. Then the small city appeared. By midday January 26, 1790, the *Washington* had dropped anchor about a mile offshore from Macao in three fathoms of water with a muddy bottom.

From the bay you couldn't notice that the buildings were on an island. Macao lay at the end of a peninsula two miles long and a half mile wide and was connected to the mainland by a causeway guarded by high double gates. Along the shore stood a row of square two- and three-story Mediterranean-style houses and buildings. Behind them, several steep hills rose above tile-roofed houses crowded into the valleys. Pine trees and green shrubs clustered around a few larger villas. A white-walled fort overlooked the bay from the peak of a hill near the center of the city. On another hill was a church. More steeples rose in the background. Though its population was only about four thousand, this was the first civilized town or city the men had seen in two years.

Kendrick's first order of business was to register the ship's arrival and collect letters from Barrell's American agents, Samuel Shaw and Thomas Randall, who had located here just two years before. In the buffeting wind, Kendrick lowered a boat into the muddy yellow-brown water and sent to the customs house for permission to enter the Typa, a sheltered area lying near the entrance to the inner harbor. A few hours later the request was denied. It was a sign of things to come.

Gray and the *Columbia* were already thirty miles up the Pearl River at Whampoa. He had arrived at Macao on November 2 and tried to take advantage of getting into the market early. Caught in the politics of the mandarins and Chinese merchants, he quickly encountered difficulties of his own.

The Praia Grande, Macao *by Thomas Allom. For nearly three hundred years, the small city of Macao was the only entry point to China for foreign merchants.*

As much as Hawaii was a raw, chaotic paradise, Macao seemed a bureaucratic nightmare. China was a nation of laws, rules, and regulations wielded by silk-robed mandarins and an army of customs officials and soldiers. As the only port open to the Fan Kwae, or "foreign devils," Macao was under the nominal oversight of a Portuguese governor, whose country had held ownership of the port since 1557. The real control, however, lay with the Chinese viceroy at Canton and the resident mandarin.

Merchants, and especially foreign merchants, had little standing in the larger scheme of things in the "Celestial Kingdom." The Chinese emperor claimed sovereignty over all things under heaven, dismissing Christian assumptions of superiority, or even equality. Further, any type of trade was considered a demeaning occupation, beneath contempt, by the Chinese gentry, literati, and government officers. The emperor, as the father of all human beings, allowed people to follow their base instincts to trade for silk, porcelain, and tea under strict regulations and penalties. Europeans who could not learn the Chinese language or understand its customs were regarded as barbarians. The official policy was that these barbarians could not be trusted or governed under the same enlightened wisdom as the Chinese people, and misrule was what was called for. Many foreign captains who found themselves considered below the level of Chinese workers believed that the only purpose of Chinese regulation was to create as much difficulty for traders and to extract as much tribute and as many gifts as possible for Chinese merchants and officials.

Once approved for trade with a "chop" permit, each ship had to be measured and have her cargo inspected. This was the task of a "hoppo" (English bastardization of the *hu-pu,* the Board of Revenue, which the bureaucrat served), who would oversee all of a ship's transactions. The hoppo exacted a personal fee in the form of gifts, such as clocks, watches, perfume, snuffboxes, or other small marketable items, and could reciprocate with gifts as well, such as jars of wine or food. The fee was called a "cumshaw," and as American traders learned, it was an essential piece of Chinese business etiquette. If the cumshaw was not paid, trade was not likely to occur.

Most legitimate trade took place upriver at Canton, a two- or three-day journey up the Pearl River from Macao. To get to Canton, Chinese personnel had to be hired: linguists and towboatmen, as well as mandarin's officers to escort the ship in vessels painted light blue with red or black eyes at the bow that were said to help guide merchants safely through shifting channels. Most ships arrived at the end of the southwest monsoon (April to September) and left again for Europe on a route around Africa's Cape of Good Hope with the northeast monsoon (October to March).

Whampoa was a dozen miles below Canton, and Gray's crew stayed there under the guns of two forts. Cargo, officers, and foreign merchants were taken the remaining distance to the Canton waterfront, where "factories" for each nation stood in a row outside the city. These were three-story whitewashed warehouses bounded by an iron fence. Trade was conducted on the first floor, and living quarters were on the second and third floors. Outside flew the flag of the particular nation inhabiting that factory. Inside the factory, life was strictly regulated. Foreign merchants could leave only on escorted walks to small shops in a few streets just beyond the compound. Entry into Canton through the city's twenty-five-foot walls was prohibited. No women or weapons were allowed in the factories. Merchants from the government-licensed "hong" would visit the first floor of the factory and offer tea, silk, porcelain, and other goods in trade for foreign cargo. The hong merchants dictated price and terms, and once up the river at Whampoa, foreign captains had little negotiating leverage. The longer they held out for a deal, the higher their costs. But there were other options.

As Kendrick would discover, beneath Macao's gilded officialdom was an equally blinding maze of clandestine transactions and smuggling that one could access with the right payments. At Macao, as in many seaports, the attitude was anything goes, and life in the small island city was filled with everything prohibited upriver. It was not yet a sinister fleshpot but was well on its way to becoming the primary port in China for drug trafficking. "Connivance fees" persuaded authorities to look the other way on ships kept as floating warehouses and foreign vessels willing to anchor in half-hidden bays. The whole arrangement seemed like a house of cards, and with one false step, all of it could come tumbling down on a foreign captain. Despite that risk, John Kendrick would soon find himself deeply immersed in clandestine China.

ON JANUARY 27, HE SENT A BRIEF LETTER to Robert Gray and Richard Howe to let them know the *Washington* had arrived and to tell them he had made an application for "liberty to enter Typa but cannot obtain it." He wanted to know the price of furs and asked for advice on how to proceed. At the factory in Canton, Gray was in his second month of struggling to sell their cargo of furs. He replied to Kendrick, sending him two letters from Joseph Barrell and undoubtedly others from home that had been posted to Barrell's agents, Shaw and Randall. Gray said he was "very sorry to inform, that our business is attended with the greatest trouble and difficulty." Mr. Randall, to whom the *Columbia* was consigned, was about to sail and could delay no longer. He positively declined to transact the business of the *Washington.* Gray recommended that Kendrick contact John McIntyre, an independent British merchant at Macao, and advised him, if the "weather be unfavorable, that you would run into dirty butter bay." He also recommended a local pilot at the custom house. The recommendations were accompanied by a warning: "Should you go there [Dirty Butter Bay] be very cautious as several vessels have been boarded by the Ladroons."

Gray gave Kendrick the name of a "Compradore (buyer) who will supply you with necessarys for two or three weeks upon Credit—which is all that is at present in our power to do—the price of Skins is from fifty to seventy dollars provided you smuggle which in this port is impossible, without great danger."

One of the letters from Joseph Barrell was dated December 12, 1787, only six weeks after the expedition had left Boston. It laid out options for Kendrick to consider at Macao, and concluded, "everything is left to your own Judgment, being on the spot, and such is the confidence we repose in your Abilities and Honor . . ." Barrell closed with the salutation "Your Friend and Employer," a phrase not found in any of his other letters.

THE NEXT DAY, JANUARY 30, Kendrick took the *Lady Washington* about fifteen miles southwest, around the south point of Montanha Island, to an inlet known as Dirty Butter Bay, or Lark's Bay. Across the bay was Montanha's Morgan Point, a hill rising more than six hundred feet. The high hills offered good protection from northeast monsoons sweeping the coast. The remote spot was also ideal for smuggling and all types of illegal activity.

As the *Washington* came into the snug bay, they found two vessels without masts moored near the sandy beach. These were hulks, floating warehouses for East India Company opium. The drug was shipped here from India in chests containing a picul (133 ⅓ pounds) and held aboard the ship until the market price peaked, guaranteeing the best profit. Although the drug would soon be strictly prohibited by the emperor and carry penalties amounting to death, about two thousand chests were sold through Macao each year. Barrell's agent Samuel Shaw, who also volunteered as American consul, said that the Portuguese governor was involved in the shipments, collecting as much as forty thousand dollars in two years, which the governor needed to support his household and administration.

Armed men kept watch over the cargo and roused themselves at the *Washington*'s approach. Kendrick's men were also armed and ready, wary of the ladrones that Gray had warned of.

Unlike the nearly barren hills and beaches of Macao, here underbrush grew luxuriantly to the water's edge. The river was the same muddy yellow-brown, carrying silt from hills far inland. Sheltered from the steady wind in Macao Roads, flies swarmed out from shore. On the Broadway River running west of the island were sampans and houseboats on which families spent their entire lives. Men stood on the narrow decks with cormorant-like birds attached to long leashes, which they sent out to dive for fish. A ring around the bird's neck prevented it from swallowing the catch. Onshore were small rice paddies and people washing clothes in the river. As soon as they anchored, Kendrick set men on armed watch until they could get more familiar with the bay. He dispatched others to find water and wood.

Unknown to him, the situation was going from bad to worse. Not only did he have to sell the expedition's cargo and protect his ship in this wayward mudhole, but he had to deal with potential hostility from the seizure of the *Argonaut*. Meares had been incredulous at the capture of his ships and men and the collapse of what seemed to be a foreordained Pacific plan. This was a huge blow to British trade and an affront to all of His Majesty's subjects. Reading Duffin's letters, he raged at Spain's audacity. But it wasn't just Spain. Meares was especially disturbed that the Americans went unmolested, and that Kendrick had used his guns in the capture of the *Argonaut*. He concluded that Kendrick had put the Spanish commandant up to seizure of the ships so that he could control the fur trade and establish an American outpost.

Before Meares left for London to place demands before the king and Parliament, word of the seizure and Kendrick's involvement had rippled through Macao. Kendrick could not be sure what to expect. The Portuguese governor was a friend of Cavalho's, who had partnered with Meares in the first voyage of the *Iphigenia*. Also, the East India Company, with which Meares was now allied, had the strongest trading presence in the port. It leased a factory at Canton and occupied four houses along the Grande Playa on the Macao waterfront. The company's local director occupied an estate that was the pride of the European community, containing ornate gardens and a prominent outcropping of rocks, known as the Rocks of Cameons. The company's agents and perhaps Cavalho as well had anticipated Kendrick's arrival.

A few days after Kendrick anchored at Dirty Butter Bay, and quite by surprise, two men arrived with an armed guard and a translator. They carried a letter from Gray saying they were interested in purchasing the furs Kendrick had on board, which consisted of "320 Whole ones, 60 Garments, and 150 pieces both large and small," in addition to the 137 skins entrusted to him by Martinez. Gray proposed that the payment be delivered to him at Canton because transporting money in boats passing up the river would offer a great risk of robbery. Kendrick refused the sale and sent back a message that he was considering bringing the *Washington* up to Canton.

Gray wrote back to discourage him: "believe me Dear Sir you will have immeasurable difficultys to struggle against at this late period of the Seson." Gray warned that, once Kendrick arrived, he would have to take whatever price was offered. He urged Kendrick to "remain below" where he would find "Merchants in abundance to take your Cargo off your hands and supply you with what ever articles you are in want of."

Two days later, Kendrick wrote to Gray that he was undecided about what he would do with the cargo and the *Lady Washington*, which a "portugeese Gentleman has it in agitation to purchase." He also asked whether "articles suitable for the North West Trade" were available, indicating his interest to return to the Northwest Coast.

Kendrick also asserted his command by asking Gray for a full account of the cargo on board the *Columbia,* and the quality of the tea, together with prices and what quantity would be sufficient to complete the ship's lading. It was an accounting he would not receive.

Fulfilling a promise made in Boston at the outset of the expedition, Kendrick sent artifacts he had gathered back to Salem for a new maritime museum (now the Peabody Essex Museum). His shipment would constitute the first native tools and artwork to arrive from the Northwest Coast. Once the shipment was off, Kendrick planned to go upriver to Canton, but he was falling ill.

Gray was about to take full advantage of the situation. In a letter to Joseph Barrell, Gray claimed that he had carried only seven hundred skins and three hundred pieces to Macao. Questions later dogged this claim. The inventory of furs taken on board the *Columbia* at Clayoquot stops abruptly at the bottom of the page, with the number "700" written in at the side in a different hand. Another inventory, taken by the *Columbia*'s agent Thomas Randall, showed that 1,215 skins were landed at Canton.

The practice of officers and crew smuggling furs ashore for their own benefit was apparently widespread, although specifically prohibited in Barrell's original orders. Furthermore, the prices of the furs fell as delays occurred over their sale. Randall was caught in a dispute between the hong merchants. The mandarin's agent intervened and requested a selection of the best furs. Eventually, Randall was forced to relinquish all the *Columbia*'s furs to the merchant Pinqua for a disappointing $21,400, approximately thirty dollars each. Nearly half of that revenue was eaten up by commissions and costs of a long stay at Whampoa, leaving a profit of only $11,241.51. With this money Gray purchased a homeward cargo of 221 chests of cheap Bohea tea. After such a dismal handling of the *Columbia*'s business, on February 9 Gray brought the ship downriver into stormy seas.

In the bay, the *Columbia* was less than a dozen miles from where the *Washington* lay. Because he hadn't heard from Gray, Kendrick sent a copy of his previous message upriver asking for an accounting. Again there was no response.

Gray avoided contact with Kendrick. He was bent on his own plans, and perhaps anticipating the honor he would receive for America's first circumnavigation. The stormy sky cleared on February 12, and Gray passed out of the harbor, taking no letters, commands, or instructions homeward.

Kendrick was infuriated when he discovered Gray's deception and insubordination, but was helpless to do anything. For weeks he was confined to ship, wracked by fever, perhaps from the foul water or from the pestilence that arrived on so many vessels. The foreigner's graveyard at Macao gave grim testimony to how common death was among sailors suffering fevers that could not be treated. At one point his men believed he was going to die. Upriver at Whampoa, Kendrick's comrade the New York revolutionary Isaac Sears, with whom he co-owned the privateer *Count d'Estang,* had been buried in 1786 after arriving with Samuel Shaw on one of the first American ships to China.

THE DAYS WERE GROWING WARM AND HUMID, while at night the temperatures dropped into the fifties. Fever-wracked and without funds, Kendrick must have mulled over the depth of the expedition's failure thus far, his own shortcomings, and the miserable situation in which he was mired. His son John had told Spanish officers that his father was sacrificing wealth for glory. And where was that glory now? Except for the furs in the hold, the *Washington* was destitute. Her sails had been confiscated as he fell into debt. Kendrick had no solid hold on any land or outposts and nothing to show for the last two years. Regrets about being so long absent from Huldah and his children with no end in sight must have depressed him, and he may have worried too about the fate of the men he'd left in the Sandwich Islands. There was opportunity, tremendous opportunity, especially with the British traders gone from the coast. But there was so much that needed to be done. In the pit of his illness, facing the bleak possibility that everything might end, he must have made promises to himself to accomplish what they had set out upon. The fever came and went, and as he had so often when events grew dire, he persevered. Somehow his constitution held, and his men were relieved when he recovered enough to come up on deck.

Prospects brightened by the first few days of spring. Martinez's prime furs sold for eight thousand dollars, and the *Washington*'s own cargo fetched a price of eighteen thousand dollars. Unknown to Kendrick, this was far better than the trade Gray had made at Canton. Flush with cash, he began to lay out an ambitious plan for the return voyage to the Northwest Coast and the Sandwich Islands.

The mornings on the island became foggy and damp. With the southwest monsoon season coming on, and still recovering his health, Kendrick took a house in Macao. The small, crowded city was a devil's paradise, filled with what dazzled foreigners and natives alike: trade, lust, and corruption, playing out amid numerous Catholic churches, Buddhist temples, and religious festivals and celebrations. Facing the bay was the An-Ma temple, dedicated to the Queen of Heaven, guardian of fishermen and sailors. On March 23 each year, thousands would gather to celebrate her birthday and ask for protection of their boats. Kendrick was fascinated by it all.

Night and day the narrow streets and alleys were an incredible melting pot of roving Pacific Islanders, Philippinos, Malays, Africans, Indians, dissolute Europeans, and wealthy merchants and gamblers, all under the watchful eyes of the mandarin and his informers. Kendrick wandered the narrow cobblestone lanes into the small stores that held a cornucopia of medicines, carved ivory and jewelry, cages filled with all kinds of birds and animals, exotic foods being cooked, fireworks shaped in rockets and pinwheels, and local wine called *samshu*.

Happy to be alive after his illness, Kendrick purchased fireworks and other trading cargo for the *Washington*. He came to know the characters of the European enclave, and spent late nights drinking among traders, gamblers, and voyagers. A charismatic figure and a man marked with a reputation by the taking of Meares's ships, the weathered American commander settled into Macao, and according to his later critics, the dissipate socializing drew him in and kept him there.

But he was making his preparations, and the project he focused on lay at the center of a plan to carry out his mission. It was something he probably thought the first time he saw the *Washington,* something he must have sworn to accomplish as he lay ill. The *Washington* was being transformed from a sloop into a brigantine, adding a second mast and a new set of sails and rigging. This would give her speed, reach, and greater maneuverability in narrow bays. It was no surprise that as the work took shape she began to look like the privateer *Fanny* he had rebuilt into a brigantine twelve years before on the shore of Dartmouth.

A channel just north of Dirty Butter Bay led around Montanha Island to the back entrance of the Typa and Macao. During the day, crew members came to Macao in the ship's boat and visited Kendrick with reports on the *Washington.* Otherwise, Kendrick traveled to the ship. Often the men came into town, drawn in part by the flower boats along the river, which held painted Chinese women and liquor. Unlike the Sandwich Islands and the Northwest Coast, such fraternizing was officially prohibited for foreigners. If the men were caught, it could mean severe punishment. Kendrick undoubtedly tried to keep the men protected and busy completing the changes to the *Washington* in time to make the season on the Northwest Coast.

The humidity thickened as spring advanced. It rained and kept raining, and soon Kendrick's good fortune turned. His house was broken into and robbed; the Chinese refused to grant him permission to leave the port; the Portuguese governor would not intervene; and he had difficulty getting provisions for his crew. He wasn't sure if this was part of the retribution from Meares and the East India Company or pressure on him to sell the *Washington.*

Stranded in port, Kendrick approached William Douglas for assistance. Douglas had just left Meares's merchant company and taken command of a New York schooner, the *Grace*. He was now sailing under an American flag, and whatever differences that remained with Kendrick were put aside. The *Washington*'s first mate, Davis Coolidge, joined Douglas as first officer on the *Grace*, and Kendrick made a deal with Douglas to have the *Grace* rendezvous with the men left at Hawaii gathering sandalwood.

Kendrick meanwhile tried to work his personal charm but could not unlock the prohibition that held him in port. Among the meager American community, Samuel Shaw and Thomas Randall had departed on their own ventures, and Kendrick's appeals to the Portuguese governor, His Excellency Lazaro da Silva Ferreira, went nowhere. He couldn't get through to Macao's Senate either. Most of the senators seemed to be merchants who were jealously protecting their friends and opportunities for their own investments.

Although Portuguese in name, the governor and nobles in the Senate had never been around the Cape of Good Hope. They were from Goa, India, and were of mixed descent. Most of the Macanese were part Portuguese, Chinese, Malay, and Indian, and spoke a local dialect barely recognizable to anyone from Lisbon. Among these men, Kendrick was a marked outsider.

ALL FOREIGN TRADERS AT CANTON were required to return to their houses at Macao in April. This swelled the city's population to about four thousand, including slaves from Africa and Timor who served and guarded the wealthy Portuguese and foreign merchants. A limited number of Chinese lived in the crowded lanes near the inner harbor. Others were restricted from residing in Macao. The English and the East India Company dominated the social scene among the Europeans, and for Kendrick, relations were cordial but duplicitous. Samuel Shaw observed: "With respect to our own [American] commerce in this quarter, which is yet in its infancy, I shall only observe, that, inconsiderable as it has hitherto been, and in this year especially, it is viewed with no small degree of jealousy by our late mother country. Gentlemen, in all parts of the world, of whatever nation they may be, can esteem, and sometimes love, one another; but Englishmen and Americans, merely as such, in any place, as at Canton, where the former have the ascendancy, can barely treat each other with civility."

Shaw, like Kendrick, saw the events in the Pacific unfolding within the context of a larger geopolitical struggle to control trade. "The English seem to be not only aiming at a monopoly of the tea-trade for Europe," Shaw wrote, "but appear to have in view the exclusive commerce of this division of the globe." Shaw pointed to British efforts to create settlements to the east and west of Macao, prohibitions against subjects in India selling ships to foreigners, and the new settlement at Botany Bay in Australia as evidence of London's intent to dominate the East.

British influence over the region was clearly growing. The East India Company's authority and accompanying audacity and reach were like an international government. Not only were British ships required to gain a license from them, but any British subject had to carry a company-approved passport, which could be revoked at a moment's notice. The company kept its own militia and armed ships, and could seize and deport any subject they wished. They could also make life extremely difficult for those who threatened their trade.

Amid his socializing in Macao, Kendrick found that the capture of the *Argonaut,* the *Princess Royal,* and the *Northwest American* had disrupted plans much larger than a British settlement on the Northwest Coast. Richard Cadman Etches and John Meares were seeking more than just an outpost in America. As Shaw had observed, they wanted to dominate the America-to-Asia trade. This included their midocean marketplace in the Sandwich Islands, and a long-awaited opening of trade with the closed nation of Japan. Meares had assurances that the inhabitants of Japan "would gladly enter into a trading intercourse" and that furs would sell there at "an immense price."

In 1785, Etches wrote to the East India Company, stating, "The

Japanese Islands would be our grand object to open a friendly intercourse with which, we have every possible hope of attaining from holding out so great a temptation as the Sea Otter Skins." Funds from these transactions would be deposited in the East India Company treasury at Canton. Etches also wrote to influential British scientist Joseph Banks on July 17, 1788, saying, "our Intention is to adopt a Permanent system of Commerce direct from this Country [England] to the N.W. Coast and from thence to the Asiatic Coast, and Islands." A few days later he wrote again to Banks, confirming: "A foundation thus laid, and as it is no longer to be doubted but there are plenty of furs to be met with, a market for their disposal wou'd be the whole to seek for, the opposite shores afford ample field, and I am perfectly satisfied that the Japan Islands may be attempted with success."

With the ships they had in transit back and forth to the Northwest Coast, Meares and Etches planned to send their first London company venture to Japan in 1791. Kendrick's participation in the seizure of the *Argonaut, Princess Royal,* and *Northwest American* crippled their whole strategy for the Pacific. As much as creating a financial collapse of the London company, the destruction of their trade strategy is what sent Meares speeding home to London and Parliament. He would find a ready audience.

About the time Kendrick was approaching Macao in January 1790, the first intelligence on the capture of the *Argonaut* and *Princess Royal* reached England. The slow-burning fuse from the taking of the ships was about to touch off the ancient blood feud between Britain and Spain.

Viceroy Revillagigedo had sent a dispatch from Mexico City to the head of the Spanish Marine and Minister of the Indies, Antonio Valdes, in Madrid, explaining what had occurred at Nootka and recommending that the British ships and men be freed. However, it was clear to Valdes in reading Colnett's confiscated papers that the British were mounting a stark challenge to Spain's dominion in the Pacific. Colnett presented a very real British threat of making claims and establishing a colony on the Northwest Coast.

The Spanish court had taken up Revillagigedo's dispatch in December, and Anthony Merry, the British chargé d'affaires in Madrid, had gotten wind of the court discussion. Merry provided the British cabinet with a vague report of a Spanish warship's confiscation of a British merchant ship in early January. And on February 10, Spain's Marquis del Campo officially notified Britain that Spain had seized a British ship that had come to take possession of Nootka. The letter described the incident and set out Spain's prior right of claim to the region. Campo demanded that those who had planned the expedition be punished.

Aside from Merry's communication, the British cabinet had no facts about the seizure. However, they were aware of Meares and Etches's activity on the Northwest Coast, that the powerful East India Company received payments from the British furs traded at Macao, and that there were larger British plans for the Pacific region. The Duke of Leeds replied to the Marquis del Campo on February 26, referring to the seizure as an "act of violence" against the law of nations and "injurous to Great Britain." Under orders from the king, he suspended all discussion of the claims made by Spain until adequate atonement was made and the vessel was released.

The Spanish court took the hostile response as a provocation of war. Their interpretation was not far off. Prime Minister William Pitt Jr. saw an opportunity to break the Family Compact between Spain and France and undermine Spain's colonial hold on the Americas.

The dispute was fundamentally over Spain's claims in the New World. Foreign Minister José Floridablanca laid out his empire's rights based on treaties with Britain in 1670 and 1713, the Papal Bull of 1493, and the 1494 Treaty of Tordesillas, which granted Spain dominion over lands from the Azores to the Philippines. British subjects were not to enter or trade in ports held by Spain. A Royal Order of 1692, and another issued by King Carlos III in 1776, probably aimed at James Cook's expedition, authorized Spanish officials to "take prisoner and prosecute by law whatsoever foreign vessel" arrived in ports on the Pacific.

The British rejected and ridiculed the Papal Bull, as well as the idea that the Spanish could claim possession of a territory by erecting a cross and then moving on. Prime Minister Pitt asserted that Spain could only claim lands it possessed through actual occupation. This was an odd position to take, since British explorers had traditionally made claims without occupying a site.

The Spanish viewed Pitt's position as a desperate move aimed at denying Spanish claims everywhere. Floridablanca had correctly understood the global reach of the conflict. The Spanish court sent orders for the ships of the Armada to begin preparing for sea. They also ordered reinforcements to be sent to Trinidad, Honduras, and Puerto Rico. In London, intelligence on Spanish mobilization at the seaport of Cadiz prompted orders from the Admiralty to prepare the fleet at Spitshead. British indignation grew.

In late April, John Meares arrived in London amid the charged atmosphere at court. He carried with him the secret letters he had received from the *Argonaut*'s supercargo, Robert Duffin. He also had depositions taken from the prisoners who had arrived on the *Columbia*. He revealed that three ships, not one, were seized and the crews imprisoned and mistreated, and that despite British rights to the region, Martinez had claimed the Northwest Coast for Spain.

Meares was ushered into the office of Secretary of State William Wyndham Grenville, who asked him to create a "memorial" describing the events and damages. Grenville was taken by Meares's claim that he had purchased tracts of land from the native people and erected buildings before Martinez arrived. This indicated to Grenville that Britain had evidence of its possession through occupation and could validate its claim to Nootka.

Grenville read the memorial to Prime Minister William Pitt and the cabinet on April 30. Pitt took the issue to King George. On May 5,

Pitt went before Parliament with an address from the king concerning the seizure of the *Argonaut* and *Princess Royal* and British grievances. The address inflamed the ancient enmity with Spain, and laid bare the larger issues at stake. House member Charles James Fox criticized the Catholic basis for Spain's claims. "In the present enlightened age the obsolete claim to territory by grant of a Pope was done away . . . We now have the opportunity, and ought to embrace it, of putting an end to the assertion of those rights forever." Talk harkened back to the War of Jenkins' Ear, declared against Spain fifty years before. Parliament voted one million pounds for gathering the fleet, and a surge toward war was on.

The warships *Pegasus, Nautilous, Termagant, Flirt,* and *Drake* were ordered to sail the same night the address was delivered. Thirty-six other ships were instructed to be prepared for sea.

Prime minister Pitt met with the Venezuelan revolutionary Francisco de Miranda to revive plans for British invasions of Chile and Mexico, as well as attacks on key ports and insurrections among colonial populations in South America. Anti-Spanish propaganda filled Britain's newspapers. John Etches wrote a distorted tract that implicated the Americans in a plot against British merchants. He charged Spain with an "insidious and mercenary conspiracy in the assistance of our revolted American colonies and the dismemberment of our empire." He also made accusations against John Kendrick, stating that the insulting capture of Colnett and the *Argonaut* was celebrated by "the anniversary of American Independence [which] was commemorated with every demonstration of joy." John Meares supported Etches and pointed to Kendrick as the architect behind Martinez's plan to seize the ships.

Impressment squads began scouring England's pubs, brothels, and lodgings, seizing men for service on warships as the preparations for global war moved quickly forward. Gouverneur Morris, a prominent member of Congress who had chaired the committee that drafted the Constitution and set up the new nation's currency of dollars and cents, was in London at the time. He witnessed what was occurring with both alarm and a sense of opportunity.

Morris was a brilliant and bullish politician who believed the pending war offered a chance for Spain, France, and America to join forces again to defeat Britain. He believed a victory would restructure the balance of power in Europe, gain American access down the Mississippi, and open trade in the West Indies. Morris wrote to America's staunchest ally in Paris, the Marquis de Lafayette: "This country is arming and I am convinced with a Determination to compel not only Spain but every other Power to subscribe to such terms as she may chuse to dictate. You will strive in vain to deprecate the Blow, therefore you must prepare to meet it. Or rather so to strike as may prevent it." He proposed to Lafayette a French attack on Holland, and playing each side against the other, he began efforts to foment the war in London as well.

Through treaties and agreements, other European nations were being drawn into the Nootka dispute. Foreign Minister Floridablanca sent a circular letter to the courts of Europe outlining the circumstances of the seizure of the British ships. Citing Britain's hostility, he sought support from Austria, Sweden, Denmark, and Russia. Most importantly, Spain needed France, its ally under the Family Compact of 1761.

King Louis XVI of France committed fourteen ships of the line. This decision infuriated revolutionaries in the National Assembly, who challenged the king's right to commit the people of France to a war. Amid that debate, France stumbled further into social chaos, with peasants burning chateaus and manor houses, and the Assembly dissolving monasteries and convents.

Behind the scenes, the Spanish reportedly sent France gold for its support. Meanwhile, the British were rumored to have made similar payments to keep France neutral.

Britain appealed to its partners in the Triple Alliance—Holland and Prussia—for support. Notices of alert were sent to military outposts in Canada, the West Indies, India, and Macao. By the middle of

June, despite the hesitation of allies, a global war was looming. Floridablanca proposed a strategic plan that included assembling troops in Cuba, encouraging rebellion in Ireland, and invading England, an attack that had been approved in an earlier plan. He also advised strengthening defenses in the Canaries, Minorca, and the Philippines.

Amid the war preparations, Meares told Pitt that the *Lady Washington* had passed through the Strait of Juan de Fuca and sailed into an inland sea, which raised the specter of the Northwest Passage and implied that the Americans might have found the elusive route in their search. Meares attempted to substantiate his claims by publishing a narrative of his voyages in 1788 and 1789, including the map showing the route of the *Washington* in the fall of 1789, sailing the entire inland shore of what would later become known as Vancouver Island.

Incendiary allegations and an ancient animosity between Spain and England motivated events at this stage and led to further escalation. As both British and Spanish warships set out to cruise the Bay of Biscay off northern Spain in the summer of 1790, only a chance confrontation was needed for the bloodshed and chaos to begin.

AT MACAO, A FIVE-MONTH VOYAGE from London, the summer monsoons were finally clearing off and the muddy hills drying out when word arrived that Spain and England were preparing for war. Fearing attack and seizure by Spanish warships out of the Philippines, the East India Company ships and other British vessels went on alert. The alarm cast a pall over the port. Kendrick was arrested by soldiers in the street and ordered to leave the city or face imprisonment. He retreated to the *Washington* at Dirty Butter Bay, unaware of the full dimension of how the taking of British ships at Nootka had shaken Europe, or how his expedition was being described at home.

CHAPTER THIRTEEN

Columbia's Homecoming

Boston

AUGUST 1790

NEWS OF THE IMPENDING WAR and the suspected involvement of the American expedition came to Robert Gray at the island of Saint Helena on his homeward passage from Macao to Boston in June 1790. In the same month, news of the king's address to Parliament, the embarkation of warships, and a description of the sweeping impressments appeared in New York and Philadelphia newspapers. On July 3, people in Boston read with alarm that "the Parliament has granted to his Britannick Majesty, two Millions, sterling, and 16,000 men, to carry on the preparations for a Spanish war . . . Spain has formed a Treaty of alliance with Austria and a strong counter-league is making against it, in which Great Britain, Prussia, and Holland are concerned." British transports were reportedly sending troops and four companies of artillery to Quebec, which stirred great concern over how far the war would spread. To raid Spanish outposts along the Mississippi and south to New Orleans and Florida, British agents were once again trying to

Thomas Jefferson embodied the drive to expand what the Founding Fathers saw as an "empire of liberty" and feared British seizure of lands west of the Mississippi. In 1813, he would write to John Jacob Astor of his outpost on the Columbia River: "I view it as the germ of a great, free, and independent empire on that side of our continent, and that liberty and self-government spreading from that as well as this side, will ensure their complete establishment over the whole." (Painting by Rembrandt Peale)

enlist the support of disaffected Americans on the "middle lands" frontier.

From London, Gouverneur Morris wrote to President Washington: "I believe that a war is inevitable; and I act on that ground." In regard to Kendrick, he urged "that it would not be amiss for the American captain, who was witness of the whole transaction, to publish a faithful narrative." Thomas Jefferson, recently returned from Paris to serve as Washington's first secretary of state, also believed that war was likely. On June 20, he wrote that the British would be satisfied "with nothing less than war, dismemberment of the Spanish empire, and annihilation of their fleet."

If fighting flared up on the North American continent, it would embroil Canada, the Floridas, and the border lands along the Mississippi. The new nation would be in great jeopardy. British officers hoped to draw in Vermont separatists and backwoods pioneers in Kentucky territory to create independent buffer states loyal to England and mount attacks on Spanish towns from Saint Louis south to New Orleans. The Spanish, likewise, were continuing efforts to create runaway border colonies occupied by independent American pioneers loyal to Spain. Once again, former American general James Wilkinson was involved with Spain, this time in partnership with a smooth-talking Irishman, James O'Fallon. Their scheme for a Spanish colony came apart when O'Fallon decided the Nootka crisis offered a better opportunity to gain British aid to attack Spain and take all of Louisiana. Indian nations were also being enticed by each side to become shock troops. Representatives of the Cherokee nation reportedly showed up in London to offer twenty thousand warriors to Britain.

As troubling as the unbridled chaos in the countryside, serious discord arose within Washington's cabinet. Jefferson favored siding with Spain and France. Alexander Hamilton opposed this and argued support for Britain. John Adams at first favored joining Spain, then recommended neutrality, as did Secretary of War Henry Knox. Jefferson finally urged delay of a decision. After sifting through the sentiments of his cabinet, Washington concluded that the United States should remain neutral as long as possible and not become entangled in foreign disputes. Jefferson ultimately concurred, stating: "If the war between Britain and Spain takes place, I think France will inevitably be involved in it. In that case, I hope the new world will fatten on the follies of the old. If we can but establish armed neutrality for ourselves, we must become the carriers for all parties as far as we can raise vessels."

The immediate goal Jefferson and others hoped to achieve by staying neutral was the opening of the Mississippi for American pioneers. But the fire Kendrick helped light at Nootka had much larger implications. It would figure not only into the long contest for the Mississippi Valley and the West, but also into the future balance of power in the Americas and Europe's shifting alliances. The Nootka crisis later became recognized as the first important diplomatic challenge to face the new government. Washington and Jefferson's policy of neutrality ultimately benefited the United States by allowing a long-term path toward stability and growth while Europe became mired in the Napoleonic Wars.

WITH THE PRESSURES OF WAR BUILDING, word of the *Columbia*'s homeward voyage arrived at New York in May aboard the ship *Federalist,* which was four months out of Canton. Gray and the *Columbia* were anticipated in Boston in July. Captain Kendrick in the *Lady Washington* was reported to be returning to the Northwest Coast. Boston's *Columbian Centinel* newspaper announced, "In the success of these intrepid navigators every heart delights." Excited by the long-awaited prospect of the *Columbia*'s circumnavigation, Joseph Barrell laid plans for a grand homecoming.

On the morning of Monday, August 9, 1790, the tall, worn sails of the *Columbia* appeared in the bay off Boston. As she approached the harbor islands, Gray fired a thirteen-gun salute, which was answered by the fort on Castle Island. The booming attracted attention along the waterfront, where a crowd began to gather. When the ship was recognized, a messenger ran to Joseph Barrell at Dock Square. From the ropewalks and chandlery shops men went down to Long Wharf. As she tied to a mooring nearby, the *Columbia* saluted them with another thirteen-gun barrage.

It was nearly three years since the *Columbia*'s men had departed. Many of them thought at times they would never see this shore again. Though it was a dear sight, the city and the waterfront were changing. Many more ships sat at anchor, the shops were bustling, and half-built hulls were taking shape in the boatyards that pocked the marsh and ran up to the North End. A phenomenal growth in marine trade was under way that would more than triple the carrying capacity of American ships between 1789 and 1792 from 123,430 tons to 411,438 tons.

Boston was enjoying a building boom. Not only were there new houses and small shops and more people; carts and wagons clogged the narrow, winding lanes and alleys. Part of the reason for all the bustle was the adoption of Gouverneur Morris's federal currency system along with the loosening of local credit. The federal government took on state and local war debts, and Congress established new protectionist policies, including a tariff on foreign-built or foreign-owned ships entering American ports, which helped give rise to Boston's shipbuilding boom. It was the beginning of a pivotal time, and some regarded it as a change as remarkable as the Revolution.

News of the *Columbia*'s arrival swept through the streets. The next day, in an event staged by Barrell, banners were hung and crowds gathered, cheering from the docks and along State Street as Robert Gray led the officers and crew in a parade onto Long Wharf and up the hill past the State House. Church bells clanged as the ragged group of men continued on to the governor's mansion. What caught everyone's eye was the young Hawaiian chief Atoo, wrapped in his brilliant yellow-and-red-feathered war cape and wearing a feathered helmet, as he walked at the head of the group with Gray.

Governor John Hancock, suffering from gout and seated in a wheelchair, held a reception for the owners, officers, and gentlemen of the ship. Lofty speeches were made extolling the first American circumnavigation. These men had crossed that largely unknown Pacific expanse, demonstrating an American reach that had been scarcely imagined before. The fact that Kendrick remained behind only added to the expedition's mystique. This was the stuff of legend and inspiration. With confidence that Americans could carry trade anywhere on the globe, visions of a new future for Boston's ships quickly took hold. All the attention may have surpassed even what Robert Gray expected. It certainly made the grim news he was about to deliver much more of a shock.

Eight months earlier, Gray had written to Barrell from Canton, echoing a letter from Kendrick that said the expedition "will not be equal to your expectations." The results were even worse than anticipated. Gray had hoped to ship six hundred chests of Bohea tea. His modest cargo of only two hundred twenty-one chests was badly stored and partially ruined by the hull's leakage on the homeward journey. Of the 21,462 pounds of tea, more than half (12,213 pounds) were damaged. Barrell and the other four owners would receive only a few thousand dollars for the tea. The debt of forty-nine thousand dollars for the expedition was nearly a total loss. To make matters worse, Thomas Randall, who carried out the transaction in China, had shipped three hundred boxes of tea aboard the *Columbia* to Samuel Parkman, one of Joseph Barrell's competitors.

In Barrell's office at the brick countinghouse at Town Dock, Gray used his newfound celebrity to blame the voyage's failure on Kendrick. Behind closed doors with the ships' owners, Gray and Haswell painted John Kendrick as careless, self-interested, and fully responsible for the expedition's economic disaster. They charged that Kendrick "had it in contemplation to cheat the Owners out of what property he has in his hands; and would have done out of all had they [Gray and Haswell] not rescued it, and brought it of [*sic*] with the Ship." In their version of events, they had saved the *Columbia* and its cargo from Kendrick's grasp.

Supported by Haswell's journal—which was undoubtedly rewritten on the homeward passage—they recited a long list of grievances and failures: Kendrick spent too long at Cape Verde; proposed to remain at the Falklands over the winter; then hazarded the voyage around Cape Horn into storms that nearly destroyed the ships. Because of his leisurely pace, they arrived at Nootka too late in the season to cruise for furs, and in the spring Kendrick did not engage the *Columbia* in trading but stayed in the sound for ten months. Gray apparently also told of Kendrick's involvement in the Nootka crisis, revealing that Kendrick had befriended the Spanish commandant Martinez, and worse, it had been the *Columbia*'s guns that were trained on the *Argonaut* when she was seized.

The one officer who could have supported Kendrick was first mate Joseph Ingraham. Gray tried to discredit Ingraham by reporting that the first mate had tried to smuggle a skin ashore at Macao. Ingraham was not there to answer. While at Whampoa, Ingraham had agreed to command a new Northwest Coast voyage for a competitor, Thomas Handasyd Perkins. He was immediately off on his venture with Perkins to secure a ship to take back to the Pacific. Of the other officers and gentlemen, the furrier, Jonathan Treat, had remained with Kendrick, as had second mate John Cordis. Richard Howe, the supercargo, who bore part of the responsibility for the trade at Macao and the failure to ensure safe storage of the homeward cargo of tea, left no record of his views.

Gray and Haswell's hostility toward Kendrick was shockingly palpable. John Hoskins, one of Barrell's young clerks, who greatly admired Kendrick, was stunned, but in no position to defend him. As he tried to reason through the charges, Hoskins made notes of the meeting and concluded: "Thus much must be acknowledged; that Captain Kendrick had two good vessels on the coast (and if his enemies are to be believed) had it in his power to make both for himself and the Owners a very handsome fortune; but he let those golden opportunities pass; and on his arrival in China was depriv'd of his largest vessel; which was his principal support . . ." Despite what was claimed, Hoskins refused to accept the whole story, concluding: "no Knavery has at present open'd."

There was no one to argue that the *Columbia,* although a sound ship, did not handle well. No one said that in the shakedown cruise to Cape Verde Kendrick saw it would be necessary to break up the hold and repack the ship. Or that to reduce dissent, Kendrick had to remove the celebrity, Simon Woodruff. He had known this sorting out would take time and raise hackles. The delay was not haphazard—he sent word back through a Boston captain that the expedition would be at Praia for three weeks. This gave him time to make his group of men into a crew, and rest and fatten them for the trials ahead, including the likelihood of scurvy. At the Falklands he had anchored in a desolate harbor, and in what seems a typical captain's ploy, proposed remaining there for the winter to get the right response—an eagerness among his officers and crew to press forward into the dangers around the Horn. Once they arrived at Nootka, he undertook care of the sick men and preparations to winter over instead of resorting to the Sandwich Islands. He then began the larger efforts of the expedition: establishing an American outpost to which the Mowachaht brought many furs, getting to know native people and their language, and learning whatever he could of the Northwest Passage. As later captains would recognize, taking a ship the size of the ungainly *Columbia* into unknown harbors and bays for furs was foolhardy. The fact that Gray nearly lost the *Washington* repeatedly on shoals, and a rock ledge, underscored the danger of risking the command ship.

Perhaps what was most telling about Kendrick's management was the fact that in an arduous voyage of this kind, in which a quarter or more of the crew commonly died, only one of the original Boston men was lost during the voyage—the astronomer John Nutting to an apparent suicide before they rounded the Horn. Although the monetary gain did not match what anyone, including Kendrick, expected, it was not out of line with that of other voyages, and unlike them, Kendrick had his eye set on establishing a base for long-term returns.

A captain less hostile than Gray might have made these points, but it was clear he had lost all sense of balance in his allegations. Like Hoskins, Barrell recognized that there was much more to the story. The scene playing out had precedents all too familiar in exploration and trade. Throughout history, ambitious captains have sought to displace their expeditions' commanders: Columbus had been undercut by his captains, Magellan was charged with horrendous crimes by his officers, and so on through a litany of voyages.

Many of these stories of treachery also had a traditional follow-up scene as well—one in which the accusers asked for a command of their own. This time was no different. Gray arrogantly proposed to take command of the *Columbia* for a second voyage to Nootka. Haswell would be his first mate and captain a schooner they would build after they arrived on the coast. Together, they dangled a description of the riches to be had with little exertion, and according to Hoskins promised "their abilities to produce a golden harvest."

The owners were divided. Two of them, John Pintard of New York and John Derby of Salem, dropped out of the venture. Samuel Brown took a new three-fourteenths share, and Crowell Hatch retained his two-fourteenths share. The share held by Charles Bulfinch, the young architect, went to his father, Dr. Thomas Bulfinch. Two Boston merchants, Davenport and McLean, put in with Robert Gray for two-fourteenths of a share in the expedition. Joseph Barrell was still inclined to support Kendrick and did not fully trust Gray, but faced with no other prospect and wanting to resolve this mystery, picked up the remaining five-fourteenths share.

The estimated cost of the new voyage was twenty-five thousand dollars. Gray, who received a total of 132 British pounds (about five hundred dollars) in pay from his three years and twenty days' service on the first voyage, somehow came up with a substantial amount of money for his joint-ownership stake (thirty-two hundred dollars for two-fourteenths).

It was at this point, perhaps in a review of accounts by Hoskins, that questions emerged about the total number of *Columbia*'s skins sold at Canton. Gray said they had sold seven hundred skins and three hundred pieces, but the inventory from Barrell's agent at Canton, Thomas Randall, showed that 1,215 skins were taken ashore. A letter Randall wrote to Alexander Hamilton said that the *Columbia* sold about 1,500 skins through him.

No direct accusations about Gray were made, but if a crew's loyalty could be used as a measure of character, it was significant that only two seamen stayed on for the second voyage: Abraham Waters, who was given a mate's position, and Joseph Barnes, who had joined the ship at Canton. Others, like Ingraham, sought new ships.

Gray got what he wanted. In the days that followed their arrival, he paraded the young Hawaiian, Atoo, in the streets of Boston in his flowing yellow-and-red-feather cape. People would stop and gape, eager to meet this exotic "Indian" from the Sandwich Islands and the first American captain to have circumnavigated the globe. Gray and Haswell, probably with Atoo in tow, were hosted in drawing rooms throughout the city, where they continued to disparage Kendrick. Word spread in the city's social circles of the commander's nefarious character. Young John Quincy Adams, who opened his first law practice in Boston on the day the *Columbia* arrived, caught wind of it. He wrote to his mother two days later that Boston was abuzz with "the arrival of the *Columbia* from an expedition which has carried her around the world. The adventurers after having their expectation raised to the highest pitch, were utterly disappointed, and instead of the immense profits upon which they had calculated, will scarcely have their outsets refunded to them. The failure has given universal astonishment and is wholly attributed to the Captain, whose reputation now remains suspended between the qualifications of egregious knavery and of unpardonable stupidity." He added that Joseph Barrell, who had once been the Adams's neighbor in Boston, "is not discouraged and intends to make the experiment once more."

Word of the voyage's financial calamity spread quickly down the coast. An extract of a Boston letter appearing in New York's *Gazette of the United States* trumpeted Gray's attack on Kendrick: "The owners of the *Columbia* wish she had sunk in Nootka Sound;—great complaints of cheatery are made; time will explain whether there has been any roguery in the business or not;—intolerable disappointment is the result of high-raised expectations I assure you."

The prospect of war made Kendrick look even worse. Boston's *Columbian Centinal* reported: "Capt. Mears, in his representation to the British Court, respecting the seizure of the British ships in Nootka Sound, insinuated that Capt. Kendrick, and the other officers of the American vessels then on the coast, advised Don Martinez to the measure." Kendrick was suspected to be the culprit responsible for the war now looming.

AT THE VILLAGE OF WAREHAM, fifty miles south of Boston, Huldah Kendrick must have been deeply anguished over the allegations of her husband's failure as commander of the expedition. All their family's sacrifice had amounted only to disaster. The fact that he was not there to answer the charges against him doubled her pain. Whatever word young Solomon brought home when he arrived aboard the *Columbia* was of no solace. And whatever she might have written to Kendrick at Macao, urging him to return, languished for nearly a year before he received it.

In their house at the Narrows, and in the store across the road, life became even harder to bear. For a time she had Solomon to help, but he was restless like his father, and soon returned to sea. He took ship with Josiah Roberts on the *Jefferson* for the Northwest, undoubtedly carrying a plea for his father to return and clear his name.

Amplified by a backdrop of impending global war, the charges against Kendrick made it seem to many that he avoided coming home to take responsibility for the failure of the expedition. But for others, the fact that Kendrick remained in the Pacific sparked excitement and eagerness to prepare ships for a voyage around the Horn to the Northwest. The American gateway into the Pacific was open, and a race to make the next season of trading was on. Joseph Ingraham found a small seventy-two-ton sloop, the *Hope,* and manned her with a crew of sixteen, including Opye, a young servant he had brought from Kauai. Acknowledging the "ill sweets" of the *Columbia*'s voyage, Ingraham launched on September 17, five weeks after he had arrived on the *Columbia*.

With Joseph Barrell's grudging support, Gray soon followed, after refitting the *Columbia*. Out of a desire to preserve his own reputation and get to the bottom of the mystery about Kendrick, Barrell placed John Hoskins in charge of the *Columbia* as supercargo. On September 25, he delivered instructions to Gray that stated: "In all matters of traffic on the northwest coast of America, China, or elsewhere, you will consult with Mr. John Hoskins . . . we therefore expect the most perfect harmony to subsist between you, your officers, and him."

Barrell was perhaps troubled by questions about where Gray had gotten the funds for his share and rumors about officers and crew smuggling furs and selling on their own accounts, and he warned: "You will constantly bear in mind the absolute prohibition against every sort of traffic, or receiving any presents on this voyage; for be assured the owners will treat every breach of the contract in this particular with the utmost severity . . . You have seen and heard the pointed manner in which every one condemns the conduct of the last; and if you have a spirit proper for this enterprise, or any regard for your own honor and rising reputation, or have respect to the sea-letters with which the President of United States has honored and indulged you, we trust you will doubly exert yourself to prevent such reflections in future." Barrell had played on his personal relationship with Washington to expedite a new sea-letter for the *Columbia*.

As Gray prepared the ship and took on what seemed like an endless load of cargo, newspapers were filled with reports of preparations for war. Despite the fact that messengers had passed and repassed between the Spanish and British courts, a war seemed inevitable. In early September, one Massachusetts newspaper reported news from an arriving packet boat: "War was declared by England against Spain the fourteenth day of July last."

What would American ships do? Fearing that the *Columbia* would be caught in the contention, Barrell instructed Gray to form "no connection with foreigners, or Americans, on the northwest coast, unless absolutely necessary; nor then, with the greatest caution."

There was no grand farewell party on board, and no speeches this time. Impatient to have the *Columbia* sail, Barrell wrote in his instructions: "If the wind is fair on the morrow, we desire and expect you will embrace it and proceed on the voyage." Following a few days of adverse winds, the *Columbia* departed Boston harbor on October 2,

Boston Harbor *by Fitz Hugh Lane. On the* Columbia's *return to Boston Harbor, Robert Gray found a new vitality brewing. Word of Gray's return and Kendrick's continuing expedition inspired other Boston merchants to set off for the Pacific.*

1790, seven weeks after her arrival. The last news before sailing may have been that the Spanish fleet was setting out to capture merchant ships, and troops and arms were pouring into the West Indies. Many speculated that West Florida and New Orleans would suffer the first attacks, bringing the prospect of war to the American coast.

POLITICAL TENSIONS WERE PEAKING in London. The naval mobilization and armament had already cost more than three million pounds, not the one million originally allotted, or the two million reported in Boston. Britain had never mobilized forces on a global scale like this before. According to one account, a total of forty-three ships and fifty-five thousand men had been readied. Everyone was anxious. Despite the magnitude of preparations and participation in maneuvers, the Dutch became reluctant to engage on behalf of Britain. And facing criticism on the one hand for inaction, and on the other for threatening an expensive and misguided war, Prime Minister Wiliam Pitt Jr. was forced to soften the language of demands aimed at humbling Spain. He needed to resolve the confrontation one way or the other. His revised terms, delivered October 14, carried an ultimatum that Spain accede to an agreement within ten days, or face attack.

Floridablanca convened a junta consisting of ministers and councilors of state to debate the ultimatum before the king. They recommended against an agreement in fear that it would allow the British to settle everywhere in Spanish territory and only postpone an inevitable war. Floridablanca was dismayed. Spain was in no position to fight a global war. King Carlos IV had not secured support from Russia or Austria. Nor had he heard from France, which was mired in her own revolutionary chaos and, like the Netherlands, would not engage. Pitt had enticed France to the sidelines by promising British neutrality in France's growing internal strife. More than just a subtle shift in position, this was a historic event. Floridablanca recognized that in their maneuvering, British emissaries had successfully destroyed the Family Compact that had been formed by the Spanish and French Bourbon kings and had countered British ambition for thirty years.

The ten-day deadline passed as the Spanish councilors debated. In London, King George III went sleepless for two days, convinced there would be a dreadful war at great cost and suffering for his people. Floridablanca, too, was anguished at the prospect of long-term damage from British warships and raiders severing the sea-borne lines of Spain's colonial wealth. To him, the paltry events at a remote harbor in the wilderness did not seem to justify a global conflict. He regarded delay and obfuscation at the risk of a sacrifice of honor as better than war. In an unexpected turnaround, Floridablanca's Supreme Council of State overrode the recommendation of the junta.

ON OCTOBER 28, BRITAIN'S AMBASSADOR, Alleyne Fitzhebert, and Count Floridablanca signed what became known as the "Nootka Convention" at the ornate palace of the Escurial north of Madrid.

The agreement committed Spain to pay damages for Meares's seized ships. Spain also pledged to restore "buildings and tracts of land . . . of which the subjects of His Britannic Majesty were dispossessed about the month of April in 1789." However, these tracts of land, claimed by John Meares, were not defined. The document was written in French, the language of diplomats, and other concessions too were open to interpretation.

Britain crowed over winning the war without firing a shot, but the conflict was far from settled. The agreement allowed British fishing, navigation, commerce, and settlement beyond the northernmost Spanish settlements. Both parties were to be allowed to navigate in the South Seas, or land at unoccupied places to trade with the natives. To Pitt, the coast above San Francisco, the ancient "New Albion" of Francis Drake, was now thrown open. To Floridablanca it meant only the area north of Nootka. The difference in translation would not be noticed until after the heat of war had dissipated and the effort to implement the agreement was carried back to the coast.

IN PARIS, GOUVERNEUR MORRIS had learned that part of the Nootka negotiations was a secret agreement between Spain and England to join in war against the revolutionaries in France. As unlikely as it seemed, Britain and Spain had become strange bedfellows out of a mutual interest in defending monarchy and the divine right of kings. To undermine this effort, Morris tried to revive his plan for France to ally with Austria, Poland, and Malta for an attack on Holland. He still hoped that war, or the threat of war, would help shift the balance of power away from Britain. If he could gain leverage by holding out American neutrality in the war, he could bargain for Britain to abandon forts in the Great Lakes, and for Spain to open the Mississippi River.

Although Morris carried instructions from George Washington to gain the American territorial concessions, he was on his own in provoking war. Without the willingness of the United States to join Spain, however, even the French leaders sympathetic to King Carlos found it impossible to advocate committing their ships and troops.

As revolutionary chaos stepped up in the streets of Paris, Morris thought the Nootka agreement marked the demise of the Spanish Empire. But he continued lobbying for a European war, which in a short time would arrive amid chaos far more horrific and enduring than anything he had envisioned.

THE CONFLICT SPARKED that July morning when Martinez and Kendrick trained their cannons on the *Argonaut* signaled a dramatic turning point. The Family Compact between France and Spain that had been in place since 1761 was broken. Spain's dominion in the Pacific was cracked and the Spanish Empire would never claim rights from the Papal Bull of 1493 again. The balance of power between France, Spain, and Britain was shifting, and Europe would be shaken to her roots. The Old World was passing away, replaced by the rise of revolutionary politics that threatened the age-old concepts of monarchy. The reverberations would soon reach around the globe, back to the raw coast of the American Northwest and the islands of the Pacific. A new stage of war for the backside of the world was about to open.

TO SECURE BRITISH RIGHTS in the Pacific and carry out the terms of the Nootka agreement, the Admiralty appointed a haughty young navy captain, George Vancouver. He was only thirty-two, but under a powdered white wig, Vancouver's long, fleshy face and broad double chin made him look a decade or more older. A career officer with no wife or children, he had spent his life since the age of thirteen serving his king and empire. As a young midshipman, he had sailed on James Cook's second and third voyages. He had been to Nootka and the Sandwich Islands and, during the American Revolution, served on the seventy-four-gun warship *Fame* in the West Indies at a time when John

Kendrick was cruising there for prizes. Like most naval officers, he had just begun to stand down from the Nootka mobilization. Although this would be his first command, the Admiralty saw him as a meticulous taskmaster, and ideally suited for the trials of this mission. His expedition was aggressive and ambitious but needed to be as subtle and secretive as possible to avoid reigniting the crisis with Spain. Espionage and acquisition of territory were to wear the guise of a diplomatic and scientific mission.

The voyage was the outgrowth of a secret plan that the Admiralty and prime minister's office had developed at the start of the Nootka crisis. The original plan consisted of an armed expedition that would establish a settlement on the Northwest Coast made up of British marines and prisoners from Botany Bay, Australia. That expedition, which included the forty-four-gun *Gorgon,* was postponed when John Meares appeared in London saying he had already established a settlement and acquired extensive lands.

Now, with an agreement in hand and not wanting to alarm the Spanish with large war frigates, Vancouver's expedition was to consist of two armed ships, the ninety-nine-foot sloop *Discovery* of 340 tons, and the eighty-foot armed tender *Chatham* of 135 tons. A supply ship, *Daedalus,* would depart later. Vancouver was to implement the Nootka agreement and receive from the Spanish the lands claimed by Meares. He was to visit and gather information on Spanish defenses to the south in California and those of the Russians to the north. He was to also seek out the "inland sea" and the Northwest Passage.

Based on the reports from Meares and others, Vancouver was to explore and acquire information on "the nature and extent of any water communication which may tend, in any considerable degree, to facilitate an intercourse for the purpose of commerce, between the northwest coast and the country upon the opposite side of the continent, which are inhabited or occupied by his Majesty's subjects." Concern about Kendrick's possible achievements were front and center. Vancouver was "required and directed to pay particular attention to the examination of the supposed straits of Juan de Fuca, said to be situated between 48 degrees and 49 degrees North Latitude, and to lead to an opening through which the sloop Washington is reported to have passed, in 1789."

The young British captain was also instructed to make claims along the Northwest Coast and examine the harbors and lands of the Sandwich Islands. The doorway that Spanish concessions had opened had to be entered quickly to prevent Spaniards and Americans from exploring and claiming critical lands. Vancouver's armed royal presence and his mission were to be the foundation for expanded merchant ventures and Britain's dominance in the North Pacific.

As Vancouver's ships prepared, the merchant *Butterworth* expedition was also getting ready. The *Butterworth* expedition contained three ships owned by a company of merchants led by Sir William Curtis. Curtis was a member of Parliament, a former mayor of London, and a strong supporter of Pitt's war policies toward Spain. Replacing John Meares and the Etches family, or perhaps taking them in as partners, his company was granted a monopoly for trade on the Northwest Coast. In order to implement the rights Vancouver was to secure, Curtis assigned William Brown, a Greenland whaling captain, to take the three ships and settle outposts at strategic locations: Staten Land near Cape Horn, Nootka or the Strait of Juan de Fuca, the Queen Charlotte Islands, and Hawaii. Aboard the thirty-gun *Butterworth,* Brown believed that part of his purpose was to drive the Americans out. His efforts at Hawaii would bring him to the center of inter-island warfare, and a fateful date with John Kendrick and the *Washington*.

Vancouver set out on April 1, 1791, from Falmouth, England, headed on a long course eastward around Africa's Cape of Good Hope. A few months later, with government support and licenses from the East India Company and South Seas Company, William Brown set off with the *Butterworth* ships headed west around Cape Horn.

CHAPTER FOURTEEN

An American Presence

China, Japan, Queen Charlotte Islands, Northwest Coast

JANUARY–JULY 1791

NEWS OF THE NOOTKA AGREEMENT wouldn't reach Macao until late in the spring or early summer. In the busy harbor the atmosphere was tense throughout the winter in anticipation of war. Two British warships and an armed frigate sat at anchor, sent from London to escort the East India merchant vessels homeward. The port was filled with Royal Navy officers and sailors expecting a Spanish attack from Manila. And rumors spread that Prussia and Holland were ready to join Britain and that a royal company called Mar del Sur had been formed to raid the coast of California and South America.

Known to be at the center of the controversy that touched off the plunge toward war, Kendrick was living aboard the *Washington* in the smuggler's haven at Dirty Butter Bay. Along the shore, spring rains were beginning to turn the hillsides green and swarms of insects were starting to hatch. A less determined man might have given up and gone home in defeat after suffering severe illness, robbery, a bureaucratic impoundment of his vessel, and arrest and threat of imprisonment. Yet Kendrick maintained his blind faith. For better or worse, he seemed to dismiss nagging daily problems, and like others in his generation of revolutionaries, perseverance and a focus on dreams larger than life carried him through.

As testimony to the trust he engendered as a captain, most of his seasoned Boston men stayed with him: the blacksmith, Jonathan Barber, his gunner James Crawford, young John Cordis, who had just turned twenty, John Maud Jr., the cooper Robert Green, carpenter Thomas Foster, and sailmaker William Bowles. For all of them, this was still the voyage of a lifetime. Together they endured, and undoubtedly made the best of the sin and solace Macao offered. And at last their luck turned.

A new Portuguese governor, Don Vasco Luis Caneiro de Sousa de Faro, was appointed by King Pedro III and took office by late 1790. Whatever hold former governor da Silva Ferreira had on Kendrick because of John Meares or the Portuguese merchant Cavalho was lifted. Finally, Kendrick could gain his clearance "chop" stamp to depart. He also had a new source of funds.

While Kendrick had missed the entire season of 1790, William Douglas and Davis Coolidge had returned from the Northwest Coast in the *Grace,* loaded with a rich cargo of furs. They had stopped at the Sandwich Islands on the way and picked up Kendrick's shipment of sandalwood. They also brought the two younger men, James Mackay and Samuel Thomas, who had been left there. From them, Kendrick learned of the massacre of the *Fair American* crew, and that Isaac Ridler remained behind amid intensifying warfare.

Douglas and Coolidge went upriver to Canton and, after selling their furs, joined Kendrick at Dirty Butter Bay. They found the *Washington* remade into a heavily armed, two-masted brigantine—the classic image of a pirate ship—with a square-rigged foremast carrying three courses of sail, and a gaff-rigged main mast with a boom extending over the stern and two courses of sail above. Her lines and sails had been replaced, and the bow was embellished with an intricately carved, eight-foot figurehead of a woman with a jade ornament in her hair and a gown almost touching the sea. As a brigantine, the *Washington* was a sailor's dream, sturdy yet flexible, with ample sail to take on the heavy seas of the North Pacific and cruise the shallow inlets of the coast. The cost of refitting the ship and maintaining his men, coupled with bribing officials and losses from the robbery, had left Kendrick drained of funds.

The windfall he had been awaiting from the thirty tons of sandalwood unfortunately shrank, because the wood turned out to be a species low in aromatic oils. Nevertheless, Douglas loaned Kendrick $2,320 for provisioning and trade goods. To address other debts, Kendrick apparently transacted a "sham sale" of the *Washington*—selling her to a merchant and then buying her back at the same price, and disclosing only the first sale. This allowed him to evade seizure of the ship and the mandarins' rule that no vessel owing money to Macanese merchants could leave port. A young Massachusetts carpenter, Amasa Delano, who would later become a legendary voyager in the Pacific, accompanied Douglas downriver from Canton and helped with final preparations of the *Washington*. He praised Kendrick for his spirit and courage, saying he was the first American in the Pacific who showed others the way. "As a seaman and a navigator," Delano noted, "he had but few equals."

Kendrick had received no further communication from Barrell. He assumed the *Columbia* was returning, but given Gray's insubordination, there was no certainty. For now, he had only a single vessel and meager resources for the expedition, but was willing to use them in bold strokes and to live off trading and bartering as he continued to build alliances and an American presence in the Pacific. His plan was a groundbreaking one, typical of the daring spirit Delano recognized. Kendrick would return to the Northwest Coast and Hawaii, but he would start with a venture to the forbidden island nation of Japan. In helping to capture Meares's ships, Kendrick had already unknowingly stifled the London company's plan to send the *Argonaut* to pioneer a market in Japan. Now he would seek to steal their thunder by trying to open the closed nation himself.

Douglas agreed to bring the *Grace* into the venture, but he apparently leaked word of the plan to the British. On several nights Douglas found himself in town talking with Captain John Blankett, commander of the seventy-four-gun HMS *Leopard,* one of the warships sent to escort British merchant ships homeward and protect them from Spanish attacks. Douglas may have been unaware that Blankett was one of the prime advocates of British trade with Japan. In a series of memos to the Lord of the Admiralty, Blankett had advocated strategies that might "cut off [Japan's] communications with other countries" and gain superiority in Japanese trade.

Clearly concerned that Britain's future efforts toward Japan might be jeopardized, Blankett sent a summary of his conversations with Douglas to the Admiralty:

> *An Adventurer by the name of Douglass who was concerned in the business of Nootka Sound has . . . made some discoveries on the NW Coast of America . . . He means to prosecute his discoveries & to collect furs as he goes on, & failing of success in finding a passage, he will go to some Islands in the vicinity of Japan to which the Japanese are said to trade, & by their means introduce himself, or his Furs to the notice of the Japanese. There can be little doubt that much can be done by way of Commerce in those Seas, & I cannot but lament that the introduction is left to such persons as may give rise to many prejudices against us, which it may not be easy to get the better of in the future.*

As a result of Blankett's urging, and prodding by the East India Company, the British court launched renewed efforts toward Japan. Coupled with Vancouver's mission, official policy on the Pacific now had a focus to ensure a dominant British role in trade.

Blankett and the British merchant fleet sailed from Macao for London in two divisions on March 20, armed for war and unaware that the crisis with Spain was over. Eleven days later, the *Washington* raised anchor and headed into the South China Sea with the *Grace*. Kendrick had been in port for fourteen months, and was exhilarated as the *Washington* slipped beyond the fishing junks on the Pearl River Delta and into the South China Sea. The men's spirits must have soared as well. The *Washington* now carried a crew of thirty-six. In addition to his original Boston men, there were also two Chinese, two Hawaiians, and British, Welsh, and Irish sailors, who later claimed to be Americans. First mate Davis Coolidge remained with Douglas on the *Grace*. The *Washington*'s new chief officer was a Welshman, John Williams. Second mate was John Redman, third mate William Bowell, and John Stoddard of Boston served as the captain's clerk.

Just before the *Washington* and *Grace* departed, the mandarins declared a complete embargo on the trade in sea otter skins. China was at war with Russia, and the mandarins feared that neutral ships would carry Russian furs to Canton. The embargo (which would last until June 1792) gave Kendrick compelling justification for the risk they were taking to open trade with Japan.

After side trips to offshore islands, on May 6 Kendrick and Douglas approached the sparsely settled Kii peninsula on Japan's south coast. They might have chosen a rural area rather than entering a port city manned by samurai troops, but they were also being driven in by mounting seas and increasingly stormy weather. The ragged black cliffs and forests of the coast were foreboding.

Japan had been a closed nation, under "Sakoku"—or self-imposed isolation—for one hundred fifty years. Portuguese vessels had first arrived in 1542, and the Dutch, English, and Spanish came in the early 1600s. Spain especially cultivated a close relationship, sending emissaries and priests from the Philippines and Mexico. In 1610, a group of twenty-three Japanese merchants and two noblemen traveled to Mexico City. But during the next two decades, conflicts mounted over the teachings of Catholic missionaries and popular conversions of Japanese villagers.

In a series of increasingly restrictive edicts, the shogun (the hereditary military leader) attempted to stop the Catholic religion from undermining Japan's culture and political system. In response, a Christian peasant revolt broke out in 1637, and more than thirty-seven thousand Japanese were eventually slaughtered. The shogun closed the nation. All Spanish, English, and Portuguese were expelled, and every ship built with European design for distant voyages was burned. The Dutch alone, who had helped attack Japanese Catholics, were allowed to remain on a three-acre compound on tiny Dashima Island in Nagasaki Bay. They were permitted two ships per year at first and then later only one. A limited trade was carried on with Chinese and Koreans through Nagasaki and offshore islands, but no one from Japan was allowed to travel abroad.

Japan's society of twenty million people—much larger than England, Spain, or the United States—was ruled by tradition-bound samurai warlords, led by the figurehead of a divine emperor at Kyoto and the Tokugawa shogun at Edo (Tokyo). The land was divided in strictly defined fiefdoms or "prefectures." The Kii peninsula was under the control of the daimyo at Wakayama Castle, seventy-five miles away by sea, or fifty miles over rugged mountain trails from the peninsula.

Kendrick and his men approached Japan with a free-wheeling notion of liberty and open trade, but were prepared for the possibility of a hostile encounter with the samurai. During his time ashore at Macao, Kendrick had collected a considerable arsenal. The *Washington* carried eight four-pound cannons, twelve swivel guns, and four small guns, plus muskets, pistols, and sabers. In the hold were cases of muskets and powder intended for the Northwest Coast and Hawaii.

Swept northward by the storm and the Kuroshio, or Black Current, the ships came in along the Kii's sheer cliffs and tall, sharp, toothlike rocks jutting from the surf. Dense forest rose above the tide-stained rock of Cape Shiomonoseki and Oshima Island, backed by green mountain chains shrouded in clouds.

Seeking shelter from what gathered into a darkening typhoon, the ships entered the channel between the village of Koza on the mainland and Oshima Island, and then moved farther into the protected bay behind the island. A copper-bottomed longboat felt the way in with a sounding lead. Onshore, the fishing village of Kushimoto stood on high ground above a narrow beach. Inside the town, frightened villagers brought frantic news of the ships to the headman, Kichigo. Any contact between Japanese people and foreign barbarians was considered a punishable offense. Those who breached the law could face exile or death. The first response of Japanese fishermen and villagers was to avoid foreign ships.

Kichigo sent a message to the daimyo at Wakayama. Nakanishi Riezaemon, the headman of the nearby Koza village, did the same. No one could recall foreign ships like this. Although a long red-and-white-striped American flag billowed from the stern of the *Washington,* they had no idea what nation it symbolized, or why the ships had come. When the storm abated, a few fishermen overcome by curiosity went out and stood alongside the ships. They found men they described as six feet tall with sharp, high noses, long hands and legs, and red eyes, which may have been the result of an outbreak of conjunctivitis (pink eye), not uncommon among crews.

Kendrick offered the fishermen food and drink, and despite the threat of punishment, they went on board. They noted with amusement a fishing pole someone had stuck in the arms of the ship's beautiful figurehead. The Chinese crewmen did not speak Japanese, but their writing was similar and they exchanged notes. Answering a series of questions, the Chinese crewmen explained, "This ship belongs to the Red Hairs from a land called America." The cargo included "copper, iron, and fifty guns," which was most likely an understatement to avoid alarm. They had been driven to port "under the stress of wind and

The Lady Washington *at Kushimoto, Japan, sketched by Hewitt Jackson.*

wave" and would not stay more than three to five days. Attempting to reassure nervous headmen in the village, they said the ships would leave as soon as the wind became favorable. "The captain's name is Kendrick," they said in closing.

Through the night, the ships fired their cannons out in the bay behind Oshima Island as a precaution against attack. The sound echoed off the hills in the dark, which unsettled the villagers even more. A silk-robed doctor was brought out to the ship and tried to communicate. The Americans perhaps thought he was an official, and waved him off. The fishermen who were allowed on board most likely traded information as well as their catch. Kendrick and Douglas soon learned that the Japanese cared nothing for wearing sea otter furs—in fact, they regarded the practice as barbaric. Contrary to rumors at Macao, a rich market in furs here was an illusion. The fishermen may have also dissuaded Kendrick from going to Osaka, a teeming city of nearly four hundred thousand people in the north. There, the two captains and their men would have faced certain arrest and confiscation of their ships.

While the wind held them in the bay, the men shot gulls or ducks to be retrieved by the ship's dog. Five men were sent ashore on Oshima to collect water from a stream in cotton (or canvas) sacks and cut trees for firewood. One local farmer who tried to stop them from taking the trees ended up running from a musket fired at his feet.

Days after Kendrick' arrival, the daimyo at Wakayama castle received the panicked messages from the Kii headmen and mobilized his troops. Perhaps after being alerted that samurai were on their way, on May 17 (about ten days after the ships arrived) the wind freshened from the west and the *Grace* and *Washington* made sail. The samurai appeared two days later. If poor weather had delayed the ships, the visit might have become America's first clash with Japan. It resulted instead in a new system of alarms and patrols for coastal villages, which increased Japan's isolation under the vigilant samurai. For the Western world it was a symbolic visit, the first by America, one that would further goad the British and build their antagonism toward Kendrick.

STRANGELY ENOUGH, JAMES COLNETT, with his penchant for misfortune, was the first one to suffer under the heightened security. Colnett had been released with the *Argonaut* and the remainder of his crew at San Blas on July 9, 1790. He wintered on the Northwest Coast and had arrived at Macao in May 1791, where he found the embargo on furs in place. Learning of Kendrick's plans to trade in Japan, he ventured there in July 1791, two months after Kendrick's visit. Colnett was immediately seized and threatened with execution if he did not depart. Then, back at Macao in November, he was arrested for disobeying the mandarins' rules about anchoring and managing his ship. Colnett was at his wits' end. He imagined once again that he would be executed or imprisoned for life in a small brick cell with only a small opening for food and water. After a disastrous two years with the *Argonaut,* the ill-fated British captain finally took ship as a passenger for London in December 1791.

A FEW DAYS AFTER LEAVING THE KII PENINSULA, Kendrick and Douglas came upon a group of islands off the Japanese coast that they named the Water Islands. They decided to separate. Douglas later ended up trading for the summer among the Russians in Alaska. He may have gone to Hawaii first, carrying homeward-bound islanders or a promised shipment of guns for Kamehameha.

Kendrick headed for the Northwest Coast. Douglas had told him that during the previous summer, the breach between Spain and England left only one other trading vessel plying the waters—the *Eleanora* under Simon Metcalfe. He also said that Martinez was gone from Nootka, replaced by Commandant Francisco de Eliza. The fort and gun batteries had been dismantled, only to be rebuilt by Eliza's force. The Russians had not yet shown up. And apparently, the new commandant had sent ships to search the Strait of Juan de Fuca for the Northwest Passage and make claims for Spain.

Carried by her expanded spread of sail and the Black Current, the *Washington* ripped across the northern Pacific in less than a month if the recorded date of her Japan visit is accurate. Kendrick must have been justly proud of his refitted little brigantine. Arcing into the lower Gulf of Alaska he came to the familiar maze of foggy islands along the coast. According to a Spanish account, in early June Kendrick arrived on the mainland coast at Bucareli Sound, the area where he had given up searching for the Northwest Passage in the fall of 1789.

Snow was still on the mountains, but the native Tsimshian people were down at their summer camps along the coast fishing for salmon. Kendrick would have tried to learn of any passage to the east, trading copper and other goods for furs as he worked his way south. After a week or so, he broke off and crossed the forty-mile channel to the Queen Charlotte Islands. He was in familiar territory now, and he and the *Washington* were known to people in several villages. As they approached Barrell's Sound and the village of Ninstints at the southern end of Anthony Island, Kendrick hoped that Coyah and Schulkinanse, the two chiefs he had locked in the gun carriage and disgraced in October 1789, had been long banished from the tribe.

They set up boarding nets and broke out pistols and muskets as they came up the sound. Anchoring a safe distance offshore from the small islet that hid the village, Kendrick fired a cannon, announcing that they had come to trade. The sound reverberated in the hills and forest, and without hesitation, men and women came off in canoes with a variety of skins. Trading was friendly, and Kendrick was told that Coyah was no longer a chief. The crew relaxed. For a couple of days a festive atmosphere prevailed and groups traveled down the coast from other villages and summer camps to take part. When Coyah appeared, he seemed to make no issue of what had happened nearly two years before. Bringing his own furs, the harsh-looking former chief mingled among the fifty warriors and women on board. Kendrick reportedly traded a blue nankin coat to him.

In the midst of the festive mood, one of the chiefs came up on the quarterdeck. Some versions of the story allege that it was Coyah. Before anyone noticed, he had climbed onto one of the two arms chests. The gunner had been cleaning weapons and inadvertently left the keys in the lock. Now the chief was holding the keys in his hand. In what appears to have been an unplanned attack, warriors surged forward, menacing Kendrick's men with double-ended knives they pulled from sheaths around their necks. As the lightly armed crew retreated, warriors in canoes crowded alongside the *Washington* and climbed on board. Crewmen brandishing pistols were told that if they fired, everyone would die. A native woman climbed onto the chains securing the mainmast and urged on the attack. The crew and officers escaped down the companionway, retreating from long bone-tipped spears that had been handed on board.

Kendrick was left on the quarterdeck alone, wielding an iron bar. Whether or not he had been the one to take the keys of the arms chest, Coyah seized the moment. He pointed to his legs and taunted Kendrick, saying, "now put me into your gun carriage." Kendrick tried to appeal to the other chiefs, but Coyah kept taunting him, confident that the warriors had control of the ship and perhaps seeking to regain prestige. Kendrick realized he could do nothing to regain the arms chest and stepped down from the quarterdeck, offering to pay the warriors to leave the ship. But there was nothing to bargain for. They had possession of the vessel and everything in it, which consisted of more than they knew, given the arsenal of muskets and powder packed in the hold.

Kendrick continued trying to reason with them. A large warrior followed him, waving a marlin spike lashed to a handle like an ax, threatening to dash out his brains. Below, the men were apparently preparing to blow up the ship rather than be captured and tortured. Kendrick was calling instructions to them. Coyah saw Kendrick edging toward the companionway, and jumped down the steps. Kendrick jumped on top of him. Coyah slashed with his knife, piercing Kendrick's shirt, and slicing his belly in two places.

The officers and men below had gathered the few arms stored in the cabins while Kendrick stalled and they fired at Coyah and other warriors coming down the companionway. Kendrick retrieved his pistols from his cabin, fired up the steps, and then led his men back on deck. They fought hand-to-hand, and about fifteen of the Haida, both men and women, were killed in the ensuing struggle on board the ship. Survivors dove from the opening in the netting and quickly began to paddle off.

A gruesome scene followed. According to the story told later, the woman who had climbed on the chains refused to yield, "urging them to action with the greatest ardour until the last moment though her arm had been previously cut off by one of the people with a hanger and she was otherway much wounded when she quitted all the natives had left the vessel and she jumpt over board and attempted to swim of but was afterwards shot though the natives had taken the keys off the arms chests yet they did not happen to be lockt. they were therefore immediately opened and a constant fire was kept up as long as they could reach the natives with their cannon or small arms after which they chased them in their armed boats making the most dreadfull havock by killing all they came across . . ."

It was a brutal retribution. Coyah's wife and child were said to be dead. The diminutive Raven clan chief had been shot in the back but escaped, and the chief Schulkinanse had a bullet lodged behind his ear. It would become an often-told story. Those who knew Kendrick found the slaughter hard to believe. One sailor's second-hand narrative alleged that Kendrick was "in liquor" at the time.

Leaving the mayhem at Ninstints, Kendrick took the *Washington* back toward Bucareli Sound. A month later, after the crew's wounds had healed, he headed home for Mawina and Fort Washington. He had no license to trade in these waters, as Martinez had advised, but he was willing to risk a confrontation with the Spaniards. He had heard nothing of the settlement between Spain and Britain and the Nootka Convention. For all he knew, a global war was in progress. They armed the cannons as they approached the entrance to Nootka Sound.

The tide and wind were with him, and Kendrick made a dramatic entrance. Only he and the steersman were on the quarterdeck as they came through the mouth of the sound and approached the inlet to Yuquot. The gun emplacement of San Rafael had its cannons perched menacingly over the sound. As the *Washington* approached, the Spanish called out through a speaking trumpet for the ship to halt. Kendrick ordered his crew to stand ready to return fire from their cannons and swivel guns. He also had each man armed with a musket, two pistols, and a saber.

A Spanish officer noted: "July 12 Captain Juan Kendrique of Boston entered this port and passed the fort with his matches lit, his men armed and the flag of his nation flying in the sloop *Washington* rigged as a brig."

The Spanish gunners held their fire, and the acting commandant, Don Ramon Saavedra, immediately sent an armed boat after the *Washington*. The wind had fallen off, and Kendrick let them approach. He was warned that the sound belonged to Spain and no one could enter or trade there without permission. In seeming defiance, he answered that they came from Macao to trade all along the coast for sea otter furs and that as soon as they finished with this task they would depart. The Spanish messengers took note of how well the ship was armed and the number of crew. Kendrick may have asked about Estevan Martinez and found he had been removed from command and would be sent back to Spain for an inquiry on the taking of Meares's ships. The *Washington* went up the sound to the anchorage at Mawina. Chastened by what had happened to Martinez, and under orders to maintain peace, Saavedra took no action. Instead, he waited for Commandant Francisco de Eliza to return from an exploration of the Strait of Juan de Fuca and the inland sea.

The summer before (1790), Eliza had sent Lieutenant Manuel Quimper Benitez del Pino into the strait in the confiscated *Princess Royal*. For two months, Lieutenant Quimper had explored both shores of the strait nearly a hundred miles inland, where he noted that the waterway branched into smaller passages between islands north, east, and south. The channels appeared to extend far into the interior. He charted the shore and islands and gave names to channels, such as "Canal Lopez de Haro." Following Eliza's orders, Quimper also went ashore to take possession of well-situated harbors. After two months he departed for Monterey.

The new commandant at San Blas, Juan Francisco de la Bodega y

Quadra, was intrigued by the charts of bays and channels that Quimper brought back. Quadra perhaps had also heard about Meares's claim that the *Washington* had sailed through the inland sea. Secret instructions he sent to Eliza ordered him to expand exploration for the passage from Juan de Fuca and along the coast north to the entrance of Bucareli, where Kendrick had just been.

Eliza left Nootka for Juan de Fuca in May, two months before Kendrick arrived. He was exploring with two ships: the sixteen-gun *San Carlos,* which was slightly larger than the *Washington,* and the thirty-five-foot schooner *Santa Saturina,* which the Spanish had assembled at Nootka.

Eliza penetrated channels beyond where Quimper had turned back, and came upon natives who warned that the people to the east would spear his men and beat them with clubs. Soon after, Eliza's longboat was attacked in the channel of Lopez de Haro, and he and his men had to fire on their attackers to escape. Ignoring the danger, Eliza pressed on. By July 22, the *San Carlos* was believed to be as far north in the inland sea as Nootka. Eliza later confirmed to Quadra that if the "oceanic passage so zealously sought by foreigners" existed, it was somewhere here, branching off from the inland sea.

AT MAWINA, KENDRICK BEGAN to enact his plans to counter the Spanish drive for domination of the region, and to secure his trade for sea otter skins and a permanent American presence. He was welcomed by the Mawina village chief Claquakinnah and his son who had learned enough English to translate well. Kendrick requested that he send for Maquinna and other chiefs.

Commandant Don Ramon Saavedra reportedly dispatched a boat to Kendrick with a gift of greens and vegetables from his garden each day. The boat allowed Saavedra's men to keep a close watch on the Americans. Kendrick was not taken in by the gesture, but nonetheless he allowed his young officers to visit Saavedra. He wrote that he himself did not come, as he was satisfied with their friendship. For some of the young officers, the adventure with Kendrick was proving a bit much. After being forced from Japan, attacked by Coyah's people, and entering the sound ready to do battle, they found themselves now engaged in trade despite the Spanish warning. They apparently feared being caught and made prisoners or dying at the hands of the Mowachaht. According to Saavedra, they feared for their lives enough to ask if they could remain at the Spanish fort. This was denied, but not before Saavedra milked them for information. They volunteered details on the armament of the *Washington* and crew, spoke of the British fleet sailing from Macao in March with armed escorts, and of the British royal company that had been formed to raid the California coast. They also told of the attack and ensuing slaughter at Ninstints.

From Saavedra they learned that the threat of war between Spain and England was over. The new San Blas commandant had sent a message to Nootka on March 12, 1791, announcing that the matter had been amicably settled and that "it has pleased His Majesty to permit the English to take part in the commerce of furs from the Puerto de Nuca to the north and to locate themselves in the port itself without prejudice to the establishment which we today possess." News of the truce between Spain and England may have alleviated some of their fears, but it did not alter Kendrick's plans. With the British also closing in on the region, he undertook a brilliant move that no other trader or nation was capable of.

The trust he had built with Maquinna, Claquakinnah, Wickaninish, and other chiefs had forged a lasting bond that did not diminish during his long stay at Macao. In fact, the ties were strengthened by the Mowachaht's frustration with continued Spanish encroachment on their land and the vital new goods Kendrick offered—muskets and powder.

After the killing of Callicum, Maquinna communicated little with the Spanish. Some of his warriors mounted sporadic attacks.

Those who traded with the soldiers asked repeatedly when they were going to leave. Kendrick's arrival created a shift. In response to his request for the chiefs to come together, Maquinna arrived at Claquakinnah's longhouse, along with Hannape, the father of one of Maquinnah's wives and the chief at Esperanza Inlet to the north. Tartoochtheatticus, Wickaninish's brother from Clayoquot, also arrived with a host of lesser chiefs.

In a nighttime celebration, Kendrick dazzled the gathering at Mawina with Chinese fireworks that lit the sky and illuminated the black water of Nootka Sound. They feasted and Kendrick spoke. In the situation they faced with foreign nations, more ships were coming, not only for trade, but with soldiers and armed men who would make claims on this place. With his usual flair for diplomacy, Kendrick apparently explained that if he held a private deed to their land, in which they maintained all their rights, neither the Spanish nor the British could claim it or encroach further. Based on what Joseph Barrell had told him, Kendrick believed that Congress would approve the purchase.

The land and everything in it was holy, and Kendrick was asking for rights to use the region as one of the Mowachaht. While words on a paper deed meant little, his offer of guns was a convincing sign of his trust. Muskets gave them the ability to enforce what they wanted, or to change or cancel the agreement. By purchasing the land, Kendrick was also bound to defend the area against Europeans or tribes outside of Maquinna's confederacy. And no one would dare trifle with Maquinna or chiefs who bought in and armed themselves. The traders would no longer feel free to raid villages and shoot at canoes.

The chiefs embraced Kendrick and his offer. In a ceremony on the deck of the *Washington* on July 20, Maquinna reportedly climbed the rigging to the masthead and pointed to the four cardinal directions, proclaiming his grant to Kendrick. The deed that was signed and witnessed read:

To all persons to whom these present shall come, I, Maquinna, the Chief, and with my other Chiefs do send greeting: Know ye that I, Maquinnah, of Nootka-sound, on the Northwest coast of America, for and in consideration of ten muskets, do grant and sell unto John Kendrick, of Boston, Commonwealth of Massachusetts, in North America, a certain harbor in Nootka-sound, called Chastacktoos, in which the brigantine Lady Washington lay at anchor, on the twentieth day of July 1791, with all the land, rivers, creeks, harbors, islands, etc. within nine miles North, East, West and South of said harbor, with all the produce of both seas and land appertaining thereto—only the said John Kendrick does grant and allow the said Maquinnah to live and fish on the said territory, as usual—and by these presents, does grant and sell to the said John Kendrick, his heirs, executors, and administrators, all the above mentioned territory, known by the Indian name Chastacktoos, but now by the name of Safe Retreat-harbor; and also does grant and sell to the said John Kendrick, his heirs, executors, and administrators, a free passage through all rivers and passages, with all the outlets which lead to and from the said Nootka-sound of which, by signing these presents, I have delivered unto the said John Kendrick. Signed with my own hand and the other Chiefs, and bearing even date, to have and to hold the said premises, etc. to him, the said John Kendrick, his heirs, executors, and administrators, from henceforth and forever, as his property, absolutely, without any other considerations whatever.

In witness whereof I have hereunto set my hand and the hands of my other Chiefs, this twentieth day of July, one thousand seven hundred and ninety-one.

Maquinnah, his X mark
Warclasman, his X mark
Hannopy, his X mark

Clophananish, his X mark
Tartoochtheeatticus, his X mark
Clackokeener, his X mark
Signed, sealed, and delivered in presence of—
John Stoddard, John Redman, Thomas Foster, William Bowles, John Maud, Jr., Florence McCarthy, John Porter, James Crawford, Robert Green, John Barber

The aptly named "Safe Retreat-harbor" agreement was at once a defensive maneuver for native people and a huge victory for Kendrick and the Americans. The deed covered Nootka Sound and surrounding land, and it reached southwest to the sea and north and east up the Tahsis and Tlupana and Muchalaht inlets where many villages lay. The boundaries formed an 18-mile square centered on Chastacktoos, and the area encompassed 324 square miles.

This was only the beginning.

KENDRICK TOOK HANNAPE up the Tahsis inlet twenty miles and met with chiefs at the traditional winter village known as Tashees. There he made an agreement for nine miles round Tashees for "two muskets and a quantity of powder." Wanting to avoid the Spanish fort at Yuquot, he took the *Washington* out the "backdoor" of Nootka Sound, entering the very narrow channel of Esperanza Inlet. He towed the ship between the forested cliffs with the longboat, waiting on the tide and watching for hidden rocks and ledges for twenty miles.

When he reached the ocean, he immediately entered Nuchatlitz Inlet to the north of Nootka Sound, where he made an agreement with Tarassom and his chiefs of New Chatleck for "two muskets, a boat's sail, and a quantity of powder." They granted a territory of eighteen miles square with the harbor of Hoot-see-ess at the center. For more muskets, powder, a boat sail, and an American flag, Kendrick purchased from Norry Youk and his chiefs on the north side of the harbor

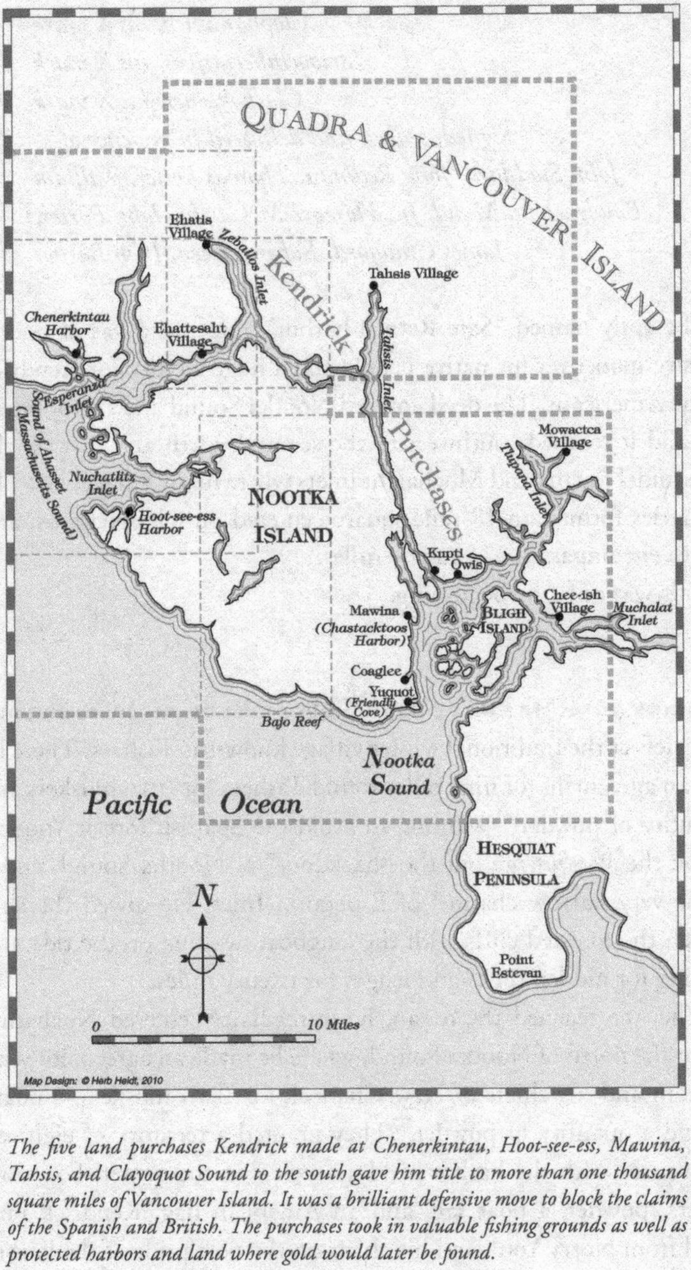

The five land purchases Kendrick made at Chenerkintau, Hoot-see-ess, Mawina, Tahsis, and Clayoquot Sound to the south gave him title to more than one thousand square miles of Vancouver Island. It was a brilliant defensive move to block the claims of the Spanish and British. The purchases took in valuable fishing grounds as well as protected harbors and land where gold would later be found.

of Ahasset another "territorial distance of eighteen miles square . . . all the lands, mines, minerals, rivers, bays, harbors, sounds, creeks, and all islands with the produce of both land and sea." The formerly named Chenerkintau Harbor would now be known as Kendrick Harbor.

Only in Maquinna's deed were the Mowachaht explicitly granted rights to continue to fish and use the land, but as a practical matter, the same condition applied to all the deeds. Kendrick did not want to displace people he saw as allies and partners who would harvest sea otters. Under these four agreements, he now owned virtually all of Nootka Island and an area around Tashees about thirty miles inland, totaling more than seven hundred square miles.

Kendrick sailed past the entrance to Nootka Sound and south to Clayoquot. When James Colnett had been there during the winter with the *Argonaut*, he told Wickaninish and his chiefs that the Spanish had "committed many Barbarities" on tribes to the south "and almost totally extirpated the whole of them off the face of the Earth." He said "they had every reason to expect the same if they suffered them to exist among them." Wickaninish responded that if the Spanish came to Clayoquot again he would trade for nothing but guns and powder. Hearing from his brother about the ceremony at Mawina, the solemn chief was awaiting Kendrick.

On August 11, Wickaninish, his brothers Tartoochtheatticus and Tooteescosettle, and two other chiefs granted Kendrick a territory "eighteen miles north, eighteen miles south, eighteen miles east and eighteen miles west" of the village of Opitsat for "four muskets, a sail, and a quantity of powder." This was all of Clayoquot Sound. While only four muskets are mentioned in the deed, in 1792 Wickaninish was said to have two hundred muskets and several barrels of powder from Kendrick. Saavedra would also observe that guns traded by Kendrick to Maquinna had made him the best-armed chief in the region.

The deals not only empowered the Mowachaht, Kendrick emerged as the most powerful trader on the coast and believed he had the ability to raise the native people against the Spanish or the English. This type of alliance was not unusual along volatile frontiers. Kendrick may have drawn inspiration from the famous mixed-blood trader Alexander McGillivray, who led the Creek nation in defense of its lands in the southwest region of Georgia, West Florida, and Alabama. McGillivray developed land titles for the tribe and played British, Spanish, and American interests off against each other for decades. Kendrick would have been well aware of McGillivray from the news published about him in Charleston, South Carolina, while he was running the Boston packet there after the Revolution.

A dozen years before the Lousiana Purchase, Kendrick held more than a thousand square miles of land on the Pacific. In a year that had begun in debt in a foul harbor near Macao, his perseverance had paid off. Settling in at Clayoquot, he constructed a new Fort Washington on an island out of reach of the Spanish and prepared for the British or whoever else might arrive.

Chapter Fifteen

Long-Awaited Return

Clayoquot Sound

August–September 1791

At noon on August 29, a ship appeared off the entrance to Clayoquot, luffing in a light breeze from the south. Natives brought word to Kendrick who came down in his longboat. Through his glass from inside the sound he could see the ship clearly. Her snub-nosed hull and three masts posed a familiar and much longed-for sight—the *Columbia*! As Kendrick set out in the late afternoon, the men of the *Columbia* noticed his launch, fired a greeting, and raised the American colors. On board with Gray was Robert Haswell, serving as first officer, and John Hoskins, the young clerk Joseph Barrell had sent along in the post of supercargo to oversee the business of the voyage.

Kendrick had no idea that Gray had thoroughly devastated his reputation in Boston. While a ship out of New England could have carried the news to Macao by the end of March, when the *Washington* sailed for Japan, the seasonal voyage for an American ship was dictated by the Canton market season and the prevailing winds. China-bound ships started well before Gray arrived home in August. Kendrick had received no news and no change in his instructions. He considered himself still under Barrell's original grant of authority to make decisions for the expedition as he saw necessary.

Kendrick's appearance was not a surprise for Gray. An hour before his boat was seen coming out of the sound, chief Hanna (Cleaskinah), who occupied the village of Ahouset near Clayoquot's entrance, paddled out and told the *Columbia*'s officers that Kendrick was in the sound in the *Washington*. While Gray and Haswell were undoubtedly uneasy about how Kendrick might receive them, Hoskins was elated.

It had been a miserable voyage for the young clerk. Soon after embarking from Boston, he discovered that Robert Gray was a bullying and vengeful captain. Gray introduced Hoskins to the men of the ship "as a spy upon his and their conduct" and told other ships the same, demeaning him at every opportunity and apparently trying to force him to leave the *Columbia*. The young clerk believed he would long have been placed "before the mast, if not turn'd ashore" if Barrell had not specifically ordered Gray to consult with him on "all matters of traffic" and to maintain "the most perfect harmony" between himself, his officers, and Hoskins. He eventually wrote that Gray interfered with the keeping of the ship's books and that he and others of the ship's officers regarded their captain "as a man of no principle" and a "Knave and a Fool."

They arrived on the coast on June 5, eight months out of Boston. Intent on a speedy voyage, Gray did not stop at Cape Verde. At the Falklands in late January, they spent eleven days preparing the ships for the passage around Cape Horn. Though it was already storm season, they luckily found winds and weather almost "what we could have wished" and made the run in three weeks. Gray kept driving hard and by late March the men began to complain of scurvy: bleeding and numb gums and swollen legs. The malady continued to spread. Ultimately, when they sighted shore in June, there were ten men in "the last stage of Scurvy." Once on shore, they buried several of them "up to the Hips in the earth, and let them remain for hours in that situation." Despite this dangerous mistreatment, abundant amounts of parsley and wild onions brought by the native people, together with doses of foul-tasting "spruce beer" and "spruce tea" laced with molasses, helped the men recover.

Later, in July, Hoskins asked people at Ninstints in the Queen Charlotte Islands if they had seen Kendrick. Only two or three weeks had passed since the *Washington*'s crew had been overwhelmed and made their brutal retaliation. Perhaps the villagers wanted to avoid talking of their attempt to take the ship, but no one mentioned the fight. They said only that Kendrick had been there. Going ashore, Hoskins found few people in the village. Many of them had cut their hair and painted their faces black in displays of mourning. Asking for Coyah, they learned that the Raven Clan leader was no longer a chief. Hoskins was told by a woman about the episode two years before when Kendrick "took Coyah, tied a rope around his neck, whipt him, painted his face, cut off his hair, and took away from him a great many skins, and then turned him ashore." She said, "Coyah was now no longer Chief, but an 'Ahliko,' or one of the lower class, they have now no head Chief, but many inferior Chiefs."

Hoskins didn't know how much credit to give the story "when it is considered our knowledge of their language is so very superficial . . . and from Captain Kendrick's well known disposition, who has hitherto treated these people more like children than an ignorant race of savages; it must therefore be supposed Captain Kendrick has been provoked by these peoples conduct to punish their Chief." The young clerk would soon find out.

AS KENDRICK'S BOAT DREW ALONGSIDE, the *Columbia* fired another salute, and the men gave three cheers. Here was the captain who had remained on the unknown side of the world and given the expedition its mystique, the man who was the reason all Americans here were called "Boston men," and who was becoming part of the legend of this coast, a captain they recognized as of a different order than Robert Gray. Still, despite the glowing welcome, Kendrick's status as the commander of the *Columbia* was anything but clear. As usual, Gray and Haswell concealed their animosity under a polite veneer. Having no idea what Kendrick was accomplishing, Haswell railed privately in his journal against his "former commander," depicting Kendrick as having done nothing during the last two years, while they had sailed around the world and returned.

Kendrick's joy at finding men he knew from home, including crewmen, on this far side of the world made up for long months of isolation. Gray's insubordination and Haswell's arrogance might have seemed insignificant at the moment, especially in light of the fact that he held title to this sound they were about to enter. There would be time to sort things out.

Kendrick spent the evening with Hoskins and the *Columbia*'s officers. Over dinner he gave a full narrative of what had happened since the *Columbia* had sailed from Clayoquot two years earlier. He talked of his travails at Macao and of entering Japan, and in answer to Hoskins's questions, he described in gory detail the attack by Coyah's people. Violence was increasing on the coast, especially as more ships arrived. Three other Boston ships were now cruising these waters: the *Hope* under Joseph Ingraham, the *Hancock* under Samuel Crowell, and the *Margaret* under James Magee. There were also five British traders, as well as the British ship *Mercury* sailing under the Swedish flag as the *Gustavus*. Most were avoiding Nootka Sound, out of fear of the Spanish, and focusing on the waters of the Queen Charlotte Islands.

Kendrick was doing well amid the growing competition. Haswell noted that after trading in the north and at Nootka and Clayoquot for two months, the *Washington* had about twelve hundred otter skins in her hold. By comparison, after cruising up and down the coast, the *Columbia* had gathered only five or six hundred, and Captain Crowell of the *Hancock* had about seven hundred skins and was planning to head to Macao in two or three weeks. Gray would not find many more furs here at Clayoquot. The natives told Hoskins they had few skins, having sold them all to Kendrick. Although he would not have spoken of it, Kendrick's status was more than just a formal holder to title of the land. During his stay at native villages, he had negotiated advance payments to local chiefs for furs yet to be gathered. A significant portion of next year's harvest of sea otters at Nootka, Clayoquot, and to the south already belonged to him. This was another benefit of the careful alliances he was taking time to build. Joseph Ingraham later commented that when trading in the region around Nootka: "Every one of the natives enquired particularly about Captain Kendrick saying they had plenty of skins for him and they would not sell them to anyone else."

WHILE THE OFFICERS WERE AT DINNER, the *Columbia* was towed to the mouth of the sound and anchored in darkness to await the tide and daylight. Kendrick left the ship late. Though he sensed something amiss, this was not a time to be rash. He would be able to talk over awkward behavior and unanswered questions at a meeting he had scheduled for the morning. At dawn, Hoskins accompanied Gray in the *Columbia*'s jolly boat inside the sound to have breakfast with Kendrick. In the bright, still morning they were rowed up a northern arm of the sound to what was apparently Fair Harbor. "We were received at a small Island which he had fortified and dignified with the appellation of Fort Washington," Hoskins wrote. The rough log outpost, consisting of living quarters and a building to store provisions, displayed an American flag on a bare pole. Beside the fortification, the *Lady Washington* had been hauled on shore to be graved in preparation for departure to Hawaii and Macao.

Hoskins and Gray bore a letter from Joseph Barrell soliciting Kendrick's cooperation with Gray and the *Columbia*. Gray was in charge of the ship. Kendrick read the letter and was stunned and dismayed by the contents. He would later write to Barrell: "Your letter per Captain Gray I received, but found it different from what I expected, as I thought to have the conducting of all your business in this part of the world . . ." He told Barrell that "had the Columbia been sent to me, it would have been much more to the benefit of the concerned, as she could have returned to America this season." Certainly if Kendrick had added a thousand furs to the *Columbia*'s cargo, her voyage would have been over by September and proved much more lucrative than the first.

But faced with the debt he owed and the plans he was in the midst of, Kendrick would not simply hand over his command and his furs to Gray. It's not clear whether Hoskins had an opportunity out of Gray's hearing to explain to Kendrick the charges made against him. In later private conversation, Hoskins may have explained in tempered terms what Gray and Haswell had said to the owners. Either way, Kendrick certainly heard the allegations later at Macao. At this point, the rationale for such a huge change may have been puzzling, and Kendrick was left questioning what course to take.

On the morning of September 20, Kendrick breakfasted again with the *Columbia*'s officers. Hoskins and Kendrick did apparently speak in private at this point. Whether it was a gesture of cooperation or a test of his remaining authority, Kendrick offered to turn over the *Washington* and one thousand sea otter skins to Hoskins as Barrell's agent. In return he asked for payment of his men's wages and the debt he had contracted in Macao of about four thousand dollars (this was apparently the debt and interest to Douglas, but not what he owed Martinez). Hoskins replied that he wasn't authorized to accept such an offer, or demand payment from him, "nor did I think any person in the Ship" had such authority, he noted. Hoskins clearly feared that the transaction would play further into Gray's hands.

At this point, Kendrick was on his own with the *Washington*. Until he received orders dismissing him, he would continue working on the outpost and the exclusive trade he was setting in place. With deeds in hand for a thousand square miles of the coast, and with future trade locked in, Kendrick wanted to establish himself more firmly in the Sandwich Islands. He would resolve matters with Joseph Barrell later.

After breakfast, Kendrick helped tow the *Columbia* to a cove that would be her winter quarters at Clayoquot. Gray and Hoskins borrowed from Kendrick's strategy on the *Columbia*'s first voyage and sought to be the first on the coast next season and to build a small sloop that Haswell would command on trading cruises.

Out of sympathy for Hoskins, Kendrick gave him a canoe as a parting gift. The young clerk, who had lost his father when he was a boy, perhaps regarded Kendrick as a father figure. In contrast to his disdain for Gray, Hoskins wrote that "during the continuance of our two vessels in port Captain Kendrick has offered and afforded us every assistance and also treated us with the most marked politeness particularly myself who am indebted for many tokens of friendship."

This time it was the *Washington* sailing from Clayoquot and leaving the *Columbia* behind. It would soon become obvious that Gray did not have the diplomatic skills to maintain good relations with Wickaninish and his people. In an incident over a coat, Gray took one of the chiefs, Wickaninish's older brother, Tootiscosettle, as a hostage and threatened to kill him. Later, Gray once again took a hostage and made threats after his Hawaiian servant, Atoo, deserted him and went into hiding with the tribe.

Native animosity toward Gray and the *Columbia* would grow. Before the end of winter, Gray discovered what he believed was a conspiracy to attack their ship and camp. In bitter retaliation, as the *Columbia* was preparing to leave the sound on March 27, 1792, Gray decided to cannonade the main summer village of Opitsat to which most inhabitants had not yet returned. One young officer, John Boit, would write:

> *I am sorry to be under the nessescity of remarking that this day I was sent with three boats, all well man'd and arm'd, to destroy the Village of Opitsatah it was a Command I was no ways tena-*

cious off, and am grieved to think Capt. Gray shou'd let his passions go so far. This Village was about half a mile in Diameter, and Contained upwards of 200 Houses, generally well built for Indians ev'ry door that you enter'd was in resemblance to an human and Beasts head, the passage being through the mouth, besides which there was more rude carved work about the dwellings some of which was by no means innelegant. This fine Village, the Work of Ages, was in a short time totally destroy'd.

Worn down by a long winter of intrigue, Hoskins wrote nothing of the destruction, and lamented only that the *Columbia*'s opportunity for "any future intercourse" here was limited.

KENDRICK, IN THE MEANTIME, made his way to the Sandwich Islands. After leaving Clayoquot on September 29 the *Washington* arrived at Hawaii about the third week of October, at the start of the *makahiki* period of peace. During the summer, talk had circulated among the trading vessels about violence and attempts to take ships in the islands. Since the spring of 1790, warfare and treachery had been nearly incessant.

Ingraham said that in May he had evaded a scheme by Kaiana to take the *Hope* at Hawaii. The small sloop and her crew of sixteen made a likely target. At Molokai, Ingraham had found Kendrick's carpenter, Isaac Ridler, who described the taking of the *Fair American* fourteen months earlier. The story sent anxiety among Ingraham's crew soaring. In fear of attack, the *Hope* fired on Kahekili as he approached with thirty canoes containing two hundred fifty warriors. Ingraham then fled to Oahu.

The *Hancock*'s captain, Samuel Crowell, told of how he stopped first at Hawaii on his voyage from Boston. He traded for furs, which, as it turned out, had been taken off the *Fair American*. When Crowell went ashore, Kaiana revealed to him "that it was his people's wish that he should kill them and seize their vessel." The sometimes duplicitous chief assured Crowell that he "would not take any advantage of people who trusted themselves within his territories." Kaiana told Crowell that he had satisfied his warriors by telling them "to wait til the morrow noon when they had his liberty to attack." He advised Crowell to leave the island as soon as possible. The *Hancock* sailed that night.

In August, the captain of the British trader *Mercury* also had a close call. At Oahu, a number of the island's most beautiful women had been brought on board by the chiefs. In the evening they lulled most of the crew and officers into a stupor. Then, while they slept, the ship's anchor cable was cut. There was immediate danger that they would be swept ashore or onto a reef. When the watch raised an alarm, "every girl on the ship clung fast to her man in a very loving manner," to stop them from getting on deck. The captain ended up shelling the village of Waikiki in a futile attempt to have the anchor returned.

The zeal to take ships and their weapons had much to do with the inter-island war.

Coming into the harbor at Kealakekua, Kendrick saw the aftermath of all the warring. More women were in mourning with their front teeth knocked out. They paddled out to the *Washington,* offering fruit, hogs, and taro, as well as themselves. Kaiana arrived and told Kendrick that Kahekili and his brother Kaeokulani had shown up on the north coast of Hawaii with a fleet of seven hundred canoes, including a double canoe armed with a cannon and foreign gunners. They were seeking revenge for Kamehameha's invasion and slaughter at the Iao River a year earlier. Kamehameha met them with his own fleet of double-hulled canoes, foreign gunners, and the *Fair American*. In a long battle off Waipio, near a lush sacred area on Hawaii's northwestern coast, the two forces clashed. People watching from shore saw the red flashes of the cannons and called it Kepuwahaulaula, which meant "Battle of the Red-Mouthed Gun." The fighting left uncountable dead. Kahekili was driven off and retreated to Maui, where he prepared for a counterattack.

Knowing he could not fight on two fronts at once, Kamehameha requested that his Hawaiian adversary, Keoua, come from his realm in the northern part of the island and make peace at a new temple Kamehameha had built. Despite suspicion about the invitation, Keoua arrived with his retinue and warriors. As he climbed from his canoe onto the beach at Kawaihae, a spear was thrown at him. In the ensuing struggle, Keoua and several of his men were killed before Kamehameha put a stop to the fight. It was a major event. Through this treachery, Kamehameha was at last king of all of Hawaii, the first step toward his proclaimed destiny to rule over all the islands.

Kaiana told Kendrick that Kamehameha was not at Kealakekua, but in the north at Hilo, organizing his government and subchiefs in the lands that had fallen to him from Keoua. Kaiana said he was left as the district chief in his stead.

Kendrick gave the usual gift of a few muskets, but he decided not to linger. If men were to be safely settled at a trading base for sandalwood and pearls, he would have to place them beyond the reach of the current turmoil. Much to Kaiana's disappointment, the *Washington* sailed from Kealakekua after only a few days.

By October 27, Kendrick was at Kauai, at the far end of the main islands from Hawaii. Keaokulani (Keao), who ruled there, was at Maui with Kahekili preparing defenses to stop Kamehameha's expected invasion. In Keao's place, Inamoo, an old chief whom Kendrick had met at Niihau two years earlier, was serving as the regent of the island and as teacher for Kaeo's twelve year-old son, Kaumaulii. The large mountain at the center of the island contained sandalwood, and with Inamoo's approval, Kendrick left three men across the channel at Niihau: his first mate, the Welshman John Williams; a young English sailor, John Rowbottom; and a feisty young Irishman, James Coleman. For eight dollars a month and a share in the profits, they were to trade for pearls and prepare cargoes of sandalwood. It was another modest beginning, but Kendrick told his men he believed that as many as twenty American ships could eventually trade between the coast and Hawaii and China. He was thinking of returning to Boston to resolve matters with Joseph Barrell and gain support for the ships.

There was an urgency building to secure the islands for American trade and passage to the East. From the Spanish at Nootka, Kendrick knew that British officials were coming to make claims on the American coast. And Douglas would certainly have shared the plans of Meares's London company. It was only a matter of time before the British reached for this gem in the North Pacific as well, and with their arrival, it was reasonable to fear they would attempt to close all these ports to Americans, as they had done in the Atlantic.

As on the Northwest Coast, Kendrick strengthened his alliances and armed native people. The conflict with Britain was closer than he might have imagined.

Part IV

Edge of Empire

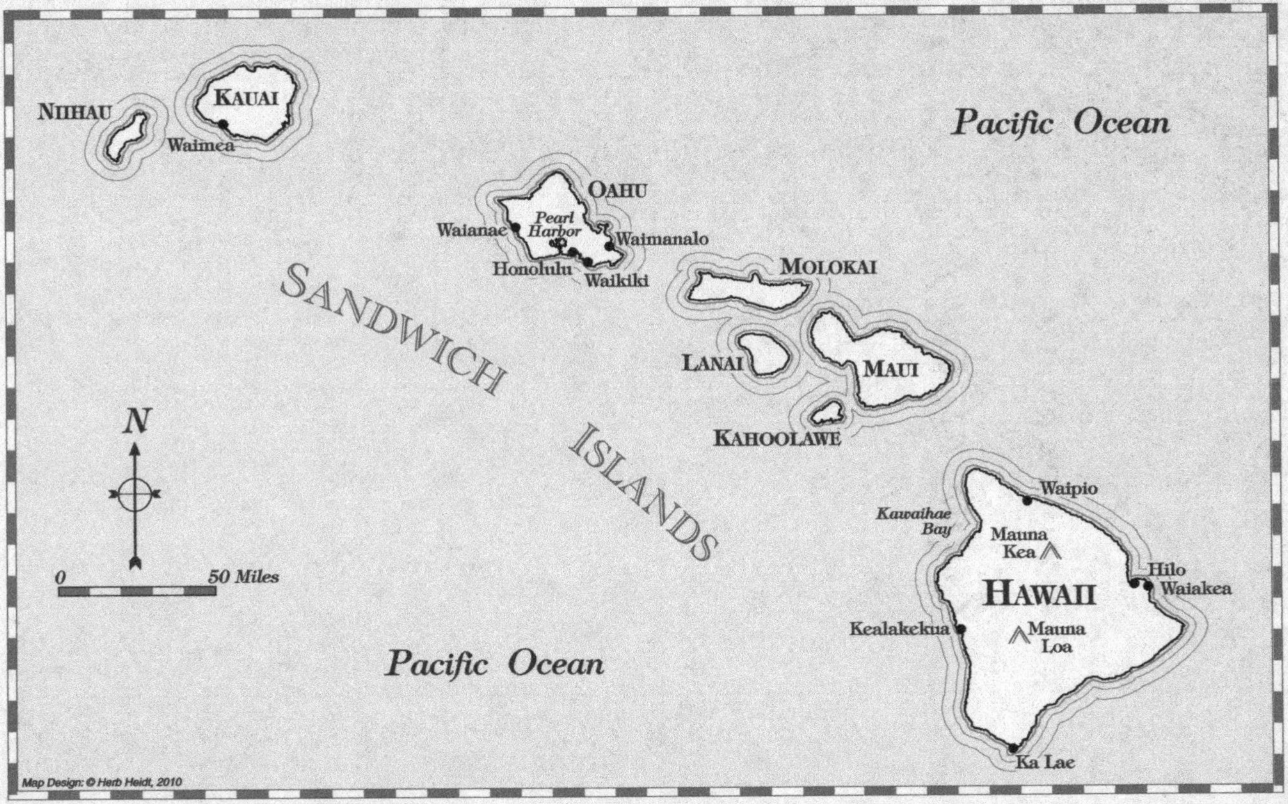
NIIHAU
KAUAI
Waimea
Pacific Ocean
OAHU
Pearl Harbor
Waianae
Waimanalo
Honolulu
Waikiki
MOLOKAI
SANDWICH ISLANDS
LANAI
MAUI
KAHOOLAWE
N
0
50 Miles
Waipio
Kawaihae Bay
Mauna Kea
HAWAII
Hilo
Waiakea
Kealakekua
Mauna Loa
Pacific Ocean
Ka Lae
Map Design: © Herb Heidt, 2010

CHAPTER SIXTEEN

A Soft War

Sandwich Islands, Northwest Coast

MARCH–SEPTEMBER 1792

AT DAYLIGHT ON MARCH 1, 1792, George Vancouver sighted the island of Hawaii lying in a haze twenty-four leagues off. As the *Discovery* and *Chatham* drew closer, the island arose with a familiar profile. From the southeast point, which appeared as a small hummock, the land increased with a gradual incline to the summit of Mauna Loa, which seemed to occupy the center of the island. Vancouver recalled being there fourteen years earlier as a junior officer. His memories included being roughed up on the beach at Kealakekua in the scuffle with natives that preceded Cook's death. As with others who had been present through those tumultuous final days, it was an event by which he marked his life.

The appearance of the two Royal Navy ships signaled the official return of the British Empire and for Vancouver an opportunity to finish Cook's work. No royal expedition had been launched into the North Pacific after Cook. Britain's sweep to the East following the American Revolution had focused first on the South Pacific and Australia. The hard

George Vancouver, a controversial figure in history, endeavored to establish Britain's hold on the North Pacific and the pathway between the Americas and the East.

lesson London had learned from defeat in the American colonies was that it would be impossible to occupy and hold each new land with military power. Britain's policy now targeted resource exploitation and development of new markets under pliable local leaders rather than systematic planting of colonies. Forts and ports would be sited only where necessary in a strategy designed to head off the Spanish and the Americans.

At the height of the Nootka crisis, John Etches had written a pamphlet charging that the Spanish "have the keys of the whole Pacific, to the exclusive monopoly of an ocean and its numerous islands, which embrace in their extent almost one half the globe." Vancouver was sent to change that. Under the cover of a diplomatic and scientific mission, he was to wage a soft war to secure the North Pacific for Britain. Vancouver was to receive "restitution of the territories which the Spanish had seized" from John Meares. He was to search for the Northwest Passage, particularly inside the Strait of Juan de Fuca where the *Washington* was said to have passed. He was to map the region and make strategic claims along the stretch of coast north of San Francisco (the region of Francis Drake's ancient claim of "New Albion") into Alaska. And he was to regard the Sandwich Islands as a priority.

The first order in his instructions from the king was to proceed with "no loss of time" to the Sandwich Islands where he was to remain during the next winter, employing his ships "very diligently in the examination and survey of the said islands."

Situated at the crossroads of the North Pacific, the islands were viewed as essential to ruling these seas. John Etches's brother and partner, the merchant Richard Etches, had raised the vision of the Sandwich Islands as an emporium between Asia and the Americas. John Meares had pushed the concept further with his belief that a prosperous colony there could someday be the home of a half-million British subjects. Investigating harbors and potential plantation lands, Vancouver would attempt to fill in those visions with detailed maps, granting British names to landmarks as the first act of possession. His efforts would increasingly come up against John Kendrick, who was seeking to ensure that neither Britain nor Spain would dominate these islands and access to trade with the East. Over time, the two captains would become entangled in deadly competition for control of the islands.

VANCOUVER WAS TO RENDEZVOUS at the islands with the supply ship *Daedalus,* sent out a few months after his departure. When he left Falmouth on April 1, 1791, disputes were still raging over interpretation of the Nootka agreement with Spain. The instructions he carried were general and somewhat vague; more detailed orders on Spanish concessions were to be delivered by the *Daedalus.* During his eleven-month voyage he had sailed eastward around Africa's Cape of Good Hope, stopping at Australia, New Zealand, and Tahiti. As they approached Hawaii, Vancouver hoped the storeship would be waiting.

The *Discovery* and *Chatham* stayed close along the shore, eager for natives to come off with fresh fruit and vegetables. The ships cut a sharp image amid the rolling swells in the morning sun. Both ships were newly designed and built in 1788, specifically for Pacific exploration and survey work. *Discovery* was a 340-ton, ninety-nine-foot sloop-of-war carrying one hundred men and seventeen marines and armed with ten four-pound cannons and ten swivel guns. The *Chatham* was an eighty-foot, 135-ton brig carrying forty-five men and ten marines and armed with four three-pound cannons and six swivel guns.

Their approach stirred excitement onshore, and at noon on March 3, five miles from Kealakekua Bay, natives came paddling out in canoes laden with hogs and fruit. Among the officers aboard the *Chatham* was James Johnstone, who had served three years earlier on John Meares's ships. He recognized the tall, handsome chief Kaiana in one of the canoes, the strapping native whose name had become common currency in London through the Nootka Crisis.

Kaiana surprised Vancouver by speaking no English. After gifts were exchanged on board, he related through a translator what had transpired after Cook's ships had left. To Vancouver, it must have sounded like a classic Elizabethan drama, a dynastic melee in which family members were embroiled in turmoil over power and conflicting predictions of destiny. Kaiana told him that after the death of the old chief, Kalaniopuu, there had been a series of battles. The chief's nephew, Kamehameha, now ruled the three northern districts: Hilo, Puna, and Ka'u. The headstrong Kaiana said he ruled the three southern districts of Hawaii: Kona, Hamakua, and Kohala, falsely implying that he was a chief equal in power to Kamehameha.

As the ships stood outside Kealakekua, the natives pointed to the spot where James Cook had been killed while trying to abduct Kalaniopuu. The sight may have unsettled Vancouver. There was no news of the *Daedalus,* although Kaiana said that four American brigs had passed through in the autumn. The *Lady Washington* had been the last, in October. Vancouver asked about chiefs he recalled, and was dismayed to learn that most of them except Kamehameha had been killed in battle. Although wars for control of the islands had occurred before Cook's arrival, Vancouver blamed the current slaughter on the "unwarrantable desires" raised by European and American traders who sold firearms. He was alarmed at the number of cannon, pistols, and muskets he saw in native hands and noted that warriors "have become very familiar [with muskets], and use these weapons with an adroitness that would not disgrace the generality of European soldiers."

Archibald Menzies, the expedition's surgeon and naturalist, observed that there had been a recent invasion from Maui (the "Battle of the Red-Mouthed Gun"), and the attentions of Kaiana and his followers "were wholly directed to warlike preparations, for nothing was now held in greater estimation or more eagerly sought after than fire arms and powder." Kaiana wanted to trade food for weapons, but Vancouver declined. Although he attributed his decision to humanitarian considerations, such trading would have violated naval policy, as well as his instructions. He also feared being overwhelmed. Vancouver knew that when Portlock and Dixon were at Kealakekua in 1786, they had to fire their cannons and muskets to clear natives off the rigging and from around their ships in order to depart. Now those same natives had muskets and small cannons of their own.

In light of the danger he perceived, Vancouver decided to leave the harbor before nightfall and to go to Oahu for news of the *Daedalus*. Kaiana warned him that Kahekili and his brother Kaeo, "with most of the chiefs of Kauai and Niihau, were at this time on a warlike expedition at Maui."

Four days later, the intrigue deepened. Vancouver bypassed Maui, and at Oahu learned that Kahekili had most of his men and firearms amassed at Maui because they expected a retaliatory invasion from Kamehameha and Kaiana. The absence of warriors on Oahu briefly restored Vancouver's sense of superiority and comfort. He anchored near the village of Waikiki and noted a welcome subservience in his reception. "The apparent docility of these people, who have been represented by former visitors as the most daring and unmanageable of any who belong to the Sandwich islands, might, probably, be attributed in a great measure to the absence of their fighting men [at Maui], and to our manifest superiority in numbers, regularity in point of order, and military government; which seemed to make a wonderful impression on all who were permitted to come on board, and who, to a man, appeared very much afraid of fire-arms."

He soon learned that there were Englishmen living at Kauai and sailed for that island looking for news of his storeship. On March 9, he arrived in the harbor where James Cook had first landed and encountered priests and commoners falling at his feet. There was no storeship waiting, and the fearful welcome Vancouver expected did not materialize. Instead he was struck by the spectacle of widespread sexual advances. Apparently, he forgot the rampant activity during Cook's stay at Hawaii. He found himself repulsed by the lewd offers and was thoroughly disgusted by the "avidity with which the men here assisted in the prostitution of the women; and the readiness of the whole sex, without any exception, to surrender their persons without the least importunity . . . no indecency that ever came under my observation, could be compared with the excessive wantonness presented." He believed this behavior "a perfectly new acquirement, taught, perhaps, by the different civilized voluptuaries, who, for some years past, have been their constant visitors." The main protagonists he believed were men serving under the American flag.

The day after their arrival, a tanned and partially clothed seaman about seventeen years old appeared in a double-hulled canoe. He came on board and greeted Vancouver, giving his name as John Rowbottom. He said "he was of Derbyshire, that he had sailed from England about five years since in an Indiaman to China, which ship he had quitted in order to engage with some of the vessels in the fur trade between North-West America and China; and that he had, ever since, been thus employed in the American service." Rowbottom said he had been left with two other men by John Kendrick of the brig *Lady Washington* to collect sandalwood and pearls. Kendrick, he said, was bound to New England, with a cargo of furs to dispose of first at Macao. The American captain was to return from his voyage to Boston and, having spent next winter on the Northwest Coast, would arrive in the islands in the autumn of 1793 to pick up the men and the cargo of sandalwood and pearls.

Embarrassed by the young man's nakedness and native-like appearance, Vancouver ordered clothes for him from the slop chest. Rowbottom had brought with him two chiefs he said could be helpful to Vancouver at Kauai and nearby Niihau. He also told Vancouver that in two days, the regent Inamoo and the young prince of the island, Kaumaulii, would arrive. Vancouver offered to take Rowbottom off the island. The sailor declined, saying that although they had been very ill treated by the natives for some time after they landed and almost starved, they now lived with Kaumaulii in a pleasant situation.

Vancouver knew John Meares had charged that Kendrick was the architect of the Spanish seizure of Colnett's ships. Now he was even more concerned after finding out that the Boston commander was a leading foreign trader who was gaining influence among the chiefs.

Rowbottom told Vancouver of the massacre of the *Fair American*'s crew, which had now become part of the lore of the islands' danger and treachery. He assured him that his well-armed ships should have no trouble. However, the next morning (Sunday, March 11) one of the chiefs, Nomateehetee, presented Vancouver with a paper containing recommendations from various captains. The first was from James Colnett, dated April 1791, which praised Nomateehetee to future visitors. Other notes from Joseph Ingraham of the *Hope,* and one from John Kendrick dated October 27, 1791, urged great caution in dealing with this islander, a warning the chief was unaware of. Vancouver craftily told him that "the paper spoke much in his praise and favor" and told him to show it to every ship that arrived.

Another one of the men left by Kendrick appeared later that morning. Vancouver was completely shocked at the sight of James Coleman, who was dressed in only a native *malo,* "which he wore with much less decency than the generality of the inhabitants." Except for the *malo,* Vancover noted, "he was perfectly naked, and the color of his skin was little whiter than the fairest of these people." Most aggravating to Vancouver, Coleman was "tattooed with a broad badge over his left shoulder meeting low down on his left side." This was similar to the marking of Kahekili's warriors. Coleman saw himself as the emissary of the young prince, and showed no deference to the British commander. Speaking with a light brogue, he delivered a message from Kaumaulii saying that the prince was on his way and would arrive the following day.

Vancouver took an immediate dislike to the young sailor and his cockiness. Rowbottom had said that Coleman was from Ireland, but when questioned by Vancouver, he insisted he was an American born in New York. "I asked him what he had done with his former clothes; to which he answered with a sneer, that they were 'hanging up in a house for the admiration of the natives'; and seemed greatly to exult in having degenerated into a savage way of life."

Coleman said the young prince wanted to know how long Vancouver intended to stay and whether his intentions were peaceable. Vancouver sent a piece of scarlet cloth as a present for the prince and said to tell him they were just taking on water and would depart as soon as that task was completed, but he would like to meet the prince and Inamoo.

Going ashore in the afternoon, Vancouver took a walk into the countryside and noted that the grassy hills to the east were on fire from a considerable height. Suspecting that the fire might be a signal to collect distant inhabitants for an attack, he ordered twenty armed men camped onshore to stay ready. According to Archibald Menzies, Vancouver made menacing threats to the natives, who promptly fled the expedition's camp. Then, as he was returning to the ship in a native canoe, Vancouver almost drowned when it overturned in the surf. Weighed down with sodden clothing, he had to swim for his life to the ship. After recovering in his cabin, he sent two armed launches to wait offshore as he worried through the night, but no attack came.

The next morning, March 12, the fire was still burning in places among broad blackened swaths on the hills. At noon, another of the *Lady Washington*'s men, John Williams, a Welshman who had been Kendrick's first mate, arrived to say that the prince was delayed and would not make an appearance until the following day. When the party finally did arrive, Inamoo came out to the ship first. He recognized Menzies, who had been there aboard the *Prince of Wales* under James Colnett a few years earlier. Relations relaxed somewhat with an exchange of presents and hogs and vegetables. Inamoo wanted to trade for muskets and pistols and powder, but Vancouver told him there was a taboo on the sale of any arms from the ship. After some consternation, the old man acquiesced.

It was a fragile atmosphere and there was obvious mistrust on both sides. Following Vancouver's delivery of two of his officers as hostages onshore, the young prince, who appeared to be eleven or twelve years old, came out in a boat, attended by thirty armed warriors, who carried swordlike iron *pahooas* and muskets wrapped in three bundles. Kaumaulii conversed politely with Vancouver through Rowbottom and Williams. The British captain was highly impressed with the young prince. Vancouver bestowed the name "George" on him in honor of the king, and imagined that he might greatly assist British merchants in the future. Wanting to thoroughly impress Kaumaulii, that night Vancouver set off a display of rockets and fireworks. Two miles offshore they could hear exclamations of "infinite surprise and admiration" from hundreds of people lining the beach.

Because he did not find the amount of supplies he had hoped for at Kauai, Vancouver sailed for Niihau at 3 A.M. on March 14. He left a letter behind for the *Daedalus* and in his journal lamented the impact that incessant war was having on the islands. The decimation of the population seemed appalling. At the time of Cook's arrival, there were thought to be three hundred thousand people in the islands. He guessed the number might now be fifty thousand. In addition to the many chiefs from Hawaii who had been killed, he noted that on Oahu, the houses at Waikiki were numerous, but many appeared to have been entirely abandoned. At Kauai, the village of Waimea was "reduced by at least two-thirds of its size since the years 1778 and 1779." There were now only grass and weeds where houses had once been numerous. The spread of venereal and other disease brought to the islands added to the impacts of warfare. Vancouver knew of the culpability of Cook's ships but blamed the traders.

His particular enmity for Kendrick emerged as he wrote, "I shall take leave of the Sandwich islands by stating the advantages which the Americans promise themselves by the commercial interests they are endeavoring to establish in these seas." John Williams had told him that Kendrick believed he could gather twenty vessels from New England for the sandalwood and fur trade to China. Vancouver mocked him, saying: "Mr. Kendrick must, undoubtedly, flatter himself" with the expectation of great profits. He doubted the quality of both the sandalwood and the pearls, and denigrated what he believed was an ill-considered and ill-prepared venture.

Under orders to sail to the Northwest Coast by March, Vancouver left Niihau on March 17, two weeks after he arrived in the islands. He had neither the time nor comfort yet to fulfill his orders to carefully survey the islands' shores and harbors. Amid the volatile warring chiefs and the encroaching Americans, he pondered how he might be able to gain these islands for Britain upon his return.

WHILE VANCOUVER WAS at the Sandwich Islands, John Kendrick lay anchored in Dirty Butter Bay. He had arrived at Macao on December 7, 1791, about five weeks from Niihau. At the smuggler's haven he found a small American flotilla gathered: Ingraham with the *Hope,* Crowell in the *Hancock,* and Coolidge with the *Grace,* and they were joined by the *Fairy* a few days later. The blustery and generous Scotsman William Douglas, who seems to have been chronically ill, died on the passage from the Sandwich Islands. Ingraham noted that Douglas had gained great profits on his voyage in 1790 when very few ships were on the coast, but that the unsettled nature of his partnerships, profits, and debts would most likely benefit only agents and opportunist merchants. Ingraham observed: "This is generally the case with the effects of any man who dies in this part of the world, for unless he has some extraordinary friend at hand most of his property will be infallibly sacrificed."

American shipmasters kept making black market payments to remain unhampered at Dirty Butter Bay. They avoided local officials and circumvented the fur embargo, selling sea otter pelts at the isolated harbor or having them smuggled upriver to Whampoa. Prices were much lower than expected: fifteen to twenty-five dollars for a prime fur. Ingraham received a price of twenty-five dollars each for a small shipment of one hundred furs. Kendrick sold one thousand furs for "twenty-one thousand Spanish head dollars."

FROM THE CIRCLE OF COMPATRIOT FUR TRADERS, Kendrick apparently heard the full story of Gray and Haswell's denunciation of him in Boston. Kendrick was no longer confused about why Gray had taken command of the *Columbia*. If Kendrick had planned to sail for New England to resolve things with Joseph Barrell and to bring back a number of ships (as Rowbottom and Williams told Vancouver), that plan was now utterly impossible. With Kendrick's reputation destroyed, he would have to acquire or build a second ship in Macao. After paying his crew and most of his debts, he began work on a small schooner to function as a tender to the *Washington*.

KENDRICK ALSO RESPONDED to the charges made against him. Eighteen months after Gray's allegations, on March 28, 1792, Kendrick wrote to Joseph Barrell from Macao: "I am confident you have been told many untruths respecting the voyage, and matters have been represented in a wrong light, neither have you had true accounts rendered into you . . ." Kendrick urged Barrell to look into the matter to verify what he was saying and promised that "you may depend on my honor and integrity . . . and further you may rely on my rendering you a proper statement of my affairs and transactions." He had acted on Barrell's instructions to proceed with his own determinations and confirmed he was "firm and steady to my first agreement, and am, content to stay and prosecute the voyage or voyages to the end . . ."

With information from Ingraham, he alleged that Gray had cheated the owners by trading on his own account on the *Columbia*'s first voyage. "I can prove that the Furs which were on board the Columbia, when she arrived at Canton was sold by Messrs. Shaw & Randle for twenty-six thousand dollars and upwards, and might have sold for much more." He wrote that "the officers even encouraged the people to follow their examples [trading on their own accounts], they have not only made their boasts, and told of it themselves."

He also described the debt the *Washington* had fallen into the previous year, and offered a generalized, ham-handed, and dismal account of his transactions that was riddled with guilt. He admitted his embarrassment, and that he had held off writing until his situation improved. He told Barrell, "I wish to convince you I have strove the utmost in my power for the benefit and interest of the concerned . . ." In what must have been a pleasant surprise to Barrell, he revealed, "In my last Voyage, I purchased of the natives five tracts of land and copies of the deeds which was signed shall be sent to you the first opportunity."

He proposed that he "continue in the employ as usual or I will take the Brig on my own account from the 16th of April 1790 and abide by all losses and gains from that date; for which I will allow you the sum of fourteen thousand dollars with an interest of 12 percent from that date until payment is made . . ." He still held out hope that his old friend would reinstate him as commander and proposed to retake the *Columbia* from Gray: "In case I am continued in the employ (as Captain and Super Cargo) and am to proceed as usual, according to our first agreement when I left Boston, I shall consider the Columbia as consigned to me, and shall expect a commission on the sales, and purchases of her cargoes of this her second voyage to the North West Coast of America."

Kendrick believed he was making a good offer, but there was little that Barrell and his partners could do. An exchange of letters would take six months each way. Whatever course they chose would have to wait another year or more before being settled. "I am now fitting out the Brig for another voyage to the North West Coast, where it is my intention to winter," Kendrick concluded, "consequently shall not be in China again until the month of November 1793." By then, he hoped the trading relationships he had in place on the Northwest Coast and in the Sandwich Islands would deliver a prosperous windfall similar to what Douglas received, or at least enough profit to bring him back to breakeven.

Kendrick entrusted the letter to young Ebenezer Dorr, who had come out with Ingraham in the *Hope* and was now Boston-bound on the *Fairy*. Robert Davis Coolidge was returning homeward too, as was the furrier Jonathan Treat. Not long after they left, plans began to change. Kendrick once again fell ill during the cold rains and dampness of the Macao winter. Ingraham told Hoskins that when he departed Macao on April 1, Kendrick was near death.

WHILE KENDRICK LAY MORTALLY ILL at Dirty Butter Bay, George Vancouver was reaching the coast of America. It was April 1792. He stalled for time as he awaited his detailed instructions on the *Daedalus*, and did not sail to Nootka but instead went directly to the coastline along present-day Oregon. There in the region of "New Albion" Vancouver began his survey and mapping, using sketches of the shoreline and logs from Meares, Barkley, and other traders, as well as information gleaned from Spanish maps. Heavy surf broke all along the coast on the trip northward, and on April 27 his ships passed an opening in the shoreline with large waves breaking in shoalwater. The naturalist Archibald Menzies noted that the muddy discoloration of the ocean indicated a sizable river. However, Meares had explored and dismissed this area, and so did Vancouver. "Not considering this opening worthy of more attention, I continued our pursuit to the N.W., being desirous to embrace the advantages of the now prevailing breeze and pleasant weather . . ." This was the entrance of "Rio de San Roque," named by Bruno Hezeta in 1774 but considered fictional by Meares and others. Ignoring the entrance of what would become known as the Columbia River, Vancouver lost a major discovery, but his attention was elsewhere. Maps that Meares and others had published showed the river Oregon—the mythical "river of the west"—entering into a sound (present-day Puget Sound) at the southeastern end of the Strait of Juan de Fuca.

Continuing along the coast, he approached the entrance of the strait with great excitement. His instructions were to explore the strait, duplicating the *Lady Washington*'s track around the island described by Meares. If he located any passage to the east, Vancouver was to purchase land and establish an outpost and fort capable of withstanding an attack by Indians, Americans, or other foreign powers. The primary aim was to gain control of "those parts which lie at the back of Canada and Hudson's Bay, as well as the navigation by such lakes as are already known [Lake of the Woods] or may hereafter be discovered."

On Saturday, April 28, offshore from the cliffs and stony beaches near the mouth of the strait, Vancouver noted that the East India Company hydrographer Alexander Dalrymple had passed along an allegation "that the Spaniards have recently found an entrance in the latitude of 47 degrees 45 minutes North, which in twenty-seven days course brought them to the vicinity of Hudson's Bay; this latitude exactly corresponds to the ancient relation of Juan de Fuca, the Greek pilot, in 1592." Vancouver excitedly noted, "This inlet could be now only ten miles from us."

The next morning at 4 A.M., "a sail was discovered to the westward standing in shore. This was a very great novelty, not having seen any vessel but our consort, during the last eight months." The ship hoisted American colors. To Vancouver's astonishment she turned out to be the *Columbia,* captained by Robert Gray, the very man he believed to have been in command of the *Lady Washington* in the fall of 1789 when the ship made her cruise up the inland sea. He saw it as an incredibly propitious event and dispatched two officers—Menzies and Peter Puget—who were on board the American vessel by 7 A.M.

Gray was surprised and perplexed by their questions about his circumnavigation of the island. He told the men that he had penetrated the strait only fifty miles, though he understood from the natives that the opening extended a considerable distance northward. He also said he had entered another entrance far to the north of Nootka—the Straits of Admiral de Fonte—and sailed more than a hundred miles to 56° north latitude without discovering a termination. Gray shared his charts, and John Boit, one of Gray's junior officers, noted that "we gave them all the information in our power, especially as respected the Straits of Juan de Fuca, which place they was in search of."

Along with this news, Menzies and Puget came back with information that Gray had just been off a river to the south at 46°10' north latitude where the current was so strong it prevented his entering despite repeated attempts over nine days. Vancouver dismissed this as the entrance they had passed on April 27, and believed that if a river were to be found there, it "must be a very intricate one, and inaccessible to vessels of our burthen, owing to the reefs and broken water."

If Gray mentioned that John Kendrick had been in command of the *Washington* in the fall when the circumnavigation through the inland sea supposedly took place, Vancouver made no note of it. He was elated that Gray denied circumnavigating the island and at the prospect that no one had sailed the inland sea. Vancouver immediately took his ships up the Strait of Juan de Fuca, finding an uninterrupted horizon to the east. On April 30, he noted, "We had now advanced further up this inlet than Mr. Gray, or (to our knowledge) any other person from the civilized world." Eager to achieve something of note, the young British commander entered a labyrinth where he had a dramatic surprise coming.

During the next month he explored eastward into the area where Meares's maps showed the Oregon River and entered a series of channels running southward. He found no river, but on June 4, the anniversary of King George's birthday, he declared that he had "long since designed to take formal possession of all the countries we had lately been employed in exploring." He went ashore at what he christened "Possession Sound" (near present-day Everett, Washington) and, discharging a royal salute from the vessels, "took possession accordingly of the coast, from that part of New Albion, in the latitude of 39 degrees 26 minutes North, and longitude 236 degrees 26 minutes East, to the entrance of this inlet to the sea, said to be the supposed Straits of Juan de Fuca, as likewise all the coast, islands, & c. within said straits, as well as on the northern and southern shores; together with those situated in the interior sea we had discovered extended from said straits in various directions . . . which interior sea I have honored with the name 'The Gulph of Georgia,' in honor of His present Majesty."

Vancouver's intent was clear, but the ceremony stood in stark contradiction to Britain's assertions to Spain during the Nootka Crisis that symbolic acts carried out on a tract of land did not constitute a valid claim, and possession was only acceptable if land were occupied and improved. Ironically, a few days earlier a Spanish ship had performed an overlapping act of possession at Neah Bay, just inside the strait's entrance, where her men were about to build the first European fort in the strait. The new fort marked only part of Spain's expanding presence.

On the morning of June 22, near the Fraser River, well north on the inland sea, Vancouver's launch, which was ahead of the ships, approached the shore to have breakfast. Vancouver noted that not far off "we discovered two vessels at anchor under the land." He thought at first they were his own ships that had come up during the night, but as they drew closer, he discovered they were Spanish vessels of war—the *Sutil* and the *Mexicana*. The commander of the *Sutil,* Dionisio Galiano, spoke a little English and told Vancouver they had left Nootka two weeks before on June 5. They were continuing the survey of the previous two years and had already mapped an area four leagues beyond this point.

Vancouver's notion of being the first European commander in these waters was shattered. Although one British Columbia historian characterized the meeting as the symbolic beginning of the decline of the Spanish Empire and the rise of Britain, it was anything but that at the time. Vancouver wrote in frank humility: "I cannot avoid acknowledging that, on this occasion, I experienced no small degree of mortification in finding the external shore of the gulf had been visited, and already examined a few miles beyond where my researches . . . had extended." In fact, many of the channels and bays he thought he was naming for the first time had already been given Spanish names.

Galiano might well have wondered what Vancouver was doing there. The Spanish pilot told Vancouver that "Senior Quadra, the commandant in chief of the Spanish marine at Saint Blas and at California, was, with three frigates and a brig, waiting my arrival at Nootka in order to negotiate the restoration of those territories to the crown of Great Britain."

Quadra had arrived at Nootka in April, the month prearranged by the British and Spanish courts to carry out the terms of the Nootka Convention. However, it made little difference to Vancouver that Quadra had been waiting six weeks. Given the Spanish presence there, and the fact that they were ahead of him in this exploration, it was urgent for Vancouver to press ahead to find something of value in the labyrinth that he could claim.

Recognizing that Galiano and Valdes possessed invaluable charts from excursions into the strait in 1790 and 1791, Vancouver proposed that they collaborate on the immense task of surveying and mapping. The two Spanish officers were reluctant to work with Vancouver's men, but their general instructions were to cooperate with the British. For three weeks, the combined group worked its way northward. They were not proceeding blindly. There were villages along the shore, and Vancouver noted that Valdes "spoke the Indian language very fluently and understood from the natives that this inlet *did* communicate with the ocean to the northward, where they had seen ships." The native men there had many muskets, and offered sea otter skins for powder. Vancouver found that they were ruled by Maquinna.

On July 13, Vancouver's boats discovered a channel northward that was said to run to the sea. It is not clear what Vancouver told Galiano and Valdes about this. On July 17, the British parted with the Spanish ships and followed officer James Johnstone through the narrow channels of what became known as Discovery Passage and the Johnstone Strait. Thomas Manby, master's mate of the *Chatham*, noted that they came upon a large village, where the natives had muskets, "pistols and cutlasses which an American vessel belonging to Boston had supplied them with in barter." After probing the mainland shore and a series of islands, they entered Queen Charlotte Sound on August 10. Vancouver became the first European captain to document a journey through the inland passage. He made his way to open ocean and headed south, four months late for his meeting with Quadra.

VANCOUVER FIRED A THIRTEEN-GUN SALUTE when he entered Nootka Sound on August 29. The guns from Fort San Miguel answered. Vancouver's spirits and expectations were high. Although he had found no Northwest Passage branching from the inland sea, he claimed that his expedition was the first to circumnavigate the immense island. In reality, the honor of the first circumnavigation fell to the *Sutil* and *Mexicana*. Vancouver had started from the mouth of the strait and had not completed the circuit; the Spanish ships had sailed from Nootka. Valdes and Galiano soon found their way through the channels and arrived in the sound three days after Vancouver. The haughty British captain ignored the fact of their achievement and was eager to get on with business. He had performed his act of possession for lands to the south, ranging from New Albion through the Strait of Juan de Fuca. Now he would try to combine those claims with Meares's reputed territories north of Juan de Fuca, thus opening the whole coast north of San Francisco to British subjects.

The *Daedalus* was waiting for Vancouver in Friendly Cove. She had come there after missing him at the Sandwich Islands and had been waiting since July 4. On board were the additional orders, which included a letter from Floridablanca dated May 12, 1791. The letter was addressed to "The governor or commander of the port at Saint Lawrence," instructing him to receive the bearer as Britain's emissary to carry out the terms of the Nootka Convention.

Juan Francisco de la Bodega y Quadra lined the shore with his troops and offered Vancouver a formal military welcome. Quadra was a career officer, fifteen years older than Vancouver, part native Peruvian, strikingly handsome, subtle, and socially adept. He presented a sophisticated contrast to Vancouver's blustery and wary demeanor. Not only was he the new commander at San Blas, but by the king's appointment, he was the leader of the Expedition of Limits, charged with setting the boundaries of Spain's empire in the Northwest. While he had waited for Vancouver to arrive, Quadra had developed a careful understanding of the situation and made additional improvements in Nootka's wilderness port.

The crude temporary military outpost started by Estevan Martinez was now a settlement of some fifteen or twenty buildings and extensive gardens. Native people casually came and went through the village, and a number of foreign vessels were in port. Using diplomatic skills lacking in previous Spanish commanders, Quadra had succeeded in repairing Martinez's breach with Maquinna and lured the Mowachaht chief back to his table. Edward Bell, the clerk of the *Chatham*, observed that Quadra was "too good a man," treating the Mowachaht "more like companions than people who should be taught subjection." Quadra had also reopened Nootka to foreign traders, and the harbor was busy that summer. While there had been only two British ships on the coast in 1790 and five in 1791, there were nine now cruising the coastal waters. There were also four ships sailing under Portuguese colors, and five Americans.

Despite Quadra's evenhandedness, a strong tension had arisen between American and British traders. William Brown of the British *Butterworth* expedition had arrived on the coast in July, and led an effort to oust the Americans from Nootka. He swore that when Vancouver's British warships arrived, the Americans would be forced to depart.

Brown was stinging from a skirmish at Clayoquot. A few weeks earlier, the natives there had refused to sell skins to him because they were saving them for John Kendrick. Brown became frustrated and sent his sailors to a Clayoquot village to rob the natives. According to Captain James Magee of the Boston trader *Margaret*, Brown's men actually cut several skins off natives' backs. Four men were killed before Wickaninish's musket-armed warriors turned out and forced the sailors to retreat, killing one and wounding several others. Captain

Magee fired a cannon to stop the fighting, and Brown accused him of firing on British vessels. Outside the sound, Brown took vengeance on Clayoquot men fishing from canoes. He hauled nine men on board, whipped them unmercifully, and threw them into the sea. The British trader *Jenny,* following the *Butterworth,* fired on them as they swam. According to a complaint Wickaninish made to Quadra, of the nine men missing, four were chiefs, and one of them his brother.

Magee told Vancouver that Brown should be charged with piracy for his attack at Clayoquot, and Brown complained of Magee and the Americans. Vancouver did nothing. He heard that Kendrick had traded the arms that were used to attack Brown's men to Wickaninish's people. A Spanish observer confirmed that Kendrick had "furnished Wickaninish with more than two hundred guns, two barrels of powder, and a considerable portion of shot, which [the Indians] have just finished using on the unhappy sailors of Captains Brown and Baker [of the *Jenny*]."

Vancouver and his officers feared the natives arming themselves here as they were doing at the Sandwich Islands. The *Chatham*'s clerk, Edward Bell, noted that Wickaninish could "turn out four hundred men arm'd with muskets and well found with ammunition . . . Their former weapons, Bows and Arrows, Spears and Clubs are now thrown aside and forgotten." At Nootka, Bell said, "it was the same way, everyone had his musket."

While Kendrick was regarded as foolish and short-sighted for trading weapons that could be turned on him and other captains, he was much more savvy than that. Kendrick had a stake in this region through his title to harbors and large tracts of land and the alliances he had built. He recognized that muskets were the only way to restrain the power of the Spanish and the British and allow the Mowachaht to protect themselves against hostile traders. His own risk was offset by the trust he had built. Just as Alexander McGillivray had successfully played British, American, and Spanish interests off against one

Friendly Cove, Nootka Sound *by H. Humphries. The Spanish settlement at Yuquot, which pushed out the Mowachat people, began to resemble a frontier village.*

another to secure land titles for the Creek nation, Kendrick could only hope that his strategy would work here as events became more volatile. Unlike McGillivray, he was not of mixed blood, and the trust he held could turn fragile.

In fact, the situation along the coast was becoming very charged. Skirmishes between traders and native people were far more frequent as more ships arrived on the coast and used violent trading tactics. After Robert Gray had destroyed Opitsat in March, he went on to kill several natives in a skirmish at Gray's Harbor in April, and then more at the north end of Vancouver Island in June, where after some difficulties, a shore party from the *Columbia* was attacked and the ship responded with cannon and musket fire. Other captains had similar skirmishes.

QUADRA DID LITTLE ABOUT THE COMPLAINTS he received concerning the simmering warfare. He tried to quell hostility between natives, traders, and the wary British with kindness and generosity. In Vancouver's case, it was a very successful seduction.

On the first evening after the arrival of the *Discovery* and *Chatham,* Quadra held a banquet upstairs in the rustic commandant's house. He treated Vancouver and his officers to wine and a five-course meal served on silver plates. As representatives of royal courts, Vancouver and Quadra had the task of executing the return of lands under the Nootka Convention of October 1790. Vancouver and his officers had expected that the handover of the building and extensive tracts owned by Meares would be a formality. The thorny difficulty, however, was determining what lands and buildings were to be restored, and exactly what area of the coast the British would have access to.

Quadra had undertaken fact-finding on the seizure of Colnett's ships from traders who had stopped at the cove. Robert Gray and Joseph Ingraham and others were invited to provide statements about events they had witnessed. By the time Vancouver sat down to dinner that evening, Quadra had a position supported by witnesses and documentation that would give the British commander nightmares.

Under the terms of the agreement, Vancouver expected to receive all of Nootka Sound and Clayoquot Sound, as well as other properties that Meares had claimed farther down the coast. Vancouver also asserted that under the terms of the agreement, Britain would have access to the entire coast north of San Francisco. Technically the line for British access was to fall north of Spain's northernmost settlement. Quadra determined that this northernmost point would be Nootka, not San Francisco.

In terms of Meares's land, Quadra directed Vancouver to the plot said to have been purchased from Maquinna. Meares's "house" no longer existed there when Martinez arrived at Nootka, Quadra explained, but he was prepared to offer the spot where the house reportedly stood.

Vancouver was astounded to realize that this plot of less than an acre was Quadra's offer. He later wrote that the location was in the northern corner of the small cove, "forming a nearly equilateral triangle not extending an hundred yards on a side, bounded in front by the sea, and on two sides by high craggy rocks." He was incredulous that this could possibly be considered "as the object of restitution expressed by the terms" of the agreement between their two nations.

Robert Duffin, who was on a merchant ship at Nootka and had sent the *Argonaut*'s letters to Meares at Macao, confirmed to Vancouver that when he returned to Friendly Cove in July 1789, Maquinna had not preserved Meares's building. On the spot where the crude house had stood "were the tents and houses of some of the people belonging to the *Columbia,* commanded by Mr. John Kendrick, under the flag and protection of the United States of America." That winter, Kendrick had burned up what was left of Meares's house as firewood.

Even more outrageous to Vancouver was that Quadra was willing to give command of the port and *use* of his buildings to Vancouver but was retaining the legal title for Spain. Quadra conducted a tour of the settlement to show Vancouver how things had been readied for him. Vancouver was beside himself. He couldn't accept the offer without Quadra yielding on the principle of ownership. He foresaw increasing problems if Britain did not have exclusive control of the entire sound. Considering the American ships on the coast and the growing hostility of the natives, he wrote, "this place would not long remain unoccupied by some one of the trading nations . . . [and] involving my Country in fresh disputes &ca., might be laid to my charge."

VANCOUVER INSISTED THAT there was a misunderstanding about what Meares had purchased from Maquinna. To dispel this idea, Quadra took Vancouver to visit Maquinna at his winter village, some twenty miles up the Tahsis Inlet. Maquinna told Vancouver that he had sold no land to John Meares, and called Meares an "*aita-aita*"—a liar. The only land he and other chiefs had sold was to Kendrick: the land around Nootka Sound, and that at Clayoquot.

At every turn, Vancouver seemed to find Kendrick frustrating British ambition: firearms traded at Hawaii and his men living with the Kauai chiefs, the *Lady Washington*'s alleged track in the Strait of Juan de Fuca that he had to follow, the arms at Clayoquot used against British traders, and after being sent halfway around the world, the harbors he was to receive were already under title in Kendrick's hands. According to Quadra and Maquinna, Britain had only a symbolic claim to the small patch of ground where Kendrick had burned the remains of Meares's house and flown the American flag.

The young British commander was uncertain how to proceed. On the way back from the visit to Tahsis, he proposed to Quadra that this immense island they were on be named "Quadra and Vancouver" Island to commemorate their negotiations. It was a subtle way to attach the British claim to the region. Quadra agreed to the offer, but he had come to believe that Nootka was a highly valuable port for the defense of California. Like Martinez he recognized that preventing British settlement would be easier than trying to eradicate outposts after they were established. He thought the way to drive foreign traders from the coast would be to infuse the region with Spanish fur traders who would offer prized abalone shells, copper, and cloth of Mexican manufacture. Quadra also began considering establishment of another Spanish settlement to the north in the Queen Charlotte Islands.

The amiable relationship Quadra had fostered with Vancouver was tested in a series of letters that passed between the *Discovery* and the commandant's house. There was no progress. Vancouver could not accept that the spot where Meares's building stood was what had been intended for restoration. "At the least," he noted, "the whole port of Nootka, of which his Majesty's subjects had been forcibly dispossessed, and at which themselves, their vessels and cargos had been captured, must have been the proposed object of restitution." He found it maddening that the best detail he had in his orders was Floridablanca's vaguely worded letter.

William Brown had brought Vancouver a dispatch from London that apparently directed Vancouver to turn over the Nootka settlement to the *Butterworth* expedition once it was in British hands. That did not appear possible now. Quadra had a much better understanding of the situation and plied his skills to politely crush the British claim. Vancouver feared he might be censured for his failure, and in a candid moment he confessed in his journal that his lack of success was due in part to "a want of sufficient diplomatic skill, which a life wholly devoted to my profession [aboard ship] had denied me the opportunity of acquiring."

Refusing to yield completely, Vancouver sent First Lieutenant Zachary Mudge on a long journey back to London and the Lords of the Admiralty. Mudge carried Vancouver's journal, surveys of the coast that had been completed (including all the work of Spanish surveyors that would be appropriated on British maps), and a letter requesting clarification of his instructions. Mudge sailed for Macao on a Portuguese trader on September 30. Vancouver also canceled plans to send the *Daedalus* to Botany Bay to pick up prisoners who were to populate a British settlement at Nootka.

There would be a long wait for any response. War had broken out in Europe. Just before Vancouver reached the American coast, France had declared war on Austria, on April 20, 1792. Prussia joined with Austria. France invaded Belgium and the Low Countries and planned to march on to Holland, similar to the strategy Gouverneur Morris had promoted two years earlier.

Like the American revolutionaries, the French Republicans wanted all harbors opened as free ports of trade. They proclaimed that all people who wanted to overthrow monarchy should rise up and join them. Carrying out this wild resolve, on the night of August 10, as Vancouver was emerging from his exploration through the "inland sea," French revolutionaries stormed the Tuileries, the royal palace on the Seine. King Louis and Marie Antoinette fled the palace and placed themselves under the protection of the Legislative Assembly. But the assembly suspended the monarchy, shocking all of Europe.

These seemingly remote events would come to undermine the positions of both Quadra and Vancouver, crumbling the edges of empire. For the fledgling United States it would have impacts from Florida and the Mississippi Valley to the Pacific Coast. The Old World's grip was loosening. For native chiefs like Maquinna and Kamehameha, and for John Kendrick, the conflagration enveloping Europe would open new possibilities on the far side of the globe.

CHAPTER SEVENTEEN

Survival and Seduction

Macao, Sandwich Islands

SEPTEMBER 1792–APRIL 1793

DURING THE LATE SUMMER, Kendrick finished constructing the tender for the *Lady Washington,* probably a thirty-six-foot sloop, called the *Avenger.* He provisioned and manned both ships. His crew included several of his original "Boston men," more recent Boston recruits, and British, Chinese, and Hawaiian sailors. Twenty-seven-year-old John Stoddard was made master of the tender. Stoddard had served as the *Washington*'s clerk for the past two years. His father was a Boston house builder and one of the revolutionaries of the 1770s. Kendrick probably knew Stoddard's father from the group of revolutionaries at St. Andrews Masonic Lodge, which both men had joined in 1778. The second mate of the tender was twenty-three-year-old David Wood III, whose grandfather had been colonel of the Massachusetts Rangers during the French and Indian Wars. Wood was in the East seeking adventure. From what he had heard, Kendrick was certain to provide it.

In September, while Vancouver was worrying about his failure with Quadra, Kendrick sailed from Macao into the South China Sea. Although his illness and building the tender had kept him in port for ten months, his plan was still to winter on the coast at Clayoquot and trade through the spring and summer. From there he would go to the Sandwich Islands in the autumn of 1793 to meet Williams, Rowbottom, and Coleman and pick up the sandalwood and pearls they had gathered. This time, he thought, with two ships and his furs purchased in advance, there was a good chance of collecting the windfall he needed.

Three days out, scattered showers fell and long rolling swells appeared, indicating a storm far offshore. It was the end of the typhoon season, and many fishing boats were out on the offshore shoals. No oracles had predicted a storm, but the breeze kicked up from the northeast and the skies steadily darkened during the next half day. Then the rain turned torrential. Kendrick might have hoped this was only a lingering tropical storm, but the signs were not good. Some of the fishing junks undoubtedly hauled for Tong-Hou Cove, a well-known island rendezvous in bad weather. If it were a typhoon, however, running for shore could make matters worse. The best course was to try to run across the path of the storm, using the leading winds to get south of it. That was the decision Kendrick apparently made now.

The ensuing hours are not difficult to envision. As the two heavily laden ships tried to run before the storm, waves began to mount. Gusts blew the tops off the heavy swells they tried to cross. Headway stalled. White water scudded over the surface in salty hard-driving rain. The storm built rapidly, too rapidly to outrun, probably the worst weather Kendrick had seen since the passage around Cape Horn. There were many things that could go wrong: weakened hull planking could split, a yard left aloft could collapse onto the deck, thrashing around like a log and hammering everything in its path, chain plates could let go, springing the foremast or mainmast.

Waves most likely built to thirty feet or more, and wallowing in the valleys of these huge seas, visibility closed down. Despite their best efforts, amid the rain and with darkness falling on the turbulent sea, they lost sight of the tender. The *Washington*'s deck became awash as they plunged into steep troughs and water surged over the deck and down her whole length. Kendrick would have called all hands below, lashing the rudder and leaving only a storm jib.

In storms such as these, sustained winds can reach 150 miles per hour, and the peak may last an hour or more, an eternity when hunkered in the dark below deck. As the waves washed over them, water leaked around the hatch covers and deck seams. For long moments the seas submerged the hull, and the thunderous howl fell muffled before rising again. The storm sail was probably soon ripped to shreds and they were left under bare poles amid the crashing waves. Worried for their own lives as well as the men on the tender, Kendrick may have thought of how they had searched in vain for the *Lady Washington* four years ago off the Horn.

Beaten with enormous force, the *Washington*'s rudder most likely snapped with a booming crack as they felt the ship lurch sideways. In a terrible moment, the ship turned under them, and everything inside that was not tied down crashed across the cabin and hold as the seas rushed down the companionway. The men trapped inside despaired as the waves punished them and they lay half underwater, frantically trying to work the pumps. But despite the beating, somehow the *Washington*'s hull of two-inch New England oak held fast. Miraculously, she remained afloat.

Hours after the ordeal began, in heaving seas and still-gusting winds, Kendrick and his exhausted men climbed out amid a dense tangle of lines and flotsam. The hull lay over on her side, half submerged. In the swamped cabin below, they searched for axes to cut away the masts. Showing incredible courage and endurance, they severed the stays, chopped off the masts, and then somehow managed to right the vessel.

They could not see the tender in the bleak daylight, but prayed for her survival. Pumping water from the ship continuously, they jury-rigged a new mast and sail and started back to Macao, finding masses of scattered wreckage from the fishing junks. Sharks were filling the waters, and survivors called out to the crippled ship. They stopped repeatedly, trying to maneuver close to the wrecks, and picked up about thirty men, but much to their torment, despite the heart-rending wails and cries, many more had to be left behind.

Seven days after the typhoon, the odd, stump-masted ship finally struggled into port at Macao. Met by the tooting of horns and the mandarin's boats, Kendrick and his crew became local heroes. If this storm was typical of typhoons that reached shore, the harbor would have been fouled with half-sunken wreckage, roofs torn from houses, mudslides scarring the hills, and the smell of rot and human waste thickening the air.

Days passed as Kendrick waited for his tender and Stoddard and Wood to appear. Arriving ships had no word of them. They had vanished without a trace, and gone with them were nine or ten men. The appreciation of those he saved couldn't balance the loss. Accepting what fate had handed them, Kendrick borrowed cash, promised shares on his next load of furs to raise money, and finally laid the *Washington* up on the beach at Dirty Butter Bay to begin repairs.

TWO MONTHS LATER, when the *Columbia* arrived, a black man came aboard and told the story of Kendrick and the typhoon. Robert Gray, returning from the streets of Macao, confirmed that he had heard the same tale. Kendrick sent a letter informing the *Columbia* of the deaths of Stoddard and Wood, but he did not seek out Gray. With all the bitterness that had settled between them, the two captains did not meet or communicate.

Despite high hopes, the *Columbia* was facing dire economic conditions. The embargo on furs had ended, and now a surplus of furs flooded the market. Hoskins wrote to Joseph Barrell on December 22, 1792, from upriver at Whampoa that "skins are very low and there is no selling them for Cash, indeed we could not get the Ship secured unless we would agree to take goods in pay . . . Skins at retail will not fetch more than thirty dollars and at wholesale from six to twenty five dollars." He expected the whole cargo would not amount to more than forty thousand dollars, and warned that the ship was leaky and needed to be hauled out and repaired, which would "make our expences at this place great."

The promises of a "golden harvest" that Gray and Haswell had made to Joseph Barrell and the other owners did not materialize. Though records of the voyage indicate sales totaling fifty thousand dollars, and one of the owners commented that the *Columbia* "made a saving voyage and some profit," Barrell's misgivings about Gray now proved justified. While still at Nootka, Hoskins had written a letter alerting Barrell that Gray had sought to cheat the owners by sending the property he was trading on his own to New York. Haswell too, Hoskins said, sought to make ten thousand dollars on his own account and "then go to England that the owners might go to hell and his wages and per centage with them." Hoskins concluded that Gray was a man "who has not even the least principle of honor or honesty but appears to be divested of every virtue, and who is in grain, if not openly a Knave and a Fool."

It was a bitter turning for those who had sided with Gray against Kendrick. "I could wish there was some person in Canton who had your orders to take the ship and cargo out of the present hands," Hoskins lamented. This could have reflected Kendrick's offer to take the *Columbia* back as Barrell's agent. It would have been a telling vindication for Kendrick, but none of the letters reached Boston in time to make a difference.

If there was any written communication between Hoskins and Kendrick at Macao, no record remains. Hoskins criticized Gray's command of the ship as "blundering along," and charged that he endangered the vessel repeatedly, running aground, shattering the keel, splitting planks, and shearing off the rudder stem. Comparing him with Kendrick, Hoskins concluded: "although he [Gray] cruiz'd the coast more; and appeared to be more persevering to obtain skins, yet his principles were no better, his abilities less, and his knowledge of the coast, from his former voyage, circumscribed within very narrow limits." On February 8, the *Columbia* made the two-day trip down the Pearl River and departed for Boston. Neither the ship nor Robert Gray ever returned to the East. Years later, Charles Bulfinch would note that the owners were disappointed that Kendrick did not turn over his furs to the *Columbia,* but nevertheless, Bulfinch said they decided to let Kendrick continue the sole conduct of their business in the Pacific.

IN THE *COLUMBIA'S* WAKE, the rumor mill was rife with talk about her voyage and conditions on the coast. Aside from hearing about Gray's skirmishing and the killing of Wickaninish's brother, Kendrick learned that Gray had discovered a river to the south of the Strait of Juan de Fuca, thought to be the mythical "Oregon" or "river of the west." After leaving Vancouver's ships at the mouth of the strait on April 29, Gray had turned south. Following a few days of skirmishing and trading at present-day Gray's Harbor, Gray took the Columbia down to the river they had tried to enter a few weeks earlier. According to fifth mate John Boit, on May 12 (according to Gray, May 11) they "saw an appearance of a spacious harbor abrest the Ship" and made a passage between breakers over two sandbars "to a fine river" which "extended to the NE as far as they eye cou'd reach, and water fit to drink as far down as the Bars, at the entrance." The beach was lined with natives who ran alongside the ship and sold them salmon and furs at very cheap rates: four otter skins for a sheet of copper, beaver skins for two spikes each, and other furs for one spike each.

They stayed until May 15, then went upriver seven or eight miles and landed "to view the Country and take possession." John Boit described the landscape in glowing terms as clear of brush and fertile for cultivation. "[T]he river abounds with excellent Salmon, and other River fish, and the Woods with plenty of Moose and Deer, the skins of which was brought us in great plenty . . . and clear ground in plenty, which with little labor might be made fit to raise such seeds as is necessary for the sustenance of inhabitants, and in short a factory set up here and another at Hancock's River in the Queen Charlotte Isles, wou'd engross the whole trade of the NW Coast (with the help a few small coasting vessels). Got 150 otter, 300 beaver, and twice the number of other land furs."

After nearly a week, they returned downriver and, following repeated attempts over a few days, cleared the turbulent surf-wracked bar into open seas on May 20. When they met Vancouver again at Nootka in September, Gray told him of their discovery, and the British commander marked it on his map, calling it "Columbia's River"—a gesture that would later win Gray a reputation as an explorer.

KENDRICK ALSO HEARD of William Brown's hostility toward Americans at Friendly Cove. The *Butterworth* expedition was said to have authorization of the British court to establish settlements, and as commander, Brown wanted to drive the Americans off the coast. It was not surprising. Among the British traders, the *Jenny* apparently collected no more than three hundred and fifty sea otter skins. And Brown's three ships were described by Vancouver's officers as "unsuccessful this, their first season . . ."

Vancouver and the British merchants were well aware that Kendrick had advance commitments for furs and that this was a significant part of their misfortune. Edward Bell, clerk of the *Chatham* noted: "Wicananish amongst others frequently receives in advance from the Masters of Vessels (particularly Mr. Kendrick) the value of from 50 to 100 Skins to be paid in a certain time which hitherto he has commonly fulfill'd and when the Butterworth & Jenny were together in that part [August 1792] I have understood they could not purchase a skin as Wickananish was making up a quantity he owed and had likewise made a promise to the person he was in debt to to keep all the skins for him over and above the sum due, that he collected."

Tied to the aggression of British traders, two warships were on the coast under the command of George Vancouver. It was said he had been sent by the king to settle the agreement made with Spain. He made claims on Nootka Sound and Clayoquot, and gave an "all or nothing" proposal to Bodega y Quadra on taking over the Spanish compound at Friendly Cove. Quadra refused. As Kendrick understood it, the Spanish commander was attempting to solidify claims too, setting up a second fort just inside the Strait of Juan de Fuca at Neah Bay, and winning a grant of land from Maquinna at Yuquot.

Much of Kendrick's information came from a new clerk who had joined the *Washington*'s crew as they made their repairs at Dirty Butter Bay. John Howell was a former English clergyman who had acted as Quadra's interpreter in discussions with Vancouver. Eager to be involved in trade, Howell was highly educated and fluent in Spanish, very unusual among the mix of sailors in the East. Howell's recent past was a string of missteps. After abandoning the clergy, he had emigrated from London to Boston where he became involved with two newspapers. Each one had promptly failed. He then made a hasty departure from town on the *Margaret* under James Magee, offering to write a history of her voyage. Now he had left Magee without producing the history, and offered his services to Kendrick. Howell's role with the *Lady Washington* and Kendrick would grow increasingly dark and curious in the events that were to unfold later.

UNBOWED BY ALL HIS SETBACKS, Kendrick rallied his crew and sailed forty miles east of Macao to Hong Kong Island, a collection of rural fishing villages and small farms. With Spain and Britain each seeking to claim lands on the Northwest Coast, Kendrick thought it best to secure the dream he and his crew were pursuing—a permanent American outpost and port on the Pacific.

At anchor in a small Hong Kong harbor, and undoubtedly with Howell's assistance, he made one of his bold moves, writing to Thomas Jefferson, the new nation's first secretary of state. The letter indicated

Kendrick's familiarity with Jefferson's endeavors to create free and open ports for commerce and his interest in expanding an "empire of liberty" that stretched to the Pacific.

> *Port Independence, On The Island Of Hong Kong, March 1, 1793*
>
> *Sir: I have the honor of enclosing to you the copies of several deeds, by which the tracts of land, therein described, situated on islands on the Northwest coast of America, have been conveyed to me and my heirs, forever, by the resident Chiefs of those districts, who, I presume, were the only just proprietors thereof. I know not what measures are necessary to be taken, to secure the property of these purchases to me and the Government thereof to the United States; but it cannot be amiss to transmit them to you, to remain in the offices of the Department of State. My claim to those territories has been allowed by the Spanish Crown, for the purchases I made at Nootka, were expressly excepted in a deed of conveyance of the lands adjacent to and surrounding Nootka-sound, executed in September last [September 1792] to El Senor Don Juan Francisco de la Bodega y Quadra, in behalf of his Catholic Majesty, by Maquinnah and the other Chiefs of his tribe, to whom those lands belonged.*
>
> *When I made these purchases, I did it under an impression that it would receive the sanction of the United States, and that, should an Act of the Legislature be necessary to secure them to me, I should find no difficulty obtaining it. The future commercial advantages which may arise from the fur-trade, besides many other branches which are daily opening to the view of those who visit the Northwest American coast, may, perhaps, render a settlement there worth the attention of some associated company, under the protection of Government. Should this be the case, the possession of lands, previously and*

> *so fairly acquired, would much assist in carrying the plan into effect. Many good purposes may be effected by the Union having possessions on that coast, which I shall not presume, Sir, to point out to you; and the benefits which have accrued to individuals, by similar purchases to those I have made, in our own States, are too well known to need a remark.*
>
> *I have the honor to be, with the utmost respect and esteem, Sir, your very humble servant. John Kendrick.*

The letter was received at the State Department with copies of the deeds seven months later on October 24, 1793. While Kendrick had been writing for government recognition, Jefferson was supporting an overland expedition to the West under the leadership of the French botanist André Michaux. This was one of Jefferson's several attempts since 1783 to encourage overland exploration to the Pacific. The journey was not sponsored by the American government, but by the American Philosophical Society. On behalf of the society, Jefferson advised Michaux to go to the headwaters of the Missouri River and pursue "the largest streams of that river, as shall lead by the shortest way, and the lowest latitude to the Pacific Ocean." The river that was called Oregon "by the latest maps . . . interlocked with the Missouri for a considerable distance, & entered the Pacific ocean, not far Southward of Nootka sound." Jefferson considered the information to be gathered of great import for science and "the inhabitants of the United States in particular, to whom your Report will open new Faiths & subject of Commerce, Intercourse, & Observation."

Interest in the region kept steadily mounting. Jefferson was aware that the Spanish were planning to explore westward from Saint Louis to the Pacific. In 1789, Diego de Gardoqui had written to Floridablanca from New York to urge such a mission. The British had also launched efforts using the *Princess Royal*'s former captain Charles Duncan, who had been at Nootka in 1786 to search for a river running westward from Hudson's Bay to the Pacific. And on behalf of a syndicate of fur traders known as the North West Company, the British fur trader Alexander Mackenzie was already on his way overland with an expedition. The time of discovery for this region seemed to be at hand.

Although Jefferson was most likely intrigued by Kendrick's efforts, Congress had taken steps to prevent individuals from making private deals for native lands that would then be acknowledged by the United States. The federal government wanted to retain its prerogative for acquiring land by negotiating treaties for concessions of large tracts. However, this land was far outside the nation's current boundaries. A new claim on the Pacific presented a whole other scale of problems. France had declared war on Britain on February 1, 1793, and a month later, on the same day Kendrick was writing to Jefferson, France had declared war on Spain. Jefferson was wrestling to keep America neutral in the war that was drawing in all of Europe and threatening American ships. Tensions were also running high with Spain along the "middle land" borders in Georgia, Kentucky, and the Ohio Valley. The frontiersman George Rogers Clark had taken a French commission. Also, the French minister to the United States, Edmund Charles Genet, was encouraging insurrection in Spanish Louisiana and the Floridas and was enlisting other Americans in the cause. Genet disclosed to Jefferson that he planned to establish an independent state in the South, connected by commerce to France and the United States.

Against this background, Kendrick's claims raised the prospect of provoking both Britain and Spain. Kendrick had been told by Joseph Barrell that the purchase of lands could be authorized by Congress after the fact. This was true, but the time for Congress to become involved and extend its territory was not ripe: annexing lands on the Pacific at this point posed too great a risk.

Unaware of the larger pressures faced by Jefferson and the Congress, Kendrick hoped for federal action on his deeds, but must have known that at best there would be a long delay. He sailed for the Northwest undoubtedly carrying cases of muskets and barrels of powder and shot with his trading cargo. Although he had little to work with, Kendrick was fully cognizant of the meager forces the two superpowers had in place at Nootka, and that he might pose a strong countervailing threat in his alliance with the native people.

DURING THE PAST FEW MONTHS, Vancouver had sailed southward to reconnoiter Spanish defenses along the California coast. He noted weak armaments and troops at San Francisco and Monterey as he partook of Spanish hospitality. In January, he sailed for Hawaii. After his failed negotiations and embarrassment at Nootka, Vancouver felt a greater sense of urgency to assert Britain's claim to the islands. He had neither the authority nor the force to take them, so the trick was to gain the approval of the chiefs and make it appear that they were asking to become one of the British Empire's possessions.

If nothing else, Vancouver had learned a valuable lesson from the seductive generosity of Quadra. Now he was about to make full use of it. On February 21, 1793, he anchored three leagues outside of Kealakekua. Kamehameha came out to the *Discovery* and, in Vancouver's eyes, welcomed him as James Cook's successor. There had been a dramatic change in Kamehameha since Vancouver had last seen the young warrior in 1779. His savage look and stern ferocity had softened. A subtle cleverness shone from his dark eyes, and he walked with a sense of grace and dignity.

Kamehameha brought Kaahumanu, his favorite queen, with him. She was about sixteen, very plump, and considered the ideal beauty. They were accompanied by her father, Keeaumoku, who had once been a chief of Maui, and an entourage of visitors of high rank who were soon crowding the ships. Kamehameha's translator and chief aide was John Young, who had been captured onshore when the *Fair American*'s crew was massacred. Vancouver offered to take him away, but Young told him that here he was a chief, at home he would be just another sailor. Through Young, Vancouver laid out his welcome and distributed an array of presents. For Kamehameha, he unfolded a special long red robe made by the ship's tailor. According to a design the captain sketched out, it was "tasseled with ribbons and bordered round with lace and particolored tape." Vancouver threw it over Kamehameha's shoulders. The king was described by Menzies as so "delighted with his present that he danced and capered about the cabin." The seduction was on.

Vancouver was somewhat reassured by Kamehameha's demonstrations of friendship, and on the morning of February 22, he brought the *Discovery* and *Chatham* into Kealakekua Bay. To ensure that no treachery would take place, Vancouver had loaded fieldpieces brought on deck and readied stands of loaded muskets on the quarterdeck. Kamehameha proceeded to the ship in a ceremonial visit, a show of state in a double canoe flanked by others in columns of five on either side. An estimated three thousand people lined the shore and paddled around the ships. In the midst of them, Kamehameha was wearing a brilliant yellow feather cloak over a printed gown, with a feathered helmet on his head. As he came on board the *Discovery,* he took Vancouver's hand and asked if he were sincerely a friend, and if the king of Great Britain favored him. Vancouver told him this was so, and Kamehameha presented four feathered helmets and ten canoes loaded with ninety hogs and a huge quantity of fruit and vegetables. Kamehameha said he would also give his treasured yellow-feathered war cloak, unlike any other in the islands, but it was only for King George III to wear.

Vancouver accepted the gifts and intensified his courtship of Kamehameha. "Convinced of the advantage, as well as the necessity, of preserving peace with these people, not only on the score of humanity, but as it respected our own present and future welfare; it became indispensably requisite that I should leave no object unattended to . . ." Vancouver gave Kamehameha more gifts, including four cows, two ewes, and a ram, which he had brought from Monterey.

Kamehameha allowed Vancouver to erect a shore camp, and on February 24, Vancouver went with an armed guard to Kamehameha's house at Kaawaloa village. The guards stationed themselves outside the courtyard of the large pili grass structure. Inside, Kamehameha's entourage sat on mats that covered the entire floor. Stacked in one corner of the house were two dozen muskets. Kamehameha told Vancouver he had gotten the guns from William Brown, master of the *Butterworth,* and that his men were afraid to use them because one had blown up when fired. Vancouver made no comment on Brown's weapons trading. Some historians believe that Vancouver and Brown may have shared a secret connection and were acting under joint orders. Brown had, after all, brought Vancouver a dispatch to turn over lands at Nootka to him. Furthermore, both Brown's and Vancouver's later operations show some degree of coordination. The *Chatham* had arrived at Kealakekua in company with the *Jackall,* and the *Butterworth* ships were "the only English vessels who had an exclusive grant from Government for trading on this coast," according to Menzies.

But common goals rather than government orders seemed to drive what would evolve into a clever joint strategy. Brown had gone ahead of Vancouver and sailed from Hawaii to the Leeward Islands in search of opportunities with Kahekili. He wrote disappointedly from Waikiki in December that he had found no whales in the vicinity that would support a whaling station there.

Menzies, meanwhile, went inland to scout opportunities for British enterprises on the big island. On a lengthy journey from Kealakekua he wrote: "It might be well worth the attention of the Government to make the experiment and settle these islands by planters from the West Indies, men of humanity, industry, and experienced abilities in the exercise of their art would here in a short time be enabled to manufacture sugar and rum from luxuriant fields of cane equal if not superior to the produce of our West Indies plantations." In addition to sugar cane, he mentioned that the climate and soil of the uplands would also be conducive to growing fruits Europeans were familiar with such as apples and peaches. What Menzies, Vancouver, and other officers believed in was a guiltless imperial dream in which native people would peacefully labor in the fields, purchase European goods, and adopt the "manners and dress" of Englishmen.

Shortly after Menzies returned from his journey, Vancouver set off a display of fireworks from shore tents. Similar to the response at Kauai a year earlier, the natives beheld the display "with utmost astonishment and admiration." Exclamations of joy, Menzies wrote, echoed around every part of the bay. With many of the chiefs gathered, Vancouver believed this was his chance to entice Kamehameha to cede Hawaii to Great Britain. Menzies noted: "Captain Vancouver was very urgent with Kamehameha to take this opportunity of declaring himself and his subjects, together with the whole island, under the dominion of Great Britain." Several chiefs brushed off the effort to give up their sovereignty. Kamehameha "positively declined unless Captain Vancouver would promise to leave one of the vessels behind at the island to assist in defending him and his people from the inroads of their enemies."

Vancouver tried to reason with Kamehameha but found the robed chief adamant. It seemed impossible to get around Kamehameha's demand for a ship, but Vancouver was not about to give up. On March 8, the British ships left Kealakekua for the Leeward Islands. Vancouver wanted to survey their harbors and fields, and perhaps hoped to incite Kamehameha's jealousy. He also sought to track down the warriors who had killed three men from the *Daedalus* when the storeship arrived late for her rendezvous with the *Discovery* the previous winter. The commander, Lieutenant Richard Hergest, her astronomer, William Gooch, and a Portuguese sailor had been attacked and murdered while they were ashore.

As Vancouver went among the Leeward Islands, he saw more devastation from the incessant warring. His sense of failure at Kamehameha's rejection deepened, as did his desire to promote the mixed purposes of British dominion and peace. "Every hour," he wrote, "produced some new intelligence, to convince me of the necessity of bringing, if it were possible, to an immediate conclusion, the ambitious pretentions of these sovereigns; being now decidedly of [the] opinion, that a continuation of such commotions [wars] would soon desolate these islands and render them incapable of affording those abundant and excellent supplies we had constantly derived, and without which the English traders would be ill qualified to maintain the commerce of north-west America."

There was no question in Vancouver's mind that British control of the islands was essential to control of trade on the Northwest Coast. This was the vital resupply point for ships sailing between the East and the Americas. If peace could be established under a British flag, he mused, captive labor would be guaranteed and the resulting agriculture and supplies from the islands for ships would be "almost inexhaustible."

But wherever Vancouver went, he found men standing in his way who served under an American flag and worked for Kamehameha or Kahekili. At Hawaii, Vancouver and Menzies had met John Smith, a British sailor who had been left by an American ship and was now a chief like John Young. At Maui, they encountered an American who said he had been empowered by Kahekili to visit ships that arrived at the island "and to order them such supplies of wood, water, and refreshments, as they might have occasion for, without their commanders having the trouble of bartering with the natives." This man also told Vancouver that Kahekili, although old and infirm, was on the way to meet him.

Kahekili arrived on the afternoon of March 13, accompanied by several canoes and no special fanfare. He came boldly alongside the ship and climbed on board with an accustomed confidence. Several chiefs followed him and constantly attended him. Vancouver judged him to be well over sixty years old (he was in his eighties) and noted that he was emaciated, with scaly skin, indicating that he drank the narcotic *awa* excessively. Kahekili's voice was faltering and he gave Vancouver several lean hogs, apologizing that his people were poor and their farms still devastated from the invasion by Kamehameha two years before in the Battle of the Dammed Waters of the Iao. In the brief occupation that followed, Kamehameha's warriors had killed or captured a vast number of villagers, taken existing food stores and hogs, destroyed irrigation systems, and wasted fields that still had not recovered. Moreover, the warriors he kept ready on the island took up much of the food supply.

Vancouver gave Kahekili and his men many presents, including a red robe similar to the one he had given Kamehameha. Kahekili seemed pleased and sent for his half-brother, Kaeo, who arrived the next afternoon from Molokai. Although Vancouver thought he recalled him as a young warrior, Kaeo appeared to be about fifty years old and suffering from the same scrofulous effects of drinking too much *awa*. To Vancouver's surprise, Kaeo remembered him and said he had kept the lock of his hair that had been given to him as a gift. When shown the lock, which was carefully wrapped in cloth and decorated with feathers, Vancouver thought it resembled his own hair, but privately noted he did not recall granting the gift.

In discussions with the two chiefs, Vancouver offered terms of peace he said were acceptable to Kamehameha, but they told him they had no faith in the integrity of the Hawaiians. If their warriors assembled at Maui for the protection of the Leeward Islands were to return home, the island would be left vulnerable "to the invasion of Kamehameha, whose unconquerably ambitious spirit would not allow him to neglect a favorable opportunity." Kaeo challenged Vancouver on his sincerity in promoting peace. Vancouver answered that foreign traders were promoting war in order to increase demand for European weapons.

Given Vancouver's surveying and intent to take possession of the islands, Kaeo may have sensed that his arguments were naive or duplicitous. The causes of war were deep, and filled with a twisted history and emotion that could not be laid only at the feet of foreign traders, or easily negotiated away. Among the interrelated rulers, a belief in destiny, a desire to right old wrongs, and a hunger for power underlay the treachery and invasions. If Vancouver had looked deeply enough he would have seen the dynastic plotting and retributions of the ruling *ali'i* families. Kahekili was rumored to be Kamehameha's father and

Kaeo his uncle. Inamoo was said to be an uncle to Kaeo. Kaiana was said to be Kaeo's slighted younger brother. Vancouver did convince Kahekili and Kaeo to send an emissary to John Young with a letter proposing peace. One of Kahekili's fierce-looking tattooed warriors was chosen for the task of delivering it. He would be killed at Hawaii.

In his own show of power, Vancouver demanded that the three or four warriors responsible for killing the men of the *Daedalus* be captured and executed. He wanted Kahekili's chiefs to perform the execution alongside the ship and for everyone to be required to witness it. Vancouver wanted the islanders to understand that any individual who committed a similar crime would be hunted down "be the distance of time ever so great, so long as the offending parties had life, or the English continued to visit these islands." Kahekili designated a chief to carry this out.

Sailing on to Oahu, on March 19 the *Discovery* encountered James Coleman, one of Kendrick's men, whom they had met the year before at Kauai. Like the American on Maui, Coleman claimed that Kahekili had given him power to regulate traffic and prevent any disturbance between the natives and the vessels that might visit Oahu. In keeping with his role, Coleman helped interrogate the three murder suspects brought aboard the *Discovery* at Waikiki. Although they protested their innocence, Vancouver's tribunal convicted them. There was a long deliberation concerning how the men were to be killed. Kahekili's chiefs wanted them taken offshore and drowned. Vancouver insisted the execution be carried out there in the harbor as an example to others. He assembled his armed men on the quarterdeck and ordered a double canoe brought to the gangway. Taking each bound prisoner down to the canoe, the chief executed him with a pistol.

A few hours after the execution, Kalanikupule appeared. He was Kahekili's son and regent of Oahu. Though he was only thirty-three years old, he too was ill, and had to be carried aboard in a chair. He confirmed the guilt of the three men. When Vancouver suggested terms of peace with Kamehameha to him, Kalanikupule answered with the same mistrust of the Hawaiian chiefs as his father, causing Vancouver to despair that peace would ever be established.

VANCOUVER APPROACHED HONOLULU HARBOR on March 23, a bay they had been told of by trading ship captains on the Northwest Coast. "In the evening observing an apparent inlet in the western side of the bay, we came to anchor before the entrance to it, and being informed while on the north-west cost of America by the masters of some of the trading vessels that a small snug harbor was situated in this side of the bay, boats were sent out early next morning to examine the passage in, but they found it so guarded by a reef a little distance from the shore that there was no access even for vessels of a small drought of water . . . The appearance of another opening was seen a little to the northward of this one, whose entrance might perhaps be more favorable, but the boats had not time to examine it, and were hoisted in . . ." This was Wai Momi, or Pearl Harbor, which would hold fateful significance for the British and Kendrick.

During the seventy-mile passage from Oahu to Kauai, Vancouver encountered three double canoes and a large single one, about sixty feet long, carrying spears, two muskets, and arm and leg bones of men killed in what was described as an "insurrection" on Kauai ten days before (March 16). Several principal chiefs had been killed. The men were going back to report to Kaeo with a few prisoners.

As they approached the island, Kendrick's former first mate John Williams "and two other sailors came off to us from Puna." Williams explained that the insurrection "was not so much against Kaeo or any of the present royal family, as against old Inamoo for his cruel and tyranic administration from which it was intended to eject him and put the young king Kaumaulii in the regency during his father's absence." Inamoo had apparently suspected he was being poisoned and conducted "frequent private assassinations for the most frivolous reasons, even among chiefs, sparing neither rank nor sex." Several of those involved were made prisoners, including one of Kaeo's favorite wives, who was among the women being transported to Oahu.

John Meares had considered Inamoo "a monster," and he looked the part as he came out to the ship. He had grown feeble since the last visit, his "limbs no longer able to support his aged and venerable person," and he too was emaciated, with his skin hanging loose. Like Kahekili, a "dry white scurf, or rather scales which overspread the whole surface of his body from head to foot, tended greatly to increase the miserable and deplorable appearance of his condition." Vancouver presented him with a scarlet cloak and a complete set of armourer's tools, but did not trust him.

The British relationship with Kauai had long been tenuous. John Meares had fired on villagers at Kauai in 1787. James Colnett had done the same in 1788, winning for the British the concealed mistrust and enmity of Kaeo and Inamoo. Vancouver was aware of this, and during his last visit, he had been anxious about a suspected attack. In light of the insurrection and the number of muskets in the hands of the natives, William Brown was also afraid to land there.

Vancouver believed the insurrection was caused by Americans advising Inamoo, and he later heard from Brown a long stream of allegations concerning the Americans. Brown wanted Vancouver to remove all foreigners from the island. Although Vancouver now regarded Kendrick as the leader of a "banditti of renegadoes," he was in no position to seize Kendrick's men, or have them and other American advisers banished. For all he had heard of the brazen American captain, he was yet to even glimpse Kendrick, who was at this time hundreds of miles to the north, following the Black Current to the American coast.

CHAPTER EIGHTEEN

A Rising Tide

Northwest Coast

MAY–SEPTEMBER 1793

BREAKERS WERE ROLLING IN on the point south of Nootka, with whitewater combing the rocky beach all the way to the entrance. It was nearly two years since Kendrick had entered Nootka Sound. He had missed the skirmishing of last summer between traders and natives, but was about to find tensions had intensified, and the tribes were fractured.

From the cannon battery on the crest of Hog Island, the gunners could see the *Lady Washington* preparing to enter the sound and sent word to Salvador Fidalgo, the latest in a series of Spanish officers to command the port. During the rainy winter, Fidalgo had increased the strength of the battery to eleven nine-pound cannons and reinforced Fort San Miguel at the mouth of the cove. As the *Washington* came abreast of the forts, Kendrick fired a salute. The Spanish gunners answered. There were no orders shouted through a speaking trumpet this time. Perhaps hoping for the festive atmosphere that prevailed under Quadra, Kendrick put out a boat to tow the *Washington* into Friendly Cove.

From the mouth of the cove, he could see that much had changed. The Spanish outpost onshore had become a crude frontier village. Tall fir trees were cleared back from the shore and on the high bank where Mowachaht houses had stood the two-story commandant's house sat surrounded by a hospital, barracks, several storehouses, blockhouses, a blacksmith shop, a bakery, and other rough dwellings. Chickens roamed the beach and the yards. In the middle of the village stood a tall wooden cross surrounded by extensive gardens fenced with stick palings. Kendrick might have looked at the nearly deserted house frames of Yuquot remaining farther along the bank and remembered the first desolate winter in 1788 when only a few Mowachaht people were there, and how Estevan Martinez had erected the first temporary fort and outbuildings. Inside the cove, the *San Carlos* lay at anchor, and smoke rose from the bakery at the edge of the beach below the commandant's house.

KENDRICK HAD MISSED MEETING VANCOUVER by several days. The *Discovery* had arrived on May 20 and found that Quadra was not there. Fidalgo told Vancouver that the mail on the *San Carlos* had letters from Quadra and viceroy Revillagigedo, but nothing for him from London. Frustrated by the lack of new instructions and eager to pursue discovery of the Straits of Admiral de Fonte, Vancouver departed for the north after only three days.

With Quadra gone, Fidalgo was facing challenges on all fronts. The viceroy in Mexico City had sent orders to warn off all ships that were not British or Spanish. While considered a prudent measure in distant viceregal offices, the order was not practical out here in the wilderness. Having armed foreign ships in the harbor provided a sense of comfort against the hostility of the Mowachaht. In Kendrick's case, however, the situation was different. His ties with Maquinna, Wickaninish, Claquakinnah, and other chiefs made him a formidable enemy. He dressed in part like the natives when among them, spoke their language fluently, and supplied them with arms. Yet he could not be easily warned off. Quadra had acknowledged the American captain's ownership of extensive lands surrounding the Spanish fort, and Kendrick's power was also magnified by a chill that gripped relations with Maquinna after Quadra left.

Fidalgo deeply mistrusted all Mowachaht. Like the British and many of his own officers, he believed that Quadra was too good to the natives. Fidalgo's friend and first pilot, Antonio Serantes, had been killed at Neah Bay, his body stripped and left in the bushes near the Spanish fort there. Fidalgo responded by firing on two canoes of the southern chief Tatooch, killing seven or eight people. His hatred and suspicion had grown to the point that when Maquinna arrived to welcome Fidalgo to the commandant's house, Fidalgo refused to allow him to enter, and ordered that all natives be kept at a distance and under close observation. The change in treatment was a stinging insult to the Mowachaht chief, who had set aside Callicum's death and other injuries to his tribe and enjoyed a constant place of honor at Quadra's table.

Bad blood between Maquinna and Fidalgo fed an unrest that was already mounting among the tribes. Given the steady onslaught of European transgressions and murders, the native people were no longer content to ask the Spanish when they were leaving. Wickaninish, Hanna, and Tatooch wanted to undertake raids and destroy the Spanish settlement. In the late summer of 1792, Maquinna was believed to have been in discussions with the three chiefs about attacking the Spanish outposts and foreign trading ships. Perhaps at some personal cost, he succeeded in holding them back. His turning point was coming though.

When Maquinna was questioned, in September 1792, about the killing of a Spanish cabin boy, he resented being treated like an enemy. Quadra was still there at the time, and Maquinna angrily told him: "You would be the first whose life would be in great danger if we were enemies. You well know that Wickaninish has many guns as well as powder and shot; that Captain Hanna [Cleaskinah, the chief at the mouth of Clayoquot] has more than a few, and that they as well as the

Nuchimanes [the tribe on the eastern side of Vancouver Island], are my relatives and allies, all of whom united make up a number incomparably greater than the Spanish, English, and Americans together, so that they would not be afraid to enter combat." The Spanish fort at Neah Bay was abandoned later that month, and Nootka was again made the focus of Spanish efforts. By early 1793, eight months after Maquinnah had made his threat to Quadra, the possibility of some type of armed conflict was very real.

Kendrick had no idea what he was walking into when he anchored in Friendly Cove. He went ashore, taking Howell with him as his translator. Fidalgo realized that this unpredictable ally of the Mowachaht was most likely bringing them more arms and powder. He attempted to take control of the situation, and the challenge grew starker. When he told Kendrick he was under orders to warn off the *Washington* from Nootka Sound, Kendrick amplified Maquinna's threat, telling Fidalgo he "would raise the Indians and drive them from their settlements" if the Spanish gave him any trouble. He left the commandant's house with that line in the sand.

Lying in the cove, in addition to the *San Carlos,* there was an American brig in terrible shape at anchor—the *Amelia* out of Providence—whose entire crew except for the captain and supercargo were recovering from severe cases of scurvy. Perhaps after seeing to the *Amelia,* Kendrick quickly left the cove for the site of his old outpost at Mawina, or Safe Harbor Retreat. It was more of a refuge than he might have thought. Awaiting him was a surprise that would soften the rising tensions for a few weeks.

A NINETY-TON SCHOONER, the *Resolution,* lay in the protected harbor flying American colors. Kendrick didn't know this vessel, but to his great amazement recognized the twenty-two-year-old second mate who came out to greet him—his son Solomon Kendrick.

It had been four years since the *Columbia* sailed from Clayoquot, taking Solomon and word of the seizure of the *Argonaut* to Macao. The blur of events since then seemed a lifetime. Although Kendrick had written home intermittently, it took six months for a letter to travel between Macao and Boston, and letters offered only a glimpse of the arduous twists of the long adventure. The curios and Chinese goods Kendrick sent homeward aboard Boston-bound ships yielded no hint of the trials he had faced, and little of the dream he was pursuing. Solomon's presence provided a sense of how far that inward journey had been. If there were tears in the weathered captain's eyes when he left his son John for duty with Estevan Martinez, there must have been more now.

Solomon was carrying letters, and brought news of Huldah at the store on the wharf. Benjamin, at seventeen, was now a seaman; Alfred was fifteen, Joseph, fourteen, and little Huldah, nearly a young lady at twelve. And next door, along the muddy street facing the tidal Narrows, Huldah's brother, Cornelius Pease, had his gaggle of girls growing toward marrying age.

The well-protected letters were nearly a year and a half old. Solomon had left Boston on November 28, 1791, aboard the 152-ton brig *Jefferson,* and rounded Cape Horn in April. At Ambrose Island, north of Juan Fernándes Island, where Gray and the *Washington* had sought drinking water in 1788, they had harvested fur seals with a cruel efficiency, securing thirteen thousand pelts. While wintering in the Marquesas, they built the *Resolution* from a frame they were carrying and, after separating from the *Jefferson* in mid-Pacific, made their way here for a rendezvous.

The *Lady Washington* settled in at Mawina, where Kendrick received a warm greeting from the chiefs who had been saving furs for him. Deer were plentiful this season, and they soon held a feast of fresh venison and salmon. Seeing his father before a fire surrounded by native people might have impressed Solomon with how much he had become a part of this place. The elder Kendrick was honored by Maquinna and other chiefs, and feared by the Spanish. And a song was being sung in the forecastles of the trading ships at night about how he and the *Washington*'s crew fought off Coyah. "The Ballad of the Bold Northwestman" served as both a celebration and a warning.

Come all ye bold Northwestmen who plough the raging main,
Come listen to my story, while I relate the same,
'Twas of the Lady Washington decoyed as she lay,
At Queen Charlotte's Island, in North America.

The song described the taking of the ship and how the desperate men below deck found only "six pistols, a gun and two small swords" while the captain stalled the attack. Rather than passively yield the arms packed in the hold and their lives, they prepared to blow up the ship:

Our powder we got ready and gun room open lay,
Our soul's we did commit to God, prepar'd for a wat'ry grave!
We then informed our captain, saying ready now are we,
He says a signal I will give, it shall be "follow me."

The song embodied the bloody spread of skirmishing and fed a spirit of racial hatred and more strife to come:

I'd have you all take warning and always ready be,
For to suppress those savages of Northwest America,
For they are so desirous some vessel for to gain,
That they will never leave it off, till most of them are slain.

There was irony in the song for Kendrick, who most likely regretted the slaughter that had occurred. At least one later captain, William Sturgis, believed that nearly all the native attacks were in retaliation for some injury and in keeping with the native code of honor that demanded retribution. It was an observation Kendrick might have shared.

Traces of his near-fatal disease months before showed in his face, along with the hard living that had begun to age him. He was part of this place now, and there was a long string of tales to share: of entering the rocky coast of Japan and the enforced isolation of a great nation; of the treachery and incredible generosity of the people of the Sandwich Islands; of Macao and the typhoon and loss of the *Avenger* and his men.

Kendrick was probably enthralled to describe the prospect of establishing an American beachhead on the Northwest Coast, and his letter to Thomas Jefferson. Solomon would see that despite all the sacrifice, his father still pursued the "glorious cause," arming native people and trying to hold off the British and the Spanish in order to establish an outpost in this corner of the continent. He would have learned that the aging captain envisioned many American ships here and a settlement that merchants would fund. The deeds gave them a choice of harbors between Clayoquot, Nootka, and Ahasett. Not only could they conduct trade for furs, they could also engage in whaling, fishing, and perhaps mining metal from these rocky shores. (Gold would later be found on the borders of Nootka Sound.) Given the mixed community in which he grew up among native people, Kendrick's vision likely included the Mowachaht.

Solomon read the deeds signed by the natives. He saw himself implied in the "heirs" who would become owners of the land, and learned that these purchases were only part of his father's strategy. In the Sandwich Islands, the American presence he sought through a similar outpost and his friendships with the chiefs would ensure America's trade route to the East. It was a hugely ambitious plan, far beyond the reach of other captains looking for riches in one or two seasons with a good cargo of furs.

Kendrick might have related that Gray had gone home with a modest profit, and Ingraham had reportedly fallen forty thousand dollars in debt with the *Hope*. James Magee had left the *Margaret* and returned homeward with Ingraham. The fact that Kendrick remained was only the beginning of what set him apart from other American shipmasters. He was the only American captain looking to the future and viewing the fur trade and this region in larger geopolitical terms. Underfunded and undermanned, he had taken immense risks. Yet he had miraculously survived and slowly built what he had now on the coast and in the islands. What he was reaching for was on the same scale as when he had received prize money from the king of France, or when he helped trigger events that pushed the world toward war in the Nootka Crisis. The odds of success in Kendrick's eyes were probably not any worse than those of a ragtag army of farmers and shopkeepers defeating one of the world's superpowers. It was all one adventurous long shot, and would demand even greater sacrifice before it was done. Given the magnitude of this dream, and the chance that it might save his father's reputation, Solomon undoubtedly saw little reason to repeat Huldah's pleas for Kendrick to come home.

He did have another urgent request to deliver, however, one that touched his father's sense of justice and allowed him to enjoy being an American ambassador for the region. After rounding Cape Horn, the *Jefferson* had stopped at Juan Fernándes Island in need of repairs. Sent ashore in the ship's boat to ask permission to anchor, Solomon found that the Spanish commandant, Don Blas Gonzales, had been stripped of his post for giving assistance to the *Columbia* in 1788. The new commandant feared he would suffer the same fate if he allowed the *Jefferson* to enter Cumberland Bay. The *Jefferson* then sailed to Valparaiso on the mainland, where Gonzales came to Solomon and lamented that he had failed in all his appeals to the viceroy for the past four years to have his reputation and position restored. Solomon carried Gonzales's written plea, begging John Kendrick and the Americans to intercede on his behalf.

For the second time in three months, Kendrick took up his pen and wrote to Secretary of State Thomas Jefferson: "On Board the Ship Lady Washington, Harbor of Maw-win-na, St. Clair's Island, North-west coast of America." Through some abuse of power by Spanish officials, Kendrick said, or "malicious statements of the facts by some secret enemies," Gonzales was charged with a crime for his "humane conduct towards me and my crew in 1788." Kendrick praised Gonzales's decision to allow him a safe harbor to repair the *Columbia* as "perfectly consistent with the amity and good understanding subsisting between the Court of Madrid and the United States." He urged that justice be done, and under "the principles of our excellent constitution as well as their native humanity," he requested Jefferson's help for Gonzales's relief. Kendrick's outrage may have been piqued by the odd similarity with his own situation of having been undercut by Robert Gray. Gonzales's plight was ultimately made known to the American chargé d'affairs in Madrid, William Carmichael. However, there is no indication that any restoration for Gonzales was ever granted.

KENDRICK UNDOUBTEDLY TOLD SOLOMON of the warring in the Sandwich Islands and the tension among tribes along the coast. They may also have spoken of the British warships and Vancouver's attempts to claim the sound and find the Northwest Passage. As long as the Mowachaht were armed, and the tribes were united, Kendrick was not worried about British or Spanish claims. But right now, Kendrick found, the tribes were enmeshed in a heated dispute.

A rift had arisen between Maquinna and Wickaninish over a promised marriage between Maquinna's daughter Apenas (who was about twelve years old) and Wickaninish's son. The marriage had been bartered in a major ceremony with thousands of the people from Clayoquot and Nootka taking part. Wickaninish came into the sound with forty canoes, carrying hundreds of people, singing and beating their paddles in time. In a steady file they entered the estuary at Coaglee, a few miles from Yuquot where Maquinna's people were camped. As they swept around Coaglee's shallow cove, every paddle of the fleet moved in unison and the sound of their drumming reverberated from the hills and forest. First Wickaninish and then Maquinna delivered speeches and the canoes came to shore. People were dressed in their best skins and blankets with saffron-colored wreaths on their heads and white down covering their hair. They sat in long rows in Maquinna's house and after dancing and feasting, a deal that was very costly for Wickaninish was finalized.

The union would help to bond the tribes and determine future leadership. But now Maquinna was balking. He wanted to wait until Apenas was older. Beneath the dispute, Maquinna may have been worried about power and prestige shifting away from him and toward the richer and stronger Wickaninish. All the chiefs were embroiled in the dispute. For Kendrick, it undermined whatever united defiance they might show to Fidalgo or Vancouver.

The weather turned to long days of heavy rain. Solomon remained at Mawina and dined regularly with his father and the *Washington*'s officers and men. Watching him among the other seamen and officers, Kendrick would have taken pride in the fact that his son was now a full-grown, sandy-haired young man, and one of the rare sailors in the world who was making his second circumnavigation. The time probably passed all too quickly. After the *Jefferson* arrived on June 22, Solomon was dispatched with the *Resolution* north to the Queen Charlotte Islands to trade and then sent south to "Gray's River."

Kendrick traded locally with the *Washington* and then left briefly for Clayoquot, perhaps in an effort to help mediate between Wickaninish and Maquinna. The dispute was threatening to turn violent. He returned to Mawina on July 13, possibly carrying some offer from Wickaninish to Maquinna, but whatever small success he might have had in these negotiations, he had no ability to control the broader sweep of events.

At the time Kendrick was returning to Mawina, Vancouver was about two hundred fifty miles to the northeast. The *Discovery* and *Chatham* were exploring an area where Vancouver hoped they were on the track of the Northwest Passage at last.

In September 1792, Jacinto Caamano, captain of the *Aranzazu,* had returned from an exploration northward and excitedly reported to Quadra that he had "entered a large Inlet going to the North East Ward which they conceived to be the Straits of Admiral de Fonte." He had traced the inlet as far as 55°30' north latitude, "where its capriciousness had so little diminished, that there were reasons to conclude from its appearance that it must penetrate a considerable way inland."

The possibility of finding the ancient passage that was said to course toward Hudson's Bay was alluring for Caamano, but ice was forming along the shores, and heavy snow already lay on the mountaintops. He reluctantly broke off and returned to Nootka. Vancouver had mulled over Caamano's news all winter. This seemed to be the same entrance that Robert Gray claimed to have sailed into for a distance of more than a hundred miles, and where Kendrick had searched. Vancouver hoped to make a vital discovery that he could announce on his return to Nootka in the fall. He also hoped that his new instructions to negotiate with Quadra would be waiting. It would soon be a year since he had dispatched Lieutenant Zachary Mudge to London.

On Saturday, July 20, the *Discovery* and *Chatham* were searching in the vicinity where Caamano had reported the opening of the strait. The weather turned gloomy. The fog was rising and falling over the rugged shoreline and a gale threatened the ships from seaward. Vancouver sought a protected harbor. As he anxiously started in among rocky islets, glimpses through the fog showed the situation to be "more intricate and dangerous" among rocks and breakers. Most captains would have headed offshore, but Vancouver continued threading his precarious course, and was suddenly told of a whaleboat appearing off the bow, rowing toward them. It turned out that she was from the *Butterworth,* sent out to help guide him into a sheltered anchorage. If this was a coincidence, as Vancouver indicated, it was one of remote chance.

At six in the evening the *Discovery* and *Chatham* anchored at 54°18' north latitude in company with the *Butterworth* and its two consorts, the sloop *Prince Lee Boo* and the schooner *Jackall*. Brown came on board following an exchange of salutes. After finding few furs to the south, where his depredations at Clayoquot had foreclosed trading, his ships had been probing this area. Not far to the north, Brown had found the reported opening in the coastline extending far inland. He said he understood from the natives there was "a very extensive inland navigation, communicating with the sea to the northward, that employed the inhabitants nearly three months in reaching its extent . . ." The opening to this channel was about nine leagues to the north-northeast.

Vancouver excitedly noted that this was probably the same channel Caamano had laid down in his chart as the Straits of Admiral de Fonte. He was eager to begin exploration, but concerned about the deep draft of his ships and hidden rocks. Brown offered the use of his small sloop, *Prince Lee Boo,* and begged Vancouver to retain her "as long as [he] should find it expedient."

As soon as the fog burned off enough the next day, they started along a range of rocky islets, with a cutter in the lead, followed by the *Prince Lee Boo, Chatham,* and *Discovery*. As the visibility continued to clear, they found themselves off a shore with "a lofty range of mountains covered in perpetual snow" and thickets of spruce running down to the water. Just south of the future border with Alaska, Vancouver named the island they were approaching "Dundas," after British home secretary Henry Dundas. This was the latest in a long string of landmarks Vancouver named in honor of royalty, high officials, and his own officers, regardless of whether they had previously been discovered and mapped with a Spanish or American name.

Westward from Dundas Island was clear ocean. To the east was a broad channel "that appeared free from interruption." Vancouver left the *Discovery* in a safe anchorage, and for the next few days the cutter and the *Prince Lee Boo* proceeded up an inlet Brown had identified. They reached a village where Brown had gotten into a dispute with the natives, and Brown told Vancouver that it had been "necessary to fire upon them from the vessels, which was attended with some slaughter."

At that point, perhaps fearing that the natives would recognize Brown's sloop and retaliate, Vancouver had the *Prince Lee Boo* return to the *Butterworth*, while he proceeded with the *Discovery*'s yawl and launch. He continued up blind channels for the next few weeks, asking small groups of natives they encountered if this was the direction of "Ewen Nass"—a great inland waterway. He received unintelligible responses, but believed that if the Strait of Admiral de Fonte existed, this was where it lay.

On August 12, far inland from the ships, Vancouver engaged in trade with one group and found his yawl blocked by a large canoe when they sought to push off. An old woman who seemed to be in charge of the canoe snatched up the lead line and lashed her canoe to the boat "whilst a young man, appearing to be the chief of the party, seated himself in the bow of the yawl and put on a mask resembling a wolf's face, compounded with the human countenance." About fifty natives waded into the shallows, surrounding the yawl. Crowding in, one of them suddenly grabbed a musket, and others took books, guns, whatever was at hand. Sensing they were in mortal danger, Vancouver leveled his musket and went forward to speak with the chief in the mask. Those surrounding the yawl immediately drew their daggers and raised their spears. The launch traveling with Vancouver had already passed into the channel. Vancouver was hoping to stall an attack, but before the launch could return with aid a skirmish broke out. Two of Vancouver's men were wounded by spears, one in the chest and thigh and the other through the thigh. A few of the natives were also wounded or killed. The British boats fled downriver and searched out a safe place to camp. The next morning, believing that they would not find the passage in this maze of channels, Vancouver turned back. With great relief they reached the ships on August 16, having traversed about seven hundred miles in twenty-three days.

About two hundred miles to the south, hostile natives had also halted another expedition. As Vancouver was just starting out to explore the inlet in his boats, the British fur trader Alexander Mackenzie was arriving overland on the banks of the Bella Coola River with six French Canadians and two native guides. The North West Company had sent the expedition from the east. They wintered over at the junction of the Peace and Smoky Rivers and started out again on May 9 when the ice in the rivers finally broke up. Arriving at the Bella Coola, Mackenzie had missed Vancouver's men in their survey boats by only six weeks. Open ocean was about forty miles to the west. Trying to reach it, Mackenzie was stopped by hostile natives. At the edge of what became known as Dean Channel, he used a mixture of bear grease and red pigment to paint a large rock with big, crude block letters: "Alex Mackenzie from Canada by land, 22d July 1793." Having accomplished his mission and fearing that he was vastly outnumbered, his small party immediately started back overland.

Upon his return, Mackenzie recommended that Hudson's Bay Company and the North West Company combine and work with the British government to form a network of outposts and forts across North America to the Pacific shore. To transport the furs to China, he urged the East India Company to join the combined fur-trading companies. Without these measures, he warned the region would be "left to the adventurers of the United States, acting without regularity or capital, or the desire of conciliating future confidence, and looking only to the interest of the moment." When the network of forts Mackenzie recommended was finally being put in place during the next decade, they would spur Thomas Jefferson to organize the initially secret mission of Lewis and Clark.

Mackenzie had determined that there were no Straits of Admiral de Fonte. Though Vancouver would have valued this information, he had begun to reach the same conclusion. By September, after searching inlets a hundred miles farther along the coast toward Baranof Island, the British commander began to believe that stories about passageways from the Straits of de Fonte in the north and de Fuca in the south were fabrications. Disillusioned, and with the winter closing in on the bleak, rocky landscape as it had on Caamano the year before, he started back to Nootka, arriving on October 5.

The *San Carlos* was the only ship in the harbor at Friendly Cove. Ramon Saavedra had taken command from Fidalgo. He told Vancouver of the ships that had arrived and sailed for China: eight American traders, seven British, two French, and one Portuguese. Kendrick and the *Lady Washington* were still at Clayoquot. The *Jefferson* and *Resolution* were preparing to winter at Barkley Sound to the south. No orders or letters had come for Vancouver since he'd left for the north in the spring, and negotiations with Quadra remained suspended.

BACK IN LONDON, British and Spanish representatives signed a second Nootka agreement on February 12, 1793, in which Spain pledged that it would pay 210,000 Spanish dollars to John Meares as compensation for loss of his ships and land. But the agreement did not attempt to clarify the terms Vancouver and Quadra wrestled with. In fact, there were no other orders issued for Vancouver. The Home Office and the Admiralty were immersed in the spreading war in Europe, which had forced England and Spain into an unlikely alliance.

Vancouver knew nothing of this yet. He remained wary of the Spanish and saw the time for his expedition running out. While he had been given this opportunity to complete James Cook's work, in his darker moments he must have felt the voyage had become a fool's errand: he was ignored by his superiors as he attempted to claim lands for which there was no clear title and spent arduous months searching for a passage that did not seem to exist.

In the absence of explicit orders, and under a growing sense of failure, events ate at him. Hampered by Kendrick and the Americans, and by those he saw as treacherous natives, the frustrated commander became desperate for some victory. The importance of the Sandwich Islands for Britain's "extension of her commerce over the Pacific Ocean" made it imperative that he succeed there. It seemed like an outrageous goal, but he continued to want "a voluntary resignation of these territories [Sandwich Islands], by formal surrender of the king and the people to the power and authority of Great Britain." Achieving such a surrender, he wrote in his journal, would create "an incontrovertible right" and prevent altercations with other nations over claims to the Sandwich Islands in the future.

Vancouver and William Brown undoubtedly discussed the situation, and what to do about the Americans. Both men believed that those under the American flag had, as Vancouver wrote, "taken up their abode with different chiefs of some power and consequence, who esteemed these people as great acquisitions, from their knowledge of firearms . . ." Whether they understood Kendrick's distribution of muskets and his loose leadership of the "banditti of renegadoes" as part of a conscious strategy is not clear. Although Kendrick had no government support and little in the way of men or resources, his ability to form alliances and support native hostility posed a grave threat to British ambition. As in the insurrection on Kauai, Vancouver saw Kendrick and his men "furthering the ambitious views of the haughty chiefs, with whom they are resident" and blocking a surrender of the islands. He would need to raise a powerful threat to sway the chiefs to come under Britain's control. The influence of the Americans and other foreigners had to be removed.

On the morning of October 8, Vancouver headed south for New Albion and the mission ports of Spanish California. He wanted to repair *Discovery* in a safe harbor with ample supplies, and to gather more intelligence and gifts to renew the seduction of Kamehameha and his chiefs.

Stalled in light winds that first day, just south of Nootka, Vancouver noted a "strange sail" to windward that he could not overtake. John Kendrick was leaving Clayquot at about the same time, and the two ships might have crossed paths, but night was coming on and the strange sail slipped off in the darkness.

Chapter Nineteen

Possession

Sandwich Islands

January–March 1794

The shade under the deep canopy of leaves cooled the forest floor on the slopes above the village of Waiakea. James Boyd, followed by a priest, picked out the tall koa trees he wanted cut. Boyd had been brought here to the north side of Hawaii by John Kendrick and placed in the service of Kamehameha to build his dream ship, a forty-ton, thirty-six-foot armed sloop. The bulky island king was ecstatic. Boyd, who had been ship's carpenter for the *Jefferson,* was probably promised whatever he wanted by Kamehameha. Kendrick also received the king's gratitude for providing Boyd.

After the priest offered a prayer to mark each tree, the cutters would chop through the creamy sapwood and red heartwood and haul the logs to the shore to season before being trimmed into a frame. Confident of the outcome, Kendrick set off through the islands to trade and meet the men he had left nearly twenty months earlier: John Williams, John Rowbottom, and James Coleman. He had learned from Kamehameha and his chiefs that Vancouver was trying to persuade them to place Hawaii under British rule. And in the Leeward Islands he was stunned to find that William Brown had already struck an agreement with Kahekili that Brown believed gave him ownership of Maui, Lanai, Molokai, and Oahu. In light of their deep animosity toward Americans, there was no telling what steps Vancouver and Brown might take to close the islands to American ships. Returning to Kealakekua, Kendrick set out to determine what he could do to disrupt their plans.

Vancouver's ships were sighted on January 9. The weather was dark and gloomy, with low-lying clouds and the shore enveloped in fog. In the early morning, as the ships labored through a heavy ocean swell, the clouds and fog broke under strong winds from the north. Vancouver stood offshore and sent in three armed boats to find an anchorage at Waiakea harbor.

When Vancouver last saw Kamehameha ten months earlier in March 1793, the understanding was that they would meet here. Vancouver waited anxiously as a few daring canoes ventured into the wind to the ship. They traded fish and brought news of his arrival back to shore. At 10 A.M., Kamehameha appeared with several other chiefs and their women, breaking through the surf in a large canoe and flying an English pennant that Vancouver had given him. The robed island king offered a hearty welcome as he climbed on board, and told Vancouver that he had been awaiting his ship for weeks. The British commander responded warmly and bestowed presents on the chiefs and their women. It began as an auspicious reunion, but within a short time the conversation turned sour.

Vancouver was told that John Kendrick had left a shipwright named Boyd on shore, and that to Kamehameha's great joy, the frame of his first vessel had been cut. Vancouver also learned that Kendrick was on the opposite side of the island at Kealakekua, where he had been attended for the past two months by Kamehameha's aide, John Young.

The British commander tried to restrain himself. At this point, Kendrick must have seemed like a prescient ghost. During the last visit, Vancouver had turned down Kamehameha's request to leave a warship

Hilo from the Bay *by James Gay Sawkins. Vancouver turned down staying at the harbor at Waiakea/Hilo and was eager to leave for Kealakekua, where Kendrick was engaged with the chiefs.*

here. Although it seemed impossible, Kendrick had found a way to deliver one. As Brown had said, there were too many Americans settled here, and at Oahu, and Kauai. They had too much influence, and were always turning up behind the scenes to reinforce the chiefs' sense of independence and sovereignty with more arms. Things seemed to be going off course right from the start.

VANCOUVER WAS EAGER to get to Kealakekua and asked Kamehameha to come with him. The island king declined. There was a *makahiki* taboo on, and he was compelled to stay within the limits of the district in which the ceremonies had commenced. In addition to religious rites and festivities, a procession went to each district of the island to collect annual taxes. No one could travel until the task had been completed and the *makahiki* taboo was lifted. Vancouver suggested that Kamehameha seek the indulgence of the priests to break the taboo. Kamehameha refused and proposed that the vessels stay near Waiakea, promising they would be well supplied.

Vancouver was caught in a dilemma. He couldn't leave Kamehameha, and he couldn't let Kendrick remain unchallenged at Kealakekua. This would be his final chance to gain these islands. The festive atmosphere at Kealakekua, where Cook had been greeted as a god, was the essential backdrop for the diplomacy and seduction he planned. Kamehameha had to be there if Vancouver were to accomplish anything. Seeing no choice, he had to risk a desperate move.

Vancouver said he couldn't stay because there was no safe harbor for his ships along this coast. Kamehameha knew this was false and didn't respond. Afraid that the king would return ashore, Vancouver then provoked his jealousy, suggesting that their friendship had cooled, and that if he had to sail without him, he "had no doubt of soon finding amongst the other islands some chief, whose assistance, protection, and authority would on all occasions be afforded." It was a clear allusion to the Leeward Island kings Kahekili and Kaeo, and the teasing threat worked. Kamehameha probably knew of Brown's new alliance with the enemy chiefs and grew distraught. He stayed overnight on the *Discovery* but would not eat. He considered himself the last person who should violate the established taboo of leaving the district at this point in *makahiki,* yet he wanted and needed Vancouver's support. Yielding to the British commander, Kamehameha sent his half-brother, Kalaimamahu, ashore to reason with the priests and ask for an indulgence to break the taboo. But before the young chief could return with an answer, the *Discovery* set out with Kamehameha and the remaining six chiefs and their consorts.

The wind continued to blow hard out of the northwest and west, creating rough seas. As they rounded the eastern end of the island, tall columns of smoke rose over the upland, indicating volcanic activity and setting off superstitious whispers about the gods among Kamehameha's entourage. As they approached Kealakekua on June 12, the wind dropped and they lay offshore through the afternoon in light rain showers. In the evening, Vancouver sent a messenger for John Young to bring out hogs and vegetables. Young appeared the next morning, but brought no hogs because of the island-wide taboo. What he did have was a letter from John Howell, an agent for Kendrick now living ashore under the protection of Keeaumoku, the chief of the Kona district. It was a letter of welcome, and rankled Vancouver further. Late in the day, as the ships lay far out in the persisting calm, Young took Kamehameha ashore.

As dusk settled, Kamehameha arrived and there was a stir in the village with his landing and word of vessels offshore. At 10 P.M. three ships appeared at the broad entrance to the harbor—Vancouver's *Discovery,* followed by the *Chatham* and the storeship *Daedalus*. Kendrick called to have the American colors hoisted.

Kamehameha had fires lit along the beach near the *Discovery*'s former anchorage. Vancouver saw the lamplight of a ship already in that spot and maneuvered in close beside her. The *Washington* and her American flag appeared in the dark with a few of her crew on deck. At last he would come face-to-face with Kendrick.

Vancouver's ships were greeted by calls from shore as they anchored. Women paddled out to them. The British commander's sense of competition with Kendrick was evident. "At this late hour many of our former friends, particularly of the fair sex," Vancouver noted happily, "lost no time in testifying the sincerity of the public sentiment in our favor." Using a strategy of lavish praise, generous gifts, and veiled threats, he was determined to pull out all the stops to sway support away from the American renegades and get what he wanted.

During the passage, Vancouver had learned that James Boyd planned to construct Kamehameha's prized new vessel on the beach at Waiakea. Dismissing the shipwright's abilities, he told Kamehameha he would have the frame transported and his carpenters would construct the ship at Kealakekua. From his own supply rooms he would provide sails, a mast, spars, caulking, and tackle. Kamehameha was delighted. Vancouver congratulated himself that there was no other favor he could have bestowed that would have pleased the island king more. He completed his takeover of the project, declaring that the vessel would be christened *Britannia,* and described her as Kamehameha's first "man-of-war." In view of his constant criticism of others supplying weapons to the natives, taking over construction of a master weapon for Kamehameha showed that Vancouver was more than willing to compromise his "humanitarian" views and skirt the limits of his own orders.

Vancouver also found during the passage from Waiakea that Kamehameha was struggling with his personal life, being estranged from his favorite queen, the teenage Kaahumanu, because of suspected adultery between her and Kaiana. Kamehameha brushed aside Vancouver's offer to help him with a reconcilation, but the British commander would later persist in playing cupid when he recognized the critical gains Kaahumanu could deliver.

VANCOUVER'S SHIPS WERE IMPRESSIVE alongside the *Washington.* The sea-worn sixty-foot, ninety-ton American brigantine was much smaller than the eighty-foot, 135-ton *Chatham,* less than half the bulk of the 340-ton, ninety-nine-foot *Discovery,* and dwarfed by the storeship *Daedalus.* Vancouver seemed to have an endless supply of trade goods to offer (except the avidly desired weapons). And with more than one hundred eighty uniformed officers and men, the British expedition vastly outnumbered the *Washington*'s polyglot crew, which probably did not number thirty.

In his typical style, Kendrick took things head on. Early on the morning after the British arrival, he appeared on the deck of the *Discovery,* accompanied by John Howell and the district chief Keaweaheulu. Vancouver was in the midst of having livestock delivered ashore as a gift: a bull and two bull calves, a cow, three rams, and three ewes he had picked up at Monterey. Vancouver was perhaps surprised at Kendrick's impressive size and his direct, casual manner as he presented himself, dressed in the best coat his sea chest had to offer. This was the brazen American. Vancouver concealed his judgment in their polite banter.

He knew that Kendrick had already sailed among the other islands to check on affairs at Oahu and Kauai. It was clear that the American captain was taking advantage of any business opportunity to build his ties with these people. He was trading for feathered war cloaks, and one he had on board his ship was said to be nine feet long and twenty-four feet wide, the largest in the islands. He had reportedly given his two stern chasers for it. He also had on board chunks of ambergris, a grayish waxy substance produced by sperm whales, treasured in the East for making perfume. One piece was said to weigh more than eighty pounds (valued at about $230 per pound). His men at Kauai were still collecting sandalwood and pearls, and he would soon set up a small operation to make molasses there, which would trade at a premium for furs on the Northwest Coast. He told Vancouver that he had been at Kealakekua for six weeks and was wintering over before returning to the Northwest Coast next spring. Howell would be staying here to manage business.

Vancouver had already met Howell at Yuquot when he acted as one of Quadra's translators in the first failed negotiations two years before. He had impressed Vancouver as highly educated and articulate, though he would be regarded by later captains as a wayward opportunist and con artist.

Wanting to probe what these men were up to, and perhaps hoping to see Kendrick's charts of the Northwest Coast, Vancouver invited them to dine with him the following day. At daylight the next morning (January 15), three large canoes "laden with forty very fine hogs, and thirty small ones, with a proportionate quantity of vegetables" came to Vancouver's three ships from Kamehameha. The period of taboo was over, and many people were gathering for the festival of *makahiki*—celebrations and games, dancing, theatrical performances, and mock battles—characterized as "a sort of Saturnalia" by the Europeans. Thousands of people flooded into the two Kealakekua villages and camped in temporary shelters on the nearly barren lowlands to the south.

That evening Kendrick and Howell went on board the *Discovery* for dinner with Vancouver and his officers. After formalities and polite conversation, Kendrick wanted to talk about William Brown and the *Butterworth* group. He understood the constraints Vancouver was under as a royal officer. Brown, on the other hand, was free to commit whatever acts he chose, apparently with Vancouver's tacit approval. There was the episode of the killings at Clayoquot and hostility toward American traders, and other actions here in the islands, especially at Kauai.

Vancouver already had Brown's side of the story. In addition to their discussions, Brown left a letter for Vancouver at Kealakekua complaining that Kendrick's men had taken up arms at Kauai in support of Inamoo. The rebellion hadn't ended with the first round of killings. After Vancouver met captives in transit to Oahu last year, Kahekili sent a party of his warriors to investigate the rebellion. Inamoo was warned of war canoes approaching, and he dispatched Kendrick's men and others with muskets to the beach. They "drove them with great slaughter from the island," Vancouver noted, "and pursued them in their flight until they left few to relate . . . the untimely fate of those who had fallen." Vancouver believed that "This melancholy event would not, most probably, have happened had not these strangers advised and assisted in perpetuation of this diabolical and unprovoked barbarity . . ."

According to Brown, Kahekili received a report of the attack from the few survivors and decided to go to Kauai. Brown offered him the use of his ships and arms. He took Kahekili aboard the *Butterworth* and sailed to Kauai, where Inamoo was brought aboard and questioned. Inamoo explained that the rebellion had not been against Keao and Kahekili, but plotters had sought to overthrow Inamoo's regency and had to be stopped. Kahekili was satisfied with Inamoo's answers. Brown used the occasion to offer Kahekili a pledge of support and protection against any attack, including an assault from Kamehameha. Kahekili signed an agreement with him in the fall of 1793 giving Brown certain rights to the Leeward Islands. From a native perspective such agreements lasted only for the chief's lifetime, but Brown believed that he was now lord of all the Leeward Islands except Kauai and Niihau.

Seated at the table with Vancouver and his officers, Kendrick produced "a copy of a letter which Mr. Brown of the Butterworth left in Decr last [December 1793] with James Coleman at Woahoo [Oahu], importing that [Kahekili] had in the most formal manner ceded to him that island together with the four islands to windward, in consideration of some valuable presents he had made to the Chief, & to render his claim more solemn & binding he had an instrument drawn up, which was signed by himself & four of his officers on the one hand & four of the principal Chiefs on the other, after which he appointed James Coleman as resident on the island of Woahoo in charge of his claim."

Coleman resented Vancouver and British tyranny, and perhaps the prospect of serving Brown, and had recently passed the copy to Kendrick. There was a general belief among American traders that Brown had approval from the Crown to establish settlements for fur trading, fishing, and whaling. Kendrick might have questioned whether Brown negotiated his agreement as a private transaction or under royal authority.

Vancouver's role in encouraging Brown to gain possession of the Leeward Islands is not known. However, Vancouver did have a motive to support the taking—it complemented his effort at Hawaii perfectly and offered a brilliant strategy to increase his leverage with Kamehameha and the district chiefs. The thirty-gun *Butterworth,* the largest ship in the islands, gave Kahekili a powerful advantage in thwarting any ambition of Kamehameha and his chiefs to rule over the Leeward Islands. The

British commander now had the opportunity to assure Kamehameha that he could control Brown, who was a subject of the king.

There is no record of what Vancouver said to Kendrick concerning Brown. Hostility toward Kendrick from Vancouver's officers was noted, however. George Hewett, surgeon's mate on the *Discovery,* wrote that when he had asked Kendrick about trading for furs on the Northwest Coast, Kendrick answered that "he would fire at a village til they brought him fifty skins & this he intended to do every time." Hewett concluded that Kendrick was "one of the worst [traders] he saw and ought to have been taken by Captain V." Hewett missed the fact that Kendrick was being wryly sarcastic and ridiculing Brown's tactics of intimidation to gather furs.

Nevertheless, Kendrick kept up his contacts with Vancouver's officers, and on January 29 they took sail together north of Kealakekua to the small cove of Keauhou. The cove held a painful secret. Up near the beach, the *Fair American* lay half hidden, secured to trees and housed over with palm fronds to preserve her hull, which was said to be leaking badly and had to be pumped out every day. She was a haunting reminder of the overriding interest of the chiefs in acquiring armed ships, and how quickly events could turn.

Three days later, on February 1, the *Discovery*'s carpenters began laying the keel of the "man-of-war" frame brought from Waiakea for Kamehameha. At this point, Kendrick may have felt something slipping from him. Not only would the ship he had arranged for Kamehameha now become a British present, but there was a shift of attention to Vancouver. For two weeks Kendrick had watched Vancouver unload a continuous stream of gifts for Kamehameha, while his officers huddled with the king and local chiefs. Vancouver had clearly reached a point where he recognized a path to make his plan succeed. He grew very confident in his relationship with Kamehameha, "in whose good opinion and confidence I had now acquired such a predominancy." Vancouver noted that he had become acquainted with his most secret inclinations and apprehensions."

By playing on Kamehameha's pride, Vancouver had succeeded in persuading him to issue a summons for every district chief to attend a grand council at Kealakekua. Vancouver wanted to relaunch the discussion about ceding the island to Great Britain.

For the grand council, Kamehameha's brother, Keliimaki, arrived from Hilo, as did Kaiana from the east, where he had apparently been avoiding the island king's wrath after being suspected of having an affair with the queen. Her father, Keeaumoku, drifted in, as did others. The last to appear was Kameeiamoku, who arrived with a thousand men in canoes streaming into the harbor amid drumming and much pomp. Vancouver now had in the harbor the two men responsible for the massacre of the *Fair American*'s crew, as well as Palea, the man said to have first stabbed James Cook. There was a certain sense of dishonor Vancouver had to swallow in order to achieve what he wanted. He had to be unusually generous and forgiving to overlook those murderous acts and welcome these men. It was a hugely symbolic gesture to heal old wounds and showed he had learned his lessons from Quadra well.

On the night of February 19, Kendrick and his men watched as all the chiefs climbed aboard the *Discovery* for a festive dinner.

This was Vancouver's test. In a conciliatory conversation, Kameeiamoku explained that the taking of the *Fair American* was in retaliation for his having been whipped and beaten by Simon Metcalf, the father of the *Fair American*'s young captain. Others confirmed this. Vancouver solemnly listened to him and shook his hand as a token of forgiveness, then presented him with gifts. A feast of consecrated pork, followed by courses of dog, fish, chicken, and vegetables, gave way to wine and ship's grog. Unaccustomed to these drinks, Kameeiamoku showed little reserve and was soon quite drunk. In a sudden rush of suspicion, he believed that Vancouver had lured him to the ship and poisoned him. He grew savage, and as he was carried from the table he uttered the words "*attoou-anni,*" indicating the treachery to his men. His armed guards appeared ready to strike Vancouver when Kamehameha broke the tension by laughing at their suspicion and drinking from Kameeiamoku's bottle. Everyone rejoined the party, but Vancouver couldn't help worrying that his whole plan would have come apart if Kameeiamoku had died from the alcohol. In the atmosphere he was weaving, British credibility and trust were essential.

For Kendrick, who was pushed to the sidelines in these events, things slipped further when a young chief had his hand split open and the tips of his two middle fingers blown off by a musket that misfired. Whether or not the gun was from the *Washington* didn't matter. When he was treated by Menzies, the lesson preached was about the untrustworthiness of the traders and how their goods could not be relied upon. It was a steady theme.

Vancouver played on the difference between the British and the Americans, saying that the natives now understood the distinction between his "little squadron and the trading vessels." He explained to them that the traders were there for their own interests and private gain, "whilst those under my command acted under the authority of a benevolent monarch, whose chief object in sending us amongst them was to render them more peaceable in their intercourse with each other; to furnish them with things that would make them a happier people; and to afford them an opportunity of becoming more respectable in the eyes of foreign visitors."

And once Vancouver had the natives' trust, he wove in fear. Beneath his bedazzled view of imperial purpose, Vancouver introduced an image far more frightening than threats from Kahekili. He told the chiefs that powerful nations looked with envious eyes upon their domains, and "the period was not very remote when they might be compelled to submit" to foreign authority. To convince them, he undoubtedly pointed to Spain's vast domain and a litany of cruelty to native people in its colonies. He said their best choice was protection under Britain as the world's greatest naval power.

The argument clearly gave the group of chiefs pause. News brought back by those who had crossed the oceans to Boston and Macao and London confirmed their islands' place in a larger world, a world far advanced and wrapped in turbulence beyond their knowing. It was not hard to imagine a hundred armed ships and thousands of soldiers with muskets and cannon.

In addition to raising the threat of subjugation to an ambitious empire, Vancouver plied his seduction on an intimate level, taking on the role of devious intermediary for Kamehameha and the teenage Kaahumanu. Vancouver learned that Kaahumanu's father, Keeaumoku, had great influence with three chiefs who posed the strongest opposition to cession of the islands to Britain. Realizing that Keeaumoku wanted his daughter restored to the royal household, Vancouver spun a sugary deceit. He convinced Kamehameha that he could bring about a reconciliation and invited the estranged queen and her parents on board under the guise of giving them special presents. He then sent a signal ashore to Kamehameha, who seemed to appear at the door of Vancouver's cabin by chance. In that moment of surprise, Vancouver joined the couple's hands, and tears and bliss followed. The only whiff of reality Vancouver admitted was that before they all left the ship, Kaahumanu pleaded that Kamehameha should be made to promise not to beat her.

Keeaumoku was won over and the island king was delighted. "The domestic affairs of Kamehameha having taken such a happy turn," Vancouver wrote, "his mind was at liberty for political considerations; and the cession of Owyhee to His Britannic Majesty became now an object of serious concern." Vancouver moved quickly.

On Tuesday, February 25, the British commander convened a historic meeting of all the leading chiefs of Hawaii on board the *Discovery* "for the purpose of formally ceding and surrendering the island of Owyhee to me for his Britannic Majesty and his heirs and successors." At dawn that day, he toured the ship to make sure all was ready. For Kendrick, the quarterdeck of the *Lady Washington* offered a prime vantage point for viewing the drama playing out.

Hours ahead of time, Vancouver had Lieutenant Peter Puget of the *Chatham* and the officers of both ships drawn up as witnesses. Kamehameha and the seven other chiefs arrived shortly before noon in full formal regalia: Keeaumoku, father of the queen and a chief of the Kona district; Kameeiamoku, the fearsome chief of Koahala; Kaiana, and Kamehameha's three brothers and a cousin.

The robed island chief rose and recited the reasons for ceding the island. He noted that several nations had now visited them. Each of these nations was too powerful for them to resist. Also, the visitors were coming more frequently and their numbers were increasing. Kamehameha expressed his fear that one of these nations would claim them and stated that it was necessary to align with one of their choosing. He said he would become a subject of Great Britain and asked who would follow. Five chiefs spoke. Keeaumoku, father of the queen, assumed the cession would happen and proposed that "when a force for their protection should be obtained from England, the first object of its employment ought to be the conquest of Mowee [Maui]." He reasoned that if a chief friendly to Hawaii were installed at Maui, the Hawaiians would have more assurance for total peace. Kaiana agreed with Keeaumoku, and proposed that an authorized guard be stationed on the island and that a war vessel or two be provided by Britain for defense by sea. All the speakers repeated that they wanted no interference with their religion or the priests, no disruption of their system of chiefs, and no change in their way of life and trade.

Vancouver apparently gave promises to meet their conditions. In addition to constructing Kamehameha's sloop *Brittania,* island historians believe that Vancouver promised Kamehameha another man-of-war armed with brass cannons. This promise was fulfilled years later. "These preliminaries being fully discussed and thoroughly understood on both sides," Vancouver wrote, the momentous climax of the courtship was at hand. According to Vancouver, Kamehameha stated again that he agreed to the cession of the island "and the whole party declared their consent by saying that they were no longer Tanata no Owyhee [the people of Hawaii], but Tanata no Britannee [people of Britain]."

Puget went ashore and proceeded to raise the British flag on a pole erected at Kaawaloa "and took possession of the island in his Majesty's name." The ships fired a salute that resounded off the cliffs and across the bay. A statement inscribed on a copper sheet presented to Kamehameha commemorated the event: "On the 25th February, 1794, Kamehameha, king of Owyhee, in council with the principal chiefs of the island assembled on board His Britannic Majesty's Sloop Discovery, in Karakakooa bay, and in the presence of George Vancouver commander of said sloop, Lieutenant Peter Puget, commander of said Majesty's armed tender Chatham, and the other officers of the Discovery; after due consideration, unanimously ceded the said island of Owyhee, to His Britannic Majesty, and acknowledged themselves subjects of Great Britain."

The event was a defeat for Kendrick, but its impact was uncertain. Britain's claim could obstruct Spain or any other nation from taking possession of Hawaii, but it was not clear what it would mean for Americans and other foreigners and their trading outposts. William Brown had charged that through the advice and example of these traders and their men, "the natives of most of the Leeward Islands had arrived at such a degree of daring insolence" that sending in small boats or anchoring near the shores was "highly dangerous." He told Vancouver that he "trusted it might be within the limits of [Vancouver's] authority to take from these islands such improper and dangerous associates."

Now, with the agreement for cession in place, Vancouver launched an effort to remove Kendrick and other traders. The British commander noted that he told Kamehameha "in the strongest terms all the bad consequences that were likely to result from those people remaining on Owyhee." But no arguments could induce Kamehameha or the other chiefs to "deliver up" these men, who included Boyd and Howell. Unlike Kendrick's men at Kauai, who had killed Kahekili's warriors, Vancouver could cite no specific charges against them, and he was afraid to cause a breach of the new agreement by compelling the men to be produced. He urged Kamehameha to trust only the two British subjects, John Young and Isaac Davis, and to prevent any other foreigners from residing or taking land on the island. The chiefs invoked their control of local matters, and the advice was turned aside. Kendrick had done his work, his relationships with the chiefs held, and the cession appeared somewhat symbolic and hollow.

It seemed that Kendrick would be able to proceed as if nothing had occurred at Hawaii, and he would ignore William Brown's claim in the Leeward Islands as well. Inamoo and Kaeo would certainly resist any high-handed efforts by William Brown to take control there. It remained to be seen what Brown would do. On the day before the cession ceremony, Brown had started back from Canton with the *Jackall* and *Prince Lee Boo,* after having sent the *Butterworth* homeward. There would soon be a reckoning with him.

UNDER A QUARTER MOON, the British expedition left Kealakekua at 3 A.M. on February 26 and proceeded along Hawaii's west coast toward the Leeward Islands to complete their survey and evaluation of the harbors and lands. Giddy with his accomplishment, Vancouver confided in his journal that he was perfectly convinced that if he had passed back and forth among the islands he could have negotiated peace (a general pacification), but unfortunately did not have the time or circumstances. The British commander was dreaming. The relative tranquility would not hold. The chiefs' dynastic ambitions would have to play themselves out. Vancouver's agreement would be of little benefit to Kamehameha in his inter-island war, and time would tell whether it would serve the interests of British merchants and imagined plantation owners.

Perhaps seeking to further dampen Vancouver's claims of British dominion in the islands, Kendrick went ahead of the *Discovery,* arriving before Vancouver at harbors and meeting with chiefs before the British captain could reach them. While Vancouver ran up the west coast of Hawaii, Kendrick sailed to Oahu and spent five days at Waikiki with

Kahekili and his chiefs. When Vancouver arrived, Kahekili and Kaeo did not come to meet him. He again encountered Kendrick and the *Washington* at Waimea on Kauai. "Having beaten around the east end of the island he arrived two days ahead of us," Vancouver noted. Here the British commander tried to pressure Kendrick into withdrawing his men, and Vancouver thought he seemed to acquiesce. However, when the *Discovery* and *Chatham* set sail from the islands on March 14, Kendrick and his men were still there.

Chapter Twenty

Last Season

Northwest Coast

April 1794–November 1794

Vancouver steered for the American coast in a last attempt to find the Northwest Passage and secure British claims. His health, his supplies, and his patience were wearing down. He had dismissed the possibility of a passage branching from the Strait of Juan de Fuca and the Straits of Admiral de Fonte and was now headed for the northern reaches of the Gulf of Alaska. "Having ascertained satisfactorily that there was not any extensive navigation eastwardly, between the 30th and 56th degrees of north latitude on this side of the American continent," he wrote, "I was led to believe, that if any such did exist, it would most probably be found communicating with Cook's River" at the northern end of the Gulf below the Kenai Peninsula.

He made the coast in April at 60° north latitude, finding ranges of "stupendous" mountains covered in snow. The green-black waters of "Cook's River" were choked with drift ice and they encountered hundreds of kayaks with Aleuts speaking Russian and offering to trade. They found the river terminated in marshes and low icy plains backed by continuous mountains. Vancouver was deeply dismayed. In a rare moment he criticized James Cook, lamenting that if the "great explorer" had "dedicated one more day to its further examination," he would have spared others from "ingeniously ascribing" a Northwest Passage to this channel. Exploring southward, he was again disappointed to find only more blind inlets and walls of ice among the bays and rivers of Prince William Sound.

In an odd parallel to the supposed chance encounter with William Brown a year earlier at a remote bay below Dundas Island, on July 3, he came across Brown and the *Jackall* near Cross Sound. Brown had just arrived on the coast, having stopped at the Sandwich Islands on his way from Canton and Macao. Vancouver may have hoped that he carried a dispatch from the Admiralty. Instead, Brown delivered devastating news.

Vancouver was stunned by "the latest accounts of the state of Europe that had appeared in China before his sailing." France had declared war on England. Louis XVI had been sent to the guillotine and there was anarchy and a reign of terror in the streets of Paris. At home, internal rebellion was stirring against King George, promoted

View of Prince William Sound and Captain Cook's Ships *by John Webber. At Prince William Sound, Vancouver continued to encounter disillusionment as mountains of snow and ice rose where waterways inland were hoped to lie.*

by discontented British subjects through "the promulgation of French doctrines, to subvert [Britain's] inestimable constitution."

Vancouver understood now why he had gotten no response from London. The world was burning with what seemed to be a crazed revolutionary fervor. Everything was in upheaval. France had also declared war against Spain and sent troops over the Pyrenees. In this strange twist of events, Britain and Spain were cast together as unlikely allies. Vancouver pondered what these events meant for their mission. The fire sweeping Europe was sure to affect the setting and holding of either empire's boundaries in the Pacific.

Vancouver undoubtedly told Brown of Kamehameha's cession of the island of Hawaii to Great Britain and of his failure to seize American residents in the islands as Brown had hoped. In the Atlantic, American merchant ships were being taken and their crews impressed for service on British vessels. But there was no prospect of that here. Seizing Kendrick's ship and crew would be too blatant an act, and reached beyond Vancouver's orders as long as the United States remained neutral.

In dark squalls and showers, Vancouver separated from the *Jackall,* and under close-reefed topsails the *Discovery* attempted to beat to windward and make her way further south.

AT NOOTKA, KENDRICK HEARD the same news of war in Europe from Ramon Saavedra. The notion of Britain and Spain as allies was baffling. Kendrick realized that his outlook could quickly turn bleak if Britain and Spain established joint control of the coast, or if the Americans were swept into war on the side of France.

As it was, the situation at Yuquot was dismal. Maquinna and his people had suffered extreme hardship during the winter and had been out of food for months. There may have been any number of causes—illnesses transmitted from the Spanish or the trading ships, poor fall salmon runs, or raiding between tribes. Maquinna's emaciated face indicated how dire the situation was for his people. Saavedra was credited with providing supplies that kept many from starving. But the rift with Wickaninish over their children's marriage continued. In his weakened condition, Maquinna feared an attack and wanted to move his village closer to the Spanish guns. Saavedra refused.

Kendrick learned that the winter at Barkley Sound for the *Jefferson* and *Resolution* did not go well either. One of the *Jefferson*'s men had been killed while he was hunting alone, and some of the *Jefferson*'s goods and equipment had been stolen. In retaliation, the *Jefferson*'s captain, Josiah Roberts, copied Robert Gray's actions and staged a raid on the village of Seshart as they prepared to depart in late March. Armed boats fired swivel guns at the houses, forcing the people to flee into the woods. The sailors then went in among the houses, taking "anything of consequence," including a great quantity of dried fish, copper, a supply of gunpowder, and one musket. They also tore down houses, smashed large canoes onshore, and rafted up others and stole them. "After having sufficient satisfaction for their depravations on us," the first mate Bernard Magee wrote, the *Jefferson* sailed from the sound.

Kendrick had no idea what part his son might have played. Solomon had already gone south in the *Resolution* to "Gray's River." From there, the schooner planned to cruise north to the Queen Charlotte Islands. Sea otter furs around Nootka and Clayoquot were getting harder to come by, and with few furs, and intertribal conflict pending at Nootka, Kendrick took the *Washington* north.

THE MISERY AT NOOTKA INCREASED after he left. In mid-May, just as the weather was beginning to turn warm, a three-day gale from the south and west struck with unprecedented ferocity. Huge swells devastated the shore and surged into the sound. In Friendly Cove, gusts rocked the ships at anchor so violently their yardarms touched the water. As the winds raged, Saavedra feared the commandant's house would be blown down. Several natives died, and the villages suffered great damage.

The British trader *Jenny* had ridden out the storm in a protected harbor near the Columbia River. She now came north and met the *Jefferson,* and Captain Roberts learned that Solomon's schooner had sailed from the Columbia River about May 1. Roberts concluded that "No vessel could survive the force of the gale at sea . . . The Resolution if she were at sea must Doubtless be lost & that it was not possible for her to live through so hard and extensive a gale."

Word of the lost ship did not reach John Kendrick. He was among the hundreds of islands of the Alexander Archipelago of southern Alaska, which he had first explored in the fall of 1789. The foggy, mosquito-infested shores and inlets were rich with furs. At the Tlingit settlement Shee-Aitka (Sitka), which would soon become a new trading center for the region, he disposed of all his trade goods, including fifty gallons of molasses his men had pressed at Kauai. By mid-July, he started south for Nootka. Perhaps having been told by native people that there was no passage eastward, or chastened by the fruitless British search, he made no further explorations for the mythical waterway. He concentrated instead on securing his American outpost.

DISMAYED BY THE NEWS of war and revolution, and with his health breaking down, Vancouver reluctantly reached a final determination about the Northwest Passage as well. On August 16, 1794, in a harbor near the southern end of Baronof Island named "Port Conclusion," he finally declared their momentus search at an end. "Following up the discoveries of De Fuca, De Fonte and a numerous train of hypothetical navigators," he had found no Northwest Passage. What he had discovered was a foggy, wild, thickly forested coastline congested with islands and countless blind inlets peopled by fierce tribes. Upon the announcement, the crew celebrated with "no small portion of facetious mirth." The next day, seeking to give import to their endless mapping, the survey crews went ashore and raised their flag. With three musket volleys, "and all the other formalities usual on such occasions" Vancouver took possession of the area from New Georgia (the mainland at the southern end of the Strait of Juan de Fuca) northwestward to Cape Spencer (Cross Sound) and all the islands within that thousand-mile stretch of coast for "His Britannic Majesty, his heirs, and successors." It was a grand symbolic gesture, and an attempt to match what he had accomplished at Hawaii.

On August 22, the ships started south to Nootka in heavy fog and adverse winds. At six in the evening on Tuesday, September 2, the *Discovery* anchored at Friendly Cove. The *Chatham* did not arrive until after dark. At anchor in the cove were the Spanish ships *Princesa, Aranzazu,* and *San Carlos* and the British traders *Phoenix* and *Prince Lee Boo,* as well as John Kendrick with the *Lady Washington*.

THE EFFECTS OF THE MASSIVE MAY STORM were still evident along the shore at Yuquot. Uprooted trees and flotsam littered the shore. Cavernous washouts marred the fields where gardens had been planted, and then replanted. A few Mowachaht houses were planked and occupied, and a stained sailcloth tent stood in the north corner of the cove on the ground John Meares had claimed. Beside it, Kendrick had the *Washington* laid up on the beach, graving her hull.

By now, Kendrick had heard of the disappearance of the *Resolution*. Loss of a ship and her crew was a fact of life at sea, but the loss of a son or a loved one left a hollow feeling of unfinished business. There were many unanswered questions. Roberts had taken the *Jefferson* to Canton in August without coming south, so there was no opportunity to ask him what search had been made, or any details of the fate of Solomon and his ten crewmates. Everything was hearsay.

Kendrick had some consolation in his anguish. His eldest son, now known as Juan Kendrick, had arrived as master of the Spanish frigate *Aranzazu*. Twenty-five years old, he had worked his way up from junior officer and pilot. During the last five years he had spent much time in Mexico, run supply trips to the California missions, and crossed the Pacific to Manila with the captured *Princess Royal.*

In an odd encounter at the Sandwich Islands, Juan and the pilot Manuel Quimper had engaged in a standoff with James Colnett, who was making his final, fateful passage to Macao after his release from San Blas. Colnett demanded they turn over the *Princess Royal* to him or he would blow them out of the water. Juan Kendrick went on board the *Argonaut* to negotiate. With his usual tragic blundering, Colnett seized him and then sent demands written in English to Quimper that no one could translate. In an attempt to end the foolishness, Quimper went on board the *Argonaut* and convinced Colnett to receive the *Princess Royal* at Macao.

The story may have amused the elder Kendrick, but it could not make the reunion with his son anything but bittersweet. There was more than the loss of Solomon. Although Juan was well stationed at the moment, he served a foreign king who was at war. Kendrick might have asked himself if it would have been better to leave both sons at home with land and a plow. He had lost good men on the *Avenger,* and now Solomon. He did not want to lose his eldest son. More than enough had been sacrificed on this far side of the world. His judgment and emotions were probably clouded. Even though it was a sailor's common fate to disappear and never be seen again, as a father, he may have held out hope that some of the crew had survived and Solomon might miraculously turn up.

What he didn't know was that the little schooner had been overwhelmed in July at a village in the Queen Charlotte Islands. All of the crew except one were massacred by a group led by Coyah, a chief named Scotsi, and his brother. Coyah had known that Kendrick's son was aboard. Juan Kendrick learned of the massacre later, and in 1798 he and others who had lost relatives or friends on the *Resolution* would exact revenge on these chiefs.

His father would hear only rumors as he focused on getting the

Washington ready for sea. Kendrick had been away from home for seven years now. This would be his fifth trans-Pacific voyage. His eldest son would have seen as no one else how the years had begun to weigh on the massive shoulders of his father. Juan had told Estevan Martinez years before that John Kendrick was sacrificing wealth for glory. The sacrifice had become much more than wealth, and he had gained no glory. Following the lead of whatever letters he had received from his mother, Juan most likely urged his father to turn homeward and, like Odysseus, at least retake his position and good name from those who had tried to destroy him.

There were many appealing reasons to go. The *Washington* had two seasons of furs in her hold, and more than eighty pounds of ambergris from Oahu (if he had not traded it to another ship). The ambergris alone was worth as much as sixteen thousand dollars. Kendrick had his trade alliances and his five deeds for much of the land along the coast. In the Sandwich Islands, his men were in place and had established friendships with the chiefs. He could head homeward and return with the ships he wanted to ply the coast, securing the American outposts and the Sandwich Island trade.

There was also a way to redeem himself with Joseph Barrell, although he was not aware of it. Waiting at Macao was a letter from Barrell. He had considered Kendrick's offer to purchase the *Lady Washington,* and wrote that if Kendrick "would send [him] to any part of the Continent 400 chests of Bohea Tea of the best quality, he paying the freight" (a total of about fourteen thousand dollars for the cargo), Barrell would discharge him.

Barrell told a partner: "I place no dependence on this, but am told he can procure the tea if he wishes it & Mr. Hoskins, who went on the second voyage of Columbia, is of the opinion that Kendrick will yet turn out an honest man . . ."

Kendrick may have taken Barrell's offer to purchase the rugged ship. But it was unlikely he would sail homeward if there were any chance of not returning to the Pacific. At the village of Wareham, or in the streets of Boston, he would be expected to act the part of a modest churchgoing merchant. He was a king here, immersed in the horrors and pleasures and ever-present dangers of a frontier. The wilderness on the far side of the world had become part of him, and his work was not yet finished. At the heart of the glory he sought, he was shaping a Pacific outpost and a legacy for the new nation.

Perhaps from the beginning of the voyage, long before he saw this coast and the islands, the dreamer in him knew there would be no turning back. Although this season had become darker and more dismal than ever before, he held to his faith in the importance of his mission. As so often happened in the bleakest moments of his life, something now appeared that would lift the cloud of misery and throw his prospects wide open.

Two days before Vancouver arrived at Nootka, the *Princesa* came into the sound carrying Brigadier General Don José Manuel Alava as newly appointed governor of Nootka. Bodega y Quadra had died of a lingering illness in Mexico, and Alava had come at last to complete negotiations with Vancouver. The Third Nootka Convention had been signed in London on January 11, 1794. As the conflagration in Europe brought Britain and Spain together as allies, the agreement became one that would allow both nations to save face. Meares's land would be handed over to Britain; Spain would dismantle the village and forts of San Miguel and San Rafael; a British flag would be raised and lowered; and then, surprisingly enough, both nations would abandon the sound.

Kendrick would be left unhampered by foreign nations on the coast. While Europe was at war, fewer British traders would appear, and he and other American vessels would have an opportunity for expanding a monopoly on trade. This would be certain to attract American merchants. And what might he expect from his letter to Jefferson, with copies of his deeds? What opportunities might lie in the fur-rich waters of southern Alaska and Sitka, or for whaling?

Both Alava and Vancouver were awaiting final instructions. The documents were expected at any time, but Alava's orders were to sail for Monterey if the packet ship did not arrive with his papers before October 15. Vancouver hauled out the *Discovery* and began repairs as they waited.

THE WEATHER DID NOT SEEM quite as gloomy during that first week in September. The rain that fell continuously during the day usually cleared in the evening. At night a light breeze drifted off the land. When the clouds broke for a few days, the crew of the *Washington* was able to make headway on their ship. By September 11, no instructions had arrived for Alava, but Juan Kendrick came to his father and said he had received orders to take the *Aranzazu* south to San Blas. He was carrying a letter from Vancouver to the Admiralty, stating that the expedition had completed its survey of the Northwest Coast and the British captain was awaiting orders on a final settlement with Spain.

In the midst of that rain and gloom, father and son embraced as they had five years before, perhaps promising to send letters through passing ships between San Blas and Macao or Kealakekua, but sure of nothing, except that the seasoned American captain would continue to pursue his costly and uncertain glory.

Once the *Washington* was repaired, Kendrick most likely went up to Mawina. Maquinna would have told him how Vancouver and Alava had come to see him at Tahsis in armed boats to explain that they were leaving. His warriors had brought out all their guns and performed a dance to celebrate, perhaps to reinforce the wisdom of the decision. Maquinna's people were well on the way to recovery from the previous winter. He might have envisioned for Kendrick how they would reclaim Yuquot, dismantling what the Spanish left behind and returning things to the way they had always been.

WITH THE APPROACH OF THE FALL EQUINOX, the weather remained unpredictable. Sudden showers and squalls blew in off the ocean and the winds increased. On the evening of Sunday, October 5, a ship appeared, which was thought to be the overdue Spanish packet but turned out to be the *Jackall*. Brown had collected a thousand prime sea otter skins in his cruise to the north. Vancouver hosted him on board and told him of the claim he had made to the thousand miles of coast for King George. Then he told him of the plan to abandon Nootka. The irony that Spain and Britain had almost gone to war over a port that would now be abandoned must have struck both men. The obvious question for Brown was who would protect him against hostility here on the coast and against interlopers in his claimed domain in the Leeward Islands, especially if Kendrick continued to expand his influence or brought in other American ships.

Vancouver's health was worsening, and Brown realized there was nothing more the British commander could do. He would be on his own. On October 15, after deciding that the Spanish packet was not coming, Vancouver had his men pack up the tents and instruments onshore. At midnight on October 16 the *Discovery* and the *Chatham* were towed out of the cove headed for Monterey. The *Princesa,* with Salvador Fidalgo and Governor Alava, departed the next day.

The *Lady Washington* lay snug in Safe Retreat Harbor at Mawina. Kendrick and several men from his original crew had outlasted all the commanders and leaders of other expeditions: Estevan Martinez, John Meares, James Colnett, Bodega y Quadra, Fidalgo, and Vancouver. And now they would contend with Brown.

Awaiting a break in the weather, and perhaps hoping for some further word of Solomon, Kendrick stayed late on the coast. Finally, taking the night breeze through Mawina's narrow channel, under stars that filled the sky and dark waters, they cruised past the forested cliffs along the shore. At the mouth of the cove below the crude log fort, only the *San Carlos* could be seen at anchor. Brown's *Jackall* and *Prince Lee Boo* had already left for Oahu.

Chapter Twenty-One

The Fire's Reach

Sandwich Islands

December 1794

THE *WASHINGTON* ANCHORED at her usual mooring beneath the immense cliff at Kealakekua. They were just yards off the beach from the stone temple and well. The "wives" of the men excitedly came on board and their familiar voices rang with the sense of a homecoming. The harbor seemed spacious with Vancouver's ships gone, although the British presence was still clear in the British flag John Young was flying outside Kamehameha's royal house. No one knew it, but half a world away the British had stepped up attacks on neutral American ships and were impressing their crews. The United States and Britain were again on the verge of war. Newspapers in Boston and New Bedford and other port cities ran a steady stream of reports on local ships being chased or seized. Britain was growing desperate, running out of men and money to conduct the war with France. On June 1, a major naval battle took place far out in the Atlantic as the British tried to stop American merchant ships carrying

The Glorious First of June *by Philippe Loutherbourg. At the close of the eighteenth century, many European nations warred over who would become the world's next hegemonic superpower. The battle on the "Glorious First of June," 1794, marked expansion in the struggle between France and Britain that threatened to draw in the United States. The global conflict was also reflected in the contest for control of the Hawaiian Islands.*

vital grain to France. The British managed to sink several French warships serving as an escort, but the grain ships made it to port. Both sides claimed the engagement as a victory.

To stay out of war, Washington sent John Jay as special envoy to London to negotiate a treaty. Jay made wildly unpopular concessions and was burned in effigy in America's town squares. On his return to New York, he would muse that it was enough fire to light his way along the coast between Boston and Phildelphia at night.

BRITAIN WAS AT THE START of a long ascendancy, but here in the Sandwich Islands, despite the British flag flying, Kendrick would concede nothing. For a few days, trade at Kealakekua proceeded in a warm, relaxed manner and Kendrick continued to build his base of support. Among the crew on board with Kendrick was a young Spaniard, Francisco Palo Marin, whom he planned to leave here to help gather sandalwood. A Kauai native whom Kendrick had nicknamed "General Washington" was also on board. He would return home to serve as one of Kendrick's men at the other end of the island chain.

Local trust in Kendrick remained high, and he was relied upon by other Americans. John Young came aboard the *Washington* and told Kendrick that the *Jefferson* had run aground when she was here a few months earlier. Her captain, Josiah Roberts, had left debts for Kendrick to pay for their stay. Several muskets were owed. Kendrick had cargo to cover the debt and didn't mind Roberts's dependence. Everything would be settled up at Macao after the new year. With the British and Spanish leaving Nootka, the *Washington*'s prospects had never been better. He could settle his outpost at Mawina next spring and establish himself firmly here in the islands. More than just fur trading, there were sandalwood and pearls and the potential for whaling. For a few placid days in the harbor it may have seemed that Kendrick and his men had reached a certain stability at last. Then came dire news from Oahu.

After three years of relative peace in the islands, warfare was breaking out. Kahekili, the last of the old Leeward Island lords, had died in July at Waikiki. The aged king left Oahu to his son Kalanikupule. The islands of Maui, Kahoolawe, Molokai, and Lanai were given to the rule of Kahekili's half-brother Kaeo, who also remained chief of Kauai. The division set off the kind of uneasiness and plotting among subchiefs that had occurred on Hawaii more than a decade before, and left both Kalanikipule and Kaeo wary and suspicious.

Adding to the rancor was the agreement Kahekili had made with Brown, giving him rights to Maui, Lanai, Molokai, Kahoolawe, and Oahu. Grants by island kings typically ended with their death, and

Kaeo most likely believed that Brown's grant was now terminated. Brown may have appealed to Kalanikupule and offered him arms and support. This would have goaded Kaeo's chiefs further. Given traditional jealousies, the potential for trouble needed little stirring.

In early November, with *makahiki* season under way, there was a lesser threat of attack from Kamehameha in Hawaii. Kaeo gathered up a large party of his warriors and started home to Kauai from Molokai where he commanded the Leeward Island defense. During the journey, he planned to stop on Oahu's northeast shore, at a traditional spot for food and rest near the village of Waimanalo.

There is some speculation that Kaeo had hostile intent. Kalanikupule's chiefs on Oahu certainly suspected it and were on edge. They spotted Kaeo's fleet of canoes approaching and prepared for an attack by digging trenches and quickly piling up earthworks.

When Kalanikupule's chiefs blocked Kaeo's canoes from landing, Kaeo's men became offended and eager for a fight. In a running skirmish with the canoes cruising along the shore, Kaeo's sharpshooter, Marc Amara, began picking out Oahu chiefs who wore brilliant feathered cloaks, and killed one of Kalanikupule's favored advisers. Kalanikupule arrived and withdrew his men to halt the fighting. The next day, he let Kaeo's canoes come ashore, and they met and cried together, renewing their trust and lamenting the death of Kahekili.

After pledging peace, Kaeo continued along the shore to the south side of the island, stopping at the villages on the way and then at Waianae on the west coast. But while he rested there he learned of a plot that had risen among his subchiefs. Eager for war on Oahu, they planned to drown Kaeo during the seventy-mile passage to Kauai. Kaeo had to decide whether to break his pledge of peace to Kalanikupule or be thrown overboard like a dog. Fighting to gain a kingdom and save his life, or dying bravely in battle, were preferable options to drowning at the hands of his own chiefs. Reluctantly, he chose to attack Kalanikupule.

Word of the pending battle spread through the islands. Men were drawn from Maui, Molokai, Lanai, and Kauai. Thousands amassed.

The outcome would have far-reaching consequences for control of the leeward domain. For William Brown, the situation was critical. If Kaeo became the victor, Brown could lose his claim to these islands, unraveling what he and Vancouver had won and jeopardizing potential fortunes that could not be regained. He quickly placed his ships, arms, and men into service for Kalanikupule.

On November 21, Brown appeared at the entrance to Honolulu Harbor, just a few miles west of Waikiki and about twenty miles to the southeast of Waianae, where Kaeo was encamped. The native people called the harbor "Kou." Brown had reputedly been the first European to enter it through a narrow channel in the reef a year earlier. Although other traders knew of the harbor, and Vancover had mentioned it, Honolulu had not appeared very noteworthy. The surrounding shore was rocky and relatively desolate, with a small, poor village, muddy beach, and random clumps of brush and a thin line of palm trees above the tide line. Higher up the slopes, scrub vegetation grew thicker and greener as it climbed to the rugged and verdant Koolau Mountains. Just to the west was the channel to Wai Momi (Pearl Harbor), which branched into three inlets entering rough terrain cut with ravines and rising ground. Despite its impoverished appearance, Honolulu was a hidden jewel, the only harbor in the islands that offered a protected anchorage and deep water close to shore. Brown had named it Fair Haven and seemed to regard the harbor as his own. This is where he wanted to cut off Kaeo's advance on Waikiki. It was about to become a killing ground.

To counter Kaeo's sharpshooters and gunners from Kauai, Brown armed Kalanikupule's gathering troops with powder and muskets and added several of his own men. Kaeo landed his forces on the beach to the west of Pearl Harbor at Ewa and marched overland. Except for rocky valleys and marshes, the shore was broad and open, offering ideal terrain for gunners. In the first encounter, at a place named Punahawele, Marc Amara killed one of Brown's men and a few other foreigners under Kalanikupule, and Kaeo's warriors routed the Oahu forces. Skirmishing continued for several days, and Kaeo steadily advanced along the shore and hills of Ewa above Pearl Harbor. Temporarily beaten, Kalanikupule collected his scattered forces along the eastern arm of Pearl Harbor between the Kalauao shore and the upper fields of Aiea. Protected by a natural ridge and cliffs to the northeast, Kalanikupule determined to halt Kaeo there in a decisive battle.

EXACTLY WHAT NEWS CAME to Kealakekua, or how much Kendrick knew, is not recorded, but he did find out that Brown had sided with Kalanikupule. While skirmishing along the shore had not been cause for alarm, Brown's involvement altered the nature of the fight. If Kalanikupule and Brown were victorious over Kaeo, they would take Kauai and Niihau. This would give Brown control over all the Leeward Islands. Brown had to be stopped at Oahu. With his habitual practice of plunging into the center of events, Kendrick took John Howell and others on board the *Washington* and sailed for Honolulu. On December 3, the *Washington* warped through the crooked, narrow channel. Brown's two ships, the *Jackall* and *Prince Lee Boo,* stood outlined against the rocky shore.

Kendrick's exact purposes are unknown, and there are widely varying accounts about the role he played. Some accounts state that Brown appealed to Kendrick for help, and he agreed to assist the British merchant for a price. But local historians, relying on information from natives who observed the battles and had a detailed understanding of the conflict between the Americans and British, say that Kendrick took no part in the fight. The appearance of the *Washington* would have provoked Brown's deep-seated hostility toward the Americans, and especially toward Kendrick, who had caused a litany of problems: the infamous capture of Colnett's *Argonaut;* the muskets provided at Clayoquot that Wickaninish used to drive Brown and his men from the sound; Kendrick's claim of lands on the Northwest Coast; Vancouver's inability to remove him and his men from the islands; and Kendrick's men and arms from Kauai opposing him now, causing the deaths of Brown's gunner and Kalanikupule's steady loss of ground. Given what they each had at stake, the coming battle held the element of a proxy war between the two men.

Kendrick's low regard for Brown and his brutal trading tactics was obvious in the sarcastic parody he had offered to Vancouver's officers. But in this remote harbor now, Kendrick was outgunned by Brown's two ships. Anchoring near the *Jackall,* Kendrick undoubtedly exchanged formalities and discussed the situation. Perhaps he wanted to dampen Brown's involvement by standing witness to the events about to occur, or to intervene at a critical moment. Going ashore, Kendrick may also have met with Kaeo and Kalanikupule as the two sides prepared for battle.

WITHIN DAYS OF KENDRICK'S ARRIVAL, Kaeo's men crossed the Pearl River and advanced on Aiea. While the *Prince Lee Boo* remained with the *Washington,* Brown took the *Jackall* up into the eastern arm of Pearl Harbor. He sent out eighteen or twenty men, eight in two armed boats, and ten or a dozen ashore led by his first mate, George Lamport.

On the morning of December 11, Kaeo reportedly came through the cultivated fields below the ravines. To the northeast, on the slopes above him, Kalanikupule's brother, Koalaukani, was positioned on the raised path from Kalauao to Aiea. Kalanikupule's uncle and war chief, Kamohomoho, occupied the shingly beach at Malei to the south, and Kalanikupule held the middle of the line in the uplands of Aiea. Just off the beach, Brown with the *Jackall* and his armed boats were positioned to shell Kaeo's troops and cut off any retreat along the shore at Pearl Harbor.

As Kaeo's thousands of warriors advanced, Koalaukani's forces descended from the path above them and broke the main column. Then, in an attempt to encircle Kaeo's forces, Kalanikupule's men came up, as did Kamohomoho's. Fighting went on through the day, and this time

Brown's gunners succeeded in killing several of Kaeo's chiefs and sharpshooters between the ravines and the beach below Aiea. In the late afternoon, with his forces in disarray, Kaeo retreated toward Pearl Harbor.

Amid the scattering forces, Brown's men noticed a small group taking shelter in a ravine near the shore. Among them, they could see the flash of a chief's vivid yellow-feathered war cape. The boats fired swivel guns and the *Jackall* poured cannon fire into the ravine. Realizing they had a chief at bay, Kalanikupule's warriors descended from the upland. They came upon Kaeo and his entourage and surrounded them. Despite being cornered, Kaeo refused to submit, and they killed him and his wives, and six or more of his chiefs and their women. Through the night, bodies were gathered from where they had fallen in the hills and piled on the beach near Paaiau. Kahulunuikaaumoku, one of the daughters of a high priest who had died with Kaeo, was thought to be dead and laid on the mound of corpses. During the night she was pecked in the eye by a bird and regained consciousness. Gathering her strength, she swam across an inlet to the farther side of Aiea and hid in the Halawa uplands, living to later tell her tale of the battle.

THE NEXT MORNING JOHN KENDRICK and one of his officers were at breakfast in his cabin below deck on the *Lady Washington*. Sunlight reflected off the water and through the transom windows, illuminating the low ceiling and the glasses of water on the narrow table. All the previous day, the boom of cannons had sounded from the west, echoing from the ravines and distant cliff faces over the lowlands. The night had fallen quiet. Word had come to the *Washington* that Kaeo was dead. Now would come a brutal turn of events.

A call sounded on deck of the approach of the *Jackall*. According to Kamehameha's aide, Isaac Davis, to celebrate Kalanikupule's victory, Brown ordered a salute to be fired. It may have also been Brown's statement of his own victorious return. Below in his cabin, Kendrick heard the blast of the *Jackall*'s first cannon. Then the second. The third came at close range. The *Jackall* was within yards of the *Washington* when a fiery explosion ripped the side of the hull, scattering round and grapeshot and spraying the deck. The captain's cabin became a smoking, splintered hole. On deck, two seamen were killed and several others were bleeding. Stunned and outraged, some of the *Washington*'s men likely went for the swivel guns and arms chest. Amid confusion and shouting, Brown claimed it was an accident. First mate James Rowan, and perhaps John Howell, stopped the men from firing on the *Jackall.*

In the shattered main cabin below the companionway, Kendrick's officer lay fatally wounded. Kendrick too had been struck. He was brought up and laid out on deck. In a native-based account, he survived a few hours and gave orders to take the *Washington* homeward. But in the story passed on by Brown's men, he was killed immediately after being struck in the head by a wad from the cannon. There was an air of disbelief that surrounded the covered shape of his large frame. After all the mortal challenges he had survived in battles at sea as a privateer, and in typhoons, hurricanes, and illness, it was this odd, unexpected blast that took him. At fifty-four years old, an age considered remarkable among men who spent their lives at sea, John Kendrick was gone.

Those who had served with him from the time they left Boston, such as young John Cordis and John Maud, found it hard to believe. In this sudden, brutal moment, they had lost their captain and the dream of returning home in glory. The legend would have no happy ending. The final work of establishing an American outpost would be left undone; no riches, no reward for all they had endured. Anchored not far from them, the *Jackall* sat like a challenge they could not avoid, and in the first few hours their outrage and disbelief passed into a brooding suspicion as conjectures became allegations.

LATE THAT AFTERNOON, the remains of Kendrick and his three unnamed men were wrapped in winding sheets and rowed ashore. In the thin line of palms beyond the beach (believed to be along what is now

South King Street in Honolulu), the crew dug graves in the packed earth. Armed crewmen gathered as John Howell most likely uttered the traditional liturgy from *The Book of Common Prayer:* "earth to earth, ashes to ashes, dust to dust . . ." Natives who watched the ceremony may have known of the animosity between the two captains. They believed that the prayer and ceremony were sorcery intended to bring about William Brown's death. Kalanikupule was allegedly warned by "Kendrick's son" to take good care of the grave or "it shall be disturbed at your peril." A young member of the crew, perhaps John Cordis, may have been the one who made the threat. That night, however, the grave was opened and robbed to obtain Kendrick's winding sheet, which the natives considered an object of power.

The crew's suspicions about the killing did not subside. In an attempt to settle the matter, an inquest was held aboard one of Brown's ships. Brown reportedly said that he had ordered three guns to be unshotted for the salute. The gunner fired the first two, and finding the third not primed, "ye Apron of ye 4th Gun was taken of, which was fir'd & being shotted with round and Grape Shot, it pierced the side of ye Lady Washington & killed Capt. Kendrick as he sat at his table, & killed & wounded many upon deck . . ." The entire question came down to the word of Brown's men, who insisted that firing the loaded cannon was an accident.

Accidents of this type were rare, and Brown's compelling motives to kill Kendrick certainly warranted suspicion. The shot was said in many accounts to have passed through "the side of the ship." If the shot passed through a porthole, as one version related, or the transom windows (both favored shots of gunners), the excuse would have appeared very thin.

But despite suspicion, and whatever allegations had been made, the *Washington*'s officers and crew had no facts to refute Brown's claim that the killing was an accident. The foreign officers who conducted the inquest on the deck of the British merchant ship found John Kendrick "a casualty," an incidental death in the battle that took place. Eager to be off and have the matter settled, Howell, who later characterized himself as Kendrick's "assistant," accepted the finding, and would soon reap rich gains from the killing. James Rowan, the *Washington*'s next in command, yielded to Howell, and the *Washington* was repaired and set off for Macao.

Although it was an isolated incident on the far side of the world, the killing of Kendrick and his three men (whether accidental or not) reflected the larger conflict taking place. It was different tinder, but the same flames, the same morning of fire that was engulfing Europe and threatening the Americas in the war for trade and territory.

WITH KENDRICK'S DEATH, Brown's outlook immediately improved. His main competition on the Northwest Coast and in the islands was gone. Maquinna and Wickaninish no longer had a steady source of powder, muskets, and lead, and the American deeds to an immense tract on Vancouver Island were shaken. Moreover, Brown now faced no outside challenge to his claim to be lord of the Leeward Islands.

He immediately demanded that four hundred hogs be slaughtered and salted for market, and took other native items as he wished. His imperious attitude provoked resentment among the Oahu chiefs. Whether or not any of them sought revenge for the killing of Kendrick, or invoked his spirit with the winding sheet that had been stolen, they considered Brown a tyrant and wanted his ships. Their retribution was swift.

Nineteen days after Kendrick's death, on January 1, 1795, a group of Kalanikupule's warriors approached the *Jackall* and *Prince Lee Boo* in a large double canoe. Most of the men on the two ships were ashore, some slaughtering and salting pork and others sent in boats to the salt ponds at Kaihikapu, where Brown was told he could take as much salt as he wanted. On attempting to return, the loaded boats stranded on a reef and had to wait for the rising tide. According to the story later passed among the ships, the double canoe full of native men "rang'd up alongside the Prince Laboo, & struck her small boat, that lay along side, & somewhat damaged her upon which Capt. Gordon run to ye gangway to blame them for it." A native working as a cook on board pushed Gordon into the water where the men in the canoe quickly killed him. They then went alongside the *Jackall* where Brown was walking the quarterdeck. Climbing on board with a long iron *pahoua*, one of the natives lunged at Brown who "seized a Swivel worm & drove the fellow of." The remaining warriors came on board and Brown tried to beat them off "but at last he was overpowered," stabbed in the neck, and pitched onto the main deck where he died.

Most of Brown's crew on shore were also killed. Those who survived eventually escaped to Kealakekua with the ships and left a tale of what had occurred and a warning for John Young that Kalanikupule planned to attack Kamehameha.

Events then took shape that many believed were foreordained. That spring, the Hawaiian king prepared his troops and several of Kendrick's men. In April, he invaded and conquered Maui, Lanai, and Molokai and moved on to Oahu, killing Kaiana and three hundred of his followers when they turned against him. Then he hunted down and killed Kalanikupule and took over all the Leeward Islands but Kauai. In time, that island too would fall under his power, fulfilling Kamehameha's prophesied destiny as king of all the islands.

CARRYING WORD OF KENDRICK'S DEATH, the *Washington* arrived at Macao in February 1795, and John Howell proceeded to rifle everything Kendrick left behind. He placed the cargo of furs with another shipmaster to sell and paid himself $1,817 in fees and inflated commissions from the proceeds. This was three times more than Robert Gray earned for the *Columbia*'s first voyage. Howell then sold the *Lady Washington* to himself for thirteen hundred dollars, a bargain price in light of Kendrick's offer of fourteen thousand dollars two years earlier. In essence, Howell took the ship and more than five hundred dollars in cash. He said nothing of the sale of the valuable ambergris Kendrick had collected, or sandalwood that had been gathered, and only mentioned the *Washington*'s pearls in passing a few years later.

On May 11, 1795, Howell sent a letter to Joseph Barrell and his partners in what would become a long course of evasion:

> *Sirs:*
>
> *I wrote to you from the island of O. Whahoo the 19th of December last, and left the letter with Captain Brown to forward via England. Eleven days after, he and Captain Gordon were both murdered there by the Chief of the Island . . . the letter was forwarded from hence by the last Fleet which sailed nearly two months ago.*
>
> *My last letter informed you of the death of Captain Kendrick, on the 12th of December at O. Whahoo . . .*

Since arriving three months earlier Howell had not had time to conduct an accounting, but claimed that "the debts he [Kendrick] accumulated were immense." As it turned out, the revenue from sale of the cargo would pay the current debt, and sale of the ship at a price similar to what Kendrick offered to Barrell would have paid the long-term debts to Martinez ($8,000) and Douglas ($2,322).

Oddly, Howell felt compelled to attack both Robert Gray and John Kendrick, telling Barrell, "I hardly ever saw a man in your N.W. employ, who was not either a fool or Rogue, and your commanders united in both these characters." He also launched into an anti-American diatribe saying, "It is absolutely necessary some steps should be taken to retrieve the character of the Americans here. Such villanies have been practiced as have sickened the Chinese from having any dealing with them on a liberal scale they would otherwise adopt." He noted that Joseph Ingraham and the *Hope*'s owners had defaulted on a bond to the hoppo Consequa for $43,821. Howell said he had joined with Chinese merchants and was preparing a trip to the Northwest Coast. He said he would send Kendrick's papers and accounts of the *Washington* when he returned.

Most important he noted, "The deeds of the Land purchased on the N.W. Coast, are in my possession. I shall leave them here to be forwarded by the first vessel of the season to Boston. If you know these lands as well as I do, you would not be very anxious about the fate of them."

Although Kendrick had written to Barrell in March 1792 that the deeds had been registered with the American consul at Macao (a task that would most likely have been entrusted to Howell as clerk), the deeds had not been registered. It was a curious game Howell was playing. He would send the *Washington* to Hawaii and the Northwest Coast in 1796 under a British captain and crew, apparently to collect the furs Kendrick had purchased in advance, and then he would continue to evade Barrell.

THE FIRST WORD of John Kendrick's death arrived at Boston on the *Jefferson,* which entered port on Monday, July 27, 1795, 168 days from China. The city was in an uproar over revelations of the details of John Jay's treaty with Britain. In exchange for neutrality and peace, Jay had sacrificed principles of open ports and free trade that had been advocated by Jefferson and other founding fathers since 1776. Equally onerous, Jay had also failed to win a ban on impressment of American sailors. Riots broke out in Boston and in New York. Up and down the coast, seaports were feverish with denunciations. At a time when Britain was wracked by internal crises and losing the war with France, Jay was seen as foolishly acquiescing to England's desired dominance on the seas. Jay had acted on the instructions of Alexander Hamilton, and the treaty had won American trade in British ports, but only for vessels of less than seventy tons (smaller than the *Lady Washington*). Secretary of State Edmund Randolph, who had been appointed after Thomas Jefferson, was dismayed by the treaty and gave up his post after being caught criticizing Washington's administration.

Those who defended the agreement, including Washington and John Adams, believed that it was the best the United States could do given the circumstances. At least for a brief time they saw it allowing a period of growth in which America could fatten on the follies of the old kingdoms. It was the price to keep America from being drawn into the spreading European conflict.

JOHN KENDRICK'S DEATH was a faint footnote to all the uproar that was occurring. A brief article appeared in Boston's *Columbian Centinel* on August 5: "Capt. Kendrick, formerly of this State, we learn, was some time since killed at Owyhee, in the Pacific Ocean, by a salute, by accident. Mr. Howell, has conducted the vessel he was in to China." The article was reprinted in New York, Philadelphia, Baltimore, and other cities.

SOUTH OF BOSTON, in the sleepy village of Wareham, the first haying was done. Across the broad marsh northeast of the Kendrick house, the tips of the marsh grass were just starting to yellow. Joseph Kendrick had turned sixteen a few weeks earlier, Alfred was seventeen, and Benjamin, at nineteen, was most likely at sea. Little Hanna, now fourteen, was her mother's companion. She would have faced the disastrous news with her. Who delivered it is unknown. If it had been difficult for Kendrick's crew to believe, here it was even more so under the double blow that Solomon too was dead, perished with ten others on the *Resolution*. The loss of a husband or son alone, even for a woman who had grown up among seafarers and accepted fate and her religion's sense of predestination, would have been hardly bearable. Now both of them were gone, and the longed-for recovery of her husband's reputation, or even a modest homecoming, would be denied.

Juan Kendrick resigned from the Spanish navy and returned home when he learned of his father's death. Unanswered questions about his father and William Brown, the fate of the deeds to the vast tract of coast, and Solomon's death must have haunted the family. In August

1798, Juan signed on as supercargo for the *Eliza,* which was headed for the Northwest. The captain was James Rowan, the *Washington*'s former first mate, and one of the officers was Samuel Burling, the brother of one of Solomon's murdered crewmates. Shortly after arriving on the coast, they hunted down the chiefs responsible for the massacre of Solomon and the *Resolution*'s crew. Juan Kendrick also sought Francisco Marin at Hawaii, and undoubtedly looked for John Howell at Macao. He found no easy answers about his father. The former English clergyman had disappeared with the *Washington*'s papers and Kendrick's deeds.

At Macao, Howell had managed in a very short time to earn a reputation for questionable business dealings. After the *Washington* returned from her 1796 voyage to the Northwest and the cargo was sold, Howell made a hasty departure from China for the Philippines in 1797. In a July monsoon, he grounded the *Lady Washington* on Luzon's Cagayan River bar and abandoned her. In an ending similar to Kendrick's barely noted demise, the hulk was later driven up the river on a flood tide, where she was stripped of anything of use and her New England oak ribs and planks slowly rotted into the mud.

In May 1798, in response to a letter from Barrell, Howell tried to hold off his inquiries with a "sketch" of an accounting. He was living in Manilla and said that he had left his papers in China. He was "in daily expectation" of them "and among them your deeds of the lands on the N.W. Coast." A year earlier he had assured Barrell that the deeds were registered at Macao and that triplicates had been made and he would forward the originals. He promised once again to transmit the deeds and documents. They were never received or found at Macao.

EVERYTHING SEEMED SO UNFINISHED. With his ships' logs and deeds missing, and his debts left unpaid, Kendrick's accomplishments on the Pacific coast and in the Sandwich Islands seemed to vanish. Unlike James Cook, or Vancouver, or a number of American captains, there was no journal that told of his seven-year odyssey. His story was scattered in letters and in logs and journals of other ships, and his reputation remained under a cloud stirred up by Robert Gray. But legends do not die as easily as those who make them, and much more lay in Kendrick's and the *Lady Washington*'s wake. The world needed to catch up. And as in life, Kendrick persevered.

His journey would become a seminal event following the American Revolution. The pioneering captain Amasa Delano, who circumnavigated the globe three times, would later say, "Capt. Kendrick was the first American that burst forth into the world and traversed those distant regions which were before but little known to the inhabitants of this part of the globe . . ." Kendrick taught others how to navigate those seas and led the American leap into the Pacific. William Sturgis, a prominent shipmaster who took part in the maritime surge into the Pacific in the early nineteenth century, called Kendrick's expedition "one of the boldest and most remarkable commercial enterprises ever undertaken from this Country." As significant as his pioneering at sea, the events Kendrick and his men helped to ignite in the Nootka Crisis caused a shift in the balance of world powers. In the view of American historian Fredrick Jackson Turner, this crisis was as important as any major battle in determining the fate of the American West and the future of the Pacific region and Asia. As the first international challenge for President Washington, the crisis also established the key American policy of neutrality in European conflicts.

All of this had great significance for the young nation. As war with Britain heated up again in the years after Kendrick's death, and the fate of the Oregon Country and the American West was contested, presidents Madison, Monroe, and Adams would turn to Kendrick's expedition, and the legacy of an American presence he left behind would take on increased meaning. He did not gain the glory or wealth he sought when they set out on that early October morning from Boston, but surviving as long as he did, he achieved something more. Kendrick's American odyssey in the Pacific shaped world events and set the stage for the next era—and through the gateway he opened others were coming.

EPILOGUE

Legacy for a New Nation

IN JANUARY 1803, President Thomas Jefferson won an appropriation from Congress for a secret overland expedition. British trading posts were being established westward across Canada as Alexander Mackenzie had recommended a decade earlier. American trade had to be established deep in the frontier to counter British outposts and claims. Jefferson's secret "Corps of Discovery" was to be led by his private secretary, Meriwether Lewis, and Captain William Clark, the younger brother of George Rogers Clark, whom Jefferson had asked to take an expedition up the Missouri in 1783. They were to explore and describe the western lands, establish trade relations with the tribes, and find a passage that would offer the most direct route to the Pacific.

In a story that has become a touchstone of American history, Lewis and Clark set out from Saint Louis on May 14, 1804, on an arduous trek of thirty-five hundred miles up the Missouri River to its headwaters and over the Rocky Mountains. In a breathtaking moment on the morning of November 7, 1805, from a high bank of the Columbia

River as the fog cleared, they caught sight of what they believed to be the blue Pacific Ocean.

Seventeen years after Kendrick and his expedition had wintered over at Nootka in 1788, the Corps of Discovery constructed their crude Fort Clatsop near the mouth of the Columbia River to wait out the snows and perhaps encounter one of the trading ships that came to the coast. The signs of American traders were broadly evident in the cast-off sailor's clothing, blankets, guns, and speech of the Clatsop and Chinook people.

From an old chief, Clark compiled a list of the captains and vessels "who visit this part of the coast for the purpose of trade." Most of them were Boston ships, and the schooner "Washilton" was noted to be a favorite. How much Lewis and Clark knew of Kendrick's expedition is uncertain, but its legacy was all around them, including the name of the river on which they camped. On the journey homeward, enthralled with what they had found and seeking a strategy that could secure this vast region, Lewis laid out a plan similar to what Joseph Barrell had envisioned and Kendrick had sacrificed so much trying to achieve.

On his arrival at Saint Louis in September 1806, Lewis immediately sent a letter to President Jefferson concluding that the United States should develop an outpost on the Columbia River that would draw furs from across the continent to ship to Canton. The nation would "shortly derive the benefits of a most lucrative trade from this source, and . . . in the course of ten or twelve years a tour across the Continent by the rout mentioned will be undertaken by individuals with as little concern as a voyage across the Atlantic is at present."

Jefferson was enthusiastic. In the dozen years since Kendrick had sent his deeds to the State Department, much had changed. Amid the hotly shifting politics of Europe, Spain had lost the vast Louisiana Territory to France. And in need of funds for war, and to keep the region from the British, Napoleon had recently sold the territory to the United

States. The immense tract, reaching from the Mississippi River to the hills of eastern Idaho, doubled the size of the nation overnight. Some in Congress believed that under old Spanish claims, the western border of the United States now extended as far as the Pacific. It would take another generation for overland migration to begin in the region, but an American maritime surge westward was already under way.

ALONG THE NORTHWEST COAST after Kendrick's death, "Boston men" came to dominate the fur trade, often gathering at Safe Harbor Retreat at Mawina. In 1800, there were eight American traders and one British ship on the coast. In 1801, twenty American and three British ships. Then, between 1802 and 1812, a total of 105 annual voyages to the coast were made by Americans. During the same period, the British made only five annual trading voyages.

At the same time, American whalers were streaming into the South Pacific. In 1791, five vessels from Nantucket and one from New Bedford came around Cape Horn to hunt whales in the "South Sea." As the number of ships increased over time, they would push their way northward, making Honolulu their primary port for supplies, repairs, and freewheeling shore leave. By 1823, as many as forty ships, most of them American, would also sit at anchor on a single day in the harbor where Kendrick died. Boston ships would also come to dominate the islands' lucrative sandalwood trade, which was managed by Francisco Marin for Kamehameha.

America's ambitious push westward would again incense Britain. In 1810, nearly twenty years after John Kendrick purchased his vast tract of land, the Winship family of Boston attempted to establish an outpost at the mouth of the Columbia River and failed due to native hostility. The following year, John Jacob Astor established the first American outpost on the banks of the Columbia at Astoria. In the War of 1812, British ships were sent to destroy any American property on the Pacific and forced Astor's outpost to be turned over to the Hudson's Bay Company.

The United States, likewise, sent the navy frigate *Essex* to destroy British ships in the "South Sea" and camps on the South American coast. This conflict would not end with the war. In June 1816, President James Madison sought to reclaim Astor's outpost and "assert American sovereignty along the [Pacific] coast." To support the American claims, he issued instructions to gather documents on Kendrick's voyage, including his deeds and the ship's log with Gray's first entry into the Columbia River.

Few of Kendrick's officers from the expedition or owners of the ships were alive to interview. Robert Davis Coolidge had died in 1795. Joseph Ingraham was lost with the American Navy brig *Pickering* in the fall of 1800. Robert Haswell disappeared with the trader *Louisa,* probably around Cape Horn, as he made his way to the Northwest Coast in 1801. Robert Gray died in 1806 of what was believed to be yellow fever on a passage from Charleston, South Carolina, leaving a widow and four daughters. Joseph Barrell died in 1804, and John Hoskins had married and moved to France to handle the Barrell family business affairs in Europe.

Barrell's son, Samuel, was able to procure letters about Kendrick's land purchases, and copies of Kendrick's deeds would be found in the State Department. Ultimately, the search ordered by Madison confirmed "in the most satisfactory manner, that Captain Kendrick did make several purchases of the Indians, of lands, on that coast, for the owners of the Columbia and Washington, whose vessels were under his command . . . The lands were taken possession of with much formality, the American flag hoisted, a bottle sank in the ground, etc., and many Chiefs present at the ceremony . . ."

The *Columbia*'s log, which contained Gray's record of entering the Columbia River in May 1792, remained eagerly sought after. The new secretary of state, John Quincy Adams, who had personal knowledge of the expedition and its participants, turned to his friend Charles Bulfinch for assistance. Bulfinch acquired a portion of the *Columbia*'s log from Robert Gray's brother-in-law, Captain Silas Atkins. Atkins copied extracts, including entries for May 7 through May 21, 1792, related to the discoveries of Gray's Harbor and the Columbia River. These were shown to Adams. Together with copies of Kendrick's deeds, the documents supported a strong American claim on the Pacific coast.

In 1818, Britain returned Astor's trading post and agreed not to interfere with American use of the Columbia River, but wanted joint rights to settle what was now known as "the Oregon Country," which stretched from northern California to the Queen Charlotte Islands. Seeking to shut out Britain, in 1819, John Quincy Adams negotiated for Spain's rights to the Oregon Country. However, Britain refused to acknowledge the agreement, claiming that Spain had relinquished her rights to the region in the Nootka settlement.

Contention over possession of the region continued into the 1820s and 1830s. Kendrick's original deeds remained missing, and the Barrell family tried to track them down by tracing John Howell to Bengal, India, where he allegedly died. To confirm what the deeds had contained, once-young sailors were summoned to given sworn statements.

They came through the streets of Boston like ghosts, old men who had stood in the wilderness on the deck of the *Washington* in the summer of 1791, or at the smuggler's haven of Dirty Butter Bay. James Tremere of Boston, age seventy-seven, recalled seeing Maquinna climb to the *Lady Washington*'s masthead to point out the four directions of the land transferred to Kendrick. Ebenezer Dorr of Roxbury, seventy-six years old, had sailed on the *Hope* with Ingraham in 1792. He said: "I had intimate acquaintance with Captain Kendrick; and, while in Lark's Bay [Dirty Butter Bay], was frequently on board his vessel . . . I recollect to have seen, inspected, and read, several deeds executed by Indians on the Northwest coast, to Captain John Kendrick . . . I recollect that muskets and clothing, copper" and other articles were given as compensation for the land. And John Cruft of Boston, age seventy-one, who had been first mate on the *Hope* and served Kendrick while the *Avenger* was being built at Macao, confirmed what Dorr had seen, having had the deeds "in my hands several times." He remembered the names of the chiefs with crosses or marks beside their names. Others verified that the deeds were on board the *Washington*.

In Hawaii, whose cession the British Parliament had never formally confirmed, John Young, in his late eighties, recalled Kendrick "as having passed several Winters" at Kealakekua. "I had much intimate acquaintance with Captain Kendrick and believed him to be a man of strict veracity," he said. He heard Kendrick "often speak of purchases of lands," which he said Kendrick had made from Indian chiefs on the Northwest Coast. "I frequently saw deeds in his possession, signed by Chiefs, who, at that time, lived at and South of Nootka-sound, and witnessed by men belonging to his vessel."

The statements were dwarfed by the larger scheme of things. Beyond these aged men the world had changed. The Spanish Empire was a shadow of its former self in the Americas, having lost Louisiana to France and then many of its Latin American colonies through wars of independence between 1810 and 1825. Britain was the ascendant power after defeating Napoleon and France, and stood firmly in the way of U.S. ambitions. As the passions associated with a presidential election mounted in 1843–44, talk of war with Britain raged again. America's confidence and expansionist fever were running high during what became known as the "furious forties." Democrat James Polk wanted to annex Texas and take possession of the Oregon Country to 54°40' north latitude, which later gave rise to the slogan "Fifty-Four Forty or Fight!" In a nation that had grown more confident and belligerent, the naive notion of carrying the American Revolution into the world through open ports and free trade had long given way to the ancient strategy of taking territory and resources. There was an underlying belief among many Americans that the United States had a foreordained right and obligation to bring republican government, free enterprise, and Christian civilization to new lands. By the end of 1845, this concept, which had begun to pervade political thinking and American culture, had a name. New York journalist John L. O'Sullivan called it "manifest destiny." While part of this confidence certainly encompassed humanitarian desires, an Old World–conquering zeal, similar to that of Spain or Britain, or other ancient nations, would drive it forward.

After he was elected, Polk chose to go to war with Mexico, and not with Britain. As Floridablanca had decided fifty years before, spending millions of dollars to go to war and lose thousands of lives for a stretch of wilderness where the sea otter trade had already played out was not worth it. Polk signed a treaty with Britain in 1846 that set the northern border of the United States at the Straits of Juan de Fuca. Britain acquiesced on American interests in lands to the south that included New Albion and San Francisco harbor, but missing from the treaty was protection of lands north of the new border that were privately owned by Americans. With the stroke of a pen, John Kendrick's land purchases were no longer a matter of concern for the United States. Attention turned south and westward.

Under the banner of "manifest destiny" the United States would take California, New Mexico, Nevada, Utah, and parts of Colorado and Arizona from Mexico in 1848; and then push farther westward, sending warships to force the opening of Japan in 1853–54, finally taking Hawaii as a protectorate in 1893, and seizing the Philippines from Spain in 1898. Historically, it was a long march from Kendrick's voyage and the first American expedition into the Pacific.

And it hasn't ended. Kendrick's odyssey still has a certain resonance today. It is easy to see the early elements of arms trading, surrogate wars, and megabusiness ventures leading to conflicts over resources scattered across the globe. In many ways, events reveal how little we have progressed from that morning of fire and the ancient drives for dominance in trade and resources. But there is much more than a wild root of imperialism in Kendrick's journey.

Kendrick's voyaging broadened Americans' consciousness and expanded their sense of horizon. He changed the perception of what was possible and became one of those rough-hewn characters who helped shape the new nation. His journey outward into the world became

America's journey. As Joseph Barrell had envisioned, the maritime surge that followed Kendrick fed the growth of the new nation. The wealth that flowed from whaling and the sandalwood trade in the Pacific funded increased shipbuilding and the early industrialization of New England. And two decades behind him, John Jacob Astor completed what Kendrick had begun in planting a dream of an American outpost on the Northwest Coast. Because of Kendrick, and others who followed, much of America's fate turned westward.

But there was no journal that captured the scope of what he had attempted and achieved. His death on the far side of the world and the scattering of his story left him off the list of iconic frontier figures such as Meriwether Lewis and William Clark. His reputation remained under a cloud, and memory of his legacy became obscured and buried over time. There is no single anecdote that captures the sweep of his seven-year odyssey. But in setting the stage for a new era, he opened the Pacific for American ships, and with his part in the Nootka crisis, he helped shake the balance of power in Europe, which affected not only the map of the Old World but American acquisition of the West. In essence, his life embodied that morning of fire at the close of the eighteenth century, and his voyaging marked a period when the new nation began to extend and define itself. Coming out of that perilous time, perhaps one of the darkest and most uncertain in U.S. history, his journey changed the way Americans saw themselves and their place in the world. For Kendrick, and for the nation, it remains an unfinished voyage.

Acknowledgments

THERE ARE MANY INDIVIDUALS and institutions to thank for their support. I am particularly indebted to the kindness of the staff at the Massachusetts Historical Society, who gave time and assistance to a fledgling project. Also in Boston, Sean Casey at the rare books department in the Boston Public Library, and the staff at the Peabody Essex Museum in Salem. At the local level, Amy Andreasson at the Eldridge Public Library in Chatham was immensely helpful in gathering microfilm and books through interlibrary loans from distant sources. Similarly, Desiree Mobed, director of the Harwich Historical Society, shared original manuscript documents and offered useful suggestions. My dear friend archeologist Beth Nelson also loaned me a manuscript copy of W. S. Nickerson's research on Native Americans which offered background on John Kendrick's family and their neighbors. Mary Malloy, a maritime historian for the Sea Education Association at Woods Hole, graciously offered use of her personal library as well as her sage advice. She said early on that the odd fact about the historical record for early mariners in the Pacific Northwest is that much of it is contained in Boston archives. While that proved true, the record that has been accumulated over time on the Northwest Coast is impressive, and I am grateful to that region's scholars whose work I have cited.

At the University of Washington special collections division, Blynne Olivieri, Pacific Northwest curator, assisted with copies of rare manuscripts. Jeff Smith, curator at the Columbia River Maritime Museum in Astoria, Oregon, provided the images of Hewitt Jackson's sketches. At the Washington State Historical Society, Fred Poyner provided similar assistance. The general archives of the Indies in the Bancroft Library at the University of California–Berkeley offered a great storehouse of documents concerning Spanish activities in the Northwest. In Hawaii, Leah Pualaha'ole Caldeira at the Bishop Museum was helpful with early documents and suggested work by native authors.

Among national repositories and archives, the Spanish Ministry of Culture has developed a state-of-the-art facility making eighty-six million digitized pages of documents plus eight thousand maps and plans available at the Archivos General de Indias in Seville, and the Archivos General de Simanicas. The sheer volume is staggering. Without access to these manuscript documents, pieces of this story would have remained missing. The world is certainly indebted for such an act of generosity and openness demonstrated by the Spanish government.

In the United Kingdom, the British Library and the National Archives at Kew contain a wealth of documents related to British efforts in the Pacific, and I thank the staffs for their diligent organization. Having lived in Washington, D.C., for many years, the Library of Congress remains one of my favorite places, and its sources were essential, particularly the journals and papers related to the expedition and the manuscript letters of Jefferson and Washington. Additionally, the libraries of the Massachusetts Maritime Academy, the Mystic Seaport Museum, and the New England Genealogical Society, as well as the Beinecke Rare Book and Manuscript Library of Yale University, University of British Columbia Library of Rare Books and Special Collections, the Hawaiian and Pacific Collection of the University of Hawaii

Library at Manoa, and Brooks Free Library also deserve my thanks for the documents they provided.

I reserve special appreciation for maritime historian Hewitt Jackson whose sketches of ships appear on the cover and throughout the book. Although Jackson passed away in 2007 at the age of ninety-three, the legacy he left will long serve to bring immediacy to the events of Pacific Northwest history. In addition to Jackson's work, the maps created by Eliza McClennen and Herb Heidt of MapWorks present masterful references for the distances crossed by Kendrick and the coasts along which he and his men sailed. Without their help, more than a few readers unfamiliar with latitude and longitude would undoubtedly be lost at sea.

For those who took part in shaping the manuscript, I also offer my appreciation: my literary agent, Larry Kirshbaum, who was as fascinated by this project as I was; Henry Ferris at William Morrow, who likewise recognized the landmark nature of the story right away; Danny Goldstein, who was terrific to work with as he shepherded the project and helped to craft its drafts and final form; and the cover designer, Richard Aquan, who produced a cover equal to the work of Hewitt Jackson. As my perennial first reader, Thom O'Connor was always willing to sail off into nearly completed chapters. And Ted Nelson, who patiently paged through a draft of the manuscript, faithfully let me know what he expected and what he delightedly found. And long before these readers, our steadfast friend Nina Solomon contributed greatly in helping give this project a start. While any errors of fact or interpretation are mine, it was these many hands that helped the book take form.

It goes without saying that the support of my family was essential as I disappeared for lengthy periods into the eighteenth century. My sons each made their own unique contributions. Evan, a budding historian, assisted with chapter notes; Colin and Trevor offered welcome distractions of baseball; and Graham provided his calm wisdom and advice when computers became balky. My wife, Carole, whose patience is now legendary, kept the light burning through late nights and steady distraction, and for that she has my deepest gratitude. The other members of our family: Mandy Gerry, Tighe, and Maeve; my brother, David; and Hector and Therese Pelletier, were always ready with a good meal and humor when the moment was needed. Absent the presence of these people, my understanding and appreciation of the world would not be sufficient to take on a project like this.

Finally, I want to acknowledge John Kendrick and those voyagers of more than two centuries ago whose story this is. These indivudals and the families they left behind received little recognition and suffered greatly for their sacrifice. To their memory and to those who continue to launch off to far corners of the world never to return home, I dedicate this book.

A Note on the Sources

THE STORY OF AMERICA'S first expedition into the Pacific has long been buried in history. The popular version handed down from the most accessible sources describes the fur trade, the discovery of the Columbia River, and Robert Gray as an explorer, circumnavigator, and American hero. While Gray deserves credit for what he accomplished (although he didn't recognize the significance at the time), the larger story is much more intriguing and valuable to an understanding of the new nation and global events. That larger story, focused on John Kendrick, is much more difficult to unearth. Given the scattering of the expedition's record, the task for research was twofold. First, to document and examine the full course of events of the expedition in order to gain a balanced perspective on Kendrick and the entire seven-year voyage. And second, to place the expedition firmly in historical context to frame the flow of events and the actions of the main players. This meant examining American, Spanish, and British perspectives, as well as the changing worlds of native people in the Pacific Northwest and Hawaii.

Fortunately, the obsession of our culture to write down and save everything yielded a rich, though far-flung, document stream. Research grew over time in a spreading arc from Boston, Harwich, and Salem,

Massachusetts, to the West Coast and Hawaii, to Macao, and the archives of Spain and Britain. The sources cited in the notes and contained in the bibliography reflect the greatly refined labor of my search. Wherever possible I have used primary sources, and attempted to point out where those and secondary sources offered conflicting views of an event, such as the death of John Kendrick. The result, I hope, contributes to a broader understanding of this seminal voyage and sparks the vital scholarship it deserves.

NOTES

PROLOGUE

1 *March 4, 1788—Through a gray:* Robert Haswell, A Voyage Round the World onboard the Ship Columbia-Rediviva and Sloop Washington (hereafter referred to as First Voyage), 29.

2 *The late eighteenth century:* Generally, see Jeremy Black, *British Foreign Policies in an Age of Revolutions, 1783–1793.* Also Warren L. Cook, *Flood Tide of Empire: Spain and the Pacific Northwest, 1543–1819,* and Peggy Liss, *Atlantic Empires: The Network of Trade and Revolution 1713–1826.*

For three hundred years: Pope Alexander VI issued the Inter Caetera Papal Bull on May 4, 1493, to address possession of non-Christian land in the New World. The dividing line between Spanish and Portuguese possessions was set one hundred leagues west of Cape Verde. The Treaty of Tordesillas, concluded on June 7, 1494, moved the dividing line to 370 leagues west of Cape Verde. This allowed Portugal to claim Brazil.

the fledgling United States: Curtis P. Nettles, *The Emergence of a National Economy, 1775–1815,* 65–69.

The commander, John Kendrick: See Josiah Paine, Edward Kenwrick: The Ancestor of the Kenricks or Kendricks of Barnstable County and Nova Scotia and His Descendants.

3 *In a historic letter:* American Commissioners to the Committee for Foreign Affairs, Passy, France, February 28, 1778. Benjamin Franklin Papers, vol. 25,

726a, American Philosophical Society and Yale University. The Treaty of Amity and Commerce between the United States and France was signed on February 6, 1778.

3 *contemporaries describe him:* Paine, Edward Kenwrick. Also Amasa Delano, *A Narrative of Voyages and Travels in the Northern and Southern Hemispheres,* 400.

"banditti of renegadoes": Robert Gray charged that Kendrick was trying to steal from the ships' owners. This led to widespread disparagement of Kendrick, as noted by John Quincy Adams and contemporary newspaper accounts. Kendrick's failure to make financial returns to the owners reinforced this characterization. George Vancouver made the reference to the American "renegadoes"; Vancouver, Vol. V, 112, 125.

4 *Kendrick remained dedicated:* Paine, Edward Kenwrick.

"Tis a wonder they were not": "Boston, May 27," *Boston Weekly News-Letter,* no. 1683 (May 20–27, 1736), 1.

5 *the whaling brig* Lydia: The Earl of Sandwich signed a Mediterranean passport for John Kendrick and the *Brig Lydia* in 1772.

took the schooner Rebecca: "New York, June 25," *Boston Evening Post,* no. 1919 (July 6, 1772), 3.

6 *the owners applied to:* Secretary of the Commonwealth of Massachusetts, *Massachusetts Soldiers and Sailors of the Revolutionary War,* 108. Also see *Independent Chronicle* 9, no. 459 (June 6, 1777), 4.

His first large prizes: Independent Ledger 1, no. 22 (November 9, 1778), 1.

engaged Benjamin Franklin: Several letters in the Benjamin Franklin Papers, including American Commissioners: Memorandum for the French and Spanish Courts, Paris, November 23, 1777. Also American Commissioners to the Committee for Foreign Affairs, November 30, 1777.

initiated into St. Andrew's lodge: Kendrick was initiated into the St. Andrews Lodge of Freemasons on December 10, 1778. Samuel Crocker Lawrence Library Archives, Grand Lodge of Massachusetts, Boston.

Kendrick bought a house, wharf, and store: David Nye to John Kendrick, November 27, 1778, for eighteen hundred pounds of lawful money. Plymouth County Registry of Deeds, Book 59, 193. Kendrick is listed in the deed as a resident of Wareham, placing the move of his family to the mainland village prior to that time, perhaps when he embarked on the *Fanny* in the summer of 1777.

built the first public school: New Age 48: 539–40.

7 *the* Count d'Estaing, *which he owned:* Secretary, *Massachusetts Soldiers and Sailors.*

7 *Southwest of the Azores:* For the details of Kendrick's capture and subsequent voyage with his men, see John Kendrick to Benjamin Franklin, June 13, 1779. The Papers of Benjamin Franklin.

He then left for the Caribbean: Charles Henry Lincoln, *Naval Records of the American Revolution, 1775–1788,* 383. It is interesting to note that Arnold Henry Dohrman, who had assisted Kendrick and his men at Lisbon, is listed as one of the owners following Kendrick's cruise. Also see "Providence, April 25," *American Journal and Advertiser* 3, no. 21 (April 25, 1781), 2.

Kendrick came ashore: "Providence, May 16," *American Journal and General Advertiser* 3, no. 127 (May 16, 1781), 2.

CHAPTER ONE

11 *the snow-crusted lane:* What is now Washington Street in Boston was called Marlborough Street in 1787. Modern-day Marlborough Street was marshland at the time.

It was early February: Charles Bulfinch became engaged in discussion about the expedition "immediately after his return" from Europe, according to biographer Susan Bulfinch in *The Life and Letters of Charles Bulfinch, Architect; with Other Family Papers,* 64. His ship arrived in Boston on January 2, 1787. See "Boston, January 2," *Massachusetts Gazette* 6, no. 292 (January 2, 1787), 3.

a detailed plan: Joseph Barrell, "Annotations on Business." Also see John Gilmary Shea and Henry Reed Stiles, "Explorations of the Northwest Coast of the United States. Report of the Claims of the Heirs of Captains Kendrick and Gray," 157.

an economic depression had settled: Jonathan Smith, "The Depression of 1785 and Daniel Shays' Rebellion." Also see Curtis P. Nettles, *The Emergence of a National Economy, 1775–1815,* 60–66.

12 *Each of those kingdoms:* Peggy Liss, *Atlantic Empires: The Network of Trade and Revolution 1713–1826,* 148.

The unrest had been spreading: George Richards Minot, *History of the Insurrections in Massachusetts in the Year Seventeen Hundred and Eighty-Six and the Rebellion Consequent Thereon.* Also Leonard L. Richards, *Shays's Rebellion: The American Revolution's Final Battle.*

Washington wrote, "I am mortified": George Washington to Henry Lee, October 31, 1786.

13 *A push was on:* The pressure was mounting for a constitutional convention to

take on the creation of a federal government rather than just reforms of the Articles of Confederation. Joseph Barrell was one of the Boston merchants strongly advocating a federal government.

13 *at the home of Thomas Bulfinch:* Bulfinch, *Life and Letters,* 64.

James Cook's journal: James Cook and James King, *A Voyage to the Pacific Ocean.*

14 *as much as one hundred and twenty:* Cook and King, *Voyage,* vol. 3, 437.

This was more than double: Based on the full seaman's wage of two to three pounds per month, with the equivalent of $2.60 to $3.30 Spanish dollars per English pound.

sent the crews of Cook's two ships: Cook and King, *Voyage,* vol. 3, 437.

Two seamen "seduced": James King, January 11, 1780, journal entry in Cook and King, *Voyage,* vol. 3, 441.

The Harriet *had gone out:* Samuel Eliot Morison, *The Maritime History of Massachusetts, 1783–1860,* 44.

"superior to any the country enjoys": Barrell, "Annotations on Business."

15 *Barrell took four shares:* Bulfinch, *Life and Letters,* 65.

hundreds of ships: Morison, *Maritime History,* 31–32.

16 *both had risked their lives:* Joseph Barrell was a member of the Sons of Liberty, and financed and provisioned privateers. John Kendrick owned and mastered privateers.

17 *It would be the first circumnavigation:* Joseph Barrell, "Orders Given Captain John Kendrick of the Ship Columbia for a Voyage to the Pacific Ocean, 1787." Also Shea and Stiles, "Explorations of the Northwest Coast."

If land could be purchased: Barrell included the purchase of lands in his orders to Kendrick; and in a letter to Thomas Jefferson of March 28, 1792, accompanying five deeds, Kendrick said he had been led to believe that Congress would authorize the purchase.

18 *he was currently mastering:* Advertisements and shipping news in Boston newspapers show the regularity of Kendrick's embarking and returning. See, for example, "Entries," *Massachusetts Centinel* 6, no. 4 (September 30, 1786), 15; "Entries," *Massachusetts Centinel* 6, no. 23 (December 6, 1786), 91; and "For Charleston, South Carolina, the Brigt. Charletown Packet, John Kendrick, master," *Massachusetts Gazette* 6, no. 288 (December 19, 1786), 4.

Barrell sent his partner John Pintard: For date of Pintard letter, see Hill, *Journals,* 514.

The following weekend: Ibid., 516–17.

18 *"bound on a voyage":* Congress passed the Northwest Ordinance of 1787 to establish the process for forming a territorial government and creating new states on July 13, 1787.

On Monday, September 24: Hill, *Journals,* 516–17.

19 *The command ship:* Samuel Deane, *History of Scituate, Massachusetts,* 20.

20 *fitting out for sea:* The armament of the *Columbia* was noted in a letter of Blas Gonzales to Viceroy Teodoro de Croix, August 1, 1788. The armament of the *Lady Washington* was noted by Estevan José Martinez in Diary of the Voyage . . . , 75.

News of the voyage appeared: See, for example, "Boston, August 13," *Massachusetts Spy* 3, no. 20 (August 16, 1787), 265; *Massachusetts Centinel* 8, no. 4 (September 29, 1787), 15; "Extract from the Journal of Congress: Monday, September 24, 1787," *Charleston Columbian Herald,* no. 326 (October 22, 1787), 2.

Signing on were: For a list of crew members, see Columbia Papers, Massachusetts Historical Society. Background on the crew is from various genealogical sources.

22 *On Friday, September 28:* The dates and actions of the ships' preparation are noted in Robert Haswell's manuscript, A Voyage Round the World Onboard the Ship Columbia-Rediviva and Sloop Washington, 1–2.

"The evening was spent": Ibid., 2.

Barrell presented Kendrick: Barrell, "Orders Given Captain John Kendrick."

CHAPTER TWO

26 *Lord Anson, seeking to raid:* Richard Walter, *Anson's Voyage Around the World: In the Years 1740–1744.*

27 *Five large Spanish warships:* Ibid., 20–23.

Four hundred miles below: Ibid., 83–84.

28 *Two nights later:* Haswell, First Voyage, 29.

29 *During the week of March 17:* Ibid., 30.

"as we lost sight of him": Walter, *Anson's Voyage,* 73.

30 *"Winds have allowed us":* Haswell, First Voyage, 30.

A month behind them: William Bligh to Sir Joseph Banks, October 13, 1789.

31 *"This Gentleman was of known abilities":* Haswell, First Voyage, 11.

he was not listed as an officer: Alan Cooke and Clive Holland, *The Exploration of Northern Canada 500 to 1920: A Chronology,* 445.

complaining of "inhuman treatment": Haswell, First Voyage, 12.

31 *As they were preparing to leave:* Ibid., 13.
they had the skills on board: Ibid., 12.
32 *At the Falklands, Haswell:* Ibid., 28.
On March 19, the ships were: Ibid., 30.
Between four and five in the morning: Ibid., 31.
33 *In the first few hours:* Ibid., 31–32.
The sloop's jib stay: Ibid., 32.

CHAPTER THREE

35 *messages about strange ships:* Richard Walter, *Anson's Voyage Around the World: In the Years 1740–1744,* 81.
Gardoqui had arrived: Frederic Austin Ogg, *The Opening of the Mississippi: A Struggle for Supremacy in the American Interior,* 421. Also David Arias, *Spanish-Americans: Lives and Faces,* 131.
36 *Gardoqui was presented:* U.S. Department of State, *The Diplomatic Correspondence of the United States of America . . . September 10, 1783–March 4, 1789,* 150–51.
Although now in decline: For a full description of the Spanish Empire and its interests in North America, see Arthur Preston Whitaker, *The Spanish-American Frontier 1783–1795: The Westward Movement and the Spanish Retreat in the Mississippi Valley.*
37 *his family bank had channeled funds:* Arias, *Spanish-Americans,* 131. Five million Turin pounds were channeled through the Gardoqui family bank to the revolutionaries. Just prior to the Declaration of Independence, at the urging of his cousin King Louis of France, King Carlos III had sent funds for munitions and supplies through a clandestine French trading company, Roderigue Hortalez and Co. More supplies and munitions were sent through the port of New Orleans, including cannons, muskets, tents, gunpowder, and cattle. And among the people of New Spain, collections were gathered for additional funds to send north to support the Americans in their rebellion.
Spain had entered the war: For a thorough treatment of Spain's involvement in the American Revolution, see J. H. Elliot, *Empires of the Atlantic World: Britain and Spain in America 1492–1830.*
In 1784, Spain shut down: Fredrick J. Turner, "The Diplomatic Contest for the Mississippi Valley," 677.
discussions had been deadlocked: Ogg, *Opening of the Mississippi.* Also Whitaker,

Spanish-American Frontier, and Turner, "The Diplomatic Contest."

38 *Britain also knew that the grant:* Ignoring Pope Alexander VI's division of the globe in 1492, Spain's inveterate English enemy made explorations and claims on the coast of North America. These claims were resolved in part by the Anglo-Spanish Peace Treaty of 1670, which allowed English colonies to occupy the coastal region north of Charleston, South Carolina. Following the American Revolution, British disputes with Spain over borders and rights in North America were passed to the independent states and Congress through rights granted by the British to the United States in the Peace Treaty of 1783.

"The cabinet of Madrid thinks": Extract from a letter by French ambassador Armand Marc, comte de Montmorin, at Madrid to French foreign minister Charles Gravier, comte de Vergennes, quoted in U.S. Congress, *State Papers and Publick Documents of the United States . . . ,* 185–86.

In 1786, Gardoqui was nearly successful: Ogg, *Opening of the Mississippi,* 434.

39 *By the summer of 1787:* W. R. Shepard. "Wilkinson and the Spanish Conspiracy," 748–66. Also Ogg, *Opening of the Mississippi,* 441–44.

40 *Ancient texts called it:* For the myths about and voyages seeking the Northwest Passage, see Samuel Purchas, *Hakluytus Posthumus or Purchase His Pilgrimes, Contayning a History of the World in Sea Voyages and Land Travells, by Englishmen and Others.*

41 *Following these stories:* For example, see 1752 map of Joseph-Nicholas de l'Isle's and 1790 map of John Meares's.

The British Parliament offered: Charles Henry Carey, *History of Oregon,* 91.

The Loyal Company of Virginia: Donald Jackson, *Thomas Jefferson and the Stony Mountains: Exploring the West from Monticello,* 8.

42 *One of his captains:* T. C. Elliott, "The Origin of the Name Oregon," 101–10. Includes Rogers's proposals of 1765 and 1772.

he wrote to George Rogers Clark: Thomas Jefferson to George Rogers Clark, December 4, 1783. It is worth noting that George Rogers Clark was the elder brother of Captain William Clark, who would co-lead the Lewis and Clark expedition twenty years later in 1803.

"We should not be surprised": Letter of Viceroy Manuel Flores to Minister Antonio Valdes. December 23, 1788, Estado 4289, Archivo General de Indias, Seville.

44 *Russian empress Catherine II:* Hubert Howe Bancroft, *History of Alaska, 1730–1885,* 281–84.

to keep an eye on: The Spanish voyages were by Juan Perez in 1774, Bruno Heceta in 1775, and Don Ignacio Arteaga in 1779.

44 *Cook concluded that a northern passage:* James Cook, *The Journals of Captain James Cook on his Voyages of Discovery.*
A number of Cook's other officers: Nathaniel Portlock as well as George Dixon and James Colnett.
larger Pacific campaign: Vincent Harlow, *The Founding of the Second British Empire, 1763–1793,* 62. The concept of a swing to the East is controversial among historians who dispute either the facts or the dating of such a movement. The overriding reality is that even if an official policy was absent, there was an unofficial focus to secure a stronger British merchant presence in the Pacific.

45 *At the City Palais:* A royal order issued November 9, 1787, addresses steps to be taken with foreign ships entering Spanish waters and makes reference to Article 10 of the Anglo-Spanish Peace Treaty of 1670, which established conditions for allowing refuge. The order is given in a document concerning the removal of Don Blas Gonzales from office: Don Pedro Vanela to Conde Campo de Alange, December 29, 1791. Estevan José Martinez, Diario de la Navegacion . . . (hereafter referred to as Martinez Diary 1788).
Conditions at the royal port: Information concerning San Blas and military operations for the port are from: Michael Thurman, *The Naval Department of San Blas: New Spain's Bastion for Alta California and Nootka, 1789–1795;* Christian I. Archer, "Spanish Exploration and Settlement of the Northwest Coast in the 18th Century"; Warren L. Cook, *Flood Tide of Empire: Spain and the Pacific Northwest, 1543–1819,* 50–51. And also documents from Archivo General de Indias, Bancroft Library, University of California, Berkeley.

46 *After studying Cook's journal:* Martinez Diary 1788.

CHAPTER FOUR

47 *Her mainmast had cracked:* A statement of these facts and other information concerning the *Columbia* at Cumberland Bay is in Blas Gonzales to Viceroy Teodoro de Croix, August 1, 1788.
Far to the southwest, Robert Gray: Gray's animosity toward Kendrick is evident in a number of his letters. In regard to breaking with Kendrick's command at this point, see Robert Gray to Joseph Barrell, July 13, 1789.
Kendrick had written orders: The orders included sailing instructions to Nootka and for trade there and at Macao, which Gray ignored. John Kendrick, Instructions to Robert Gray, February 1788.

48 *Three weeks after parting:* Robert Haswell, A Voyage Round the World On-

board the Ship Columbia-Rediviva and Sloop Washington (hereafter referred to as First Voyage), 33.

49 *Twenty years before:* Ibid., 38.

Several hundred miles north: These are the islands of Saint Ambrose and Saint Felix.

on the morning of May 3: Haswell, First Voyage, 40.

50 *During the next three weeks:* Ibid., 42–43.

He had been ordered by Joseph Barrell: Joseph Barrell, Orders Given Captain John Kendrick of the Ship Columbia for a Voyage to the Pacific Ocean, 1787.

This was the island: Daniel Defoe based his story on Selkirk's four-year experience, which had first been recorded by Richard Steele in *The Englishman* in 1711.

51 *Lord Anson had taken refuge there:* Walter, *Anson's Voyage Around the World: In the Years 1740–1744,* 103–6.

From the fort, the governor: Blas Gonzales to Viceroy Teodoro de Croix, August 1, 1788.

52 *He quickly summoned an officer:* Ibid. Juanes's observations and description of what subsequently occurred at Juan Fernándes Island were included in Blas Gonzales's report to Viceroy Teodoro de Croix.

Although royal law dating from 1692: Teodoro de Croix to Mexican Viceroy Manuel Flores, July 31, 1788. This law was complicated by the Anglo-Spanish Peace Treaty of 1670, Article 10, which allowed a ship refuge under certain conditions.

53 *Four days after the Americans arrived:* Gonzales to de Croix, August 1, 1788.

54 *"fatiguing passage of eighty-six days":* John Kendrick to Joseph Barrell, May 28, 1788.

the thirty-four-gun Santa Maria: Josef Munos to Captain General Higgins, August 3, 1788.

"We cannot ignore the strangers": De Croix to Flores, July 31, 1788.

55 *Kendrick would enlist Thomas Jefferson:* Fredric W. Howay, *Voyage of the Columbia to the Northwest Coast, 1787–1790 and 1790–1793,* 154–55.

de Croix sent a warning: De Croix to Flores, July 31, 1788. The letter instructed commanders of coastal ports to "secure these ships and their people."

"A ship named Columbia": Manuel Flores's instructions to Estevan Martinez, Estevan José Martinez, Diary of the Voyage.

57 *This was the curse:* There are many eighteenth-century writings on scurvy, which espouse various theories and cures. James Cook was one of the few who found a preventive measure through packing dried soup and brewing spruce beer, which his crew detested. Aboard the American expedition, Haswell apparently knew the

value of salad and greens to ward off scurvy, as indicated in his journal, but they did not prevent the disease for the crew of the *Washington* during the trip to the North Pacific. Until the mid-nineteeth century, when the use of limes became prevalent in the British navy, this disease took a heavy toll on long voyages.

58 *John Hammond and Hanse Lawton:* Discharge and Wage Accounting, Columbia Papers. Massachusetts Historical Society.

59 *"not very delicate eating":* Haswell, First Voyage, 44.

On July 31 came the surprise: Ibid., 46.

on the morning of August 2: Ibid., 47.

60 *noted that they were "well-limbed":* Ibid., 49.

61 *A "very fine looking fellow":* Ibid., 53.

It wasn't until the evening: Ibid., 56.

"these were the most acceptable things": Ibid., 57.

62 *"the women wearing nothing":* Ibid., 64.

an "amazing number of the natives": Ibid., 58.

a war dance, "accompanied": Ibid., 59.

63 *"turning a clump of trees":* Ibid., 61.

64 *"hoops and houlings":* Ibid., 63.

65 *The next morning, August 18:* Ibid., 65–66.

CHAPTER FIVE

66 *Martinez had sailed north:* Estevan José Martinez. Diario de la Navegacion . . . (hereafter referred to as Martinez Diary 1788).

67 *at the mouth of Prince William Sound:* Warren L. Cook, *Flood Tide of Empire: Spain and the Pacific Northwest, 1543–1819,* 123.

Problems with his officers: See complaint of Lopez de Haro filed against Martinez, Gonzalo Lopez de Haro to Viceroy Flores, October 28, 1788.

Three Saints Bay on Kodiak Island: de Haro to Flores, October 28, 1788. Also Cook, *Flood Tide,* 124.

68 *Another Russian ship:* Hubert Howe Bancroft, *The Works of Hubert Howe Bancroft,* vol. 33, *History of Alaska, 1730–1885,* 266.

An expedition from Siberia: Bancroft, *History of Alaska,* 282. Billings was appointed by Empress Catherine II on August 8, 1785, to command "A Secret Astronomical and Geographical Exploration . . . between Asia and America."

The Russians were intent: Martinez Diary 1788.

69 *"last breath in the service":* Estevan Martinez to Viceroy Manuel Flores, December 5, 1788.

70 *eager to be the first to bring news:* de Haro to Flores, October 28, 1788.
"our just and preeminent right": Flores instructions for Martinez 1789 expedition, in Manuel Antonio Flores to Estevan José Martinez, December 23, 1788. Also Martinez, Diary of the Voyage . . . (hereafter referred to as Martinez Diary 1789).

71 *"a small packet":* Martinez Diary 1789, 7.
royal standing orders allowed him: Real Cedula de 29 de Noviembre 1692, referenced by Viceroy de Croix in Teodoro de Croix to Mexican Viceroy Manuel Flores, July 31, 1788.

CHAPTER SIX

76 *John Hammond, had succumbed:* John Hammond died September 19. Hanse Lawton would die September 28. John Kendrick to Don Estevan José Martinez, May 8, 1789, and Ship Columbia Discharge and Wage list September 1790 showing dates of death.
Gray had arrived at Nootka: Robert Haswell, A Voyage Round the World onboard the Ship Columbia-Rediviva and Sloop Washington (hereafter referred to as First Voyage), 74–75.

77 *Haswell complained in his journal:* Ibid., 76–77.
103 days from Masafeuro to New Albion: Departure and arrival dates from Haswell, First Voyage, and Kendrick, noted in Haswell, First Voyage, 80–81. This shows that the two vessels made approximately the same forward progress during the nearly seventy-five-hundred-mile journey.

78 *James Cook had arrived here:* The ships arrived Monday, March 30, 1778. James Cook and James King, *A Voyage to the Pacific Ocean . . .*, vol. 2, 265. Also see James Cook, *The Journals of Captain James Cook on his Voyages of Discovery.*
according to legend, the natives: For background on the diverse perceptions of this contact, see Daniel W. Clayton, *Islands of Truth: The Imperial Fashioning of Vancouver Island,* 23.
Three canoes approached Cook's ships: For Cook's description of the arrival and first encounters, see Cook and King, *Voyage,* vol. 2, 265–67.

79 *on a single note, drawing it out:* There are several varying firsthand accounts of the initial encounter with native people at Nootka. See, for example, James Burney journal, March 30, 1778; Lieut. James King journal, March 30, 1778; Cook, *Journals,* March 30, 1778.
Cook was apparently using a Spanish map: Cook had on board Spanish maps of the Pacific. He noted his awareness that Spanish ships had explored this coast

in 1774 or 1775 and claimed that they "had not been at Nootka . . ." See Cook and King, *Voyage*, vol. 2, 332. For a description of the Spanish arrival offshore at Nootka in 1774, see José Mariano Mozino, *Noticias de Nutka: An Account of Nootka Sound in 1792*, 65–66. Also see Dagny Hansen, "Captain Cook's First Stop on the Northwest Coast: By Chance or Chart?"

79 *"itchmenutka"*: Tradition has held this to be one explanation of the origin of the name. Another is that Cook drew a circle in the sand to signify the sound and asked what it was; he was told by a puzzled native that what he had just done meant "to go around."

stories of magnificent profits: Cook and King, *Voyage*, vol. 3, 437.

The first British trading ship: Robert Greenhow, *The History of Oregon and California, and the Other Territories on the North-West Coast of North America*, 165–66. The *Captain Cook* and the *Experiment* under Prince Charles's godson, James Strange, came in 1786, as did Cook's former officers George Dixon and Nathaniel Portlock in the *King George* and the *Queen Charlotte*. An Austrian-flagged ship of the East India Company, *Imperial Eagle*, under Charles Barkley, visited the sound in 1787, as well as John Meares's ships, *Prince of Wales* and *Princess Royal*, under James Colnett and Charles Duncan.

80 *"within forty yards of us"*: Haswell, First Voyage, 79.

81 *Believing the* Columbia *lost:* Ibid. Despite their intense rivalry Meares and Kendrick would never meet.

the village name Yuquot: Frederic W. Howay, *Voyages of the Columbia to the Northwest Coast; 1787–1790 and 1790–1791*, 59, fn 4.

October 1, 1788, was the anniversary: Haswell, First Voyage, 80.

82 *They left the cove on October 14:* Ibid., 81. The plundering of the village and canoes at the time the Americans arrived demonstrates the violence already being practiced on the people of Nootka.

83 *"flocked to us in great numbers"*: Haswell, First Voyage, 82.

84 *Although some sailors:* Eliot Fox-Povey, "How Agreeable Their Company Would Be."

"cleansing a naked young Woman": Cook, *Journals*, vol. 3, 1095.

86 *luxurious sea otter furs:* There are many traders' descriptions of the appeal of sea otter furs. See, for example, William Sturgis, *"A Most Remarkable Enterprise": Lectures on the Northwest Coast Trade and Northwest Coast Indian Life*, 3.

The natives' ornaments differed: There are a number of descriptions of the people of Nootka. See, for example, Haswell, First Voyage, 97–98, and Mozino, *Noticias de Nutka*, 13–16.

87 *Legend says his father:* Mozino, *Noticias de Nutka*, 31.

87 *Maquinna and his people being cannibals:* While the fear of cannibalism was widespread, and specific observations were noted, those who examined the allegations found only ritual practices of human sacrifice. Mozino, *Noticias de Nutka,* 22, fn 11.

Maquinna's people "eat the flesh": Haswell, First Voyage, 104.

88 *By the middle of November:* Ibid., 82–83.

89 *There were twenty-two villages:* Archer, "Seduction before Sovereignty," 143.

on the night of December 11: Haswell, First Voyage, 83–84.

90 *perhaps flour pudding:* Later crews that wintered over at Clayoquot found they could obtain blackberries and "whortle berries" into the winter months. Plum duff, a flour pudding, was a sailor's favorite, and whortleberries would have made a likely substitute for this holiday repast.

"You were always on the side": Joseph Barrell to Nathaniel Barrell, December 20, 1787, and "Roster and Vote of the Committee of Twenty-Five," February 3–4, 1788. Vol. 6, 1411. Also: *Massachusetts Gazette,* October 30, 1787, 171.

91 *The only news families had received:* "Extract of a Letter from New London, dated April 16," *Independent Chronicle and the Universal Advertiser* 21, no. 1069 (April 23, 1789), 3.

On January 13, an alarm went up: Haswell, First Voyage, 84–85.

on January 28, a large canoe appeared: Ibid., 86.

92 *Maquinna's arrival was not recorded:* The first formal meetings described by visitors to Nootka took place inside Maquinna's house, with exchange of gifts, dancing and drumming, and a meal.

94 *"I am of [the] opinion":* Haswell, First Voyage, 68.

95 *these people appeared taller:* Ibid., 107.

96 *Haswell rapturously determined:* Ibid., 109.

"no land to obstruct the view": Ibid., 111.

97 *built a "Good house":* Ibid., 123.

98 *After the sloop passed:* Ibid., 125.

a strange ship appeared: Ibid., 125, and Estevan José Martinez, Diary of the Voyage . . . , 75.

CHAPTER SEVEN

99 *He had started out from San Blas:* Estevan José Martinez, Diary of the Voyage . . . (hereafter referred to as Martinez Diary 1789), 17.

not this small American sloop: Ibid., 7.

100 *Viceroy Flores had given Martinez:* Martinez stated that he had no orders to take

Kendrick's ships, and at other times that he had orders to take them or that he planned to take them. The confusion can be explained by his not having explicit written orders, but being allowed to take these ships under standing orders. The royal order of 1692 allowed Martinez to treat all foreign ships as enemies. (See Teodoro de Croix to Mexican Viceroy Manuel Flores, July 31, 1788.) Also, while Flores did not commit to writing a specific order for taking the American ships (which could have risked a diplomatic incident), he may have given specific oral orders. The end result in either case is that Martinez was free to interpret what "more powerful arguments" would mean.

100 *"get rid of him":* Martinez Diary 1789, 29.

101 *"was a Portuguese, the first mate":* Ibid., 76.

102 *"this gentleman endeavored":* Robert Haswell, A Voyage Round the World Onboard the Ship Columbia-Rediviva and Sloop Washington (hereafter referred to as First Voyage), 126.

Meares's new business partner: John Meares to Robert Funter, February 3, 1789, in James Colnett, *A Voyage to the North West Side of America: The Journals of James Colnett, 1786–1789,* 18–19.

aggressively proposing trade: The Journal of Captain James Colnett Aboard the Argonaut, April 26, 1789–November 3, 1791, 306, Appendix II. Containing the license of the South Sea Company under which Colnett was sailing.

"possession of all new discovered parts": Martinez Diary 1789, 120.

103 *In the harbor at Friendly Cove:* William Douglas, "Extract of the Journal of the Iphigenia" (hereafter referred to as Douglas Journal), in John Meares, *The Memorial of Lt. John Mears of the Royal Navy . . . ,* 59.

"We sang the Salve": Martinez Diary 1789, 79.

104 *"On the morning of the [5th] of May":* Haswell, First Voyage, 143–44.

Kendrick told him another half-truth: Kendrick confirmed what he had told Martinez in a letter a few days later. John Kendrick to Don Estevan José Martinez, May 8, 1789.

105 *After lunch, Martinez accompanied:* Martinez Diary 1789, 80; Douglas Journal, 60.

106 *Martinez had tossed abalone:* Martinez Diary 1789, 81.

"In answer to your request": Kendrick to Martinez, May 8, 1789.

"their brother who had come": Martinez Diary 1789, 83–84.

107 *The celebrations continued:* Martinez Diary 1789, 86–87. There is a divergence in the record of what occurred the next day. Martinez places himself at Yuquot. Douglas claims that Martinez took his bedding on the morning of May 11 and went to stay overnight with Kendrick. Douglas Journal, 62–63.

107 *Douglas later claimed:* Ibid., 63–64.

Meares would allege: Ibid. This allegation was based on what Douglas suspected.

War of Jenkins' Ear: In this war between Britain and Spain, the primary engagements were from 1739 to 1741, with some trailing skirmishes continuing to 1748. The source of the conflict was an incident in which a British merchant ship or privateer was boarded by the Spanish *garda costa* in the Caribbean, and the ship's captain, Robert Jenkins, allegedly had his ear sliced off by the Spanish captain. When displayed to Parliament, the severed ear touched off the volatile relations between the two countries.

108 *Douglas's Portuguese instructions:* "Extract of Letter from Mr. Meares to Captain William Douglas, February, 1788," in Meares, *Memorial,* 33–34. Also Douglas Journal, 63.

109 *"As soon as I was on board":* Douglas Journal, 62.

Forty armed Spanish men: Ibid., 62–63.

The Treaty of Paris concluding: This treaty between Spain, Britain, France, and Portugal granted Britain extensive lands (such as Canada), boosting its international presence and ambitions.

111 *"his orders were to take":* Douglas Journal, 68.

"he might act as he thought proper": Ibid., 70.

112 *"set her on fire":* Ibid., 76.

"the Spanish Ship": Haswell, First Voyage, 143.

113 *The log house and forge:* While Kendrick would occupy this site, which he called Fort Washington, intermittently over the next five years, the harbor at Mawina, which he would later purchase from Maquinna, naming it Safe Retreat Harbor, became a favorite anchorage of American trading vessels in the coming decades.

114 *Two days earlier, on June 15:* Martinez Diary 1789, 106.

"we discovered that the straits": Haswell, First Voyage, 142.

115 *"I have recalled that in the year '74":* Martinez Diary 1789, 104.

Charles Barkley, commanding: Robert Greenhow, *The History of Oregon and California, and the Other Territories on the North-West Coast of North America,* 171.

116 *Martinez held a special dinner:* Martinez Diary 1789, 111.

117 *The morning of Wednesday, June 24:* Ibid., 112.

118 *On the morning of Sunday, June 28:* Ibid., 114.

CHAPTER EIGHT

120 *"Should you go into the Port":* Thomas Hudson to James Colnett, July 3, 1789, in James Colnett, *The Journal of Captain James Colnett aboard the Argonaut from April 26, 1789 to November 3, 1791,* 55.

"He was entrusted to prevent": Estevan José Martinez, Diary of the Voyage . . . (hereafter referred to as Martinez Diary 1789), 120.

Colnett responded that he was: Joseph Ingraham, *Joseph Ingraham's Journal of the Brigantine Hope on a Voyage to the Northwest Coast of America, 1790–1792,* 221.

121 *"in a friendly manner":* Martinez Diary 1789, 121.

122 *"I divined his intentions":* Martinez Diary 1789, 120. Also Colnett, *Journal,* 309–10.

"we would have had a bad neighbor": Estevan José Martinez to Viceroy Manuel Antonio Flores, July 13, 1789. Also Martinez Diary 1789, 209.

"all the assistance in his power": Colnett, *Journal,* 319.

"a man of honour, Nephew": Ibid., 319–21.

"would go in on those declarations": Ibid., 319–20.

"It was late and thick weather": James Colnett to the ambassador of Great Britain, May 1, 1790, in Colnett's, *Journal aboard the Argonaut,* 319–21.

123 *The* Argonaut*'s bow was tied:* Martinez Diary 1789, 122.

124 *"giving us to understand":* Ibid., 123.

"He informed me he bore": Ibid.,124.

125 *"My friend, in the present":* Ibid., 125.

"I received an order from Don Martinez": Colnett, *Journal,* 311.

"I have no thought of doing so": Martinez Diary 1789, 126. Colnett, *Journal,* 311–12.

126 *"although he did not understand":* Colnett, *Journal,* 98.

shouted, "Goddamn Spaniard": Martinez Diary 1789, 127.

"I now saw, but too late": Colnett, *Journal,* 98.

"It was impossible to make any": Robert Duffin to John Meares, July 12, 1789, in John Meares, *The Memorial of Lt. John Mears of the Royal Navy . . .*, 79.

127 *"[A]n Officer that had been":* Colnett, *Journal,* 60.

"this will undoubtedly occasion": John B. Treat to Samuel Breck, July 14, 1789.

129 *"There is ground for believing":* Martinez Diary 1789, 132.

130 *"If Captain Cook had lived":* Ibid., 136. See 132–36 for full statement.

"sextant, charts, and drawing paper": Colnett, *Journal,* 179.

131 *Colnett was overcome with despair:* Robert Duffin to John Meares, July 13, 1789, in Meares, *Memorial,* 83.

131 *In the British version of events:* Deposition of William Graham, May 5, 1790, in Meares, *Memorial,* 34–41.

He had also heard that Callicum: Martinez Diary 1789, 144.

133 *"if his crew offered any resistance":* Ibid., 141.

"Mr Jaques, As I am a Prisoner": Colnett, *Journal,* 62.

"to use all care": Martinez Diary 1789, 142.

"Yard Rope rove to hang": Colnett, *Journal,* 62.

134 *"Martinez Pisec!":* Martinez Diary 1789, 144.

135 *in a touching scene:* This was described by one of Martinez's officers, Josef Tobar y Tamariz, "Report of Don Josef Tobar y Tamariz, First Mate of the Royal Navy, to His Most Excellent Lordship and Viceroy of New Spain, August 29, 1789," 118.

"not by any means equal": John Kendrick to Joseph Barrell, July 13, 1789.

CHAPTER NINE

137 *"a distance of five or six miles":* Estevan José Martinez, Diary of the Voyage . . . (hereafter referred to as Martinez Diary 1789), 148.

"I treated this enemy as a friend": Ibid., 224.

138 *Gray had written a letter:* Robert Gray to Joseph Barrell, July 13, 1789.

140 *The* Washington*'s first mate:* The men who remained with Kendrick can be determined from those on the voyage pay list minus those who returned with Gray, and also from those recorded as witnesses on Kendrick's deeds in 1791.

a total of twenty-one men: Gray said that Kendrick had twenty men on board. Robert Gray to Joseph Barrell, December 18, 1789.

Kendrick pressured the most experienced: "Information of William Graham," in John Meares, *The Memorial of Lt. John Mears of the Royal Navy . . .* , 34–41.

threatened to leave them onshore: Ibid., 41.

142 *What Kendrick did next:* The earliest part of the controversy was between John Meares and George Dixon, who refuted Meares's claims. Robert Gray and Vancouver entered into it as well, positing that Kendrick did not make the indicated circumnavigation. Historian Robert Greenhow, in *The History of Oregon and California . . .* , concluded in 1840 that Kendrick had accomplished the circumnavigation of Vancouver Island. Charles Fredric Newcombe, a British Columbia physician and ethnologist, believed that he disproved Greenhow's reasoning in a memorial published in 1914 (see C. F. Newcombe, ed., "The First Circumnavigation of Vancouver Island").

"The Straits of Juan de Fuca": James Colnett, *The Journal of Captain James Col-*

nett aboard the Argonaut from April 26, 1789 to November 3, 1791, 192.

"It's the general Opinion of Capt. Duncan": Colnett, *Journal,* 400, fn 370.

143 *According to John Meares:* John Meares, *Voyages Made in the Years 1788 and 1789 . . . ,* lvi.

Backing up his statements: When challenged on the Washington's circumnavigation of the island, Meares said he had a source who got the information directly from Kendrick at Macao. "Mr. Neville, who was continually with him [Kendrick] during that interval, and received the particulars of the track from him, was so obliging as to state it to me." Contained in Meares, "An Answer."

144 *The next confirmed report of Kendrick:* Martinez Diary 1789, 221–22.

145 *"an almost endless task":* Robert Haswell, A Voyage Round the World onboard the Ship Columbia-Rediviva and Sloop Washington (hereafter referred to as First Voyage), 142.

147 *What fascinated the* Washington*'s crew:* Haswell, First Voyage, 129. Also John Boit, 11.

"always ready and willing": John Hoskins, The Narrative of a Voyage, 51.

"a little diminutive savage-looking fellow": Ibid., 56.

148 *The native version of the story:* Ibid., 51.

CHAPTER TEN

150 *The* Argonaut *arrived at San Blas:* James Colnett, *The Journal of Captain James Colnett aboard the Argonaut from April 26, 1789 to November 3, 1791,* 67. Also Warren L. Cook, *Flood Tide of Empire: Spain and the Pacific Northwest, 1543–1819,* 194.

"every case of the cargo": Colnett, *Journal,* 65.

"half Starved and [bathed in]": Ibid., 67.

151 *"It being a Market day":* Ibid., 69.

"which was it not for the Turkey Bustards": Ibid., 70.

152 *read with alarm a letter:* Estevan José Martinez to Viceroy Manuel Antonio Flores, July 13, 1789.

Count Juan Vincente de Revillagigedo: Cook, *Flood Tide,* 195.

First mate James Hansen committed suicide: Colnett, *Journal,* 73.

153 *"We now had no remedy left":* Ibid., 78.

Robert Gray was en route to China: John Meares, *The Memorial of Lt. John Mears of the Royal Navy . . . ,* includes letters and statements from prisoners who arrived at Macao on the *Columbia*.

CHAPTER ELEVEN

158 *officers of arriving ships:* Ebenezer Dorr on the women of the Marquesas, April 17, 1791, in Joseph Ingraham, *Joseph Ingraham's Journal of the Brigantine Hope on a Voyage to the Northwest Coast of America, 1790–1792,* 47, fn 1.

"which abounds in everything": Estevan José Martinez, Diary of the Voyage . . . (hereafter referred to as Martinez Diary 1789), 211–12.

159 *"the grand emporium of Commerce":* Richard Cadman Etches to East India Company Court of Directors, April 29, 1785, in Vincent T. Harlow, *The Founding of the Second British Empire, 1763–1789,* 421–24.

providence intended the islands: John Meares, *Voyages Made in the Years 1788 and 1789 . . . ,* xcv.

160 *Barrell rode out to Worcester:* George Washington, *The Diaries of George Washington,* vol. 5, 472–73, fn 2.

"that the day will arrive": Ibid. Also George Washington to Joseph Barrell, June 8, 1788.

the snowy peak of Mauna Kea: Mauna Kea, at 13,796 feet above sea level, is about one hundred feet taller than Mauna Loa to the east. It is the tallest mountain in the world when measured from the sea floor.

161 *oral histories tell of:* Edward Joesting, *Kauai: The Separate Kingdom,* 10–11.

Cook had stopped at Tahiti: Tahiti had been "discovered" by the Spanish in 1606 but according to British tradition did not receive a European visitor until Captain Samuel Wallis in 1767. Cook claimed that Wallis had discovered Tahiti. Cook, vol. 2, 241.

When he asked about islands: Ibid., 180.

Cook is commonly recognized: Ibid., 191. Cook sighted the islands on January 18, 1778. However, he found the natives in possession of small bits of metal, which they had fashioned into tools. One piece was guessed to have been the point of a broadsword, leading some of the crew "to think we had not been the first European visitors of these islands. But, it seems to me, that the very great surprise expressed by them, on seeing our ships . . . cannot be reconciled with such a notion." Ibid., 240.

local historians believe: See Abraham Fornander, *The Polynesian Race: Its Origin and Migrations, and the Ancient History of the Hawaiian People to the Times of Kamehameha I,* 158. Also Darlene E. Kelley, "Foreign Contact with Hawaii before Captain Cook."

Estevan Martinez mentioned Gaetano: Estevan José Martinez to Viceroy Manuel Antonio Flores, July 13, 1789.

162 *one officer described as "tasting":* Alexander Home, master's mate. James Cook, *The Journals of Captain James Cook on his Voyages of Discovery . . .*, 565.

Off the eastern end of the island: Ibid., 191–92.

163 *there was panic and debate:* Sheldon Dibble, *History of the Sandwich Islands*, 31, 34–35.

they were temples of Lono: Ralph S. Kuykendall, *Hawaiian Kingdom: Foundation and Transformation 1778–1854*, vol. 2, 8.

Voyage records show that more: The *Resolution*'s pay book records showed sixty-six men with confirmed venereal disease.

Cook decreed that no women: Cook, *Journals*, vol. 2, 196.

One man carried off a butcher's cleaver: Ibid., 195.

Another was shot and killed: Ibid., 197–98.

164 *the natives knew their disease:* "March 1779: As soon as they got on board, one of the men began to tell us, that we had left a disorder amongst their women, of which several persons of both sexes had died. He was himself afflicted with venereal disease." James Cook and James King, *A Voyage to the Pacific Ocean . . .*, vol. 3, 89.

165 *Kealakekua—the "pathway of the gods":* Following the pronunciation of James Cook, the British and American captains called this bay "Karakakooa."

This was the annual four-month period: For background on the *makahiki* celebrations, see Kuykendall, *Hawaiian Kingdom*, vol. 1, 7–9.

"singing and shouting and exhibiting": Cook and King, *Voyage*, vol. 3, 2–3.

Cook found villagers falling: Ibid., 5–7.

According to officers' accounts: Ibid., 10–11. Also Fornander, *Polynesian Race*, 189.

"these people will oblige me": Cook and King, *Voyage*, vol. 3, 40.

166 *killing him and four marines:* Ibid., 45–46.

wanted Cook's body returned: Ibid., 65.

His skull was said to be: Ibid., 68.

Two warriors' heads were cut off: The retaliation for Cook's killing continued off and on for days, resulting in the village of Waipunauloa being burned and priests and others killed. General retaliation: Ibid., 54–75; the incident of the severed heads: Ibid., 75.

who made a brief visit in May 1786: Nathaniel Portlock, *A Voyage Round the World . . .*, 63–64. Also see James Colnett, *The Journal of Captain James Colnett aboard the Argonaut from April 26, 1789 to November 3, 1791*, 323, fn 395. Dixon also believed that Kealakekua was unsafe and may have communicated this information to Colnett when they met at Nootka.

168 *a system of religious instructions:* Kuykendall, *Hawaiian Kingdom,* vol. 1, 7–9.
Life was a journey: George Kanahele, *Ku Kanaka Stand Tall: A Search for Hawaiian Values,* 32.
the first who stabbed Cook: Kuykendall, *Hawaiian Kingdom,* vol. 1, 19, fn 27. Vancouver said this man was living on an estate in eastern Hawaii belonging to Kahowmotoo. George Vancouver, *A Voyage of Discovery to the North Pacific Ocean and Round the World . . . ,* vol. 5, 55.
169 *"seemed not to esteem chastity":* Ingraham, *Journal,* 47.
"that few could but admire": Ebenezer Dorr, A Journal of a Voyage from Boston Round the World . . . , entry for April 17, 1791; Ingraham, *Journal,* 47, fn 1.
even James Cook was seduced: Dibble, *History,* 33; Fornander, *Polynesian Race,* 162.
171 *Richard Howe, warned:* Richard Howe, September 7, 1789.
as a fearless warrior: Kuykendall, *Hawaiian Kingdom,* vol. 1, 429–30.
172 *The old island lord was rumored:* Fornander, *Polynesian Race,* 260.
174 *one tale says it was a coincidence:* Dibble, *History,* 68; James Jackson Jarves, *History of the Hawaiian or Sandwich Islands,* 155; William De Witt Alexander, *A Brief History of the Hawaiian People,* 134.
people called the mako'u: David Malo, *Hawaiian Antiquities (Mooleo Hawaii),* 74.
one of the most savage faces: Jarves, *History,* 171.
175 *the carpenter Isaac Ridler:* Ingraham, *Journal,* 78–79.
With two younger crew members: Ingraham mentions two crewmen. A threatening letter Simon Metcalfe sent ashore is addressed to Ridler, Mackay, and Thomas. See Bruce Cartwright, "Some Early Foreign Residents of the Hawaiian Islands."
"During the stay of these three weeks": John Kendrick Recommendation for Kaiana, December 11, 1789.
176 *opened fire with grapeshot:* Ingraham, *Journal,* 82.
177 *He was left for dead:* Ibid., 79.
"to take ample revenge": Letter of Simon Metcalfe to Isaac Ridler et al., March 22, 1790; included in Bruce Cartwright "Some Early Foreign Residents of the Hawaiian Islands," 25th Annual Report of the Hawaiian Historical Society, 58.
teaching his warriors how to fire: Ibid., 82.
178 *The battle became known as Kepaniwai:* Kuykendall, *Hawaiian Kingdom,* vol. 1, 35.

CHAPTER TWELVE

180 *By midday January 26:* John Kendrick to Robert Gray and Richard S. Howe, January 27, 1790.

He had arrived at Macao: "Deposition of the Officers and Men of the Schooner North West American," in John Meares, *The Memorial of Lt. John Meares of the Royal Navy . . .*, 52.

181 *Europeans who could not learn:* Ernest John Eitel, *Europe in China: The History of Hong Kong from the Beginning to the Year 1882,* 12–13.

182 *misrule was what was called for:* Kenneth Scott Latourette, *The History of Early Relations between the United States and China, 1784–1844,* 20–21.

Most ships arrived at the end: Eitel, *Europe in China,* 8.

183 *The hong merchants dictated:* J. Wade Caruthers, *American Pacific Ocean Trade: Its Impact on Foreign Policy and Continental Expansion, 1784–1860,* 77.

On January 27, he sent: Kendrick to Gray and Howe, January 27, 1790.

"very sorry to inform": Robert Gray to John Kendrick, January 29, 1790.

184 *"everything is left":* Joseph Barrell to John Kendrick, December 12, 1787.

around the south point: "The Water Islands are two small islands close off the South end of Montanha; one mile N.W. ¾ N. from them lies another small island, having a little bay called Lark's Bay, betwixt it and the West point of Montanha, with 2 ½ fathoms in it at low water": James Horsburgh, *The India Directory, or, Directions for Sailing to and from the East Indies, China, Australia . . .*, 362. S. Wells Williams, *The Chinese Commercial Guide, Sailing Instructions,* 9, gives the same location: "Inside Islet, having a small inlet called Lark bay, between it and Morgan point (608 feet above the sea), the west extreme of Montanha."

floating warehouses for East India Company: Rev. J. C. Thomson, "Historical Landmarks of Macao."

185 *the Portuguese governor was involved:* Samuel Shaw, *The Journals of Major Samuel Shaw: The First American Consul at Canton, with the Life of the Author,* 238.

186 *It leased a factory at Canton:* Sir Lindsey Ride and May Ride, *An East India Company Cemetery: Protestant Burials in Macao,* 58.

"320 Whole ones": Robert Gray to John Kendrick, January 30, 1790.

Kendrick refused the sale: No document extant, but see Gray's response of February 4.

Gray wrote back to discourage him: Robert Gray to John Kendrick, February 4, 1790.

186 *Two days later, Kendrick wrote:* John Kendrick to Robert Gray and Richard S. Howe, February 6, 1790.

187 *Kendrick sent artifacts:* Kendrick reportedly sent back to Rev. William Bentley of Salem a variety of artifacts, the first Northwest Coast artifacts received in New England. These included bows and arrows, bark cloth, a "squaw's fan," bone fishhooks, and a woven conical hat. Mary Malloy, *Souvenirs of the Fur Trade: Northwest Coast Indian Art and Artifacts Collected by American Mariners, 1788–1844,* 98, 102–3.

he was falling ill: Hoskins wrote, "almost immediately upon his arrival he was seized with a violent fever; which caused for his life for some time to be despaired of: and which prevented his going to Canton in person, as he had previously intended." John Hoskins, The Narrative of a Voyage, 6.

The inventory of furs: Inventory of furs, Columbia Papers. The issue of Gray not recording the actual amount of skins brought ashore and sold was addressed later by Kendrick as well as by Barrell's agent Thomas Randall. Randall's accounting is also included in the Columbia Papers.

188 *Because he hadn't heard from Gray:* John Kendrick to Robert Gray, February 9, 1790.

Gray passed out of the harbor: Richard S. Howe and Robert Gray to Joseph Barrell, June 16, 1790. Also Hoskins, Narrative, 103.

New York revolutionary Isaac Sears: Shaw, *Journals,* 235.

His son John had told: Josef Tobar y Tamariz, "Report of Don Josef Tobar y Tamariz, First Mate of the Royal Navy, to His Most Excellent Lordship and Viceroy of New Spain, August 29, 1789," 118.

189 *Night and day the narrow streets:* Shaw, *Journals,* 168–72.

Kendrick purchased fireworks: He would later use the fireworks in impressive displays for natives on the Northwest Coast and in the Sandwich Islands.

190 *according to his later critics:* Robert Gray leveled charges that Kendrick sought to cheat the owners of the *Columbia* and gratify his own pleasure.

His house was broken into: Hoskins, Narrative, 103.

191 *"With respect to our own":* Shaw, *Journals,* 354.

192 *"The English seem to be":* Ibid., 353.

Meares had assurances: John Meares, *Voyages Made in the Years 1788 and 1789 . . . ,* lxxxiii–v.

"The Japanese Islands would be": David MacKay, *In the Wake of Cook: Science, Exploration and Empire 1780–1801,* 63.

193 *"our Intention is to adopt":* Howay, "Four Letters," 125–39.

193 *their first London company venture:* John Meares wanted the *Argonaut* returned to China in the autumn of 1791 so that she could be dispatched to Japan. "Extracts of Letter from Mr. Mears to Captain Colnett, Dated Macao, 25 April, 1789," in Meares, *Memorial,* 29.

Viceroy Revillagigedo had sent: Warren L. Cook, *Flood Tide of Empire: Spain and the Pacific Northwest, 1543–1819,* 195, fn 128, cites letter of Revillagigedo to Valdes, August 27, 1789.

194 *Merry provided the British cabinet:* Anthony Merry to the Duke of Leeds, Madrid, January 4, 1790, in John Norris, "The Policy of the British Cabinet in the Nootka Crisis," 562, fn 3.

on February 10, Spain's Marquis del Campo: Cook, *Flood Tide,* 205.

195 *"take prisoner and prosecute":* Daniel Clayton, *Islands of Truth: The Imperial Fashioning of Vancouver Island,* 184.

prompted orders from the Admiralty: Jeremy Black, *British Foreign Policy in an Age of Revolutions, 1783–1793,* 236. Also "Late Foreign Intelligence. London. May 9–15," *Boston Herald of Freedom* 4, no. 34 (July 27, 1790), 153.

He carried with him: See attachments to Meares, *Memorial.*

Grenville read the memorial: Black, *British Foreign Policy,* 236.

196 *Pitt went before Parliament:* Robert Greenhow, *The History of Oregon and California and the Other Territories on the North-West Coast of North America,* 203.

"In the present enlightened age": James Marshall and Carrie Marshall, eds. *Pacific Voyages: Selections from Scots Magazine 1771–1818,* 74.

The warships Pegasus, Nautilous: "Spain," *Litchfield* (CT) *Weekly Monitor* 5, no. 261 (June 28, 1790), 2.

"insidious and mercenary conspiracy": Etches, "An Authentic Statement."

197 *"This country is arming":* Max M. Mintz, "Gouverneur Morris, George Washington's War Hawk," 651–61.

Behind the scenes: Howard V. Evans, "The Nootka Sound Controversy in Anglo-French Diplomacy—1790," 609–40.

198 *Floridablanca proposed a strategic plan:* Ibid., 222–23.

publishing a narrative: Meares, *Voyages.*

Kendrick was arrested: Hoskins, Narrative, 103.

CHAPTER THIRTEEN

199 *a description of the sweeping:* "Spanish War," *New-York Daily News,* no. 462 (June 19, 1790), 2. Also "Spanish War," *Federal Gazette and Philadelphia Evening Post,* June 21, 1790, 2.

199 *"the Parliament has granted":* "Boston, July 3," *Portland* (ME) *Cumberland Gazette,* July 12, 1790, 1.

British transports were reportedly: "Late Foreign Intelligence, London. May 9–15," *Boston Herald of Freedom* 4, No. 34 (July 27, 1790), 153.

200 *"I believe that a war":* Gouverneur Morris to George Washington, May 29, 1790.

"with nothing less than war": Thomas Jefferson to Thomas Mann Randolph Jr., June 20, 1790.

hoped to draw in: Jeremy Black, *British Foreign Policy in an Age of Revolution 1783–1793,* 237–38.

201 *came apart when O'Fallon:* Arthur Preston Whitaker, *Spanish-American Frontier 1783–1795: The Westward Movement and the Spanish Retreat in the Mississippi Valley,* 141–42.

Representatives of the Cherokee: David Humphreys to Thomas Jefferson, October 20, 1790. Also Fredrick J. Turner, "The Diplomatic Contest for the Mississippi Valley," *The Atlantic,* May 1904.

"If the war between Britain and Spain": Thomas Jefferson to E. Rutledge, July 4, 1790.

It would figure not only: Turner, "Diplomatic Contest," 676.

The Nootka crisis later became: Ibid., 680.

202 *Captain Kendrick in the* Lady Washington: "Boston, May 19," *Concord Herald* 1, no. 23 (June 15, 1790), 3.

"In the success of these": "Late Foreign Intelligence."

On the morning of Monday, August 9: Justin Winsor, *The Memorial History of Boston, Including Suffolk County Massachusetts, 1630–1880,* vol. 4, 208.

more than triple: Wade J. Caruthers, *American Pacific Ocean Trade: Its Impact on Foreign Policy and Continental Expansion, 1784–1860,* 72.

203 *new protectionist policies:* The Tonnage Act of 1789 placed a duty of fifty cents per ton on foreign-built or foreign-owned vessels entering American ports. The duty on American vessels was only six cents per ton. Curtis P. Nettles, *The Emergence of a National Economy, 1775–1815,* 239.

change as remarkable as: Jacqueline Barbara Carr, "A Change 'as Remarkable as the Revolution Itself': Boston's Demographics, 1780–1800," 583–602.

in his brilliant yellow-and-red-feathered: Susan Ellen Bulfinch, *The Life And Letters of Charles Bulfinch, Architect; with Other Family Papers,* 66.

"will not be equal": Robert Gray to Joseph Barrell, December 18, 1789.

204 *Behind closed doors:* John Hoskins, The Narrative of a Voyage, 6–7.

"had it in contemplation": Ibid., 6.

204 *Gray apparently also told:* In response to these charges, Barrell in his instructions to Gray for the next voyage warned against forming such relationships.

205 *"Thus much must be acknowledged":* Hoskins, Narrative, 7.

207 *"their abilities to produce":* Ibid., 8.

The owners were divided: John Boit, "A New Log of the Columbia," 2.

Gray, who received a total: Discharge and Wages list, September 1790, Columbia Papers.

A letter Randall wrote: Thomas Randall to Alexander Hamilton, August 14, 1791.

208 *"the arrival of the* Columbia*":* John Quincy Adams, *Writings of John Quincy Adams,* vol. 1, 518. Entry for August 14, 1790.

"The owners of the Columbia*":* "Extract of a Letter from Boston, August 10," *New York Gazette of the United States* 2, no. 38 (August 21, 1790), 567.

"Capt. Mears, in his representation": "Captain Meares; British Court; Don Martinez," *Boston Columbian Centinel* 14, no. 1 (September 15, 1790), 3.

209 *Acknowledging the "ill sweets":* Joseph Ingraham, *Joseph Ingraham's Journal of the Brigantine Hope on a Voyage to the Northwest Coast of America, 1790–1782,* 1–2.

"In all matters of traffic": Joseph Barrell to Robert Gray, September 25, 1790.

210 *"War was declared by England":* "Something More of War," *Massachusetts Spy* 19, no. 909 (September 2, 1790), 3.

"no connection with foreigners": Barrell to Gray, September 25, 1790.

"If the wind is fair": Letter of Joseph Barrell to Robert Gray, September 25, 1790.

211 *The last news before sailing:* "British Advices, via Philadelphia: London July 13," *New York Daily Gazette,* no. 538 (September 16, 1790), 886.

The naval mobilization and armament: Expenses were reported as 3,072,114 pounds in "Accounts as far as can be made up, of the expences of the armament on account of the Dispute with Spain, up to November 11, 1790, presented to the House of Commons." James Marshall and Carrie Marshall, eds., *Pacific Voyages: Selections from Scots Magazine, 1771–1808,* 92–93.

212 *His revised terms:* Warren L. Cook, *Flood Tide of Empire: Spain and the Pacific Northwest, 1543–1819,* 232, fn 74.

King George III went sleepless: Ibid., 241, fn 91.

Floridablanca, too, was anguished: Ibid., 232–33.

In an unexpected turnaround: See Jeremy Black, *British Foreign Policy in an Age of Revolutions, 1783–1793,* 250. Also figuring into Floridablanca's problems was the opposition he faced from the queen, who had gained great influence over government policies. The U.S. chargé d'affairs in Madrid, William Carmichael, wrote to Thomas Jefferson, "This government is weak; the ministry is in a ticklish situation; the Queen governs with caprice; the people begin to dispute their sovereigns; and altho' they have no chiefs to look up to, the dissatisfaction is general . . ." This uncertainty was made even greater in view of the fact that the queen was about to give birth and there was fear she would die. See William Carmichael to Thomas Jefferson, January 24, 1791.

212 *Alleyne Fitzhebert, and Count Floridablanca:* Black, *British Foreign Policy,* 250.

213 *mutual interest in defending monarchy:* Cook, *Flood Tide,* 232.

To undermine this effort: Max Mintz, "Gouverneur Morris, George Washington's War Hawk." Also Jared Sparks, *The Life of Gouverneur Morris: With Selections from His Correspondence and Misc. Papers.*

215 *Vancouver's expedition was to consist:* George Vancouver, *A Voyage of Discovery to the North Pacific Ocean and Round the World . . .* , vol. 1, 49–50.

"the nature and extent": Ibid., 60.

"required and directed": Ibid., 62–63.

216 *The young British captain was:* Ibid., 58.

the merchant Butterworth *expedition:* J. F. G. Stokes, "Honolulu and Some New Speculative Phases of Hawaiian History," 61–62, 96–98.

CHAPTER FOURTEEN

217 *Prussia and Holland were ready:* Henry R. Wagner, *Spanish Explorations in the Strait of Juan de Fuca,* 193.

218 *A new Portuguese governor:* http://www.friesian.com/newspain.htm.

They had stopped at the Sandwich Islands: Joseph Ingraham, *Joseph Ingraham's Journal of the Brigantine Hope on a Voyage to the Northwest Coast of America, 1790–1792,* 83–84.

They found the Washington *remade:* Mary Malloy, Hisayasu Hatanaka, and Mitsanori Hammano, "The Lady Washington at Oshima Island, Japan in 1791," 10.

219 *Douglas loaned Kendrick $2,320:* John Howell to Joseph Barrell, May 11, 1795.

apparently transacted a "sham sale": John Kendrick to Joseph Barrell, March 28, 1792.

"As a seaman and a navigator": Amasa Delano, *A Narrative of Voyages and Travels in the Northern and Southern Hemispheres,* 400.

220 *Douglas found himself in town:* John Blankett to Admiralty First Lord Chatham, April 9, 1791.

strategies that might "cut off": John Blankett, "Sea of Japan Report," December

1774, Sandwich Papers, Montagu F.5/38 quoted in Margaret Stevens, *Trade, Tactics and Tenacity*, 25.

220 *"An Adventurer by the name":* Blankett to Chatham, April 9, 1791.

official policy on the Pacific: David MacKay, *In the Wake of Cook: Science, Exploration and Empire 1780–1801,* 192. Also Howard Terrell Fry, *Alexander Dalrymple (1737–1808) and the Expansion of British Trade.*

221 *Blankett and the British merchant fleet:* Wagner, Extract of "Navigation by Pantoja," in *Spanish Explorations,* 193. Also Delano, *A Narrative,* 42.

Eleven days later, the Washington: John Hoskins, The Narrative of a Voyage, 103. Pantoja notes Kendrick's departure from Macao as April 1. Wagner, *Spanish Explorations,* 193.

two Chinese, two Hawaiians: Wagner, *Spanish Explorations,* 192. Also signatures on Kendrick's deed of July 21, 1791.

who later claimed to be Americans: Vancouver conversation with James Coleman. George Vancouver, *A Voyage of Discovery to the North Pacific Ocean and Round the World . . . ,* vol. 1, 383–84.

The Washington*'s new chief officer:* Identification of officers was made by John Cruft. See Affadavit of John Cruft, November 18, 1839, in John Gilmary Shea and Henry Reed Stiles, "Explorations of the Northwest Coast of the United States. Report of the Claims of the Heirs of Captains Kendrick and Gray," 172, and deed of July 20, 1791, showing those men as witnesses.

The embargo (which would last): Ingraham, *Journal,* 175; James Colnett, *A Voyage to the North West Side of America: The Journals of James Colnett, 1786–1789,* 297, fn 26.

on May 6 Kendrick and Douglas: Howard F. Van Zandt, *Pioneer American Merchants in Japan,* 1.

Portuguese vessels had first: Donald F. Lach and Edwin J. Van Kley, *Asia in the Making of Europe,* Vol. III, Book 4, 1848.

a group of twenty-three: Zelia Nuttall, "The Earliest Historical Relations between Mexico and Japan."

222 *a Christian peasant revolt:* Nutall, "Earliest Historical Relations," 8–11.

They were permitted two ships: Foster Rhea Dulles, *Yankees and Samurai: America's Role in the Emergence of a Modern Japan: 1791–1900,* 2.

223 *Seeking shelter from what gathered:* Information about this visit is drawn from several sources, including Jim Mockford, "The Lady Washington at Kushimoto, Japan, in 1794," 83–89, and Malloy, Hatanaka, and Hammano, "Lady Washington." The original source is the report of a contemporary samurai, Sakamoto Tenzan, who published an account of the visit, *Kinan Younou,* in

1799, which was translated by Malloy and her coauthors.

223 *Kichigo sent a message:* Mockford, "Lady Washington," 87–88; Van Zandt, *Pioneer American Merchants,* 5.

Although a long red-and-white-striped: The official U.S. flag with placement of stars and stripes was not formalized until 1818.

They found men they described: Malloy, Hatanaka, and Hammano, "Lady Washington," 10.

"This ship belongs to the Red Hairs": The note in Chinese still exists in Japanese archives. Dulles, *Yankees and Samurai,* 1.

225 *the men shot gulls or ducks:* Malloy, Hatanaka, and Hammano, "Lady Washington," 10.

one that would further goad: General concern is evident in the letter of Captain John Blankett to the British Admiralty. Two months after Kendrick's departure, James Colnett would be seized, and a later British mission to Japan would fail. The Admiralty dispatched William Robert Broughton to survey the Japanese coast in the HMS *Providence* in 1794. Not until 1853 would U.S. Admiral Matthew Perry sign the first modern port agreement with the shogun, officially opening Japan to trade.

Colnett had been released: For Colnett's release, see James Colnett to Viceroy Revillagigedo, July 8, 1790, in Warren L. Cook, *Flood Tide of Empire: Spain and the Pacific Northwest, 1543–1819,* 291.

226 *After a disastrous two years:* Colnett, *Voyage,* 4.

Kendrick and Douglas came upon a group: Hoskins, Narrative, 104.

the Washington *ripped across:* If the dates cited by the sources are correct, the *Washington* departed from the Water Islands about May 20 and arrived on the coast at 52°58' on June 13. See Hoskins, Narrative, 104. In contrast, Haswell says the passage took eight weeks, which places the departure from Japan in mid-April: Robert Haswell, A Voyage on Discoveries on the Ship Columbia Rediviva (1791–1792), 7–8.

Kendrick arrived on the mainland: Wagner, Extract of "Navigation by Pantoja," in *Spanish Explorations,* 193. Also Hoskins, Narrative, 104.

227 *In the midst of the festive mood:* Variant sources describe this attack. Hoskins, who heard it directly from Kendrick, is used as the primary source here, along with additional information from Ingraham. See Hoskins, Narrative, 105–7; Ingraham, *Journal,* 180–81; Wagner, *Spanish Explorations,* 191–92; John Bartlett, "A Narrative of Events in the Life of John Bartlett of Boston, Massachusetts, in the Years 1790–1793 . . . ," 320–21.

228 *"now put me into your gun carriage":* Hoskins, Narrative, 105.

228 *piercing Kendrick's shirt:* Wagner, *Spanish Explorations,* 193; Hoskins, Narrative, 106.

229 *"urging them to action":* Hoskins, Narrative, 106.

Coyah's wife and child: Ingraham, *Journal,* 204.

One sailor's second-hand narrative: Bartlett, "Narrative of Events," 320.

Kendrick took the Washington: Bartlett reports seeing the *Washington.* Bartlett, "Narrative of Events," 307.

As the Washington *approached:* Wagner, *Spanish Explorations,* 191.

230 *they came from Macao:* Ibid., 192.

After two months he departed: Quimper left Nootka on May 31, 1790, to examine the straits, and departed the straits for Monterey on August 4.

231 *Secret instructions he sent:* "Secret Instructions to Lieutenant Don Franscisco de Eliza, Commandant of the Puerto de Nutca and the Frigates Concepcion and Princesa, Juan Francisco de la Bodega y Quadra, San Blas, February 4, 1791," in Wagner, *Spanish Explorations,* 137.

By July 22, the San Carlos: Extract from "Voyage by Eliza," in Wagner, *Spanish Explorations,* 133.

"oceanic passage so zealously sought": Ibid. Also H. H. Bancroft, *History of the Northwest Coast, 1543–1800,* 248, quoting letter from Eliza to Quadra, August 1791.

232 *According to Saavedra, they feared:* Wagner, Extract of "Navigation by Pantoja," 192.

the British royal company that had been: Ibid., 193.

"it has pleased His Majesty": Wagner, *Spanish Explorations,* 140.

233 *Tartoochtheatticus, Wickaninish's brother:* See signatories on Kendrick's deed for those who were present. For additional background see Daniel W. Clayton, *Islands of Truth: The Imperial Fashioning of Vancouver Island,* 114 on Hannope and on Clahquakinnah at Mawina; 144 on Tartoochtheatticus.

In a ceremony on the deck: Affidavit of James Tremere, October 30, 1830, in Shea and Stiles, "Expeditions," 172–73.

234 *To all persons to whom these present:* For the text of the deeds, see Shea and Stiles, "Expeditions," 168.

235 *the area encompassed 324 square miles:* An erroneous total for the area of Kendrick's land as described in the five deeds has been passed down historically as "4 degrees of latitude or 240 square miles." That stretch of latitude is 240 linear miles. Even without a formal survey and plot plan, the dimensions given in the deeds indicate the relative area of each tract. The land area of the first

deed from Maquinna to Safe Retreat Harbor (Mawina) based on the formula for the area of a square 18 miles on a side or 324 square miles. The other four deeds total more than 1,500 square miles, taking in three major sounds and more than 1,000 square miles of land on western Vancouver Island. An alleged "missing" deed for the area around Gray's Harbor contributes to the "4 degrees of latitude," but is not included in the estimate of more than fifteen hundred square miles..

235 *he took the* Washington *out:* Hoskins, Narrative, 107.

237 *he told Wickaninish and his chiefs:* James Colnett, *The Journal of Captain James Colnett aboard the Argonaut from April 26, 1789 to November 3, 1791,* 192. Colnett told the same story to Maquinna: Colnett, *Journal,* 208.

in 1792 Wickaninish was said to have: José Mariano Mozino, *Noticias de Nutka: An Account of Nootka Sound in 1792,* 70–71.

Saavedra would also observe: Clayton, *Islands of Truth,* 122.

238 *famous mixed-blood trader Alexander McGillivray:* McGillivray was a very high-profile native leader in the South and entered into a landmark treaty with President Washington, the first that attempted to guarantee lands for native tribes. See: "New York, August 21," *Boston Gazette,* August 30, 1790, 2. This treaty was ignored by the State of Georgia, which sought to sell off native lands for development. Kendrick would also have learned of McGillivray as his packet passed in and out of Charleston: "Charleston, S.C. January 5th," *Massachusetts Spy* 15, no. 728 (March 31, 1785). In this article McGillivray issued an open letter that states in part: "You wish to have our trade; but let us ask you, where are we to find skins to buy your goods with, after you have taken from us our hunting ground."

CHAPTER FIFTEEN

240 *He considered himself still:* Kendrick's original instructions to make determinations based on the conditions he found himself in were repeated in Joseph Barrell's letter of December 12, 1787, which Kendrick received at Macao in January 1790.

Kendrick's appearance was not: Robert Haswell, A Voyage on Discoveries on the Ship Columbia Rediviva (hereafter referred to as Second Voyage), 7.

"as a spy upon his and their conduct": John Hoskins to Joseph Barrell, August 21, 1792.

ordered Gray to consult with him: Joseph Barrell to Robert Gray, September 25, 1790.

240 *the ship's officers regarded:* Hoskins to Barrell, August 21, 1792.
"what we could have wished": John Hoskins, The Narrative of a Voyage, 25.
by late March the men began to complain: John Boit Journal, 7.
"the last stage of Scurvy": Ibid., 9.
"up to the Hips in the earth": Ibid., 10.

241 *"took Coyah, tied a rope":* Hoskins, Narrative, 51.

242 *railed privately in his journal:* Haswell, Second Voyage, 8.
Over dinner he gave a full narrative: Hoskins, Narrative, 103–7.
about twelve hundred otter skins: Haswell, Second Voyage, 109.
about seven hundred skins: Ibid., 3.

243 *A significant portion of next year's harvest:* Joseph Ingraham, *Joseph Ingraham's Journal of the Brigantine Hope on a Voyage to the Northwest Coast of America, 1790–1792*, 223.
"We were received at a small Island": Hoskins, Narrative, 109.
"Your letter per Captain Gray": John Kendrick to Joseph Barrell, March 28, 1792.

244 *Kendrick offered to turn over:* Hoskins to Barrell, August 21, 1792.

245 *"during the continuance":* Hoskins, Narrative, 117.
Gray took one of the chiefs: Ibid., 32.
"I am sorry to be under": Boit, Remarks, 27.

246 *"any future intercourse":* Hoskins, Narrative, 169.
After leaving Clayoquot: Historians who have criticized Kendrick for not cruising and trading more avidly ignore the fact that he had a different method of gathering furs, paying in advance and collecting them at specific locations. F. W. Howay, in particular, criticizes Kendrick for being lackadaisical about trading and sailing late from Clayoquot. Kendrick was clearly spending time among the native people, and would not have wanted to arrive at Hawaii until the start of the *makahiki* period in October or November.
talk had circulated among the trading vessels: The desire to have a small armed vessel was high in the armament race among the islands. Despite the imagined or real attacks, there were no reported efforts to take the *Lady Washington*. See notes below concerning other vessels.
Ingraham then fled to Oahu: Ingraham, *Journal*, 85–86.
"that it was his people's wish": Hoskins, Narrative, 85–86.

247 *"every girl on the ship clung fast":* John Bartlett, "A Narrative of Events in the Life of John Bartlett of Boston, Massachusetts, in the Years 1790–1793 . . . ," 311–13.

247 *called it Kepuwahaulaula:* Ralph S. Kuykendall, *Hawaiian Kingdom: Foundation and Transformation 1778–1854,* vol. 1, 37.

248 *By October 27, Kendrick was at Kauai:* George Vancouver, *A Voyage of Discovery to the North Pacific Ocean and Round the World . . .* , vol. 1, 383.

Kendrick left three men: Ibid., 378–85.

he believed that as many as twenty: Ibid., 407.

CHAPTER SIXTEEN

253 *George Vancouver sighted the island:* George Vancouver, *A Voyage of Discovery to the North Pacific Ocean and Round the World . . .* , vol. 1, 347.

which seemed to occupy the center: Archibald Menzies, *Hawaii Nei, 128 Years Ago: Journal of Archibald Menzies,* 13.

254 *Britain's policy now targeted:* Graham MacDonald, "Exploration of the Pacific," 515.

255 *"have the keys of the whole Pacific":* John Etches, writing as "Argonaut," "A Continuation of an Authentic Statement of All the Facts Relative to Nootka Sound, Its Discoveries, History, Settlement, Commerce and the Public Advantages to be derived from It."

"restitution of the territories": Vancouver, *Voyage,* vol. 1, 49.

instructions from the king: Ibid., 58.

the merchant Richard Etches: Richard Cadman Etches to East India Company Court of Directors, April 29, 1785, in Vincent T. Harlow, *The Founding of the Second British Empire, 1763–1789,* 421–24.

the home of a half-million British subjects: John Meares, *Voyages Made in the Years 1788 and 1789 . . .* , 210.

256 *more detailed orders:* Vancouver, *Voyage,* 59.

Both ships were newly designed: Ibid., 47–50.

natives came paddling out: Menzies, *Hawaii Nei,* 13.

257 *was dismayed to learn:* Vancouver, *Voyage,* 406.

"unwarrantable desires": Vancouver, *Voyage,* 404.

"have become very familiar": Ibid., 403.

"were wholly directed": Menzies, *Hawaii Nei,* 14.

258 *"with most of the chiefs of Kauai":* Vancouver, *Voyage,* 352.

they expected a retaliatory invasion: Ibid., 361.

"The apparent docility": Ibid., 362.

"avidity with which the men": Ibid., 377–78.

259 *"he was of Derbyshire":* Ibid., 378.
would arrive in the islands: Ibid., 379.
now lived with Kaumaulii: Menzies, *Hawaii Nei,* 30.
260 *and one from John Kendrick:* Vancouver, *Voyage,* 383.
"which he wore with much less decency": Ibid., 384.
"tattooed with a broad badge": Menzies, *Hawaii Nei,* 32.
"I asked him what he had done": Vancouver, *Voyage,* 384.
261 *After recovering in his cabin:* Menzies, *Hawaii Nei,* 33.
John Williams, a Welshman: Vancouver calls him Richard Williams. *Voyage,* 388.
262 *Vancouver bestowed the name:* Ibid., 400.
"infinite surprise and admiration": Ibid., 397–98.
He left a letter behind: The letter was left with Kaiana at Hawaii. Ibid., 353. William De Witt Alexander notes that the *Daedalus* arrived on May 7, 1792, at Oahu, *A Brief History of the Hawaiian People,* 135.
"reduced by at least two-thirds": Vancouver, *Voyage,* 405. Disease is also suspected to have played a major role in the decline of population. Venereal disease, in addition to fatality for those infected, has been assumed to have made many women and men sterile.
"I shall take leave": Ibid., 407.
"Mr. Kendrick must, undoubtedly": Ibid. Despite Vancouver's mockery, the sandalwood trade would become extensive and highly profitable, although within a few decades it would also become oppressive work for the villagers and heavily damaging to the environment.
263 *He had arrived at Macao:* Joseph Ingraham, *Joseph Ingraham's Journal of the Brigantine Hope on a Voyage to the Northwest Coast of America, 1790–1792,* 179. Also see John Kendrick to Joseph Barrell, March 28, 1792.
Scotsman William Douglas, who seems: Ingraham, *Journal,* 176, on death of Douglas; 178, on the ships at Lark's Bay.
"This is generally the case": Ibid., 182.
"twenty-one thousand Spanish head dollars": Kendrick to Barrell, March 28, 1792. Also see Ingraham, *Journal,* 177–186, on embargo, amount of furs in port, smuggling, and dealings with the Portuguese.
264 *"I am confident you have been told":* Kendrick to Barrell, March 28, 1792.
265 *"I am now fitting out the Brig":* Ibid.
266 *Kendrick was near death:* John Hoskins to Joseph Barrell, August 21, 1792.
"Not considering this opening": Vancouver, *Voyage,* vol. 2, 34.
267 *"those parts which lie":* David MacKay, *In the Wake of Cook: Science, Exploration*

and Empire 1780–1801, 96, citing Home Office 42/17 December 1790, Grenville to Lords of the Admiralty H.O. 28/7, 392–99.

267 *"that the Spaniards have recently found":* Vancouver, *Voyage,* vol. 2, 34.

"This inlet could be now only ten miles": Ibid., 40.

"a sail was discovered": Ibid., 41.

though he understood from the natives: Ibid., 42.

"we gave them all the information": Boit indicates the date as April 28, 1792, while Vancouver's log states April 29. John Boit, Remarks on the Ship Columbia's Voyage from Boston (on a Voyage, Round the Globe), 29.

268 *"must be a very intricate one":* Vancouver, *Voyage,* vol. 2, 58.

"We had now advanced further": Ibid., 56.

"long since designed": Ibid., 169.

269 *a Spanish ship had performed:* Warren L. Cook, *Flood Tide of Empire: Spain and the Pacific Northwest, 1543–1819,* 349.

"we discovered two vessels at anchor": Vancouver, *Voyage,* vol. 2, 209.

the Sutil *and the* Mexicana: The ships were forty-six-foot schooners of less than fifty tons, ideal for shallow-water surveys. They had been dispatched from San Blas as part of Alexandro Malaspina's Pacific exploration for Spain. For full background on these ships and their voyages, see Henry R. Wagner, *Spanish Explorations in the Strait of Juan de Fuca.* Also John Kendrick, *The Voyage of the Sutil and Mexicana, 1792: The Last Spanish Exploration of the Northwest Coast of America.*

and had already mapped an area: Vancouver, *Voyage,* vol. 2, 209–10.

"I cannot avoid acknowledging": Ibid., 210.

"Senior Quadra, the commandant": Ibid., 211.

270 *"spoke the Indian language":* Ibid., 220.

Vancouver's boats discovered: Edward Bell, "A New Vancouver Journal, Edward Bell," 13.

"pistols and cutlasses which an American vessel": Thomas Manby, *Journal of the Voyages of the HMS Discovery and Chatham,* entry for July 20, 1792. For those who might believe that Kendrick made the circumnavigation, this poses a tantalizing revelation.

they entered Queen Charlotte Sound: Vancouver, *Voyage,* vol. 2, 308. Vancouver entered the area that had been visited and named by the ship *Experiment* out of Bengal in August 1786.

271 *In reality, the honor of the first:* Wagner, *Spanish Explorations,* 55.

found their way through the channels: Cook, *Flood Tide,* 355.

The Daedalus *was waiting:* Vancouver, *Voyage,* vol. 2, 335.

271 *On board were the additional orders:* Ibid., 349.

272 *"too good a man":* Bell, "New Vancouver Journal," 25.

William Brown of the British Butterworth: Ingraham wrote, "It was now hinted about in Friendly Cove among those who chose to pay attention to it that as soon as the English men-of-war arrived there would be no more American flags flying." Ingraham, *Journal,* 227.

273 *According to a complaint:* Ibid., 225–26.

"furnished Wickaninish with more": José Mariano Mozino, *Noticias de Nutka: An Account of Nootka Sound in 1792,* 71.

"turn out four hundred men": Bell, "New Vancouver Journal," 40–41.

274 *he went on to kill several natives:* For the April skirmish, see Boit, Remarks, 31. For the June attack, ibid., 37.

275 *Quadra had a position supported:* Quadra's documentation included a statement made by Joseph Ingraham and Robert Gray. Ingraham, *Journal,* 217–22.

"forming a nearly equilateral triangle": Vancouver, *Voyage,* vol. 2, 374.

276 *"as the object of restitution":* Ibid., 374–75.

"were the tents and houses": Ibid., 372.

"this place would not long remain": Vancouver to Bodega, September 1, 1792, in Wagner, "Narrative," 18.

277 *be named "Quadra and Vancouver" Island:* By the mid-nineteenth century the name Quadra and Vancouver Island would be changed on British charts to Vancouver Island, and except for the scattering of Spanish place names, the appropriation of the land and the Spanish legacy would be complete.

Like Martinez he recognized that: Cook, *Flood Tide,* 390.

Quadra also began considering: Ibid., 391.

"At the least," he noted: Vancouver, *Voyage,* vol. 2, 375.

William Brown had brought Vancouver: J. F. G. Stokes, "Honolulu and Some New Speculative Phases of Hawaiian History," 91–94.

278 *Vancouver also canceled plans:* Cook, *Flood Tide,* 388.

CHAPTER SEVENTEEN

281 *The best course was to try:* Tropical cyclones that cross into the South China Sea have a high probability of passing within 180 nautical miles of Hong Kong. The over-ocean threat extends for a radius of 180 miles. See Dennis C. Perryman, Richard Gilmore, and Ronald E. Englebretson, "The Decision to Evade or Remain in Port."

282 *sustained winds can reach:* For typhoon information, see S. Campbell, "Typhoons Affecting Hong Kong: Case Studies."

282 *The hull lay over on her side:* The story of the *Washington* being caught in a typhoon is contained in John Boit, Remarks on the Ship Columbia's Voyage from Boston (on a Voyage, Round the Globe), 52.

283 *Days passed as Kendrick waited:* The notice of the deaths of John Stoddard and David Wood III appeared nearly a year later in "Deaths," *Boston Columbian Centinel* 19, no. 42 (August 8, 1793), 3.

a black man came aboard: Boit, Remarks, 52.

"skins are very low": John Hoskins to Robert Gray and Joseph Barrell, December 22, 1792.

284 *records of the voyage indicate:* There are several summations of the profits of the *Columbia*'s second voyage. Boit recorded that the sea otter furs sold for ninety thousand dollars, an average of forty-five dollars each. Boit, Remarks, 53. This does not match Hoskins's statement of twenty-five dollars per fur maximum (Hoskins to Barrell, December 22, 1792) or the later statement by the owners that it was a "saving voyage and some profit." Boit's statements appear at odds with more careful accounts at times.

"made a saving voyage": Susan Bulfinch, *The Life and Letters of Charles Bulfinch, Architect; with Other Family Papers,* 68–69.

Gray had sought to cheat: John Hoskins to Joseph Barrell, August 21, 1792.

"blundering along": Letter of Robert Haswell to Joseph Barrell, August 21, 1792.

"although he [Gray] cruiz'd the coast": John Hoskins, The Narrative of a Voyage, 7.

285 *Charles Bulfinch would note:* Affidavit of Charles Bulfinch, April 21, 1838.

"saw an appearance of a spacious harbor": Boit, Remarks, 32. Gray recorded the day as May 11, which has become the officially recorded date of the *Columbia* entering the river.

"to view the Country": Boit, Remarks, 33. F. W. Howay notes that the words "to take possession" were inserted later. Howay, *Voyages of the Columbia to the Northwest Coast; 1787–1790 and 1790–1791,* 398, fn 3. Although Hoskins stated that he and Gray went ashore and took possession (see U.S. Congress, Senate, Committee on Public Lands, Report No. 335 [Felch Report], 10), such an event, without witnesses or the participation of other crew members does not seem likely. However Gray's discovery of the river was acknowledged by Quadra and Vancouver and withstood later dispute from Britain.

"[T]he river abounds": Boit, Remarks, 33.

286 *Gray told him of their discovery:* Ibid., 34. Other than by Vancouver, not much notice was taken of the discovery at the time, but together with Kendrick's deeds, it would later support U.S. claims to the region.

286 *Brown wanted to drive the Americans:* Warren L. Cook, *Flood Tide of Empire: Spain and the Pacific Northwest, 1543–1819*, 345.

Among the British traders: Edward Bell, "A New Vancouver Journal, Edward Bell," 58.

"unsuccessful this, their first season": Ibid., 59.

"Wicananish amongst others": Ibid., 64.

287 *Much of Kendrick's information:* F. W. Howay, "The Ship Margaret: Her History and Historian."

288 *his interest in expanding:* Jefferson later stated: "I view it as a germ of a great, free & independent empire on that side of the continent." Thomas Jefferson to John Jacob Astor, November 9, 1813. Also see Gordon S. Wood, *Empire of Liberty: A History of the Early Republic, 1789–1815*.

"Port Independence, On The Island": U.S. Congress, Felch Report, 17.

289 *The letter was received:* John Gilmary Shea and Henry Reed Stiles, "Explorations of the Northwest Coast of the United States. Report of the Claims of the Heirs of Captains Kendrick and Gray," 168.

"the largest streams of that river": Thomas Jefferson to André Michaux, January 23, 1793.

The British had also launched: Howard Terrell Fry, *Alexander Dalrymple (1737–1808) and the Expansion of British Trade*, 219.

290 *The federal government wanted:* U.S. Congress, Felch Report, 13. For background on early U.S. land laws affecting acquisition see Paul W. Gates, *History of Public Land Law Development* (Washington, D.C.: U.S. G.P.O., November 1968).

Genet disclosed to Jefferson: Merrill D. Peterson, *Thomas Jefferson and the New Nation: A Biography*, 497.

Kendrick had been told by Joseph Barrell: This conclusion can be drawn from Joseph Barrell's instructions to Kendrick and Kendrick's letter to Thomas Jefferson.

but the time for Congress: In addition to the other conditions mentioned, Jefferson left office in December 1793. No action was taken on Kendrick's deeds at that time.

291 *to reconnoiter Spanish defenses:* Vancouver's duplicity did not go unnoticed. In answer to a question about his activities, Vancouver told Governor Joseph Joaquin de Arrillaga that his voyage was a scientific one for the good of humanity, and that his coming to Monterey was for the purpose of making necessary repairs and pursuing botanical investigations. Arrillaga recorded the response. Papeles de Estado 20 N. 5642, Archivo General de Indias, Seville.

he anchored three leagues: Archibald Menzies, *Hawaii Nei, 128 Years Ago: Journal of Archibald Menzies*, 63.

292 *"tasseled with ribbons":* George Vancouver, *A Voyage of Discovery to the North Pacific Ocean and Round the World . . .*, vol. 3, 64.

"delighted with his present": Menzies, *Hawaii Nei,* 64.

An estimated three thousand people: Ibid., 67.

Kamehameha said he would also give: Ibid., 68.

"Convinced of the advantage": Vancouver, *Voyage,* vol. 3, 223.

293 *Kamehameha told Vancouver:* Menzies, *Hawaii Nei,* 73.

Some historians believe that Vancouver: Speculation appears based on the secret plan of early 1790 for establishing settlements and the interactions of the two captains. No documentation has come to light. J. F. G. Stokes, "Honolulu and Some New Speculative Phases of Hawaiian History," 92–95.

"the only English vessels": Menzies, *Hawaii Nei,* 129.

he had found no whales: William Brown to Sir William Curtis, December 1792.

"It might be well worth": Menzies, *Hawaii Nei,* 79.

294 *"with utmost astonishment":* Ibid., 93.

"Every hour," he wrote: Vancouver, *Voyage,* vol. 3, 302.

295 *"almost inexhaustible":* Ibid., 303.

Kahekili arrived on the afternoon: Ibid., 305.

296 *"to the invasion of Kamehameha":* Ibid., 306.

297 *"be the distance of time":* Ibid., 309.

executed him with a pistol: Menzies, *Hawaii Nei,* 123–24.

298 *causing Vancouver to despair:* Ibid., 124.

a bay they had been told of: Vancouver, *Voyage,* vol. 3, 361–63.

"In the evening observing": Menzies, *Hawaii Nei,* 126.

"and two other sailors": Ibid., 128.

"was not so much against Kaeo": Menzies, *Hawaii Nei,* 133–34; Vancouver, *Voyage,* vol. 3, 373.

299 *considered Inamoo "a monster":* John Meares, *Voyages Made in the Years 1788 and 1789.*

"limbs no longer able to support": Ibid., 376.

regarded Kendrick as the leader: Vancouver, *Voyage,* vol. 5, 112, 124.

CHAPTER EIGHTEEN

300 *From the cannon battery:* There has been a common misconception about the location of the Spanish installations. Estevan Martinez described San Miguel on Observatory Island at the opening of Friendly Cove. Just west of it he described the gun battery of San Rafael on Hog Island. See Estevan Martinez,

Diary of the Voyage . . . , 106–7, 166, and 170. Both installations were first constructed in June 1789 and reconstructed in 1790–1793.

301 *The Spanish outpost onshore:* There are variant descriptions of the Spanish compound at Yuquot in 1792. Joseph Ingraham wrote that the "village" consisted of sixteen buildings. See *Joseph Ingraham's Journal of the Brigantine Hope on a Voyage to the Northwest Coast of America, 1790–1792,* 213–14. John Boit reported fifty buildings, perhaps including native houses. Boit, Remarks on the Ship Columbia's voyage from Boston (on a Voyage, round the Globe), entry for July 25, 1792, 44. This description follows "Plan of the Port of Nootka" shown in Warren L. Cook, *Flood Tide of Empire: Spain and the Pacific Northwest, 1543–1819,* fig. 46.

Vancouver departed for the north: He arrived on May 20, 1793, and departed on May 23. George Vancouver, *A Voyage of Discovery to the North Pacific Ocean and Round the World . . .* , vol. 3, 428.

The viceroy in Mexico City: Ibid., 424.

302 *when Maquinna arrived:* Marshall, "Dangerous Liaisons."

in discussions with the three chiefs: Ibid., 169.

"You would be the first": José Mariano Mozino, *Noticias de Nutka: An Account of Nootka Sound in 1792,* 56.

303 *The Spanish fort at Neah Bay:* The date of abandonment was September 29, 1792. Cook, *Flood Tide,* 386.

"would raise the Indians": John Howell to Joseph Barrell, December 23, 1796.

A ninety-ton schooner: The *Resolution* arrived at Nootka five weeks before the *Jefferson*. Bernard Magee, Log of the Jefferson, June 22, 1793.

305 *"The Ballad of the Bold Northwestman":* The ballad was printed on a broadside by L. Deming in Boston between 1832 and 1836. F. W. Howay. "Ballad of the Bold Northwestman: An Incident in the Life of Captain John Kendrick," *Washington Historical Quarterly,* 1929, 71–72.

William Sturgis, believed that nearly all: William Sturgis, *"A Most Remarkable Enterprise": Lectures on the Northwest Coast Trade and Northwest Coast Indian Life.*

307 *Solomon carried Gonzales's written plea:* F. W. Howay, "John Kendrick and His Sons."

"On Board the Ship Lady Washington": U.S. Congress, Senate Committee on Public Lands, Report No. 335 (Felch Report), 20.

308 *A rift had arisen between Maquinna:* Archer, "Seduction before Sovereignty," 158.

The marriage had been bartered: Menzies Journal, May 21, 1793.

309 *a deal that was very costly:* Ibid.

309 *Solomon remained at Mawina:* Magee, Log.

310 *"entered a large Inlet":* Menzies Journal, September 8, 1793, 120–21.

in the vicinity where Caamano: Vancouver, *Voyage,* vol. 4, 112. This was the area north of Ketchikan which the Spanish called "Bucareli" and Vancouver renamed "Clarence Strait."

"more intricate and dangerous": Vanouver, *Voyage,* vol. 4, 113.

311 *"a very extensive inland navigation":* Ibid., 114.

this was probably the same channel: Ibid., 113.

"as long as [he] should find it": Ibid., 114–15.

"that appeared free from interruption": Ibid., 116.

"necessary to fire upon them": Ibid., 114, 120.

312 *On August 12, far inland:* Ibid., 170–75.

"whilst a young man, appearing: Vancouver, *Voyage,* vol. 4, 172. Remainder of scene 170–75.

having traversed about seven hundred miles: Ibid., 191.

313 *"Alex Mackenzie from Canada":* Charles Henry Carey, *History of Oregon,* 153–54.

"left to the adventurers": Robert Greenhow, *The History of Oregon and California and the Other Territories on the North-West Coast of North America,* 265.

314 *stories about passageways from the Straits:* Ibid., 270–71.

Nootka, arriving on October 5: Ibid., 290.

He told Vancouver of the ships: Despite Fidalgo's orders, many trading vessels continued to stop at Nootka. Eighteen trading ships would visit the coast in 1793. Cook, *Flood Tide,* Appendix E: Nationality of Vessels Visiting the Northwest Coast, 1774–1820.

The Jefferson *and* Resolution *were preparing:* Magee, Log, September 7, 1793.

No orders or letters had come: Vancouver, *Voyage,* vol. 4, 289.

315 *Britain's "extension of her commerce":* Vancouver, *Voyage,* vol. 5, 50.

"a voluntary resignation": Ibid., 51.

"taken up their abode": Ibid., 112.

"furthering the ambitious views": Ibid., 113.

316 *"strange sail":* Ibid., 293. It should be noted that large heavy sloops like Vancouver's do not sail well to windward. He could not have caught the "strange sail" if he wanted to, and certainly would not have recorded that he tried and failed.

CHAPTER NINETEEN

318 *At 10 A.M., Kamehameha appeared:* Vancouver, Voyage, vol. 5, 5.

318 *Kendrick had left a shipwright:* Ibid., 29.
Kendrick was on the opposite side: Menzies, *Hawaii Nei, 128 Years Ago: Journal of Archibald Menzies,* 139.
319 *Vancouver was eager to get:* Vancouver, *Voyage,* 6–7.
320 *he couldn't stay because:* Ibid., 7.
"had no doubt of soon finding": Ibid., 8–9.
But before the young chief could return: Ibid., 11–12.
321 *Young appeared the next morning:* Menzies, *Hawaii Nei,* 143.
At 10 P.M. three ships appeared: Vancouver, *Voyage,* 14–15.
"At this late hour": Ibid., 15.
322 *From his own supply rooms:* Ibid., 29–30.
no other favor he could have bestowed: Ibid., 29.
estranged from his favorite queen: Vancouver wrote that she was with her parents at Kealakekua while Kamehameha was at Waiakea. According to Menzies she was left at Waiakea and later brought to Kealakekua. Menzies, *Hawaii Nei,* 146.
more than one hundred eighty: There were 156 officers and sailors and 27 marines. For the full roster of expedition members, see Thomas Manby, *Journal of the Voyages of the HMS* Discovery *and* Chatham.
Early on the morning after the British: Menzies, *Hawaii Nei,* 146.
323 *ambergris, a grayish waxy substance:* Vancouver, *Voyage,* 121–22.
He had impressed Vancouver: Ibid., 115.
opportunist and con artist: Charles Bishop, *The Journal and Letters of Captain Charles Bishop on the North-West Coast of America, in the Pacific and in New South Wales, 1794–1799,* xxxii.
Vancouver invited them to dine: Menzies, *Hawaii Nei,* 146.
"laden with forty very fine hogs": Vancouver, *Voyage,* 17.
324 *characterized as a "sort of Saturnalia":* James Jackson Jarves, *History of the Hawaiian or Sandwich Islands,* 81.
Brown left a letter for Vancouver: Vancouver, *Voyage,* 115, 125.
"drove them with great slaughter": Ibid., 126.
"This melancholy event would not": Ibid., 125–26.
325 *Inamoo was brought aboard:* Ibid., 126.
Kahekili signed an agreement: Kahekili signed the agreement ceding Oahu and perhaps Kauai. See Gavan Daws, *Shoal of Time: A History of the Hawaiian Islands,* 38.
"a copy of a letter which Mr. Brown": John Scofield, *Hail, Columbia: Robert Gray, John Kendrick, and the Pacific Fur Trade,* 308. Scofield cites Archibald Menzies, *Journal.*

325 *that Brown had approval from the Crown:* Joseph Ingraham, *Joseph Ingraham's Journal of the Brigantine Hope on a Voyage to the Northwest Coast of America, 1790–1792,* 222–24; Ralph S. Kuykendall, *Hawaiian Kingdom: Foundation and Transformation 1778–1854,* vol. 1, 226–30.

326 *"he would fire at a village":* Daniel W. Clayton, *Islands of Truth: The Imperial Fashioning of Vancouver Island,* 85.

Up near the beach, the Fair American: Menzies, *Hawaii Nei,* 148–49, 173.

on February 1, the Discovery's *carpenters:* Vancouver, *Voyage,* vol. 5, 30.

"in whose good opinion": Ibid., 40.

327 *to issue a summons:* Ibid., 27–28.

He grew savage: Ibid., 61.

328 *Vancouver couldn't help worrying:* Ibid., 60–62.

"little squadron and the trading vessels": Ibid., 52.

"the period was not very remote": Ibid., 53.

329 *The only whiff of reality:* Ibid., 46.

"The domestic affairs of Kamehameha": Ibid., 47.

"for the purpose of formally ceding": Ibid., 90–91.

330 *"when a force for their protection":* Ibid., 93.

and that a war vessel or two: Ibid., 93–94.

Vancouver promised Kamehameha: Kuykendall, *Hawaiian Kingdom,* vol. 1, 42.

"These preliminaries being fully: Vancouver, *Voyage,* vol. 5, 94.

331 *"and took possession of the island":* Ibid., 95.

"the natives of most of the Leeward Islands": Ibid., 114.

But no arguments could induce Kamehameha: Ibid., 114–15.

332 *he was perfectly convinced:* Ibid., 83–84.

Kendrick sailed to Oahu: Ibid., 121.

333 *"Having beaten around the east end":* Ibid., 124.

tried to pressure Kendrick: Ibid., 122.

Kendrick and his men were still there: Ibid., 133.

CHAPTER TWENTY

334 *"Having ascertained satisfactorily":* George Vancouver, *A Voyage of Discovery to the North Pacific Ocean and Round the World . . . ,* vol. 5, 135–36.

"stupendous" mountains: Ibid., 170.

335 *if the "great explorer":* Ibid., 213–14.

came across Brown and the Jackall: At 59°6' north latitude. Ibid., 354.

Brown had just arrived on the coast: One American trader's log reports Brown at the Sandwich Islands, where he might have picked up communications left by Vancouver. John Boit, Remarks on the Ship Columbia's Voyage from Boston (on a Voyage, round the Globe), October 16, 1795. Boit says Brown was back at Oahu in February 1794 where he entered "Fair Haven" harbor and remade the two sloops—one into a ship and the other into a cutter.

335 *"the latest accounts of the state":* Vancouver, *Voyage,* 355.

336 *In dark squalls and showers:* Ibid., 355–56.

At Nootka, Kendrick heard: The *Aranzazu* had arrived bringing news and dispatches to Saavedra, who also reported them to Vancouver when he arrived. Vancouver, *Voyage,* vol. 6, 71.

337 *But the rift with Wickaninish:* Archer, "Seduction before Sovereignty," 158.

"anything of consequence": Bernard Magee, Log of the Jefferson, March 31, 1794.

a three-day gale: Magee, Log, August 2, 1794. The storm raged from May 15 to May 18.

338 *By mid-July, he started south:* Ibid., July 17, 1794.

On August 16, 1794, in a harbor: Vancouver, *Voyage,* vol. 6, 38.

339 *"and all the other formalities":* Ibid., 39.

On August 22, the ships started south: Ibid., 59–60.

Roberts had taken the Jefferson: Magee, Log, August 21, 1794.

His eldest son, now known as Juan Kendrick: Warren L. Cook, *Flood Tide of Empire: Spain and the Pacific Northwest, 1543–1819,* 414.

340 *Juan Kendrick learned of the massacre:* Samuel Burling, Log of the Eliza (1798–99).

341 *Waiting at Macao was a letter:* This letter was in answer to Kendrick's offer of March 28, 1792.

"would send [him]": Joseph Barrell to John Kendrick.

"I place no dependence on this": John Scofield, *Hail, Columbia: Robert Gray, John Kendrick, and the Pacific Fur Trade,* 300.

342 *Two days before Vancouver arrived at Nootka:* Alava arrived on August 31, 1794. Cook, *Flood Tide,* 416.

Bodega y Quadra had died: Vancouver, *Voyage,* vol. 6, 65.

The Third Nootka Convention: Convention for the Mutual Abandonment of Nootka.

Alava's orders were to sail for Monterey: Vancouver, *Voyage,* vol. 6, 65–68.

343 *The weather did not seem:* Ibid., 72–73.

By September 11, no instructions: Ibid., 73.

344 *Brown had collected:* Ibid., 91.

Vancouver's health was worsening: Vancouver's complaints about his health began to enter his journal when he arrived back on the coast. He would die in 1798, before completing work on the journals. His gravestone mentions nothing of the Royal Navy to which he had dedicated his life.

344 *the* Discovery *and the* Chatham *were towed:* Vancouver, *Voyage,* vol. 6, 93.

CHAPTER TWENTY-ONE

345 *the British had stepped up attacks:* Merrill D. Peterson, *Thomas Jefferson and the New Nation: A Biography,* 545.

On June 1, a major naval battle: The battle became known as "The Glorious First of June." Britain claimed victory for capturing and sinking seven French ships. France also claimed victory because the American grain ships survived to make port. See Robert Gardner, ed., *"The Glorious First of June" Fleet Battle and Blockade: The French Revolutionary War, 1793–1797.*

346 *To stay out of war:* John Jay had previously served as secretary of state for the Congress of the Confederation and become mired in controversy over his recommendation to accept Spain's shutdown of the Mississippi River in 1787. At the time of being appointed envoy to London he was Chief Justice of the United States.

347 *a young Spaniard, Francisco Palo Marin:* Ross H. Gast, *Don Francisco de Paula Marin: A Biography,* 3–5.

A Kauai native: Ebenezer Townsend, "Extract of the Diary of Ebenezer Townsend, Jr., Supercargo of Sealing Ship Neptune on Her Voyage to the South Pacific and Canton."

the Jefferson *had run aground:* Bernard Magee, Log.

Kahekili, the last of the old: Peter Mills, *Hawaii's Russian Adventure: A New Look at Old History,* 85.

348 *Kaeo gathered up a large party:* Abraham Fornander, *The Polynesian Race: Its Origin and Migrations, and the Ancient History of the Hawaiian People to the Times of Kamehameha I,* 262.

Kalanikupule arrived and withdrew: Ibid., 262–63.

Kaeo continued along the shore: Ibid., 263.

Reluctantly, he chose to attack: Ibid.; also William De Witt Alexander, *A Brief History of the Hawaiian People,* 141.

349 *On November 21, Brown appeared:* Ralph S. Kuykendall, *Hawaiian Kingdom: Foundation and Transformation 1778–1854,* 46.

Brown had named it Fair Haven: Alexander, *A Brief History,* 141.

In the first encounter: Alexander, *A Brief History,* 141; Fornander, *Polynesian Race,* 264.

350 *Kaeo steadily advanced:* Fornander, *Polynesian Race,* 264.

On December 3, the Washington: Alexander, *A Brief History,* 141.

there are widely varying accounts: As might be expected, Kendrick's legend generated divergent tales of events. Three main sources provided descriptions of what occurred in December 1794: John Young, Isaac Davis, and native observers. Visiting captains became secondary sources who created variant versions, and writers attempting to make sense of the conflicting statements have created further variations of the stories. The primary conflicts are: whether Kendrick assisted Brown and Kalanikupule in the warfare on December 12; whether Kendrick requested a salute from Brown to celebrate the victory; and whether the firing of the *Jackall*'s loaded cannon was accidental. The version of events incorporating native observations, recorded by Dibble and his researchers in the 1830s and reported by Judge Fornander and Ralph Kuykendall, has been relied upon in this work because it complies closely with existing historical relationships. Consistent with the hostility between Brown and Kendrick, Dibble states explicitly that Kendrick took no part in the warfare, gives Kendrick no part in the salute, and makes no mention of the "accidental" loading of the cannon, saying only that the inquest found Kendrick a "casualty" of the battle. Some accounts say that Kendrick joined Brown. Other accounts go so far as to say that Kendrick, and not Brown, participated in the warfare. The versions in which Kendrick was engaged in warfare apparently arise from descriptions given to John Young by Brown's men.

Kendrick took no part in the fight: Sheldon Dibble, *History of the Sandwich Islands,* 68; Fornander, *Polynesian Race,* 264–65; Kuykendall, *Hawaiian Kingdom,* 46.

351 *He sent out eighteen or twenty men:* Alexander, *A Brief History,* 141; Charles Bishop, *The Journal and Letters of Captain Charles Bishop on the North-West Coast of America, in the Pacific and in New South Wales, 1794–1799,* 102.

On the morning of December 11: Fornander, *Polynesian Race,* 264.

cut off any retreat along the shore: Ibid., 264–65; Kuykendall, *Hawaiian Kingdom,* 46.

352 *they killed him and his wives:* Fornander, *Polynesian Race,* 265.

Kahulunuikaaumoku, one of the daughters: Ibid., 265–66. Her tale was apparently told to Dibble's researchers before 1837, or to Fornander's native sources.

According to Isaac Davis: Bishop, *Journal and Letters,* 102–3; Dibble, *History,* 68.

353 *Late that afternoon:* Dibble, *History,* 68–69.

354 *Kalanikupule was allegedly warned:* Dibble, *History,* 69; Fornander, *Polynesian Race,* 266.

The gunner fired the first two: Boit relates John Young's version of Kendrick's killing, stating that Kendrick was "met with a very friendly reception by Capt. Brown" when he arrived at Honolulu. Young places Kendrick in the warfare and has Kendrick requesting a salute from Brown. John Boit, *Log of the Union: 1794–1796,* 70–72.

"ye Apron of ye 4th Gun": Ibid., 72.

found John Kendrick "a casualty": Dibble, *History,* 69.

355 *as Kendrick's "assistant":* John Howell to Joseph Barrell, May 28, 1798, itemizing his wages as "assistant."

He immediately demanded: Fornander, *Polynesian Race,* 267.

on January 1, 1795: Ibid. Also Alexander, *A Brief History,* 142–43.

"rang'd up alongside the Prince": Boit, *Log of the Union,* 72.

356 *paid himself $1,817:* Wages $900 per year—double what Gray had been paid—and a commission on the sale of the furs, $840. The commission of 5 percent was double what Howell would charge other ships two years later. John Howell to Joseph Barrell, May 28, 1798.

Howell then sold the Lady Washington: Howell to Barrell, May 11, 1795.

357 *"the debts he [Kendrick] accumulated":* Joseph Ingraham, *Joseph Ingraham's Journal of the Brigantine Hope on a Voyage to the Northwest Coast of America, 1790–1792,* 182.

358 *Although Kendrick had written to Barrell:* John Kendrick to Joseph Barrell, March 28, 1792.

The first word of John Kendrick's death: "Courier's Marine Journal," *Courier* 1, no. 9 (July 29, 1795), 35. No ship from China is reported as arriving at Boston between July 27 and August 5, when the first notice of Kendrick's death was published. John Howell said that he arrived in Macao with the Washington in "early February" 1795. The *Jefferson* had been 168 days at sea, placing its departure from Macao on February 8.

Up and down the coast: Peterson, *Thomas Jefferson,* 547.

Those who defended the agreement: David McCullough, *John Adams,* 456–57.

359 *A brief article appeared:* "Deaths," *Columbian Centinel* 23, no. 43 (August 5, 1795), 3.

Juan Kendrick resigned: Gast, *Don Francisco,* 4–5.

In August 1798, Juan signed on: Ibid., 5. Also F. W. Howay, "The Ship Eliza at Hawaii in 1799," and Samuel Burling, Log of the Eliza (1798–99).

360 *Juan Kendrick also sought Francisco Marin:* Gast, *Don Francisco,* 5.

360 *he grounded the* Lady Washington: Jim Mockford, "The Lady Washington at Kushimoto, Japan, in 1791." Mockford cites The Journal of Daniel Paine, 1794–1797, 59.

"in daily expectation": John Howell to Joseph Barrell, May 28, 1798.

361 *"Capt. Kendrick was the first American":* Amasa Delano, *A Narrative of Voyages and Travels in the Northern and Southern Hemispheres,* 400.

EPILOGUE

362 *In January 1803:* "Thomas Jefferson Confidential Message to Congress." Jefferson requested twenty-five hundred dollars for a small expedition west "for the purpose of extending the external commerce of the United States." This was in addition to military pay. The cost for the expedition would ultimately total thirty-nine thousand dollars.

his private secretary, Meriwether Lewis: Lewis had a history of prior involvement with the western expedition. When he was eighteen years old he applied to lead the expedition west that had been given to André Michaux and was later canceled. Merrill D. Peterson, *Thomas Jefferson and the New Nation: A Biography,* 763.

on the morning of November 7, 1805: Meriwether Lewis and William Clark, *The Lewis and Clark Journals: An American Epic of Discovery,* William Clark entry, November 7, 1805. Also see facsimile pages online at http://lewisandclarkjournals.unl.edu/.

363 *"who visit this part of the coast":* Ibid., William Clark entry, January 1, 1806.

schooner "Washilton": Ibid., William Clark note attached to January 1, 1806. There is no record of John Kendrick's entering the Columbia River, although his additional rumored land deed was said to be for the area around adjacent Gray's Harbor.

"shortly derive the benefits": Meriwether Lewis to Thomas Jefferson, September 23, 1806, in *Thomas Jefferson and Early Western Explorers,* transcr. and ed. Gerard W. Gawalt, Manuscript Division, Library of Congress, General Correspondence Series 1, 912. Also see Donald Jackson, *Thomas Jefferson and the Stony Mountains: Exploring the West from Monticello,* 200.

364 *Some in Congress believed:* U.S. Congress, House Committee on Commerce and Manufacturers, "No. 178, Exploration of Louisiana," March 8, 1804.

In 1800, there were eight: Warren L. Cook, *Flood Tide of Empire: Spain and the Pacific Northwest, 1543–1819,* Appendix E: Nationality of Vessels Visiting the Northwest Coast, 1774–1820.

364 *In 1791, five vessels:* Curtis P. Nettles, *The Emergence of a National Economy, 1775–1815,* 219.

By 1823, as many as forty ships: James Morton Callahan, *American Relations in the Pacific and Far East, 1784–1900,* 39, fn 4.

managed by Francisco Marin for Kamehameha: Ross H. Gast, *Don Francisco de Paula Marin: A Biography,* 40–43, 46–47.

In the War of 1812: Callahan, *American Relations,* fn 3; 25.

365 *sent the navy frigate* Essex: Ibid., 25–27.

In June 1816, President James Madison: Congressional Globe, 25th Congress, 2nd Session: 56 (May 1838). Also *American State Papers: Foreign Relations,* 662–65; 3:85–86, 126, 185–86.

"in the most satisfactory manner": B. Joy to Secretary of State James Monroe, November 28, 1816, in U.S. Congress, Senate Committee on Public Lands, Report No. 335 (Felch Report), 31–32.

from Robert Gray's brother-in-law: John Boit, "A New Log of the Columbia," 5.

366 *These were shown to Adams:* Letter of JQA to Charles Bulfinch, December 1, 1817, in Felch Report, 32. It's important to note that the original log from which the copies were made in 1817 had been destroyed as waste paper by 1837. Boit, "A New Log," 5.

In 1818, Britain returned Astor's: Anglo-American Convention of 1818.

Seeking to shut out Britain: Adams-Onus Treaty of 1819.

James Tremere of Boston: Sworn statement, October 30, 1838, Felch Report, 28.

Ebenezer Dorr of Roxbury: Sworn statement, November 16, 1839, Felch Report, 25.

John Cruft of Boston: Sworn Statement, November 18, 1839, Felch Report, 26.

367 *John Young, in his late eighties:* Sworn statement, July 26, 1835, Felch Report, 27.

"manifest destiny": John L. O'Sullivan, "The True Title." O'Sullivan wrote that the claim to the Oregon Country "is by right of our manifest destiny to overspread and to possess the whole of the continent which Providence has given us for the development of the great experiment of liberty and federated self-government entrusted to us . . ." This first recorded use of the term echoed a long-held sentiment concerning the destiny of the United States, which was preceded by the "westering" impulse among colonists. It also foreshadowed events for the next century and beyond.

Bibliography

Books

Adams, John Quincy. *Writings of John Quincy Adams.* Vol. 1. Edited by Worthington Chauncy Ford. New York: Macmillan, 1913.

Alexander, William De Witt. *A Brief History of the Hawaiian People.* New York: American Book Company, 1891.

Allen, Gardner Weld. *Massachusetts Privateers of the Revolution.* 2 vols. Boston: Houghton Mifflin, 1913.

Arias, David. *Spanish-Americans: Lives and Faces.* Victoria, BC: Trafford, 2005.

Bancroft, Hubert Howe. *History of the Northwest Coast, 1543–1800.* Vol. 1. San Francisco: A. L. Bancroft, 1884.

———. *The Works of Hubert Howe Bancroft.* Vol. 33, *History of Alaska, 1730–1885.* San Francisco: A. L. Bancroft, 1886.

Bartlett, John. "A Narrative of Events in the Life of John Bartlett of Boston, Massachusetts, in the Years 1790–1793, During Voyages to Canton and the Northwest Coast of North America." In *The Sea, the Ship, and the Sailor: Tales of Adventure from Log Books and Original Narratives,* 287–337. Salem, MA: Marine Research Society, 1925.

Bishop, Charles. *The Journal and Letters of Captain Charles Bishop on the North-West Coast of America, in the Pacific and in New South Wales, 1794–1799.* Edited by Michael Roe. Cambridge, England: University Press, 1967.

Black, Jeremy. *British Foreign Policy in an Age of Revolutions, 1783–1793.* Cambridge: Cambridge University Press, 1994.

Boit, John. *Log of the Union, 1794–1796.* Edited by Edmund Hayes. Boston: Massachusetts Historical Society, 1981.

Briggs, Vernon L. *History of Shipbuilding on North River, Plymouth County, Massachusetts.* Boston: Coburn Brothers, 1889.

Broughton, William Robert. *A Voyage of Discovery to the North Pacific Ocean Performed in His Majesty's Sloop Providence and Her Tender in the Years 1795, 1796, 1797, 1798.* London: T. Cadell and W. Davies, 1804.

Bulfinch, Susan Ellen, ed. *The Life and Letters of Charles Bulfinch, Architect; With Other Family Papers.* Boston: Houghton Mifflin/Riverside Press, 1896.

Callahan, James Morton. *American Relations in the Pacific and Far East, 1784–1900.* Baltimore: John Hopkins Press, 1901.

Carey, Charles Henry. *History of Oregon.* Chicago: Pioneer Historical Publishing, 1922.

Caruthers, J. Wade. *American Pacific Ocean Trade: Its Impact on Foreign Policy and Continental Expansion, 1784–1860.* New York: Exposition Press, 1973.

The Chinese Repository, vols. 1–5. Canton: 1834. Reprint: Boston: Adamant Media, 2005.

Clayton, Daniel W. *Islands of Truth: The Imperial Fashioning of Vancouver Island.* Vancouver: UBC Press, 2000.

Colnett, James. *The Journal of Captain James Colnett aboard the Argonaut from April 26, 1789 to November 3, 1791.* Edited by Fredric W. Howay. Toronto: Champlain Society, 1940.

———. *A Voyage to the North West Side of America: The Journals of James Colnett, 1786–1789.* Edited by Robert Galois. Vancouver: UBC Press, 2004.

Conway, Moncure Daniel. *Omitted Chapters of History Discovered in the Letters and Papers of Edmund Randolph.* New York: G. P. Putnam's Sons, 1889.

Cook, James. *The Journals of Captain James Cook on His Voyages of Discovery; The Voyage of the Resolution and Discovery, 1776–1780.* Edited by J. C. Beaglehole. 3 vols. Cambridge, England: Hakluyt Society, 1967.

Cook, James, and James King. *A Voyage to the Pacific Ocean: Undertaken by the Command of His Majesty for Making Discoveries in the Northern Hemisphere to Determine the Position and Extent of the West Side of North America; Its Distance to Asia; and the Practicality of a Northern Passage to Europe . . .* 3 vols. London: W. & A. Strahan, 1784. James Cook is the author of volumes 1 and 2, James King the author of volume 3.

Cook, Warren L. *Flood Tide of Empire: Spain and the Pacific Northwest, 1543–1819.* New Haven: Yale University Press, 1973.

Cooke, Alan, and Clive Holland. *The Exploration of Northern Canada 500 to 1920: A Chronology.* Toronto: Arctic History Press, 1978.

Dalrymple, Alexander. *Plan for Promoting the Fur-Trade, and Securing It to This*

Country, by Using the Operations of the Hudson's Bay Company. London: George Biggs, 1789. Reprint Osiris/I Ehrlich, 1975.

Daws, Gavan. *Shoal of Time: A History of the Hawaiian Islands*. Honolulu: University of Hawaii Press, 1974.

Deane, Samuel. *History of Scituate, Massachusetts*. Boston: James Loring, 1831.

Delano, Amasa. *A Narrative of Voyages and Travels in the Northern and Southern Hemispheres*. Boston: E. G. House, 1817.

Dibble, Sheldon. *History of the Sandwich Islands*. Lahainaluna, HI: Press of the Mission Seminary, 1843.

Drucker, Philip. *Indians of the Northwest Coast*. New York: McGraw-Hill/American Museum of Natural History, 1955.

Dulles, Foster Rhea. *America in the Pacific: A Century of Expansion*. Boston: Houghton Mifflin, 1932.

———. *Yankees and Samurai: America's Role in the Emergence of a Modern Japan: 1791–1900*. New York: Harper & Row, 1965.

Egnal, Marc. *A Mighty Empire: The Origins of the American Revolution*. Ithaca: Cornell University Press, 1988.

Eitel, Ernest John. *Europe in China: The History of Hong Kong from the Beginning to the Year 1882*. Hong Kong: Kelly and Walsh, 1895.

Elliot, J. H. *Empires of the Atlantic World: Britain and Spain in America 1492–1830*. New Haven: Yale University Press, 2006.

Ellis, Joseph. *His Excellency George Washington*. New York: Alfred A. Knopf, 2004.

Fisher, Robin. *Contact and Conflict: Indian-European Relations in British Columbia, 1774–1890*. Vancouver: UBC Press, 1992.

Fisher, Robin, and Hugh Johnston, eds. *From Maps to Metaphors: The Pacific World of George Vancouver*. Vancouver: UBC Press, 1993.

Forbes, David W. *Hawaiian National Bibliography, 1780–1900*. Vol. 1, *1780–1830*. Honolulu: University of Hawaii Press, 1999.

Ford, Paul Leicester, ed. *The Works of Thomas Jefferson*. Federal Edition. 12 vols. New York: G. P. Putnam's Sons, 1904–1905. Online Library of Liberty, http://oll.libertyfund.org.

Fornander, Abraham. *The Polynesian Race: Its Origin and Migrations, and the Ancient History of the Hawaiian People to the Times of Kamehameha I*. Vol. 2. London: Trubner, 1880.

Foster, Thomas A. *Sex and the Eighteenth Century Man: Massachusetts and the History of Sexuality in America*. Boston: Beacon Press, 2006.

Franklin, Benjamin. *The Papers of Benjamin Franklin*. Edited by William B. Willcox. Vol. 25, 726a. American Philosophical Society and Yale University, 1986.

Fry, Howard Terrell. *Alexander Dalrymple (1737–1808) and the Expansion of British Trade*. Toronto: University of Toronto Press, 1970.

Gardner, Robert, ed. *"The Glorious First of June" Fleet Battle and Blockade: The French Revolutionary War, 1793–1797*. London: Chatham, 1996.

Gast, Ross H. *Don Francisco de Paula Marin: A Biography* and *The Letters and Journal of Francisco de Paula Marin*. Edited by Agnes C. Conrad. Honolulu: University Press of Hawaii/Hawaiian Historical Society, 1973.

Giunta, Mary A., ed., and J. Dane Hartgrove, asst. ed. *Documents of the Emerging Nation: United States Foreign Relations 1775–1789*. National Historical Publications and Records Commission. Wilmington: Scholarly Resources, 1998.

Graham, Gerald S. *Seapower and British North America, 1783–1820: A Study in British Colonial Policy*. Boston: Harvard University Press, 1941.

Greenhow, Robert. *The History of Oregon and California and the Other Territories on the North-West Coast of North America*. Washington, DC: U. S. Senate, 1840. 2nd ed. Boston: Charles C. Little and James Brown, 1845.

Harlow, Vincent T. *The Founding of the Second British Empire, 1763–1793*. Vol. 2. London: Longmans Green, 1964.

Haycox, Stephen, James Barnett, and Caedmon Liburd, eds. *Enlightenment and Exploration in the North Pacific, 1741–1805*. Seattle: University of Washington Press, 1997.

Hill, Roscoe R., ed. *Journals of the Continental Congress, 1774–1789*. Vol. 33 (1787). Washington, DC: Library of Congress, 1936.

Howay, Fredrick W., ed. *Voyages of the Columbia to the Northwest Coast: 1787–1790 and 1790–1791*. Boston: Massachusetts Historical Society, 1941. Reprint, Portland: Oregon Historical Society Press, 1990.

Hutchins, Thomas. *Historical Narrative and Topographical Description of Louisiana, and West Florida*. Philadelphia: 1784. Reprint, Gainesville: University of Florida Press, 1968.

Ingraham, Joseph. *Joseph Ingraham's Journal of the Brigantine Hope on a Voyage to the Northwest Coast of America, 1790–1792*. Edited by Mark D. Kaplanoff. Barre, MA: Imprint Society, 1971.

Jackson, Donald. *Thomas Jefferson and the Stony Mountains: Exploring the West from Monticello*. Urbana: University of Illinois Press, 1981.

Jarves, James Jackson. *History of the Hawaiian or Sandwich Islands*. Boston: James Munroe, 1844.

Jewett, John R. *Journal, Kept at Nootka Sound*. Boston: Printed for the author, 1807.

Joesting, Edward. *Kauai: The Separate Kingdom*. Honolulu: University of Hawaii Press, 1984.

Kamakau, Samuel, Mary Kawena Pukua, and Dorothy B. Barrere. *Tales and Traditions of the People of Old*. Honolulu: Bishop Museum Press, 1991.

Kanahele, George. *Ku Kanaka Stand Tall: A Search for Hawaiian Values*. Honolulu: University of Hawaii Press, 1993.

Kendrick, John. *The Voyage of the Sutil and Mexicana, 1792: The Last Spanish Exploration of the Northwest Coast of America*. Spokane: Arthur H. Clark, 1992.

Kuykendall, Ralph S. *Hawaiian Kingdom: Foundation and Transformation 1778–1854*. Honolulu: University of Hawaii Press, 1938.

Lach, Donald F., and Edwin J. Van Kley. *Asia in the Making of Europe*. Vol. 3, book 4. Chicago: University of Chicago Press, 1994.

Latourette, Kenneth Scott. *The History of Early Relations between the United States and China, 1784–1844*. New Haven: Yale University Press, 1917.

Ledyard, John. *Voyage to the Pacific Ocean and in Quest of a Northwest-Passage between Asia and America; Performed in the Years 1776, 1777, 1778 and 1779*. Hartford: Nathaniel Patten, 1783.

Lewis, Meriwether, and William Clark. *The Lewis and Clark Journals: An American Epic of Discovery*. Edited by Gary E. Moulton. Lincoln: University of Nebraska Press, 2003.

Lincoln, Charles Henry. *Naval Records of the American Revolution, 1775–1788*. Manuscript Division, Library of Congress. Washington, DC: Government Printing Office, 1906.

Liss, Peggy. *Atlantic Empires: The Network of Trade and Revolution 1713–1826*. Baltimore: Johns Hopkins University Press, 1983.

MacKay, David. *In the Wake of Cook: Science, Exploration and Empire 1780–1801*. London: Croom-Helm, 1985.

Malloy, Mary. *"Boston Men" on the Northwest Coast: The American Maritime Fur Trade, 1788–1844*. Fairbanks: University of Alaska Press, 1998.

———. Souvenirs of *the Fur Trade: Northwest Coast Indian Art and Artifacts Collected by American Mariners, 1788–1844*. Cambridge, MA: Peabody Museum of Archaeology and Ethnology, 2000.

Malo, David. *Hawaiian Antiquities (Mooleo Hawaii)*. Honolulu: Bishop Museum Press, 1971.

Manby, Thomas. *Journal of the Voyages of the HMS Discovery and Chatham*. Fairfield, WA: Ye Galleon Press, 1992.

Marshall, James, and Carrie Marshall, eds. *Pacific Voyages: Selections from Scots Magazine, 1771–1808*. Portland, OR: Binfords and Mort, 1960.

McCullough, David. *John Adams*. New York: Simon & Schuster, 2001.

Meany, Edmond S. *History of the State of Washington*. New York: Macmillan, 1909.

———. *Vancouver's Discovery of Puget Sound*. London: Macmillan, 1907.

Meares, John. *The Memorial of Lt. John Meares of the Royal Navy: Dated 30th April, 1790, and Presented to the House of Commons, May 13, 1790, Containing Every Particular Respecting the Capture of the Vessels in Nootka Sound*. Fairfield, WA: Ye Galleon Press, 1985.

———. *Voyages Made in the Years 1788 and 1789, from China to the North West Coast of America to Which Are Prefixed, an Introductory Narrative of a Voyage Performed in 1786 from Bengal, in the Ship Nootka, Observations on the Probable Existence of a North West Passage, and Some Account of the Trade between the North West Coast of America and China, and the Latter Country and Great Britain*. London: Logographic Press, 1790.

Menzies, Archibald. *Hawaii Nei, 128 Years Ago: Journal of Archibald Menzies*. Edited by William Fredrick Wilson. Honolulu, 1920.

———. *Menzies' Journal of Vancouver's Voyage: April to October 1792*. Edited by C. F. Newcombe. Memoir No. 5. Victoria, BC: Archives of British Columbia, 1923.

Merk, Frederick. *The Oregon Question: Essays in Anglo-American Diplomacy and Politics*. Cambridge, MA: Belknap Press/Harvard University Press, 1967.

Mills, Peter. *Hawaii's Russian Adventure: A New Look at Old History*. Honolulu: University of Hawaii Press, 2002.

Minot, George Richards. *History of the Insurrections in Massachusetts in the Year Seventeen Hundred and Eighty-Six and the Rebellion Consequent Thereon*. Boston: J. W. Burditt, 1810.

Morison, Samuel Eliot. *The Maritime History of Massachusetts, 1783–1860*. Boston: Houghton Mifflin, 1961.

Mozino, José Mariano. *Noticias de Nutka: An Account of Nootka Sound in 1792*. Edited by Iris Higbie Wilson. Seattle: University of Washington Press, 1970.

Murphy, Orville T., and Charles Gravier, Comte de Vergennes: *French Diplomacy in the Age of Revolution 1719–1787*. Albany: State University of New York Press, 1982.

Nettles, Curtis P. *The Emergence of a National Economy, 1775–1815*. Vol. 2, *The Economic History of the United States*. New York: Harper & Row, 1962.

Newcombe, C. F., ed. *The First Circumnavigation of Vancouver Island*. Archives of British Columbia Memoir No. 1. Victoria, BC: W. H. Cullin, 1914.

Ogg, Frederic Austin. *The Opening of the Mississippi: A Struggle for Supremacy in the American Interior*. New York: Macmillan, 1904.

Peterson, Merrill D. *Thomas Jefferson and the New Nation: A Biography*. New York: Oxford University Press, 1970.

Phillips, Paul Chrisler. *The West in Diplomacy of the American Revolution.* New York: Russell & Russell, 1967.

Portlock, Nathaniel: *A Voyage Round the World, but More Particularly to the Northwest Coast of America, Performed in 1785, 1786, 1787, and 1788 in the King George and Queen Charlotte, Captains Portlock and Dixon.* London: John Stockdale and George Goulding, 1789.

Purchas, Samuel. *Hakluytus Posthumus or Purchase His Pilgrimes, Contayning a History of the World in Sea Voyages and Land Travells, by Englishmen and Others.* London: Printed by William Standsby for Henrie Fetherstone, 1625.

Richards, Leonard L. *Shays' Rebellion: The American Revolution's Final Battle.* Philadelphia: University of Pennsylvania Press, 2002.

Ride, Sir Lindsey, and May Ride. *An East India Company Cemetery: Protestant Burials in Macao.* Edited by Bertrand Mellor. Hong Kong: Hong Kong University Press, 1996.

Scofield, John. *Hail, Columbia: Robert Gray, John Kendrick, and the Pacific Fur Trade.* Portland: Oregon Historical Society Press, 1993.

Secretary of the Commonwealth of Massachusetts. *Massachusetts Soldiers and Sailors of the Revolutionary War,* vol. 9. Boston: Wright and Potter, 1902.

Shaw, Samuel. *The Journals of Major Samuel Shaw: The First American Consul at Canton, with the Life of the Author.* Edited by Josiah Quincy. Boston: Wm. Crosby and H. P. Nichols, 1847.

Sparks, Jared. *The Life of Gouverneur Morris: With Selections from His Correspondence and Misc. Papers,* vol 2. n.p.: Gray & Bowen, 1832.

Sterling, Elspeth P., Dorothy B. Barrere, Catherine C. Summers, and M. Kelly, ed. *Index to the Ruling Chiefs of Hawaii by S. M. Kamakau.* Honolulu: Bernice P. Bishop Museum, 1974.

Steven, Margaret. *Trade, Tactics, and Territory: Britain in the Pacific, 1783–1823.* Melbourne: Melbourne University Press, 1983.

Sturgis, William. *"A Most Remarkable Enterprise": Lectures on the Northwest Coast Trade and Northwest Coast Indian Life.* Edited by Mary Malloy. Marstons Mills, MA: Parnassus Imprints, 2000.

Thurman, Michael. *The Naval Department of San Blas: New Spain's Bastion for Alta California and Nootka, 1789–1795.* Cleveland: Arthur H. Clark, 1967.

Turner, Fredrick Jackson. *The American Nation, a History: Rise of the New West, 1819–1829.* Vol. 14. New York: Harper Brothers, 1906.

U.S. Congress. *State Papers and Publick Documents of the United States, from Accession of George Washington to the Presidency, Exhibiting a Complete View of Our Foreign Relations Since That Time.* Vol. 10. 3rd ed. Boston: Thomas B. Wait, 1819.

———. Senate, Senate Document 470, 25th Congress, 2nd Session (Linn Report includes Affidavit of Charles Bulfinch, April 21, 1838), June 6, 1838. United States Public Documents, serial number 318.

———. Senate. Committee on Public Lands. Report No. 335 (Felch Report). 32nd Cong., 1st sess., *Reports of the Committees of the Senate of the United States*, vol. 2. Washington, DC: A. Boyd Hamilton Printer, 1852.

———. House. Committee on Commerce and Manufacturers. "No. 178. Exploration of Louisiana," March 8, 1804. *American State Papers: Miscellaneous*, 390.

U.S. Department of State. *The Diplomatic Correspondence of the United States of America . . . September 10, 1783–March 4, 1789*, vol. 3. Washington, DC: Blair & Reeves, 1837.

Van Dyke, Paul A. *The Canton Trade: Life and Enterprise on the China Coast, 1700–1845*. Hong Kong: Hong Kong University Press, 2005.

Van Zandt, Howard F. *Pioneer American Merchants in Japan*. Tokyo: Lotus Press, 1980.

Vancouver, George. *A Voyage of Discovery to the North Pacific Ocean and Round the World; in Which the Coast of the North-west America Has Been Carefully Examined and Accurately Surveyed; Undertaken by His Majesty's Command, Principally with a View to Ascertain the Existence of Any Navigable Communication between the North Pacific and North Atlantic Oceans; and Performed in the years 1790, 1791, 1792, 1793, 1794 and 1795*. Vols. 1–6. London: John Stockdale, 1801.

Wagner, Henry R. *Spanish Explorations in the Strait of Juan de Fuca*. New York: AMS Press, 1971.

Walter, Richard. *Anson's Voyage Around the World: In the Years 1740–1744*. London: Rivington, 1901. Reprint, New York: Dover Publications, 1974.

Washington, George. *The Diaries of George Washington*. Edited by Donald Jackson and Dorothy Twohig. 6 vols. Charlottesville: University Press of Virginia, 1979.

Whitaker, Arthur Preston. *Spanish-American Frontier 1783–1795: The Westward Movement and the Spanish Retreat in the Mississippi Valley*. Boston: Houghton-Mifflin, 1927.

Williams, Glyn. *Voyages of Delusion: The Quest for the Northwest Passage*. New Haven: Yale University Press, 2003.

Winsor, Justin, ed. *The Memorial History of Boston, Including Suffolk County Massachusetts, 1630–1880*. 4 vols. Boston: James R. Osgood, 1881.

Wood, Gordon S. *Empire of Liberty: A History of the Early Republic, 1789–1815*. New York: Oxford University Press, 2009.

ARTICLES

Archer, Christian I. "Spanish Exploration and Settlement of the Northwest Coast in the 18th Century," *Sound Heritage* 7 (January–March 1973): 33–53.

———. "Seduction before Sovereignty: Spanish Efforts to Manipulate the Natives in Their Claims to the Northwest Coast." In Robin Fisher and Hugh Johnston, eds., 143, *From Maps to Metaphors: The Pacific World of George Vancouver*. Vancouver: UBC Press, 1993.

Bell, Edward. "A New Vancouver Journal, Edward Bell," *Washington Historical Quarterly* 6, no. 1 (January 1915).

Boit, John. "A New Log of the Columbia." Edmond S. Meany, ed. *Washington Historical Quarterly* 12, no. 1. Seattle: University of Washington Press, 1921.

Calvert, Peter. "Sovereignty and the Falklands Crisis." *International Affairs* 59, no. 3: 405–13.

Campbell, S. "Typhoons Affecting Hong Kong: Case Studies." *Hong Kong: The Hong Kong University of Science and Technology*, April 2005.

Carr, Jacqueline Barbara. "A Change 'as Remarkable as the Revolution Itself': Boston's Demographics, 1780–1800." *New England Quarterly* 73, no. 4 (December 2000): 583–602.

Cartwright, Bruce. "The First Discovery of Honolulu Harbor," *31st Annual Report of the Hawaiian Historical Society*, 1922.

———. "Some Early Foreign Residents of the Hawaiian Islands," *25th Annual Report of the Hawaiian Historical Society*, 1916.

Clark, Dan E. "Manifest Destiny and the Pacific." *Pacific Historical Review* 1, no. 1 (March 1932): 1–17.

Cleland, Robert Glass. "The Early Sentiments for the Annexation of California: An Account of the Growth of American Interest in California 1835–1846." *Southwestern Historical Quarterly* 18, no. 1 (July 1914).

Cloud, Barbara. "Oregon in the 1820s: The Congressional Perspective." *Western Historical Quarterly* 12, no. 2 (April 1981): 145–64.

Cobban, Alfred. "British Secret Service in France, 1784–1792." *English Historical Review* 69, no. 271 (April 1954): 226–61.

Deutsch, Herman J. "Economic Imperialism in the Early Pacific Northwest." *Pacific Historical Review* 9, no. 4 (December 1940): 377–88.

Durey, Michael. "William Wickham, the Christ Church Connection and the Rise and Fall of the Security Service in Britain, 1793–1801." *English Historical Review* 121 (June 2006): (492): 714–45.

Elliot, T. C. "Jonathan Carver's Source for the Name of Oregon." *Oregon Historical Quarterly* 23 (1922): 53–69.

———. "Origin of the Name Oregon." *Oregon Historical Quarterly* 22 (1922): 91–105.

Evans, Howard V. "The Nootka Sound Controversy in Anglo-French Diplomacy—1790." *Journal of Modern History* 46, no. 4 (1974): 609–40.

Fireman, Janet L. "The Seduction of George Vancouver: A Nootka Affair." *Pacific Historical Review* 56, no. 3 (August 1987): 427–33.

Fox-Povey, Eliot. "How Agreeable Their Company Would Be: The Meaning of the Sexual Labor of Slaves in the Nuu-chah-nulth—European Sex Trade at Nootka Sound in the Eighteenth Century." *British Columbia Historical News* 36, no. 3 (Summer 2003): 2–10.

Graebner, Norman A. "Maritime Factors in the Oregon Compromise." *Pacific Historical Review* 20, no. 4 (1951): 331–45.

Hansen, Dagny. "Captain Cook's First Stop on the Northwest Coast: By Chance or Chart?" *Pacific Historical Review* 62, no. 4 (November 1993): 475–84.

Howay, F. W. "Ballad of the Bold Northwestman: An Incident in the Life of Captain John Kendrick." *Washington Historical Quarterly* (1929): 71–72.

———. "Four Letters from Richard Cadman Etches to Sir Joseph Banks, 1788–92." *British Columbia Historical Quarterly* 6, no. 2 (April 1942): 125–39.

———. "John Kendrick and His Sons." *Quarterly of the Oregon Historical Society* 23, no. 4 (December 1922).

———."The Ship Eliza at Hawaii in 1799." *42nd Annual Report of the Hawaiian Historical Society,* 1933

———. "The Ship Margaret: Her History and Historian." *35th Annual Report of the Hawaiian Historical Society,* 1929.

Howay, F. W., and Albert Matthews. "Some Notes Upon Captain Robert Gray." *Washington Historical Quarterly* 21 (January 1930).

Igler, David. "Diseased Goods: Global Exchanges in the Eastern Pacific Basin, 1770–1850." *American Historical Review* 109, no. 3.

Johnson, John J. "Early Relations of the United States with Chile." *Pacific Historical Review* 13, no. 3 (1944): 260–70.

Kelley, Darlene. "Foreign Contact with Hawaii before Captain Cook: Keepers of the Culture, a Study in Time of the Hawaiian Islands." *Statewide County Hawaii Archives News* (December 15, 2008).

Landin, Harold W. "Some Letters of Thomas Paine and William Short on the Nootka Sound Crisis." *Journal of Modern History* 13, no. 3 (1941): 357–74.

MacDonald, Graham. "Exploration of the Pacific." *Journal of Interdisciplinary History* 24, no. 3 (Winter 1994): 509–16.

Malloy, Mary, Hisayasu Hatanaka, and Mitsanori Hammano. "The *Lady Washington* at Oshima Island, Japan in 1791." *Quarterdeck* 18, no. 1 (Fall 1991).

Manning, W. R. "The Nootka Sound Controversy." *Annual Report of the American Historical Association for 1904*. Washington, DC, 1905.

Marshall, Yvonne. "Dangerous Liaisons." In Robin Fisher and Hugh Johnston, eds., 171–73, *From Maps to Metaphors: The Pacific World of George Vancouver*. Vancouver: UBC Press, 1993.

Mathes, Valarie Sherer. "Wickaninish, a Clayoquot Chief, as Recalled by Early Travelers." *Pacific Northwest Quarterly* (July 1979): 110–20.

Mintz, Max M. "Gouverneur Morris, George Washington's War Hawk." *Virginia Quarterly Review* (Autumn 2003): 651–61.

Mockford, Jim. "The Lady Washington at Kushimoto, Japan, in 1794." In *The Early Republic and the Sea: Essays on the Naval and Maritime History of the Early United States*. Edited by William S. Dudley and Michael J. Crawford. Washington, DC: Brayey's, 2001.

Norris, John M. "The Policy of the British Cabinet in the Nootka Crisis." *English Historical Review* 70, no. 277 (1955): 562–80.

Nuttall, Zelia. "The Earliest Historical Relations between Mexico and Japan." *American Archaeology and Ethnology* 4, no. 1 (1906).

Perryman, Dennis C., Richard Gilmore, and Ronald E. Englebretson. "The Decision to Evade or Remain in Port." In *Typhoon Havens Handbook for the Western Pacific and Indian Ocean; Hong Kong*. Monterey, CA: U.S. Naval Research Laboratory, 1993.

Porter, Edward G. "The Discovery of the Columbia River." *New England Magazine*, New Series 6 (June 1892): 472–88.

Seed, Patricia. "Taking Possession and Reading Texts: Establishing the Authority of Overseas Empires." *William and Mary Quarterly* 49, no. 2 (April 1992): 183–209.

Shea, John Gilmary, and Henry Reed Stiles. "Explorations of the Northwest Coast of the United States. Report of the Claims of the Heirs of Captains Kendrick and Gray." *Historical Magazine and Notes and Queries Concerning the Antiquities, History and Biography of America*, Second Series 8 (September 1870): 155–75.

Shepard, W. R. "Wilkinson and the Spanish Conspiracy." *American Historical Review* 9 (July 1904): 748–66.

Smith, Jonathan. "The Depression of 1785 and Daniel Shays' Rebellion." *William and Mary Quarterly*, Third Series 5, no. 1 (January 1948): 77–94.

Stokes, J. F. G. "Honolulu and Some New Speculative Phases of Hawaiian History." *42nd Annual Report of the Hawaiian Historical Society* (1933): 61–102.

Taylor, Paul S. "Spanish Seamen in the New World during the Colonial Period." *Hispanic American Historical Review* 5, no. 4 (November 1922): 631–66.

Thomson, Rev. J. C. "Historical Landmarks of Macao." *Chinese Recorder and Missionary Journal* 18 (November 1887): 426.

Tobar y Tamariz, Josef. "Report of Don Josef Tobar y Tamariz, First Mate of the Royal Navy, to His Most Excellent Lordship and Viceroy of New Spain, August 29, 1789." In *Observations on California, 1772–1790,* by Father Luis de Sales, translated and edited by Charles N. Rudkin. Los Angeles: Glen Dawson.

Toville, Freeman M. "Chief Maquinna and Bodega y Quadra." *British Columbia Historical News* 34, no. 4 (Fall 2001): 8–14.

Turner, Fredrick J. "The Diplomatic Contest for the Mississippi Valley." *Atlantic,* May 1904.

Wheeler, Mary E. "Empires in Conflict and Cooperation: The 'Bostonians' and the Russian-American Company." *Pacific Historical Review* 40, no. 4 (1971): 419–41.

NEWSPAPERS

"Boston, May 27." *Boston Weekly News-Letter,* no. 1683 (May 20–27, 1736).

"New York, June 25." *Boston Evening Post,* no. 1919 (July 6, 1772), 3.

"New York, June 25." *Providence Gazette; And Country Journal* 11, No. 444 (July 11, 1772).

(Advertisement) Independent Chronicle 9, no. 459 (June 6, 1777): 4.

"Received of the Honorable John Holker . . ." Independent Ledger 1, no. 22 (November 11, 1778), 1.

"Providence, April 25." *American Journal and Advertiser* 3, no. 21 (April 25, 1781), 2.

"Providence, May 16." *American Journal and General Advertiser* 3, no. 127 (May 16, 1781), 2.

"Charleston, S.C. January 5th." *Massachusetts Spy* 15, no. 728 (March 31, 1785).

"Entries." *Massachusett Centinel* 6, no. 4 (September 30, 1786).

"Entries." *Massachusetts Centinel* 6, no. 23 (December 6, 1786), 91.

"For Charleston, South Carolina, the Brigt. Charletown Packet, John Kendrick, master." *Massachusetts Gazette* 6, no. 288 (December 19, 1786), 4.

"Boston, January 2." *Massachusetts Gazette* 6, no. 292 (January 2, 1787), 3.
"Boston, August 13." *Massachusetts Spy* 3, no. 20 (August 16, 1787), 265.
"Extract from the Journal of Congress: Monday, September 24, 1787." *Charleston Columbian Herald,* no. 326 (October 22, 1787), 2.
"Boston, August 13." *Massachusetts Centinel* 8, no. 4 (September 29, 1787), 15.
Massachusetts Gazette, October 30, 1787, 171.
"Extract of a Letter from New London, Dated April 16." *Independent Chronicle and the Universal Advertiser* 21, no. 1069 (April 23, 1789), 3.
"Boston, May 19." *Concord Herald* 1, no. 23 (June 15, 1790), 3.
"Spanish War." *New-York Daily News,* no. 462 (June 19, 1790), 2.
"Spanish War." *Federal Gazette and Philadelphia Evening Post,* June 21, 1790, 2.
"Spain." *Litchfield* (CT) *Weekly Monitor* 5, no. 261 (June 28, 1790), 2.
"Boston, July 3." *Portland* (ME) *Cumberland Gazette,* July 12, 1790, 1.
"Late Foreign Intelligence, London. May 9–15." *Boston Herald of Freedom* 4, no. 34 (July 27, 1790), 153.
"Extract of a Letter from Boston, August 10." *New York Gazette of the United States* 2, no. 38 (August 21, 1790), 567.
"New York, August 21." *Boston Gazette,* August 30, 1790, 2.
"Something More of War." *Massachusetts Spy* 19, no. 909 (September 2, 1790), 3.
"Captain Meares; British Court; Don Martinez." *Boston Columbian Centinel* 14, no. 1 (September 15, 1790), 3.
"British Advices, via Philadelphia: London July 13." *New York Daily Gazette,* no. 538 (September 16, 1790), 886.
"Deaths." *Boston Columbian Centinel* 19, no. 42 (August 8, 1793), 3.
"Courier's Marine Journal." *Courier* 1, no. 9 (July 29, 1795), 35.
"Deaths." *Boston Columbian Centinel* 23, no. 43 (August 5, 1795), 3.
"British Claim to the Oregon Fur Trade between the N.W. Coast of America and China. From Fisher's Colonial Magazine for January." *Niles' National Register* 14, no. 3 (March 18, 1843), 40–42.
O'Sullivan, John L. "The True Title," *New York Morning News* (December 27, 1845).

Manuscripts, Letters, Journals, Diaries, Pamphlets

Barrell, Joseph. "Annotations on Business." In U.S. Congress. Senate Committee on Public Lands. Report No. 335 (Felch Report).
———. "Orders Given Captain John Kendrick of the Ship Columbia for a Voyage

to the Pacific Ocean, 1787." In U.S. Congress. Senate Committee on Public Lands. Report No. 335 (Felch Report).

———. Joseph Barrell to John Kendrick, December 12, 1787. Columbia Papers. Massachusetts Historical Society.

———. Joseph Barrell to Nathaniel Barrell, December 20, 1787. *Massachusetts Volumes of the Documentary History of the Ratification of the Constitution,* vol. 5, 490.

———. Joseph Barrell to Robert Gray, Boston, September 25, 1790. Columbia Papers. Massachusetts Historical Society.

Blankett, John. Letter of John Blankett to Admiralty First Lord Chatham, April 9, 1791. Pitt Papers, 30/8/365, 219–22. Public Record Office (Kew).

Bligh, William. William Bligh to Sir Joseph Banks, October 13, 1789. Log and Letters of William Bligh Pertaining to the Mutiny on the Bounty, National Library of Australia.

Boit, John. Remarks on the Ship Columbia's Voyage from Boston (on a Voyage, round the Globe). John Boit's Journals. Massachusetts Historical Society.

Brigham, William Tufts, et al. Accounts of the Sandwich Islands, 1784–1889. Manuscript Collection. Massachusetts Historical Society.

Brown, William. William Brown to Sir William Curtis, December 1792.

Burling, Samuel. Log of the Eliza (1798–99). Manuscript Collection. Massachusetts Historical Society.

Burney, James. James Burney Journal, March 30, 1778.

Carmichael, William, to Thomas Jefferson, January 24, 1791.

Croix, Teodoro de. Teodoro de Croix to Mexican Viceroy Manuel Flores, July 31, 1788. Estado 20.N. 39. Archivo General de Indias, Seville.

Dorr, Ebenezer. A Journal of a Voyage from Boston Round the World . . . John Carter Brown Library, Providence, RI.

Earl of Sandwich. Mediterranean passport, John Kendrick/*Brig Lydia*, 1772. Manuscript Division. G. W. Blount Library, Mystic Seaport, Mystic, CT.

Etches, John, writing as "Argonaut." "An Authentic Statement of All the Facts Relative to Nookta Sound; Its Discovery, History, Settlement, Trade, and the Probable Advantages to be Derived from It; in an Address to the King." London: S. W. Fores, 1790.

———. "A Continuation of an Authentic Statement of All the Facts Relative to Nootka Sound, Its Discoveries, History, Settlement, Commerce and the Public Advantages to be Derived from It . . ." London: S. W. Fores, 1790.

Flores, Manuel. Viceroy Manuel Flores to Minister Antonio Valdes, December 23, 1788. Estado 4289. Archivo General de Indias, Seville.

———. Manuel Antonio Flores to Estevan José Martinez, December 23, 1788. Archivo General de Indias, Bancroft Library, University of California, Berkeley.

Franklin, Benjamin. Observations Concerning the Increase of Mankind, 1751 (published 1755).

Gonzales, Blas. Blas Gonzales to Viceroy Teodoro de Croix, August 1, 1788. SGU Leg. 6895, Archivo General de Simancas, Seville.

Gray, Robert. Robert Gray to Joseph Barrell, July 13, 1789. Columbia Papers. Massachusetts Historical Society.

———. Robert Gray to Joseph Barrell, December 18, 1789. Columbia Papers. Massachusetts Historical Society.

———. Robert Gray to John Kendrick, January 29, 1790. Columbia Papers. Massachusetts Historical Society.

———. Robert Gray to John Kendrick, January 30, 1790. Columbia Papers. Massachusetts Historical Society.

———. Robert Gray to John Kendrick, February 4, 1790. Columbia Papers. Massachusetts Historical Society.

Haswell, Robert. A Voyage Round the World Onboard the Ship Columbia-Rediviva and Sloop Washington (1787–1789). Microfilm Edition. Massachusetts Historical Society.

———. A Voyage on Discoveries in the Ship Columbia Rediviva (1791–1792). Manuscript Collection. Massachusetts Historical Society.

Hoskins, John. The Narrative of a Voyage. Manuscript Collection. Massachusetts Historical Society.

———. John Hoskins to Joseph Barrell, August 21, 1792. Columbia Papers. Massachusetts Historical Society.

———. John Hoskins to Robert Gray and Joseph Barrell, December 22, 1792. Columbia Papers. Massachusetts Historical Society.

Howard, J. G. *History of the Lousiana Purchase.* Callaghan & Company, 1902.

Howe, Richard S. Richard Howe to John Kendrick, September 7, 1789. Columbia Papers. Massachusetts Historical Society.

———. Richard S. Howe and Robert Gray to Joseph Barrell, June 16, 1790. Columbia Papers. Massachusetts Historical Society.

Howell, John. John Howell to Joseph Barrell, May 11, 1795. Columbia Papers. Massachusetts Historical Society.

———. John Howell to Joseph Barrell, December 23, 1796. Columbia Papers. Massachusetts Historical Society.

———. John Howell to Joseph Barrell, May 28, 1798. Columbia Papers. Massachusetts Historical Society.

Humphreys, David. David Humphreys to Thomas Jefferson, October 20, 1790.

Jefferson, Thomas. Thomas Jefferson to George Rogers Clark, December 4, 1783. Thomas Jefferson Papers, Series 1, General Correspondence. Library of Congress.

———. Thomas Jefferson to Thomas Mann Randolph Jr, June 20, 1790. Thomas Jefferson Papers, Series 1, General Correspondence, 613–14. Library of Congress.

———. Thomas Jefferson to E. Rutledge, July 4, 1790. Thomas Jefferson Papers. Series 1, General Correspondence, 782. Library of Congress.

———. Thomas Jefferson to André Michaux, January 23, 1793. Thomas Jefferson Papers, Series 1, General Correspondence, 694. Library of Congress.

———. "Thomas Jefferson Confidential Message to Congress, January 18, 1803." Thomas Jefferson Papers, Series 1, General Correspondence, 841. Library of Congress.

———. Thomas Jefferson to John Jacob Astor, November 9, 1813. Thomas Jefferson Papers, Series 1, General Correspondence, 1322. Library of Congress.

Kendrick, John. Instructions to Robert Gray, February 1788. Columbia Papers. Massachusetts Historical Society.

———. John Kendrick to Joseph Barrell, May 28, 1788. Columbia Papers. Massachusetts Historical Society.

———. John Kendrick to Don Estevan José Martinez, May 8, 1789. Columbia Papers. Massachusetts Historical Society.

———. John Kendrick to Joseph Barrell, July 13, 1789. Columbia Papers. Massachusetts Historical Society.

———. John Kendrick Recommendation for Kaiana, December 11, 1789. *Historia*, vol. 69. Archivo General de la Nacion, Mexico City.

———. John Kendrick to Robert Gray and Richard S. Howe, January 27, 1790. Columbia Papers. Massachusetts Historical Society.

———. John Kendrick to Robert Gray and Richard S. Howe, February 6, 1790. Columbia Papers. Massachusetts Historical Society.

———. John Kendrick to Robert Gray and Richard S. Howe, February 7, 1790. Columbia Papers. Massachusetts Historical Society.

———. John Kendrick to Robert Gray, February 9, 1790. Columbia Papers. Massachusetts Historical Society.

———. John Kendrick to Joseph Barrell, March 28, 1792. Columbia Papers. Massachusetts Historical Society.

Lopez de Haro, Gonzalo. Gonzalo Lopez de Haro to Viceroy Flores, October 28, 1788. Estado 20–34, Archivo General de Indias, Seville.

Magee, Bernard. Log of the Jefferson. Manuscript Collection. Massachusetts Historical Society.

Martinez, Estevan José. Diario de la Navegacion que de orden de Rey Nuestro Senor . . . en el presente ano de 1788 del 8 marzo al 5 diciembre. Audencia de Mexico 1529 (90-3-18) Kibre Calendar of Documents, Archivos General de Indias, Bancroft Library, University of California, Berkeley.

———. Diary of the Voyage which I, Ensign of the Royal Navy, Don Estevan José Martinez, am going to make to the port of San Lorenzo de Nuca, in command of the frigate Princesa and the packet San Carlos, by order of his excellency Don Miguel Antonio Florez, Viceroy, Governor, and Captain General of New Spain, in the present year of 1789. Trans. Joseph Ingram Priestley. University of Washington (microfilm), 1915.

———. Estevan José Martinez to Viceroy Manuel Flores, December 5, 1788. Gobierno 1492–1858. Archivo General de Indias. Bancroft Library, University of California, Berkeley.

———. Estevan José Martinez to Viceroy Manuel Antonio Flores, July 13, 1789. Gobierno 1492–1858. Archivo General de Indias. Bancroft Library, University of California, Berkeley.

Meares, John. "An Answer to Mr. George Dixon, & c. by John Meares; in which the Remarks of Mr. Dixon are fully considered and refuted." London, 1791.

Morris, Gouverneur. Gouverneur Morris to George Washington, May 29, 1790. George Washington Papers, 1741–1799. General Correspondence, Series 4, 526–536. Library of Congress.

Mozino, Joseph Marina. Relation de la ysla de Mazarredo . . . 1793. Beinecke Rare Book and Manuscript Library, Yale University.

Munos, Josef. Josef Munos to Captain General Higgins, August 3, 1788. Estado 7102. Archivo General de Simancas, Seville.

New Age (journal). Washington, DC: Washington Supreme Council 33, Ancient and Accepted Scottish Rite of Freemasonry Southern Jurisdiction, USA. Library of Congress (microform).

Nickerson, W. S. Some Lower Cape Cod Indians. Manuscript copy.

Paine, Josiah. Edward Kenwrick: The Ancestor of the Kenricks or Kendricks of Barnstable County and Nova Scotia and His Descendants. Yarmouth, MA: Charles W. Swift, 1915.

Papeles de Estado 20 N. 5642, Archivo General de Indias, Seville.

Randall, Thomas. Thomas Randall to Alexander Hamilton, August 14, 1791. Alexander Hamilton Papers, General Correspondence, 1734–1804. Manuscript Division, Box 4. Library of Congress.

Sanchez, Fray Francisco Miguel. *Historio Compuesta de todo lo acaesido en la expedic-con hecha al Puerto de Nuca ano de 1789*. Beinecke Rare Book and Manuscript Library, Yale University.

Schuchert, Charles. "Biographical Memoir of Joseph Barrell, 1869–1919." Paper presented to the National Academy of Sciences Annual Meeting, 1925.

Townsend, Ebenezer. "Extract of the Diary of Ebenezer Townsend, Jr., Supercargo of Sealing Ship Neptune on Her Voyage to the South Pacific and Canton." *Hawaiian Historical Society Reports*, no. 4.

Treat, John B. John B. Treat to Samuel Breck, July 14, 1789. Samuel Breck Papers. Library Company of Philadelphia.

Vanela, Don Pedro. Don Pedro Vanela to Conde Campo de Alange, December 29, 1791. Archivo General de Simancas, Seville, Spain.

Washington, George. George Washington to Henry Lee, October 31, 1786. George Washington Papers, 1741–1799. Series 2, Letterbook 13, 205. Library of Congress.

———. George Washington to Joseph Barrell, June 8, 1788. George Washington Papers, 1741–1799. Series 2, Letterbook 15, 134–35. Library of Congress.

MAPS AND SAILING DIRECTIONS

De l'Isle, Joseph-Nicholas map of North America, 1752.

Hayes, Derek. *Historical Atlas of the Pacific Northwest: Maps of Exploration and Discovery*. Seattle: Sasquatch Books, 2000.

Horsburgh, James. *The India Directory, or Directions for Sailing to and from the East Indies, China, Australia* . . . . London: Wm. H. Allerton, 1852.

Meares, John. *A Chart of the Interior Part of North America Demonstrating the Very Great Probability of an Inland Navigation from Hudson's Bay to the West Coast*. In John Meares, *Voyages Made in the Years 1788 and 1789* . . . . London: Logographic Press, 1790.

Ortelis, Abraham. *Theatrum Orbis Terrarum*. Antwerp: Giles Coppens de Deist, 1570.

Ray, R. C. *The Coast of British Columbia including Juan de Fuca Strait, Puget Sound, Vancouver and Queen Charlotte Islands*. Hydrography Office of the U.S. Navy. Washington, DC: Government Printing Office, 1891.

Williams, S. Wells. *The Chinese Commercial Guide, Sailing Instructions*. Hong Kong: A. Shortrede, 1863.

Index

CPSIA information can be obtained
at www.ICGtesting.com
Printed in the USA
LVHW041411100322
713072LV00006B/126

9 780061 700194